Instructor's Resource Manual

to Accompany

Medical Language

Second Edition

Susan Turley, MA(Educ), BSN, RN, RHIT, CMT
Adjunct Professor, School of Health Professions,
Wellness, and Physical Education
Anne Arundel Community College
Arnold, Maryland

Pearson

Boston   Columbus   Indianapolis   New York   San Francisco   Upper Saddle River
Amsterdam   Cape Town   Dubai   London   Madrid   Milan   Munich   Paris   Montreal   Toronto
Delhi   Mexico City   Sao Paulo   Sydney   Hong Kong   Seoul   Singapore   Taipei   Tokyo

www.pearsonhighered.com

10 9 8 7 6 5 4 3 2 1
ISBN-13: 978-0-13-505766-7
ISBN-10:   0-13-505766-3

CONTENTS

PREFACE

Thank you for adopting *Medical Language*! The goal of this textbook is to immerse your students in the real world of medicine. I propose to do this by way of various visual, auditory, and pedagogical features throughout the textbook and the student and instructor's resources. Combined with your instructional expertise and guidance, this textbook and these resources will help your students discover the way to become fluent in medical language. By taking full advantage of what this textbook and these resources have to offer, you and your students will discover a system of learning medical language that is simple and yet comprehensive.

By selecting *Medical Language* as your textbook you have given yourself access to a wide variety of excellent text-specific instructional tools. In the pages of this preface that follow, I introduce you to the most advanced instructor resources of any medical terminology textbook on the market today.

Annotated Instructor's Edition

This is an annotated version of the textbook that contains every page of the student edition but with margin material to help enrich the instructional experience. It includes the following:

- An array of teaching strategies and tips
- Interesting facts and anecdotes
- Extra content, such as word derivations, not covered in the textbook
- Answers to each chapter's Chapter Review Exercises.

Instructor's Resource Manual

This contains a wealth of material to help faculty plan and manage the course. It includes the following:

- The Art and Craft of Teaching. This section discusses various teaching techniques to ensure that students learn the material effectively. It also highlights classroom management techniques that help to make learning enjoyable.
- Nearly 100 ready-made worksheets that can be used for quizzes or homework assignments.
- A sample course syllabus.
- Answers to each chapter's worksheet questions and puzzles.

Instructor's Resource DVD-ROM

This disk provides many resources in an electronic format. It includes the following:

- A complete 5,063-question test bank that allows instructors to generate customized exams and quizzes.
- A comprehensive, turn-key lecture package in PowerPoint format that contains discussion points and a powerful library of images, animations, and videos.

- Classroom response sections with questions and highlighted correct answers to support immediate learning and feedback.
- PowerPoint content to support instructors who are using Personal Response Systems ("clickers").
- A complete image library that includes every photograph and illustration from the textbook.

Student Media

With the purchase of this textbook students have access to an immersive media study experience. Log on to www.myhealthprofessionskit.com using the access code inside the front cover. You will be transported to Medical Terminology Interactive—a virtual world of fun quizzes, word games, videos, and other self-study challenges.

- Build an avatar to get started. Explore your medical bag where you'll find reference materials, Spanish translations, flashcards, and more.
- Start in the lobby and navigate to the elevator where you'll select a floor correlated to the chapter you want to study.
- When you arrive on that floor, you'll enter one of three rooms described below. Each room has clickable objects that will activate a different activity.

  1. **Medical Records Room.** Here you will find exercises related to spelling, pronunciation, and transcription.
  2. **Laboratory.** This is where you will be able to watch a variety of videos to help you study and also practice with a variety of flashcards.
  3. **Examination Room.** This is the place to play a variety of educational games and quizzes such as Word Surgery, Racing Pulse, and Speedway.

- Finally, if you're ready for the ultimate challenge in our virtual hospital, visit the ER. This stands for Exam Review and here you'll be transported to the set of a medical terminology quiz show where you can customize your own gaming experience. Practice and enjoy as you become an ER champ!

  The Medical Terminology Interactive experience allows students to track their own progress chart as they proceed through the various floors and rooms. It also allows students to email the results of their work to instructors.

THE ART AND CRAFT OF TEACHING

George Bernard Shaw once said, "He who can, does; he who cannot, teaches." This tongue-in-cheek comment on poor teachers compels us to strive to be better. We may start out not knowing a lot about teaching techniques, but that doesn't mean we should continue in that state. It is the responsibility of each teacher to continually improve and refine his or her teaching techniques.

Please take some time to read the following material on the art and craft of teaching and allow it to influence your teaching.

Teaching Styles

This list shows the natural progression from beginning teaching techniques to a more mature and effective teaching style.

1. **Subject-centered teaching.** This teaching style places the subject matter on a pedestal. If there are 30 chapters in the book, then all 30 must be covered before the end of the course. If one chapter is especially long, it still must be covered in the same amount of time given to other, smaller chapters. The order of the chapters can never be varied from what is found in the Table of Contents.

2. **Teacher-centered teaching.** This teaching style places the teacher on a pedestal. Each chapter covered must be presented by the teacher who is the sole source of information. The teacher knows all aspects of the subject; the students know nothing. Lecture is the preferred method of presenting material and students cannot be expected to learn in any other way. The lecture is always about telling students something, and there is very little dialogue coming from the students to the teacher. The teacher feels the role of the teacher is to initiate and the role of the student is to respond, because discovering knowledge is beyond the power of the average student. The teacher asks few questions and views spontaneous questions from students as an interruption to the flow of the lecture. The teacher's authority is the final word and students' questions are viewed as a challenge to his or her authority rather than an opportunity for further study.

Beginning and experienced teachers can become trapped in either of the two teaching styles described above. Fortunately, enthusiasm and caring in the classroom cover a multitude of teaching sins! Students can still learn a lot about medical language even when the teacher uses either of these teaching styles. However, the teacher should always be striving to embrace the third teaching style described below.

3. **Student-centered teaching.** This teaching style places the student on a pedestal. The teacher actively considers the students' needs in planning the course material. The teacher consciously follows Maslow's Hierachy of Needs (as described in the

next section) to direct course activities. Students are encouraged to ask questions, do research projects, form study groups, and so on. The teacher should provide opportunities to help students realize that they can give intelligent answers based on life experience and general fund of knowledge. For example, "What is it called when your tonsils are red and inflamed?" [tonsillitis]. "What is the surgical procedure to remove your tonsils?" [tonsillectomy].

Use group participation to "piece together" answers to questions. Keep rewording the question to stimulate thinking and show there is more than one way to look at things. Ask "why" questions and then provide the answer to show connections and relationships in the course material.

Maslow's Hierarchy of Needs

This adaptation of Maslow's Hierarchy of Needs is a graphic representation that depicts the full spectrum from students' most basic needs to the highest need, self-fulfillment. Needs are met from the bottom of the pyramid to the top, and a need higher on the pyramid cannot be met until all of the needs below it have been fulfilled. This section describes how a teacher can best meet these needs.

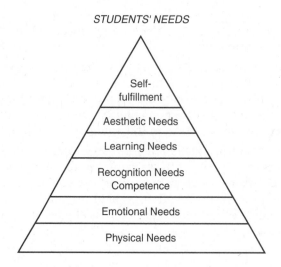

STUDENTS' NEEDS

- Self-fulfillment
- Aesthetic Needs
- Learning Needs
- Recognition Needs Competence
- Emotional Needs
- Physical Needs

Physical Needs

Learning stops when the physical needs of the student have not been met. Make sure the temperature and lighting in the room are conducive to learning. Take one or more breaks during a long session. Inform students where the restrooms are on the first day of class. If the class continues during lunch or dinner hours and food is not allowed in the classroom, discuss ways that students can work around this.

Emotional Needs

Learning stops when the emotional needs of the student have not been met. On the first day of class, allay fears about the course. Teach students specific ways they can ensure their success (flashcard review, designated study time in small segments, involve family members, etc.). Do not allow any student to belittle another student. Do not have students grade each others' test papers. Encourage group activities to break the ice with students who do not know each other, but discourage cliques.

Recognition Needs and Competence

Keep an open atmosphere that allows student questions of any type. All questions are an opportunity for learning. Inspire student self-confidence by taking each question seriously and complimenting the student who thought to ask it ("Oh, that was a very good point!"). Allow students who are familiar with a medical condition to share their point of view about it.

Learning Needs

When the physical needs, emotional needs, and recognition/competence needs of students are being met, then, and only then, will the learning needs be met. Students need to learn the course materials in a way that they can recall that information and apply it to real-life situations in the medical field. In many cases, students need to be taught how to learn before they can begin to learn.

Aesthetic Needs

Above the need for learning is the need to have an aesthetic experience. This relates to feeling connected and responding to the beauty and emotion of the world around us as opposed to having a purely intellectual connection. The aesthetic needs of the student are not difficult to meet because the human body is full of wondrous things and the field of medicine is compelling in the emotions of life and death that it deals with every day. The textbook includes the famous painting *The Starry Night* by Vincent van Gogh to illustrate the possible side effects of the cardiac drug digitalis in Chapter 5, "Cardiology." It also includes the famous drawing of the skeleton by Andreas Vesalius in Chapter 8, "Orthopedics (Skeletal)." Other paintings can be obtained from art history books and shown to the class when teaching the following chapters:

Chapter 5, "Cardiology"
The Doctor's Wife, by Frans van Mieris
Shows a doctor feeling the patient's pulse. It was not until the invention of watches with a second hand, around 1700, that the pulse rate could be accurately measured.

The Dropsical Woman, by Gerard Dou
Shows the same type of scene as *The Village Doctor*. The title of the painting leads to a discussion of word origins. "Dropsy" is an old word for "congestive heart failure."

Chapter 11, "Urology"
The Village Doctor, by David Teniers
Shows the doctor examining a urine specimen. It was not unusual for the doctor to also taste the urine as part of the examination.

Chapter 16, "Otolaryngology"
Portrait of an Old Man and a Young Boy, by Domenico Ghirlandaio
Shows the medical condition of rhinophyma on the old man.

Chapter 18, "Oncology"
The First Operation under Ether, by Robert Hinckley.
It shows the first successful demonstration of surgical anesthesia at Massachusetts General Hospital. It shows a young man (Gilbert Abbott) unconscious after ether anesthesia. He is seated in a chair while a tumor is being removed from his jaw.

Self-Fulfillment

The final step of Maslow's Hierarchy of Needs is self-fulfillment. The empowered student has fulfilled his or her own learning needs and implemented that knowledge in the practice of a career and success in life.

Poor Teaching Techniques

Aristotle said, "All men, by nature, desire to know." But poor teachers can thwart the efforts of even the most dedicated students. During her long career as a student and an educator, the author has encountered the following poor teaching techniques. Read this section to make sure these *do not* describe your teaching! If they do, follow the *Solution* given.

Boring

The teacher lacks enthusiasm, does not change the inflection of his or her voice, and stands behind a podium without moving.

Solution: Be passionate! Get excited about the material and how it applies to a career in the healthcare field. Let your voice reflect this! Move around the class as you teach, from side to side, and even teach from the back of the classroom occasionally. Even if you have taught this medical terminology course 10 times and it seems boring to you, this is the first time your students will have heard it. Good teaching involves a little bit of acting. Sometimes you have to act like you are interested even when you are not! Be sure to get a good night's sleep and come to class with plenty of energy because good teaching is active and demands energy. Inject humor into your lectures and include classroom activities as described in the margins of the *Annotated Instructor's Edition* (AIE).

Insecure

The teacher stands in front of the students and reads from the text-book, offering few additional comments or insights.

Solution: Learn the material well enough so that you are not reading from the textbook but only glancing at it to keep your place. Collect interesting medical facts to share during class or use some of the ones presented in the margins of the *Annotated Instructor's Edition* for each chapter.

Technically challenged

The teacher has not kept up with the latest technology advances in the classroom. Not only does the teacher not know how to operate PowerPoint slides, but he or she does not know how to use the over-head projector and create overheads, may not be computer literate, and cannot create the course syllabus, handouts, and tests.

Solution: Pick one area of technology at a time and master it. It's your job to do that and do it right!

Not relevant

The teacher does not make a strong connection between what is being learned in class and the real world.

Solution: Bring in newspaper articles and report what you hear on the news or relevent TV shows. Bring in medical reports. Do your own research on the Internet to find out what's new in medicine. These Internet sites are particularly helpful:

www.webmd.com

www.sciencentral.com

www.nlm.nih.gov (National Library of Medicine and Medline Plus)

www.news-medical.net

www.medicineNet.com

www.cbsnews.com/sections/health.html (CBSHealthWatch)

http:/pubs.ama-assn.org (*Journal of the American Medical Association*)

www.nejm.org (*New England Journal of Medicine*)

www.eurekalert.org (comprehensive Web site of new advances in medicine and health)

www.personalmd.com

Digressive   The teacher presents little course material but always seems to have time to talk about personal concerns and myriad other subjects.

Solution: Make the majority of what you present course material and sprinkle in anecdotes and activities sparingly. Remember, students are paying you to provide them with a comprehensive experience in medical terminology.

Careless   The teacher feels that the presentation of the material is the equivalent of learning. This mirrors the expression, "If you build it, they will come" by saying "If you teach it, they will learn."

Solution: It is the teacher's responsibility to make sure students learn the material by using good teaching techniques. It is also the teacher's responsibility to administer tests to make sure students have retained the material.

The Teacher's Role

"My job as a teacher is to empower my students, to demystify a subject for them, and so to give up my power over them. If I am doing my job, by the end of the semester my students are independent of me. I strive every semester to give my students power, even though when I succeed I inevitably disempower myself. I hate that feeling of powerlessness at the end of the semester. And I love it!"

Source: Peter G. Beidler, *Distinguished Teachers on Effective Teaching.* San Francisco: Jossey-Bass, 1986.

The teacher's role has many facets:

Gardener   One who tills and cultivates the fertile soil of students' minds, plants the seeds of knowledge, and then watches as understanding blossoms

Potter   One who shapes and molds students' thoughts and opinions

Dietitian   One who feeds students' minds with good information and then poses critical questions to help students digest that information

Builder   One who lays a foundation of knowledge in the subject and then helps students build on it throughout the course

Electrician   One who connects all the vital links of knowledge and then turns on the switch and watches for that "ah-ha" moment when the lightbulb goes on to illuminate students' minds

"Teaching is a craft, and as with any craft, one's performance can be bettered by careful attention to detail. Choosing textbooks, assigning papers, preparing for class, testing, grading, learning to improvise despite the best-laid plans—these are all important skills well worth your continuing attention. Yet the center of all teaching and learning is the interaction between the teacher and the learner. Developing as a teacher can be described as becoming wiser and less judgmental, more generous, less arrogant and yet more confident; being more honest with oneself and students and subject matter; taking more risks; showing forth without showing off; being impatient with ignorance but not appalled by it."

Source: Kenneth Eble, *The Craft of Teaching: A Guide to Mastering the Professor's Art.* San Francisco: Jossey-Bass, 1988, pp. xvii, 212.

Great Beginnings: What to Do on the First Day of Class

For most teachers, the longest, loneliest minute of life occurs in facing a class for the first time, when students quiet down and look up expectantly. Where to begin and what to do on the first day of class can seem both overwhelming and perplexing, particularly to an inexperienced teacher. The tips below can help you provide a smooth introduction to a medical terminology course for all of your students. Your efforts will produce students who can work confidently and productively in the weeks ahead.

1. **Provide a relaxed atmosphere.** Begin by assessing your classroom, its equipment, lighting, temperature, and so on, to ensure that it is conducive to learning. A modified version of Maslow's Hierarchy of Needs is presented here to clarify the point that physical comfort must be established before the student can progress to the next level. Fear and anxiety caused by unclear expectations for performance can prevent students from reaching the level where learning takes place.

Get acquainted. Rather than immediately plunging into course content and requirements, take a few minutes to allow students to become acquainted with each other. Ask them to stand and introduce themselves and state what they hope to gain from the course. A slightly longer version of this involves having students take out a blank piece of paper and write down the following things: name, why they are taking the course, something interesting about themselves (like their hobbies), and their greatest fear about the course. Then collect these papers. Call out the name on each paper and have the student raise his or her hand. That way you can put a face with the student's name. Take some notes on each paper to help you remember who is who. Students often sit in the same spot in the classroom each time and by the third week, you should be calling each student by his or her correct name. If the student has an interesting hobby, share it with the class and make a brief comment. Finally, take a moment to review all of the papers to identify the students' greatest fears. Then summarize them for the entire class and tell how you will help them overcome these fears. By developing a cooperative atmosphere in which students feel a part of the group and not isolated, you can help allay fears. Research has shown that a strongly supportive peer group in a learning situation helps students to cope successfully with the frustrations inherent in learning a new subject.

Slow and steady. As a new teacher, I remember that my only thoughts on the first day of class dealt with how much material needed to be covered and the short time that I had to do it. I wrongly felt that if I didn't plunge right in to work on the first day that I would fall so far behind in presenting the material that I could never catch up for the rest of the course. That was a misperception on my part, but I am sure it caused quite a few anxious moments for my overwhelmed students.

When you do begin to present course material, proceed at a slower-than-normal pace. When every part of an instructional process is new, students need extra time to understand detailed instructions. Speak slowly and allow pauses during which students can digest what you have presented. There is nothing more frustrating than having a teacher present course requirements so quickly that they become impossible to remember. Your students will not be able to immediately see patterns of learning in your course and will not be able to initiate their own learning/studying process if your presentation is hurried and pressured.

Address student anxiety. Every learner, regardless of age, has feelings of anxiety when confronted with a new learning situation, particularly if the learning involves being graded or evaluated in any way. It is important for the teacher to acknowledge this anxiety and discuss it with the group in order to help defuse it. Humorous sayings on the chalkboard (such as "Does medical terminology give you cephalalgia?") can provide a release of tension for students. One simple exercise that acknowledges the difficulty of learning a new skill is to ask students to fold their arms across their chests in the usual way that is comfortable for them. Then ask them to fold their arms with the other arm on the top. This usually provokes laughter and strange arm movements as the difficulty of this seemingly simple task becomes apparent. The teacher should then remind students that learning medical terminology is a mental skill that takes some time to properly coordinate and that they should not feel frightened or frustrated if their efforts do not immediately produce perfect results. Share this Khmer (Cambodian) proverb with them: "A journey of 1,000 miles begins with a single step."

2. **Provide general, then specific, information.** First, present the big picture (the entire course) before you discuss the details. This will give students a framework on which to hang the details you discuss later. Go over the information in the course syllabus and weekly reading assignments very slowly, reading it aloud while students follow along. Read through at least three weeks to show the repeating structure of the course objectives and assignments. This helps students get a sense of continuity within the course.

   Explore the textbook and student media. Display and discuss the required textbook. Students will then know if they have purchased the correct textbook, and your positive comments about why this textbook was selected will generate confidence.

   Some students are so worried about a course that it prevents them from doing anything but what the instructor specifically says for them to do. On their own, they may fail to explore the textbook and enjoy what it has to offer. For all students, however, it is also helpful to go through the textbook chapter names and sections so that they do not feel intimidated and, when you give them their first assignment, they have the tools they need to do it and can confidently say, "Oh, I know where that section is in the textbook!" Go from cover to cover in the textbook, pointing out sections that the student will need to use during the course (brief table of contents, index, answer key, glossary of word parts, etc.). Ask students to look up the meaning of several word parts in the Glossary and look in the Index to find on what page "appendectomy" and "rhinorrhea" are located in the text. Be sure to point out special features of the textbook that make learning easier or more interesting (Word Alert boxes, A Closer Look, cartoons, etc.). You can do this by going through "Dive Into Something Different" on pages viii–xiii, which elaborate on these special features. A number of teachers follow up this in-depth review with a brief quiz on the syllabus and parts of the textbook the following week. They have found that this approach has lowered their attrition rate dramatically.

   If possible, run the student media during class and show how easy it is to navigate through it to allay the fears of some students who are technophobic. Also demonstrate some of its features and games to entice students to make it an integral part of their learning experience. Mention that Pearson's technology is advanced and much richer than that of any other medical terminology book publisher on the market, and how fortunate the students are for their school to have picked this textbook that contains this student media. Tell students who are not computer savvy to find a child, family member, or friend who can quickly show them how to use this student media.

3. **Be enthusiastic.** A major airline advertises, "We love to fly, and it shows!" Like that airline, an instructor who loves to teach will show it, and one who has a love for the subject will not be able to hide it. Nothing is more important to teaching than an enthusiasm for the subject. That enthusiasm will be contagious. This is especially important in medical language because learning word parts and vocabulary is often associated with boring repetition and mind-numbing drill.

4. **Introduce the concepts of good study habits.**

   Take advantage of small blocks of time. Have students explore the Web site www .exploratorium.edu/memory/index.html. "The Memory Exhibition" Web site contains activities to test your memory—and some things you can try to help you remember things better.

   Urge students to keep their flashcards with them and study them while they wait to pick up their children from an activity, stop at a red light, or sit in a doctor's waiting room. Emphasize the importance of using every available moment. The successful student is the one who is best able to identify a study moment and seize it. Tiny study moments add up and contribute more to long-term retention than does a single, memorize-until-you-drop study session.

Involve family. Urge students to get family members involved in what they are learning. Even small children can enjoy helping as they hold up a flashcard printed from the student media that accompanies the textbook. Use water-soluble markers to label body parts on family members.

Summary

In short, make the first day of class a relaxed, confidence-building, memorable experience for your students. "We tend to forget how difficult it is for [students]. ... Our grasp of our subject matter is apt to become automatic. ... It is our duty to assume nothing and explain everything."

This material was adapted from the following articles:

Susan Turley, "Great Beginnings: What to Do on the First Day," *Perspectives on the Medical Transcription Profession,* Fall 1991, pp. 4–5.

Ellen Drake, "Teaching Medical Terminology," *Perspectives on the Medical Transcription Profession,* Fall 1992, pp. 12–15.

Classroom Management Techniques

Chapter Questions and Exercises

Give extra credit to every student who can show that they completed all the chapter exercises. This includes the anatomy-labeling exercises and word-building exercises in the middle of the chapter as well as the final section of Chapter Review Exercises. You do not need to check for correct or incorrect answers (that is the student's job). You are just rewarding diligent study habits that pay off in better test scores and more knowledge retained at the end of the course. Some students may want to resell their textbook and may not want to write in it. Stress to them that doing the exercises right in the textbook is a very helpful learning tool and that many students want to keep their textbook as a very useful reference book as they finish their other studies and later during their careers.

Weekly Spelling Practice

Select one of the following techniques to reinforce spelling each week for the chapter being studied.

Beanbag Spelling Toss. The members of the class stand in a circle. The first player, who is holding the beanbag, pronounces a medical word from the chapter while tossing the beanbag to another student. The student catching the beanbag must quickly spell the word. If the student spells the word correctly, then he or she thinks of and pronounces a new medical word while tossing the beanbag to another student, and so on. If the student cannot spell the word correctly, the student is eliminated, gives the beanbag to the instructor, and sits down. The instructor then pronounces a medical word while tossing the beanbag to another student and the game continues. The game is over when only one player remains standing.

Scrabble. Bring in a standard Scrabble game board set. The rules of the game are modified in that only medical words are allowed. Players work together in groups of two or three. Players may use a medical dictionary or the textbook to verify the correct spelling (but only half of the points are awarded). Option: Players can be required to define the words as they play them.

Spelling Bee. Divide the class into three or four equal groups. Have each group line up at the whiteboard at the front of the class. At the same time, give students at the head of each group a different word to spell. They should write it on the whiteboard. If the word is spelled correctly, the student stays standing with his or her group but goes to the end of the group. If the word is spelled incorrectly, the student must sit down. The group with the last person left standing wins the spelling bee and a few points can be given to each member of that group.

Gridlock. Use the grid below to review chapter terminology. Draw two identical grids on the board. Divide the class into two groups. Each group should stand at the board and collectively think of and write words from the chapter that begin with the initial letters on the grid. The team that thinks of the most words wins, but misspelled words do not count.

M	
E	
D	
I	
C	
A	
L	
W	
O	
R	
D	

Hangman. This game reinforces spelling but also pronunciation and the definitions of medical words. Pick one student to be the hangman. He or she mentally picks a medical word that is at least eight letters in length, goes to the board, and draws a scaffold and a noose and a series of blanks indicating the number of letters in the word. Going around the room, each student calls out a letter. If the letter is present in the word, the hangman writes it in the appropriate blank. If the letter is not present, the hangman draws a body part. As the game progresses, the body should be drawn in six steps (head, torso, left leg, right leg, left arm, right arm). The student who guesses the word before the hangman picture is completed is declared the winner, but only if he or she can also correctly pronounce the word and define it. If so, then that student becomes the hangman for the next round.

Weekly Pronunciation Practice

Select one of the following techniques to reinforce pronunciation each week for the chapter being studied.

Parroting. Using the comprehensive "see and say" pronunciation guide in the Pronunciation Checklist, say each word, and then have the students as a group repeat the pronunciation to you. This promotes active listening and helps them to develop competence in their pronunciation of medical words aside from the standard times of practice that occur as they study the chapter or use the student media. Alternatively, give the pronunciation of one word and then have the students as a group give the pronunciation of the next word.

Hieroglyphics. Randomly pick and write a few of the "see and say" pronunciations on the board and see if students can pronounce the medical word.

Beach Ball Blast. If students seem to be tired and unable to concentrate on the lecture, stop the class and surprise them with this activity. Have each of them quickly pick out four medical words from the chapter. Specify that at least one should be a long medical word.

Have them quickly review the pronunciations of the words they picked (they can say them out loud to practice the pronunciations). It is okay if some students pick some of the same words. As they are doing this, quickly blow up an inflatable beach ball. Tell them each time the beach ball comes to them they are to punch or hit it to another student (or pick it up and punch it if it falls to the floor) and, at the same time, they are to correctly pronounce one of the vocabulary words they have picked. They are not to catch the ball, just react to it and punch or hit it away. The next time the ball comes to them, they are to punch or hit the ball while pronouncing their second vocabulary word. Continue this until most students have pronounced at least three of their words. Start the activity by hitting the ball high in the air toward the back row of students while you say the word for the medical specialty of the chapter you are currently studying. If the activity is done correctly, the ball should be moving quickly around the room and there should be lots of medical words being pronounced.

Weekly Chapter Test

Each week, the class should cover one chapter of material and take a test on that material the following week at the beginning of class. This keeps the learning segments at a size that is manageable and prevents students from falling behind and doing poorly (which can happen when the course only has one large midterm examination and one large final examination). The test should be taken in the first 30 minutes of class, and then the answers quickly reviewed. I often allow students to skip one weekly test that does not count toward their grade to allow for unforeseen events such as illness and family emergencies.

Weekly Spelling Test

For each chapter, provide students with a list of 20 spelling words to study. Then, next week, at the conclusion of the weekly chapter test, have students turn their test paper over and number the back for the spelling test. Pronounce each spelling word and use it in a sentence. Include at least 10 of the spelling words.

Weekly Pronunciation Test

Assign 20 words from the Pronunciation Checklist. Any time before the next weekly test, tell each student to call your office or home and leave a message on your answering machine in which they give their name and then pronounce the list of words.

Take-Home Test

If you don't have time to cover every chapter, consider using a take-home test to be completed during the mid-semester break or over the course of several class sessions. This would be an open-book test.

Comprehensive Review Before the Final Examination

Some colleges require that a comprehensive final examination be given. This is a good strategy to make sure students review and relearn material from the entire course. This leads to better retention of course material for the future when the student is on the job. However, a final examination can cause students great anxiety. Devote some of your final class time to helping students prepare for the final examination by using this fun exercise.

Have each student make up 10 *Jeopardy*-like questions the week before the final review. The questions can be based on anything and everything studied during the whole course. Have students write the answer on one side and the question on the other side of an index card. Questions are always phrased as an answer and the answer is then always given in the form of a question.

Answer: Ren/o- and nephr/o- [on the front of the index card]

Question: What are the two combining forms that both mean *kidney?*

For the final review class, collect all the index cards and shuffle them. Divide the students into two or three teams and have them remain standing. Read an index card "answer" to each group. The group members can help each other come up with the answer in the form of a question and write it on the board. If they are correct, give them another "answer" to work on. The first group to write 10 correct questions on the board wins.

Interesting Quotations to Use During Class

The beginnings of all things are small.—Cicero

A journey of 1,000 miles begins with one step.—Khmer (Cambodian) proverb

The distance is nothing; it is only the first step that is difficult.—Marquise Du Deffand (1697–1780)

Learning is a continuous process of combining the familiar with the new.—Stanford C. Ericksen (1974)

If we succeed in giving the love of learning, the learning itself is sure to follow.—Sir John Lubbock

Perfection is the child of time.—Joseph Hall (1574–1656)

Knowledge is power.—Francis Bacon (1500s)

Learn from the mistakes of others—you can't live long enough to make them all yourself.—Anonymous

Examinations are formidable even to the best prepared, for the greatest fool may ask more than the wisest man can answer.—Charles Colton (1888–1965)

Intelligent thinking is the basis of all great endeavors.—Anonymous

Genius is one percent inspiration and ninety-nine percent perspiration.—Thomas Alva Edison (1874–1931)

Whatever is worth doing at all is worth doing well.—Philip Chesterfield (1694–1773)

Nothing great was ever achieved without enthusiasm.—Ralph Waldo Emerson (1803–1882)

If you're going to do it, do it RIGHT.—Lee Iacocca

I have not failed; I have discovered 50,000 things that will not work.—Thomas Alva Edison (1874–1931)

Getting an idea should be like sitting on a tack; it should make you get up and do something about it.—Herbert Prochnow

If you would hit the mark, you must aim a little above it.—Henry Wadsworth Longfellow (1807–1882)

He who aims at nothing will likely hit it.—Anonymous

The secret of success is constancy of purpose.—Benjamin Disraeli

Ambition, energy, and perseverance are the levers that move obstacles in our path.—Ida Scott Taylor (1894)

The best way to escape from a problem is to solve it.—Brendan Frances

Life is a daring adventure, or it is nothing.—Helen Keller

The most important thing in life is to love what you're doing, because it's the only way you'll ever really be good at it.—Donald Trump

"Mnifty" Mnemonic Devices

Many of us are familiar with the term *mnemonic device* (pronounced "ne-MAWN-ik"). Certainly we have all used mnemonic devices in one way or another throughout our lifetimes. Do you remember learning these mnemonic devices?

"Roy G. Biv" (red, orange, yellow, green, blue, indigo, violet) to remember the colors of the rainbow

There are two *s*'s in "dessert" because you always want two helpings of dessert. This mnemonic helps you differentiate between the spelling of "dessert" and "desert."

"**M**y **v**ery **e**xcellent **m**other **j**ust **s**erved **us** **n**ine **p**izzas" to remember the names of the planets (Mercury, Venus, Earth, Mars, Jupiter, Saturn, Uranus, Neptune, Pluto)

A mnemonic device is simply a memory aid that helps link the unfamiliar with the familiar, so that we can retrieve information from our brains more quickly. Using mnemonic devices and learning how to construct them helps students remember the spellings of the many new words they have to learn in medical terminology.

1. **First-letter cues.** To spell difficult words or to remember long lists, use the letters of the word or the first letters of each of the words in the phrase to construct a sentence. For example, the spelling of "rhythm" is difficult to remember, but constructing the sentence, "Ruby had yams; Tommy had muffins" can help you remember. Anatomy students use "Every child must nap" to remember the four major types of body tissues (epithelial, connective, muscle, nerve).

2. **Imagery link.** Linking medical words to mental images makes them easier to remember. "Dysphagia" and "dysphasia" are frequently confused, and are more easily remembered by linking "dysphagia" with "gag" and "dysphasia" with "speech."

3. **Associate spelling with "logical order."** To remember the difference between "perineal" and "peroneal," associate the word with its order of appearance in the body from head to toe: the perineal area (external genital area) comes before the peroneal area (leg area). Also, the "i" (in perineal) comes before the "o" (in peroneal) alphabetically.

4. The CD-ROM of the textbook contains several good mnemonic devices for each chapter. Encourage students to develop their own as well!

This textbook's student media shares many mnemonic devices for each chapter, but the ones that students make up themselves are the ones they often remember best. Give two extra credit points for each good mnemonic that a student submits (limit 10 points throughout the course). Share the best ones with the rest of the class. Mnemonic devices can be in the form of an abbreviation where each letter stands for something, or in the form of a riddle, a poem, or a song. For example, a medical terminology student created this mnemonic to remember the order of the small intestine (duodenum, jejunum, ileum): "**D**ogs **e**at **J**unk and don't get **Ill**."

Source: Adapted from Linda Campbell, "Using Mnemonic Devices," *Perspectives on the Medical Transcription Profession,* Fall 1991.

All of the Above

Test questions:
   A) are not easy to construct.
   B) can mean different things to the teacher and student.
   C) may inaccurately test students' knowledge.
   D) can give away the correct answer.
   E) All of the above.
   [The correct answer is "E) All of the above."]

When I first began teaching, my immediate priorities were to quickly develop a course syllabus, select an appropriate textbook, and research additional lecture material for each class. Sometimes in the week-to-week busyness of class preparation, I would have to construct a test. Often I found myself doing this hurriedly and late at night. Some last-minute preparation is certainly unavoidable for a new teacher or even for an experienced teacher developing and presenting a course for the first time. However, last-minute test preparation is not conducive to thoroughness and may inaccurately test students' knowledge.

It is important to recognize some of the finer points of test construction. As in all areas of teaching, we grow in our ability to teach as well as to evaluate students' learning. The writing of test questions is something of an art, the perfection of which depends on two factors: knowledge of the mechanics/techniques of proper test construction, and the time to practice and refine those techniques.

1. **Draw from course objectives.** No course syllabus is complete without a list of course objectives. Chapter objectives can be found at the beginning of every chapter in the textbook. The test must be drawn from these same objectives. Consider the following example in which the test questions do *not* correlate with the chapter objectives.

   Chapter Objectives
   List the main structures of the cardiovascular system.
   Identify common diseases of the cardiovascular system.

   Test Questions
   Give a brief history of the discovery of the circulatory system.
   Identify five common radiology procedures performed on the circulatory system.

2. **Consider time and scope.** Consider the length of the testing time period and the scope of the material that is to be tested. It is common to include too many questions for the time allowed. It is also common to pick questions that focus too much attention on one area of content. It may be helpful to keep a chart as you prepare a test and check off each subject area when you finish its test questions.

3. **Vary the types of questions used.** There are several test question formats that can be used to approach the material in different ways. These formats include multiple choice, true/false, matching, fill in the blank, short answer, sequencing, selection, and case studies. Not every question format is suitable to each testing situation. However, the use of several different test question formats is preferred.

Multiple-Choice Questions

This format is widely used but can be inaccurate if a question is not constructed properly. When constructing a chapter test, make sure that all of the answers (correct and incorrect) are from that chapter's material. All of the answers must be plausible and constructed in such a way that the sentence structure does not give a clue as to the correct answer. Consider the following example in which the sentence structure is faulty, making it easy to determine the correct answer.

> A ronguer is an _____ instrument.
>   A) neurologic
>   B) cardiovascular
>   C) orthopedic
>   D) gastrointestinal
> [Answer: C) orthopedic. The use of "an" clues the student that the correct answer must begin with a vowel, and only one answer begins with a vowel.]

Because multiple-choice formats allow the student to guess the right answer, it is best to include five answers rather than four to reduce the probability of a correct guess from 25 percent to 20 percent.

Beginning test writers tend to shy away from the first alternative [a.] being the correct answer. In fact, the third position [c.] tends to be the correct answer a disproportionate number of times. The goal should be to have the correct answer appear in each position an equal number of times. The position of the correct answer should be selected randomly. No pattern of the correct answer position should be apparent in the test.

True–False Questions

This format is also widely used, but is more restricted in the scope of information it can test. It is best to avoid test questions that contain the words *always, never,* or *none,* as this provides a clue that the answer is probably false. True–false questions also provide an opportunity for students to guess at the answer with a 50 percent chance of being correct. Therefore, this type of question should be used sparingly.

Matching Questions

This format can test relationships and the ability to classify. It is best not to provide an exact match between the number of items in Column 1 and those in Column 2. An uneven match makes students evaluate each item based on its own merits rather than just matching it to whatever is left over. Never continue the matching columns from the bottom of one page to the top of another. Make sure that the entire matching question appears on just one page.

One twist on the matching question is to use this format (answers provided):

Column 1		Column 2
1. A is caused by B	3, 4	femur: bone
2. A is a source of B	5	MI: elevated CPK-MB
3. A is made of B	2	pancreas: insulin
4. A is a type of B	1	stroke: blood clot
5. A is proven by B	1, 5	syphilis: Treponema

This format requires a bit of thinking on the part of the student. It is very important that the teacher review and explain this type of question and how to employ thinking strategies to answer it correctly *before* presenting it in a testing situation.

Fill-in-the-Blank Questions

This format effectively measures memorization of specific facts but cannot measure understanding or relationships. If the question is not well constructed, students may have a difficult time trying to guess what should go in the blank. The teacher may also inadvertently give a clue to the correct answer by making a long or short blank line.

Short-Answer Questions

This format is similar to that of fill-in-the-blank questions but differs in that there is no line drawn to write in the answer.

Sequencing Questions

This format is particularly useful in testing anatomy in which there is a well-defined sequence of structures. Example:

Arrange the structures of the urinary tract in the correct anatomical order, beginning with the flow of blood in the renal artery and ending with the production of urine. Pick from these structures to complete the sequence.

Renal artery   ureter   glomerulus   renal pelvis [etc.]

Renal artery   →   _____   →   _____   →   _____ [etc.]

Selection Questions

In this format, students are asked to select only those answers that correspond to a particular category, disease condition, and so on. Example:

Circle those drugs used to treat cardiac arrhythmias.

Nexium	Procan-SR	Corgard
Lasix	Lipitor	Avodart

Case Studies

This format presents the opportunity to test not only students' knowledge of facts but their understanding of relationships. Case studies should be used sparingly on tests because they are time-consuming. Case studies should be presented in class to allow students to develop the skills needed to correctly answer questions associated with a case study.

Summary

A final thought on test construction. Just as there is no perfect student and no perfect teacher, there is also no perfect test question. A question that seems perfectly clear to the teacher may be confusing to a student. Teachers should make every effort to word questions clearly and to use only terminology that has been presented in class or in the textbook. The wise teacher will listen to the student who has a logical explanation for a "wrong" answer. It is not heresy to admit that there might be more than one correct interpretation of the wording of a question and to give the student a point back for that question.

Source: Adapted from Susan Turley, "All of the Above," *Perspectives on the Medical Transcription Profession*, Fall 1990, pp. 8–10.

When Is an Adult an Adult?

Students in a medical terminology course can range in age from 18 to 55 years of age or more. This is a wide span and it behooves the teacher to be aware of the differences and similarities of these students and the practical challenges this presents when teaching adult learners.

Traditional educational research has extensively addressed the question of what constitutes an adult learner, what personal characteristics are common to adult learners, and what basic characteristics can be attributed to them. Two schools of thought attempt to describe the adult learner.

The first school of thought views adult learners as a generic group with similar characteristics based on their sharing of adulthood. Malcolm S. Knowles, an educational researcher, is one of the main proponents for this group. According to Knowles, the foundation of modern adult learning theory is based on several key assumptions that ascribe particular attributes to all adult learners. In general, these assumptions state that all adults are motivated, inquiring, mature, self-directed, experienced, and have attained a formal operational level of thought processes.

- **Motivated.** Adult learners are more motivated to learn. They often have a sense of urgency and are more willing to make sacrifices in their pursuit of learning.
- **Inquiring.** Adult learners are less willing to accept the authority of the teacher as the final and sole source of knowledge. Adult learners demand that teachers be accountable and that coursework be meaningful.
- **Mature.** Adult learners are more mature in the behavior and attitudes they bring to the learning experience. Their goals are more clearly defined, and they take their studies seriously. Adult learners have a strong self-concept and confidence gained from coping with the responsibilities of adult life.

- **Self-directed.** Adult learners are self-directed in their pursuit of knowledge. They value the right to make independent decisions about their own learning needs.
- **Experienced.** Adult learners bring to the classroom a rich background of varied experiences. This past learning becomes a touchstone for relating to new learning. In contrast to younger learners, adult learners possess sophisticated insights springing from their knowledge of the world of work and from the skills they have acquired there.
- **Formal operational.** Adult learners function at the level of formal operational thinking and are able to deal with abstract concepts as well as concrete (hands-on) learning.

There is considerable uncertainty from other authors (from the second school of thought) as to whether all adult learners can be so categorically labeled and whether this labeling accurately reflects a true picture of *any* individual adult learner. Stephen D. Brookfield, a professor and author in the field of adult education, notes that individual learning behaviors are so idiosyncratic as to cast considerable doubt on any general assertions about adults as learners. Although some adult learners may be highly self-directed, many adults regress in a classroom situation to relive their role as passive childhood learners. Some are even visibly intimidated, and it is unrealistic to claim that self-directed learning is a commonality across the spectrum of adult learners. Brookfield cautions not to assume that all adults will enter a course as self-directed learners or will even want to become so with the assistance of the teacher.

While some adult learners possess a wide range of learning experiences, some minority, poor, and disadvantaged adult learners come from an environment that did not foster critical thinking and a self-directed attitude toward learning.

For those adult learners who do possess a rich variety of experiences, it still cannot be said that this is a positive resource to learning. Life experiences can enrich and enlarge an individual's perception of self and society, but they can also result in mental habits and biases that tend to close the mind to new ideas and alternative ways of thinking.

While some adult learners have a strong self-concept and confidence, other adult learners are hesitant and lack confidence in their ability to learn. While some adult learners have clear goals and take their studies seriously, others have goals and priorities that are poorly defined.

Some adult learners may actively participate in the learning process, while others may sit back and expect to be spoon-fed by the instructor. This calls to mind the title of the infant nutrition book *Feed Me, I'm Yours*.

So when is an adult an adult? For some students, maybe never. We must, then, acknowledge the flaw of attempting to put the same labels on all adult learners. We must remember that adult learners come with all different levels of motivation, curiosity, maturity, and independence. Our job as teachers is to recognize each student as an individual with distinct strengths and weaknesses, to praise their strengths, correct their weaknesses, and help them on their journey to become an adult learner.

Source: Adapted from Susan Turley, "When Is an Adult an Adult?," *Perspectives on the Medical Transcription Profession*, Winter 1990–91, pp. 25–27.

SAMPLE COURSE SYLLABUS

Instructor: (Teacher's name here)
E-mail: (Teacher's e-mail address here)
Course Text: Turley, Susan. *Medical Language,* 2/e (Pearson, 2011)

Course Goals

1. Give the medical meaning of prefixes, suffixes, and combining forms for each body system.
2. Demonstrate the ability to use word parts to build medical words.
3. Analyze the meaning of medical words for each body system.
4. Correctly make plural and adjective forms of medical words.
5. Demonstrate the ability to interpret medical words in the context of medical reports.
6. Pronounce and spell medical words correctly for each body system.
7. Translate common abbreviations, acronyms, and slang terms for each body system.
8. Make a personal commitment to learning medical terminology.
9. Describe methods of time management and good study habits and apply them to this course.

Course Outline and Weekly Learning Objectives

Week 1: Chapter 1, The Structure of Medical Language

1. Identify the five skills of medical language communication.
2. Describe the origins of medical language.
3. Recognize common Latin and Greek singular nouns and form their plurals.
4. Describe characteristics of combining forms, suffixes, and prefixes.
5. Give the medical meaning of common word parts.
6. Build medical words from word parts and divide medical words into word parts.
7. Spell and pronounce common medical words.
8. Describe the format and contents of common medical documents.
9. Dive deeper into the structure of medical language by reviewing the activities at the end of this chapter and online at Medical Terminology Interactive.

Week 2: Chapter 2, The Body in Health and Disease

1. Define approaches used to organize information about the human body.
2. Identify body directions, body cavities, body systems, and medical specialties.
3. Describe various categories of diseases.
4. Describe techniques used to perform a physical examination.
5. Describe categories of healthcare professionals and settings in which health care is provided.
6. Give the medical meaning of word parts related to the body, health, and disease.
7. Build medical words about the body, health, and disease from word parts and divide and define words.
8. Spell and pronounce medical words about the body, health, and disease.
9. Dive deeper into the body, health, and disease by reviewing the activities at the end of this chapter and online at Medical Terminology Interactive.

Note: The following weeks correlate to specific body systems and medical specialties. The weekly learning objectives are the same for each of these weeks.

Weekly Learning Objectives for Weeks 3–15

1. Identify the structures of the [gastrointestinal] system.
2. Describe the process of [digestion].
3. Describe common [gastrointestinal] diseases and conditions, laboratory and diagnostic procedures, medical and surgical procedures, and drug categories.
4. Give the medical meaning of word parts related to the [gastrointestinal] system.
5. Build [gastrointestinal] words from word parts and divide and define [gastrointestinal] words.
6. Spell and pronounce [gastrointestinal] words.
7. Analyze the medical content and meaning of a [gastroenterology] report.
8. Dive deeper into [gastroenterology] by reviewing the activities at the end of this chapter and online at Medical Terminology Interactive.

Week 3:   Chapter 3, Gastroenterology/Gastrointestinal System
Week 4:   Chapter 4, Pulmonology/Respiratory System
Week 5:   Chapter 5, Cardiology/Cardiovascular System
Week 6:   Chapter 6, Hematology and Immunology/Blood and the Lymphatic System
Week 7:   Chapter 7, Dermatology/Integumentary System
Week 8:   Chapter 8, Orthopedics/Skeletal System
Week 9:   Chapter 9, Orthopedics/Muscular System
Week 10: Chapter 10, Neurology/Nervous System
Week 11: Chapter 11, Urology/Urinary System
Week 12: Chapter 12, Male Reproductive Medicine/Male Genitourinary System
Week 13: Chapter 13, Gynecology and Obstetrics/Female Reproductive System
Week 14: Chapter 14, Endocrinology/Endocrine System
Week 15: Chapters 15 and 16, Ophthalmology/Eye and Otolaryngology/Ears, Nose, and Throat

Independent Study Chapters throughout the Course
    Chapter 17   Psychiatry
    Chapter 18   Oncology
    Chapter 19   Radiology and Nuclear Medicine
Final Examination

Course Management

Attendance

Students are expected to be present for all class sessions. We all, on occasion, have times when illness or family situations prevent us from attending class. You need not provide the instructor with an explanation or a note or a reason for your absence. No points are deducted for missing a class lecture. However, regular attendance promotes success, and absenteeism may adversely affect your overall grade.

If you are absent from a class, it is *your* responsibility to find out what you missed, to copy notes from another student, and to ask the instructor for the handouts. Being absent does not excuse you from being responsible for learning any subject matter that was presented or discussed, whether in the textbook or during class time.

Basis for a Final Grade

Weekly Test. A test will be given weekly (beginning on the third week). Each weekly test will cover the material presented in class or assigned in the textbook during the previous week(s). There are no makeup tests under any circumstances. In calculating your final grade for the course, your one lowest weekly test grade will be automatically dropped. In addition to that, if you are absent and miss one test (or circumstances left you unprepared and you elect not to take one test), that one test will be omitted from your grade and will not count against you.

Take-Home Tests. Occasionally a chapter test will be a take-home test that you complete at home over 1–2 weeks and then turn in. These are open-book tests.

Homework. Occasional homework assignments may be given. Late homework assignments are not accepted unless you were absent from class on the day that the assignment was due.

Optional Extra Credit Work. If you complete all the chapter review exercises by writing directly in the textbook, you can receive 3 extra points per chapter. Show your textbook to your instructor to receive credit.

During the course, you may submit mnemonic devices (memory aids) that you think of yourself to help you remember the course material (like the sequence of body structures in the GI system, etc.). Each is worth 2 points, and you may submit up to 5 during the course for a possible total of 10 points.

Comprehensive Final Examination. This is a college requirement for passing this course. If you have a scheduling conflict at the time the Final Examination is scheduled, you must make prior arrangements with your instructor for a copy of the Final Examination to be sent to the college Testing and Tutoring Center, and the Final Examination must always be taken before the regularly scheduled classroom Final Examination.

Grading Scale

89.5–100%	A
79.5–89.4%	B
69.5–79.4%	C
Below 69.4%	F

Let's Keep in Touch

The instructor will inform you of your midterm grade before it is turned into the Records and Registration Office. Students with a low C or below at midterm will be referred by the instructor to the Counseling Center.

You may ask the instructor what your current grade is at any time during the course.

Don't be afraid to ask your instructor for help in clarifying the expectations of the course and/or how to improve your grade. It is your responsibility to do this.

IMPORTANT: If you feel confused, anxious, not "on track," or concerned about anything about the course, immediately speak to your instructor via e-mail or before class or during class break. Believe it or not, every student feels that way from time to time! It's a normal response to the stress of learning something new!

Drop/Withdraw

Your instructor has given you a dates sheet that gives the last date to withdraw from the course. If you decide to drop/withdraw from this course, it is your responsibility to notify the Records and Registration Office at the college and complete paperwork to formally drop/withdraw. If you do this before the Final Drop Date for the semester, the course will be taken off your transcript. If you drop/withdraw after that, you will receive a "W" on your transcript for this course. If you do not complete the paperwork at the Records and Registration Office, you will receive an F on your transcript for this course.

The Structure of Medical Language

Measure Your Progress: Learning Objectives

After reading this chapter, the student should be able to

- Identify the five skills of medical language communication.
- Describe the origins of medical language.
- Recognize common Latin and Greek singular nouns and form their plurals.
- Describe characteristics of combining forms, suffixes, and prefixes.
- Give the medical meaning of common word parts.
- Build medical words from word parts and divide medical words into word parts.
- Spell and pronounce common medical words.
- Describe the format and contents of common medical documents.
- Dive deeper into the structure of medical language by reviewing the activities at the end of this chapter and online at Medical Terminology Interactive.

It All Starts with Word Building

Medical language is all about medical words and their word parts. Jump right into this chapter by learning some of the combining forms and their definitions that you will encounter in this chapter.

append/o-	appendix
arthr/o-	joint
cardi/o-	heart
cutane/o-	skin
esthes/o-	sensation; feeling
gastr/o-	stomach
hem/o-	blood
hepat/o-	liver
laryng/o-	larynx (voice box)
mamm/o-	breast
neur/o-	nerve
pneumon/o-	lung; air
psych/o-	mind
thyroid/o-	thyroid gland
tonsill/o-	tonsil
trache/o-	trachea (windpipe)
urin/o-	urine; urinary system
ven/o-	vein

Word Search

Complete this word search puzzle that contains Chapter 1 words. Look for the following words as given in the list below. The number in parentheses indicates how many times the word is found in the puzzle.

communication	medical (2)
CPR	origin
diagnosis	patient
EPR (2)	plural
etymology (2)	prefix
Greek	record (2)
HIPAA	suffix
language	treatment
Latin (3)	word (2)
listen (2)	

```
A  P  S  R  T  C  W  O  R  D  R  O  C  E  R
G  R  E  E  K  L  I  S  T  E  N  O  P  Z  P
X  E  S  C  G  Q  R  N  C  Y  M  S  R  L  E
K  F  W  O  R  D  E  T  Y  M  O  L  O  G  Y
V  I  H  R  V  I  B  K  U  C  L  R  J  M  G
D  X  H  D  T  L  A  N  G  U  A  G  E  E  O
P  I  I  A  R  A  I  O  N  L  T  D  W  L  L
O  F  P  U  L  C  J  S  I  H  I  P  A  A  O
R  F  A  E  A  I  G  M  T  C  N  W  T  R  M
I  U  A  T  L  D  F  O  A  E  L  I  N  U  Y
G  S  I  F  Q  E  O  L  L  P  N  C  D  L  T
I  O  T  N  E  M  T  A  E  R  T  X  Z  P  E
N  H  I  R  V  B  D  I  A  G  N  O  S  I  S
```

Crossword Puzzle

ACROSS

1. A _____ is an allied health professional who responds to emergency calls in the community.

5. Medical words are derived from the _____ and Latin languages.

7. The prefix "_____" means against.

8. The prefix "_____" means slow.

9. The combining form "_____" means vein.

11. A _____ is the process of using an instrument to examine the stomach.

14. A _____ _____ is the foundation of a medical word

16. Medical language skill #4 involves writing (or typing) and the ability to correctly _____ words.

DOWN

1. The combining form "_____" means lung.

2. The suffix "_____" means one who specializes in.

3. In this textbook, you will study medical _____.

4. It is important to be able to spell medical words correctly when you _____ them in the patient's medical record.

6. _____ is the study of the heart.

10. A tumor on a nerve is a _____.

12. The suffix "_____" means surgically created opening.

13. The _____ history and family history are two headings in the patient's medical record.

15. The suffix "_____" means process of cutting or making an incision.

Underline the Accented Syllable

Read the medical word. Then review the syllables in the pronunciation. Underline the primary (main) accented syllable in the pronunciation.

1. anesthesia   (an-es-thee-zee-ah)

2. subcutaneous   (sub-kyoo-tay-nee-us)

3. neuroma   (nyoo-roh-mah)

4. cardiomegaly   (kar-dee-oh-meg-ah-lee)

5. hypothyroidism   (hy-poh-thy-royd-izm)

6. appendectomy   (ap-pen-dek-toh-mee)

7. neurology   (nyoo-rawl-oh-jee)

8. postnasal   (post-nay-zal)

9. pneumonia   (noo-moh-nee-ah)

10. polyneuritis   (pawl-ee-nyoo-ry-tis)

11. psychosis   (sy-koh-sis)

12. tachycardia   (tak-ih-kar-dee-ah)

13. tonsillectomy   (tawn-sih-lek-toh-mee)

14. endotracheal   (en-doh-tray-kee-al)

15. colostomy   (koh-laws-toh-mee)

Word Surgery

Read the medical word. Break the medical word into its word parts, and give the meaning of each word part. Then give the definition of the medical word.

1. arthropathy

   Suffix and its meaning: _____

   Prefix and its meaning: _____

   Combining form and its meaning: _____

   Medical word definition: _____

2. bradycardia

   Suffix and its meaning: _____

   Prefix and its meaning: _____

   Combining form and its meaning: _____

   Medical word definition: _____

3. cardiomegaly

   Suffix and its meaning: _____

   Prefix and its meaning: _____

   Combining form and its meaning: _____

   Medical word definition: _____

4. postnasal

   Suffix and its meaning: _____

   Prefix and its meaning: _____

   Combining form and its meaning: _____

   Medical word definition: _____

5. endotracheal

   Suffix and its meaning: _____

   Prefix and its meaning: _____

   Combining form and its meaning: _____

   Medical word definition: _____

6. gastrointestinal

Suffix and its meaning: _____

Prefix and its meaning: _____

Combining form and its meaning: _____

Combining form and its meaning: _____

Medical word definition: _____

7. epidermal

Suffix and its meaning: _____

Prefix and its meaning: _____

Combining form and its meaning: _____

Medical word definition: _____

8. hypothyroidism

Suffix and its meaning: _____

Prefix and its meaning: _____

Combining form and its meaning: _____

Medical word definition: _____

9. intravenous

Suffix and its meaning: _____

Prefix and its meaning: _____

Combining form and its meaning: _____

Medical word definition: _____

10. pericardial

Suffix and its meaning: _____

Prefix and its meaning: _____

Combining form and its meaning: _____

Medical word definition: _____

11. pneumonia

Suffix and its meaning: _____

Prefix and its meaning: _____

Combining form and its meaning: _____

Medical word definition: _____

12. polyneuritis

   Suffix and its meaning: _____

   Prefix and its meaning: _____

   Combining form and its meaning: _____

   Medical word definition: _____

13. subcutaneous

   Suffix and its meaning: _____

   Prefix and its meaning: _____

   Combining form and its meaning: _____

   Medical word definition: _____

14. tonsillectomy

   Suffix and its meaning: _____

   Prefix and its meaning: _____

   Combining form and its meaning: _____

   Medical word definition: _____

15. urination

   Suffix and its meaning: _____

   Prefix and its meaning: _____

   Combining form and its meaning: _____

   Medical word definition: _____

Chapter Quiz

1. Effective communication involves:

    A. reading and writing.

    B. listening and speaking.

    C. thinking and analyzing.

    D. All of the above.

2. A prefix:

    A. can be found at the beginning of a medical word.

    B. can be found at the end of a medical word.

    C. is present in every medical word.

    D. is combined with a consonant.

3. A root followed by a vowel (usually an *o*) is known as a:

    A. stem.

    B. combining form.

    C. suffix.

    D. prefix.

4. Which of the following is a combining form?

    A. ven/o-

    B. urin/o-

    C. gastr/o-

    D. All of the above.

5. Which of the following is a suffix?

    A. peri-

    B. -ar

    C. pneumon/o-

    D. cardi/o-

6. When building a medical word:

    A. use a combining form plus a suffix.

    B. start with a suffix.

    C. end with a prefix.

    D. use a prefix immediately followed by a suffix.

7. When analyzing the word "cardiology," we find:

    A. a prefix and suffix.

    B. combining form and a suffix.

    C. a suffix meaning lungs.

    D. a prefix and a combining form.

8. A prefix often gives information about:

    A. location or direction.

    B. amount, number, or speed.

    C. degree or quality.

    D. All of the above.

9. Medical words can have:

    A. no word parts.

    B. a prefix plus a combining form and a suffix.

    C. no prefix.

    D. All of the above.

10. To analyze a medical word, begin:

    A. with the prefix.

    B. with the combining form.

    C. with the suffix.

    D. with the combining vowel.

FILL IN THE BLANK

1. The prefix that means around is _____.

2. The prefix that means below; deficient is _____.

3. When a medical word ends in "-um," make it plural by changing the "-um" to

    _____.

4. HIPPA stands for _____

5. Although CPR can stand for cardiopulmonary resuscitation, in the context of medical records it means _____.

6. _____ is the abbreviation for diagnosis.

7. The plural of bronchus is _____.

8. The word part "post" in postnasal is a _____.

TRUE/FALSE

_____ 1. Prefixes and suffixes modify the meaning of the combining form.

_____ 2. Occasionally a medical word contains two prefixes.

_____ 3. The prefixes "a-" or "an-" mean painful.

_____ 4. Analyzing a medical word begins by finding the meaning of the prefix.

_____ 5. "Gastrointestinal" contains two prefixes and one suffix.

_____ 6. To make the plural form of "phalanx," change the "-nx" to "-nxes."

_____ 7. An informed consent is a document that describes the purpose of the proposed surgery and informs the patient of alternatives, risks, and possible complications.

_____ 8. In the "see-and-say" method of pronunciation used in the textbook, the syllable that is emphasized (accented syllable) is in capital letters.

_____ 9. The etymology of a medical word is how it is pronounced.

_____ 10. The suffixes "-ic," "-al," "-ar," and "-ous" all mean "pertaining to."

Pronunciation Checklist

Read each word and its pronunciation. Practice pronouncing each word. Verify your pronunciation by listening to the Pronunciation List on Medical Terminology Interactive. Check the box next to the word after you master its pronunciation.

- ❏ abdominal (ab-DAWM-ih-nal)
- ❏ alveolus (al-VEE-oh-lus)
- ❏ alveoli (al-VEE-oh-lie)
- ❏ anesthesia (AN-es-THEE-zee-ah)
- ❏ antibiotic (AN-tee-by-AWT-ik)
- ❏ apex (AA-peks)
- ❏ apices (AA-pih-seez)
- ❏ appendectomy (AP-pen-DEK-toh-mee)
- ❏ areola (ah-REE-oh-lah)
- ❏ areolae (ah-REE-oh-lee)
- ❏ artery (AR-ter-ee)
- ❏ arthritis (ar-THRY-tis)
- ❏ arthropathy (ar-THRAWP-ah-thee)
- ❏ aspermia (aa-SPER-mee-ah)
- ❏ atria (AA-tree-ah)
- ❏ atrium (AA-tree-um)
- ❏ bacteria (bak-TEER-ee-ah)
- ❏ bacterium (bak-TEER-ee-um)
- ❏ bilateral (bi-LAT-er-al)
- ❏ bladder (BLAD-er)
- ❏ bradycardia (BRAD-ee-KAR-dee-ah)
- ❏ bronchi (BRONG-kigh)
- ❏ bronchus (BRONG-kus)
- ❏ bursa (BER-sah)
- ❏ bursae (BER-see)
- ❏ calculus (KAL-kyoo-lus)
- ❏ calculi (KAL-kyoo-lie)
- ❏ calices (KAL-ih-seez)
- ❏ calix (KAY-liks)
- ❏ carcinoma (KAR-sih-NOH-mah)
- ❏ carcinomata (KAR-sih-NOH-mah-tah)
- ❏ cardiac (KAR-dee-ak)
- ❏ cardiology (KAR-dee-AWL-oh-jee)
- ❏ cardiomegaly (KAR-dee-oh-MEG-ah-lee)
- ❏ colonoscope (koh-LAWN-oh-skop)
- ❏ colostomy (koh-LAWS-toh-mee)
- ❏ communication (koh-MYOO-nih-KAY-shun)
- ❏ conjunctiva (CON-junk-TY-vah)

- ❏ conjunctivae (CON-junk-TY-vee)
- ❏ cortex (KOR-teks)
- ❏ cortices (KOR-tih-seez)
- ❏ decubitus (dee-KYOO-bih-tus)
- ❏ decubiti (dee-KYOO-bih-tie)
- ❏ dementia (dee-MEN-shee-ah)
- ❏ diagnoses (DY-ag-NOH-seez)
- ❏ diagnosis (DY-ag-NOH-sis)
- ❏ digestion (dy-JES-chun)
- ❏ digestive (dy-JES-tiv)
- ❏ diverticula (DY-ver-TIK-yoo-lah)
- ❏ diverticulum (DY-ver-TIK-yoo-lum)
- ❏ drug (DRUHG)
- ❏ dysphagia (dis-FAY-jee-ah)
- ❏ endotracheal (EN-doh-TRAY-kee-al)
- ❏ epidermal (EP-ih-DER-mal)
- ❏ epididymides (EP-ih-dih-DIM-ih-deez)
- ❏ epididymis (EP-ih-DID-ih-mis)
- ❏ etymology (ET-ih-MAWL-oh-jee)
- ❏ euthyroidism (yoo-THY-royd-izm)
- ❏ fibroma (fy-BROH-mah)
- ❏ fibromata (FY-broh-MAH-tah)
- ❏ ganglia (GANG-glee-ah)
- ❏ ganglion (GANG-glee-on)
- ❏ gastric (GAS-trik)
- ❏ gastrointestinal (GAS-troh-in-TES-tih-nal)
- ❏ gastroscopy (gas-TRAWS-koh-pee)
- ❏ glomerulus (gloh-MAIR-yoo-lus)
- ❏ glomeruli (gloh-MAIR-yoo-lie)
- ❏ gyrus (JY-rus)
- ❏ gyri (JY-rye)
- ❏ haustra (HAW-strah)
- ❏ haustrum (HAW-strum)
- ❏ heart (HART)
- ❏ helices (HEE-lih-seez)
- ❏ helix (HEE-liks)
- ❏ hemiplegia (HEM-ee-PLEE-jee-ah)
- ❏ hepatic (heh-PAT-ik)

- ❏ hemolysis (hee-MAWL-ih-sis)
- ❏ hila (HY-lah)
- ❏ hilum (HY-lum)
- ❏ hypertension (HY-per-TEN-shun)
- ❏ hypothyroidism (HY-poh-THY-royd-izm)
- ❏ index (IN-deks)
- ❏ indices (IN-dih-seez)
- ❏ intercostal (IN-ter-KAWS-tal)
- ❏ intestinal (in-TES-tih-nal)
- ❏ intracardiac (IN-trah-KAR-dee-ak)
- ❏ intranasal (IN-trah-NAY-zal)
- ❏ intravenous (IN-trah-VEE-nus)
- ❏ irides (IHR-ih-deez)
- ❏ iris (EYE-ris)
- ❏ labia (LAY-bee-ah)
- ❏ labium (LAY-bee-um)
- ❏ language (LANG-gwij)
- ❏ laparotomy (LAP-ah-RAW-toh-mee)
- ❏ laryngitis (LAIR-in-JY-tis)
- ❏ leiomyoma (LIE-oh-my-OH-mah)
- ❏ leiomyomata (LIE-oh-my-OH-mah-tah)
- ❏ malnutrition (MAL-noo-TRISH-un)
- ❏ mammogram (MAM-oh-gram)
- ❏ mammography (mah-MAWG-rah-fee)
- ❏ medical (MED-ih-kal)
- ❏ mitocondria (MY-toh-CON-dree-ah)
- ❏ mitochondrion (MY-toh-CON-dree-on)
- ❏ mononucleosis (MAWN-oh-noo-klee-OH-sis)
- ❏ muscular (MUS-kyoo-lar)
- ❏ muscle (MUS-el)
- ❏ neurology (nyoo-RAWL-oh-jee)
- ❏ neuroma (nyoo-ROH-mah)
- ❏ nuclei (NOO-klee-eye)
- ❏ nucleus (NOO-klee-us)
- ❏ ova (OH-vah)
- ❏ ovum (OH-vum)
- ❏ paranoia (PAIR-ah-NOY-ah)
- ❏ patella (pah-TEL-ah)

- patellae (pah-TEL-ee)
- pelvic (PEL-vik)
- pelvis (PEL-vis)
- pericardial (PAIR-ih-KAR-dee-al)
- petechia (peh-TEE-kee-ah)
- petechiae (peh-TEE-kee-ee)
- phalanges (fah-LAN-jeez)
- phalanx (FAY-langks)
- phobia (FOH-bee-ah)
- physician (fih-ZISH-un)
- pneumonia (noo-MOH-nee-ah)
- polyneuritis (PAWL-ee-nyoo-RY tis)
- polyneuropathy (PAWL-ee-nyoo-RAWP-ah-thee)
- postnasal (post-NAY-zal)
- premenstrual (pree-MEN-stroo-al)
- psychiatry (sy-KY-ah-tree)
- psychology (sy-KAWL-oh-jee)
- psychotherapy (SY-koh-THAIR-ah-pee)
- psychosis (sy-KOH-sis)
- quadriplegia (KWAH-drih-PLEE-jee-ah)
- respiration (RES-pih-RAY-shun)
- ruga (ROO-gah)
- rugae (ROO-gee)
- scapula (SKAP-yoo-lah)
- scapulae (SKAP-yoo-lee)
- sclera (SKLEER-ah)
- sclerae (SKLEER-ee)
- sinus (SY-nus)
- sperm (SPERM)
- spirometry (spih-RAWM-eh-tree)
- subcutaneous (SUB-kyoo-TAY-nee-us)
- sulcus (SUL-kus)
- sulci (SUL-sigh)
- tachycardia (TAK-ih-KAR-dee-ah)
- testes (TES-teez)
- testis (TES-tis)
- therapist (THAIR-ah-pist)
- thorax (THOR-aks)
- thrombi (THRAWM-by)
- thrombus (THRAWM-bus)
- tonsillectomy (TAWN-sih-LEK-toh-mee)
- tonsillitis (TAWN-sih-LY-tis)
- transvaginal (trans-VAJ-ih-nal)
- trigeminal (try-JEM-ih-nal)
- urinary (YOO-rih-NAIR-ee)
- urination (YOO-rih-NAY-shun)
- uterine (YOO-ter-in)
- vein (VAYN)
- vena (VEE-nah)
- venae (VEE-nee)
- venous (VEE-nus)
- vertebra (VER-teh-brah)
- vertebrae (VER-teh-bree)
- villus (VIL-us)
- villi (VIL-eye)

Answer Key

Word Search

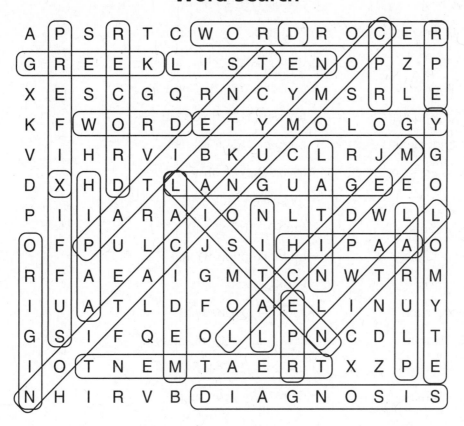

Crossword Puzzle

Underline the Accented Syllable

1. anesthesia   (AN-es-<u>THEE</u>-zee-ah)

2. subcutaneous   (SUB-kyoo-<u>TAY</u>-nee-us)

3. neuroma   (nyoo-<u>ROH</u>-mah)

4. cardiomegaly   (KAR-dee-oh-<u>MEG</u>-ah-lee)

5. hypothyroidism   (HY-poh-<u>THY</u>-royd-izm)

6. appendectomy   (AP-pen <u>DEK</u>-toh-mee)

7. neurology   (nyoo-<u>RAWL</u>-oh-jee)

8. postnasal   (post-<u>NAY</u>-zal)

9. pneumonia   (noo-<u>MOH</u>-nee-ah)

10. polyneuritis   (PAWL-ee-nyoo-<u>RY</u>-tis)

11. psychosis   (sy-<u>KOH</u>-sis)

12. tachycardia   (TAK-ih-<u>KAR</u>-dee-ah)

13. tonsillectomy   (TAWN-sih-<u>LEK</u>-toh-mee)

14. endotracheal   (EN-doh-<u>TRAY</u>-kee-al)

15. colostomy   (koh-<u>LAWS</u>-toh-mee)

Word Surgery

1. arthropathy

   Suffix and its meaning: -pathy *disease; suffering*

   Prefix and its meaning: none

   Combining form and its meaning: arthr/o- *joint*

   Medical word definition: Disease of the joint

2. bradycardia

   Suffix and and its meaning: -ia *condition; state; thing*

   Prefix and its meaning: brady- *slow*

   Combining form and its meaning: cardi/o- *heart*

   Medical word definition: Condition of a slow heart (rate)

3. cardiomegaly

   Suffix and its meaning: -megaly *enlargement*

   Prefix and its meaning: none

   Combining form and its meaning: cardi/o- *heart*

   Medical word definition: Enlargement of the heart

4. postnasal

   Suffix and its meaning: -al *pertaining to*

   Prefix and its meaning: post- *after; behind*

   Combining form and its meaning: nas/o- *nose*

   Medical word definition: Pertaining to behind the nose

5. endotracheal

   Suffix and its meaning: -al *pertaining to*

   Prefix and its meaning: endo- *innermost; within*

   Combining form and its meaning: trache/o- *trachea (windpipe)*

   Medical word definition: Pertaining to within the trachea

6. gastrointestinal

   Suffix and its meaning: -al *pertaining to*

   Prefix and its meaning: none

   Combining form and its meaning: gastr/o- *stomach*

   Combining form and its meaning: intestin/o- *intestine*

   Medical word definition: Pertaining to the stomach and the intestines

7. quadriplegia

   Suffix and its meaning: -ia *condition; state; thing*

   Prefix and its meaning: quadri- *four*

   Combining form and its meaning: pleg/o- *paralysis*

   Medical word definition: Condition of four (limbs) with paralysis

8. hypothyroidism

   Suffix and its meaning: -ism *process; disease from a specific cause*

   Prefix and its meaning: hypo- *below; deficient*

   Combining form and its meaning: thyroid/o- *thyroid gland*

   Medical word definition: Disease from a specific cause of deficient thyroid gland

9. intravenous

   Suffix and its meaning: -ous *pertaining to*

   Prefix and its meaning: intra- *within*

   Combining form and its meaning: ven/o- *vein*

   Medical word definition: Pertaining to within a vein

10. pericardial

    Suffix and its meaning: -al *pertaining to*

    Prefix and its meaning: peri- *around*

    Combining form and its meaning: cardi/o- *heart*

    Medical word definition: Pertaining to around the heart

11. pneumonia

    Suffix and its meaning: -ia *condition; state; thing*

    Prefix and its meaning: none

    Combining form and its meaning: pneumon/o- *lung; air*

    Medical word definition: Condition of the lung

12. polyneuritis

Suffix and its meaning: -itis *inflammation of; infection of*

Prefix and its meaning: poly- *many; much*

Combining form and its meaning: neur/o- *nerve*

Medical word definition: Inflammation of many nerves

13. subcutaneous

Suffix and its meaning: -ous *pertaining to*

Prefix and its meaning: sub- *below; underneath; less than*

Combining form and its meaning: cutane/o- *skin*

Medical word definition: Pertaining to underneath the skin

14. tonsillectomy

Suffix and its meaning: -ectomy *surgical excision*

Prefix and its meaning: none

Combining form and its meaning: tonsill/o- *tonsil*

Medical word definition: Surgical excision of the tonsils

15. urination

Suffix and its meaning: -ation *a process; being or having*

Prefix and its meaning: none

Combining form and its meaning: urin/o- *urine; urinary system*

Medical word definition: A process of (making) urine

Chapter Quiz

MULTIPLE CHOICE

1. D	4. D	7. B	9. D
2. A	5. B	8. D	10. C
3. B	6. A		

FILL IN THE BLANK

1. peri-

2. hypo-

3. a (or –a)

4. Health Insurance Portability and Accountability Act

5. computerized patient record

6. Dx

7. bronchi

8. prefix

TRUE/FALSE

1. True

2. True

3. False (they mean without)

4. False (begin with the suffix)

5. False (two combining forms and one suffix)

6. False (change "-nx" to "-nges.")

7. True

8. True

9. False

10. True

CHAPTER 2

The Body in Health and Disease

Measure Your Progress: Learning Objectives

After reading this chapter, the student should be able to

- Describe approaches used to organize information about the human body.
- Identify body directions, body cavities, body systems, and medical specialties.
- Describe various categories of diseases.
- Describe techniques used to perform a physical examination.
- Describe categories of healthcare professionals and settings in which health care is provided.
- Give the medical meaning of word parts related to the body, health, and disease.
- Build medical words about the body, health, and disease from word parts and divide and define words.
- Spell and pronounce medical words about the body, health, and disease.
- Dive deeper into the body, health, and disease by reviewing the activities at the end of this chapter and online at Medical Terminology Interactive.

It All Starts with Word Building

Medical language is all about medical words and their word parts. Jump right into this chapter by learning some of the common combining forms and their definitions that you will encounter in this chapter.

abdomin/o-	abdomen	medic/o-	physician; medicine
anter/o-	before; front part	medi/o-	middle
caud/o-	tail (tail bone)	palliat/o-	reduce the severity of
cav/o-	hollow space		
cephal/o-	head	path/o-	disease; suffering
congenit/o-	present at birth	pelv/o-	pelvis (hip bone)
coron/o-	structure that encircles like a crown	physi/o-	physical function
		poster/o-	back part
crani/o-	cranium (skull)	proxim/o-	near the center or point of origin
dist/o-	away from the center or point of origin		
		pulmon/o-	lung
		sagitt/o-	going from front to back
dors/o-	back; dorsum		
eti/o-	cause of disease	scop/o-	examine with an instrument
extern/o-	outside		
front/o-	front	spin/o-	spine; backbone
gnos/o-	knowledge	spir/o-	breathe
heredit/o-	genetic inheritance	super/o-	above
iatr/o-	physician; medical treatment	surg/o-	operative procedure
idi/o-	unknown; individual	symptomat/o-	collection of symptoms
ili/o-	ilium (hip bone)	therap/o-	treatment
infect/o-	disease within	thorac/o-	thorax (chest)
infer/o-	below	tom/o-	cut; slice; layer
intern/o-	inside	umbilic/o-	umbilicus; navel
later/o-	side	ventr/o-	front; abdomen
lumb/o-	lower back		

Word Search

Complete this word search puzzle that contains Chapter 2 words. Look for the following words as given in the list below. The number in parentheses indicates how many times the word appears in the puzzle.

acute
anatomy
anterior (2)
body
caudad
cavity (2)
coronal
cranial
distal
dorsal

etiology
health
hospitals
iliac
medial
prognosis
prone (2)
quadrant
sign

```
A  C  U  T  E  T  I  O  L  O  G  Y
N  I  L  I  A  C  A  U  D  A  D  T
T  O  S  L  A  T  I  P  S  O  H  I
E  A  C  E  N  O  R  P  B  W  S  V
R  N  R  G  U  O  P  Z  D  I  Q  A
I  A  A  I  N  L  X  I  S  O  U  C
O  T  N  E  T  H  S  O  L  C  A  O
R  O  I  R  E  T  N  A  A  A  D  R
Z  M  A  A  A  G  S  H  I  V  R  O
N  Y  L  L  O  R  I  A  D  I  A  N
W  T  I  R  O  C  G  M  E  T  N  A
H  C  P  D  K  Z  N  S  M  Y  T  L
```

Crossword Puzzle

ACROSS

1. _____ is the study of the function of the structures of the human body.

7. Moving from the body toward the end of a limb is referred to as moving in a _____ direction.

8. A disease or condition that has no identifiable cause is referred to as _____.

9. _____ is the medical specialty that deals with the ears, nose, and throat.

10. The combining form "_____" refers to the front of the body or abdomen.

DOWN

2. The _____ _____ is a vertical plane that divides the body into left and right sections.

3. The abbreviation D.O. stands for Doctor of _____.

4. The pituitary, thyroid, and adrenal glands are all part of the _____ system.

5. The medical specialty of _____ includes the lymphatic system and the white blood cells and their ability to recognize and destroy disease-causing organisms and abnormal cells.

6. The combining form "_____" refers to the head.

Underline the Accented Syllable

Read the medical word. Then review the syllables in the pronunciation. Underline the primary (main) accented syllable in the pronunciation.

1. acute   (ah-kyoot)

2. cardiovascular   (kar-dee-oh-vas-kyoo-lar)

3. congenital   (con-jen-ih-tal)

4. endocrine   (en-doh-krin)

5. genital   (jen-ih-tal)

6. hypochondriac   (hy-poh-con-dree-ak)

7. iatrogenic   (eye-at-roh-jen-ik)

8. integumentary   (in-teg-yoo-men-tair-ee)

9. neonatology   (nee-oh-nay-tawl-oh-jee)

10. neoplastic   (nee-oh-plas-tik)

11. ophthalmology   (off-thal-mawl-oh-jee)

12. orthopedics   (or-thoh-pee-diks)

13. physiology   (fiz-ee-awl-oh-jee)

14. psychiatry   (sy-ky-ah-tree)

15. pulmonology   (pul-moh-nawl-oh-jee)

Word Surgery

Read the medical word. Break the medical word into its word parts and give the meaning of each word part. Then give the definition of the medical word.

1. physiology

   Suffix and its meaning: _____

   Prefix and its meaning: _____

   Combining form and its meaning: _____

   Medical word definition: _____

2. auscultation

   Suffix and its meaning: _____

   Prefix and its meaning: _____

   Combining form and its meaning: _____

   Medical word definition: _____

3. congenital

   Suffix and its meaning: _____

   Prefix and its meaning: _____

   Combining form and its meaning: _____

   Medical word definition: _____

4. dermatology

   Suffix and its meaning: _____

   Prefix and its meaning: _____

   Combining form and its meaning: _____

   Medical word definition: _____

5. dorsal

   Suffix and its meaning: _____

   Prefix and its meaning: _____

   Combining form and its meaning: _____

   Medical word definition: _____

6. geriatrics

Suffix and its meaning: _____

Prefix and its meaning: _____

Combining form and its meaning: _____

Combining form and its meaning: _____

Medical word definition: _____

7. idiopathic

Suffix and its meaning: _____

Prefix and its meaning: _____

Combining form and its meaning: _____

Combining form and its meaning: _____

Medical word definition: _____

8. microscopic

Suffix and its meaning: _____

Prefix and its meaning: _____

Combining form and its meaning: _____

Combining form and its meaning: _____

Medical word definition: _____

9. obstetrics

Suffix and its meaning: _____

Prefix and its meaning: _____

Combining form and its meaning: _____

Medical word definition: _____

10. ophthalmology

Suffix and its meaning: _____

Prefix and its meaning: _____

Combining form and its meaning: _____

Medical word definition: _____

11. palpation

    Suffix and its meaning: _____

    Prefix and its meaning: _____

    Combining form and its meaning: _____

    Medical word definition: _____

12. prognosis

    Suffix and its meaning: _____

    Prefix and its meaning: _____

    Combining form and its meaning: _____

    Medical word definition: _____

13. sagittal

    Suffix and its meaning: _____

    Prefix and its meaning: _____

    Combining form and its meaning: _____

    Medical word definition: _____

14. therapist

    Suffix and its meaning: _____

    Prefix and its meaning: _____

    Combining form and its meaning: _____

    Medical word definition: _____

15. urology

    Suffix and its meaning: _____

    Prefix and its meaning: _____

    Combining form and its meaning: _____

    Medical word definition: _____

Chapter Quiz

MULTIPLE CHOICE

1. The plane that is an imaginary surface dividing the body into left and right sides is the:

   A. coronal plane.

   B. sagittal plane.

   C. transverse plane.

   D. abdominal plane.

2. The opposite of anterior is:

   A. interior.

   B. exterior.

   C. posterior.

   D. sagittal.

3. The words medial and lateral refer to:

   A. body planes.

   B. directions.

   C. the head and tail.

   D. the transverse plane.

4. The wrist is distal to the:

   A. elbow.

   B. knee.

   C. thumb.

   D. fingers.

5. The opposite of superficial is:

   A. deep.

   B. caudal.

   C. cephalad.

   D. transverse.

6. The regions of the abdominopelvic area include:

    A. the left and right hypochondriac regions.

    B. the umbilical region.

    C. the right and left lumbar regions.

    D. All of the above.

7. Which of the following is the study of blood?

    A. immunology

    B. dermatology

    C. orthopedics

    D. hematology

8. Which of the following medical specialties refers to the study and treatment of cancer?

    A. pharmacology

    B. pediatrics

    C. geriatrics

    D. oncology

9. Auscultation:

    A. uses a stethoscope.

    B. examines the ear.

    C. is a type of disability.

    D. causes cancer.

10. An ambulatory surgical center is:

    A. a facility where minor procedures are performed.

    B. a traditional inpatient hospital.

    C. where hospice services are delivered.

    D. a special pharmacy.

FILL IN THE BLANK

1. The word that means showing no symptoms is _____.

2. A _____ _____ is a healthcare professional who performs some of the duties of a physician.

3. _____ is when a healthcare professional examines the body by pressing on the body part to feel for masses or enlargement.

4. Superior refers to a structure that is _____ a reference point.

5. The umbilical region refers to the area around the _____.

6. A small central area of the thoracic cavity that contains the trachea, esophagus, and heart is known as the _____.

7. Gastroenterology focuses attention on the _____ system.

8. The _____ plane divides the body into front and back sections.

9. Standing erect with head up and arms at the sides and palms facing forward is known as the _____ position.

10. _____ is the word that refers to the patient's back side.

TRUE/FALSE

_____ 1. Symptoms and signs that are less severe in intensity than acute are called subacute.

_____ 2. The suffix "-ation" means "a process; being or having."

_____ 3. The predicted outcome of treatment is the diagnosis.

_____ 4. Ancillary care departments include radiology, clinical laboratory, and physical therapy.

_____ 5. A neoplasm is always a cancerous (malignant) growth.

_____ 6. The medical specialty that deals with medicine and drugs is known as radiology.

_____ 7. Ophthalmology is the study of the ear and hearing.

_____ 8. The lumbar cavity is within the ribs.

_____ 9. The transverse plane is an imaginary plane that divides the body into superior and inferior sections.

_____ 10. When an x-ray camera is placed in front of the chest and the x-rays enter from the patient's back, this is called an anteroposterior view.

Pronunciation Checklist

Read each word and its pronunciation. Practice pronouncing each word. Verify your pronunciation by listening to the Pronunciation List on Medical Terminology Interactive. Check the box next to the word after you master its pronunciation.

❏ abdominal cavity
  (ab-DAWM-ih-nal KAV-ih-tee)
❏ abdominopelvic cavity
  (ab-DAWM-ih-noh-PEL-vik
  KAV-ih-tee)
❏ acute (ah-KYOOT)
❏ ambulatory
  (AM-byoo-lah-TOR-ee)
❏ anatomical
  (AN-ah-TAWM-ih-kal)
❏ anatomy (ah-NAT-oh-MEE)
❏ ancillary (AN-sih-LAIR-ee)
❏ anterior (an-TEER-ee-or)
❏ anteroposterior
  (AN-ter-oh-pohs-TEER-ee-or)
❏ asymptomatic
  (AA-simp-toh-MAT-ik)
❏ auscultation
  (AWS-kul-TAY-shun)
❏ cardiology
  (KAR-dee-AWL-oh-jee)
❏ cardiovascular
  (KAR-dee-oh-VAS-kyoo-lar)
❏ caudad (KAW-dad)
❏ cavity (KAV-ih-tee)
❏ cephalad (SEF-ah-lad)
❏ chronic (KRAW-nik)
❏ communicable disease
  (koh-MYOON-ih-kah-bl
  dih-ZEEZ)
❏ congenital disease
  (con-JEN-ih-tal dih-ZEEZ)
❏ coronal plane
  (kor-OH-nal PLAYN)
❏ cranial cavity
  (KRAY-nee-al KAV-ih-tee)
❏ degenerative disease
  (dee-JEN-er-ah-tiv dih-ZEEZ)
❏ dentistry (DEN-tis-tree)
❏ dermatology
  (DER-mah-TAWL-oh-jee)
❏ diagnosis (DY-ag-NOH-sis)
❏ dietetics (DY-eh-TET-iks)
❏ disability (DIS-ah-BIL-ah-tee)
❏ disease (dih-ZEEZ)
❏ distal (DIS-tal)
❏ dorsal (DOR-sal)
❏ endocrine (EN-doh-krin)
  (EN-doh-krine)

❏ endocrinology
  (EN-doh-krih-NAWL-oh-jee)
❏ environmental
  (en-VY-rawn-MEN-tal)
❏ epigastric (EP-ih-GAS-trk)
❏ etiology (EE-tee-AWL-oh-jee)
❏ exacerbation
  (eg-ZAS-er-BAY-shun)
❏ external (eks-TER-nal)
❏ frontal plane
  (FRUN-tal PLAYN)
❏ gastroenterology
  (GAS-troh-en-ter-AWL-oh-jee)
❏ gastrointestinal system
  (GAS-troh-in-TES-tih-nal
  SIS-tem)
❏ geriatrics (JAIR-ee-AT-riks)
❏ gynecology
  (GY-neh-KAWL-oh-jee)
❏ health (HELTH)
❏ hematology
  (HEE-mah-TAWL-oh-jee)
❏ hereditary disease
  (heh-RED-ih-TAIR-ee
  dih-ZEEZ)
❏ horizontal plane
  (HOR-ih-ZAWN-tal PLAYN)
❏ hospice (HAWS-pis)
❏ hypochondriac
  (HY-poh-KAWN-dree-ak)
❏ hypogastric (HY-poh-GAS-trik)
❏ iatrogenic disease
  (eye-AT-roh-JEN-ik dih-ZEEZ)
❏ idiopathic disease
  (ID-ee-oh-PATH-ik dih-ZEEZ)
❏ iliac (IL-ee-ak)
❏ immunology
  (IM-myoo-NAWL-oh-jee)
❏ infectious disease
  (in-FEK-shus dih-ZEEZ)
❏ inferior (in-FEER-ee-or)
❏ inguinal (ING-gwih-nal)
❏ inspection (in-SPEK-shun)
❏ integumentary system
  (in-TEG-yoo-MEN-tair-ee
  SIS-tem)
❏ internal (in-TER-nal)
❏ lateral (LAT-er-al)
❏ lumbar (LUM-bar)

❏ lymphatic system
  (lim-FAT-ik SIS-tem)
❏ macroscopic
  (MAK-roh-SKAWP-ik)
❏ medial (MEE-dee-al)
❏ medicine (MED-ih-sin)
❏ microscope (MY-kroh-skohp)
❏ microscopic
  (MY-kroh-SKAWP-ik)
❏ midsagittal plane
  (mid-SAJ-ih-tal PLAYN)
❏ muscular system
  (MUS-kyoo-lar SIS-tem)
❏ neoplastic disease
  (NEE-oh-PLAS-tik dih-ZEEZ)
❏ nervous system
  (NER-vus SIS-tem)
❏ neurology
  (nyoo-RAWL-oh-jee)
❏ nosocomial disease
  (NOS-oh-KOH-mee-al
  dih-ZEEZ)
❏ nutritional disease
  (noo-TRISH-un-al dih-ZEEZ)
❏ obstetrics (awb-STET-riks)
❏ oncology (ong-KAWL-oh-jee)
❏ ophthalmology
  (OFF-thal-MAWL-oh-jee)
❏ orthopedics
  (OR-thoh-PEE-diks)
❏ otolaryngology
  (OH-toh-LAIR-ing-GAWL-
  oh-jee)
❏ palliative (PAL-ee-ah-tiv)
❏ palpation (pal-PAY-shun)
❏ pathogen (PATH-oh-jen)
❏ pediatrics (PEE-dee-AT-riks)
❏ pelvic cavity
  (PEL-vik KAV-ih-tee)
❏ percussion (per-KUSH-un)
❏ pharmacology
  (FAR-mah-KAWL-oh-jee)
❏ physician (fih-ZISH-un)
❏ physiology
  (FIZ-ee-AWL-oh-jee)
❏ plane (PLAYN)
❏ posterior (pohs-TEER-ee-or)
❏ posteroanterior
  (POHS-ter-oh-an-TEER-ee-or)

- preventive (pree-VEN-tiv)
- prognosis (prawg-NOH-sis)
- prone (PROHN)
- proximal (PRAWK-sih-mal)
- psychiatry (sy-KY-ah-tree)
- pulmonology
  (PUL-moh-NAWL-oh-jee)
- quadrant (KWAH-drant)
- radiology
  (RAY-dee-AWL-oh-jee)
- recuperation
  (ree-KOO-per-AA-shun)
- refractory
  (ree-FRAK-tor-ee)
- rehabilitation
  (REE-hah-BIL-ih-TAY-shun)
- remission (ree-MISH-un)
- reproductive system
  (REE-proh-DUK-tiv SIS-tem)

- respiratory system
  (RES-pih-rah-TOR-ee SIS-tem)
  (reh-SPYR-ah-tor-ee)
- sequela (see-KWEL-ah)
- sequelae (see-KWEL-ee)
- skeletal system
  (SKEL-eh-tal SIS-tem)
- spinal cavity
  (SPY-nal KAV-ih-tee)
- stethoscope
  (STETH-oh-skohp)
- subacute (SUB-ah-KYOOT)
- superior (soo-PEER-ee-or)
- supine (soo-PINE) (SOO-pine)
- surgeon (SER-jun)
- surgery (SER-jer-ee)
- symptom (SIMP-tom)
- symptomatology
  (SIMP-toh-mah-TAWL-oh-jee)

- transverse plane
  (trans-VERS PLAYN)
- umbilical (um-BIL-ih-kal)
- urinary system
  (YOO-rih-NAIR-ee SIS-tem)
- urology (yoo-RAWL-oh-jee)
- ventral (VEN-tral)
- viscera (VIS-er-ah)
- syndrome (SIN-drohm)
- technician (tek-NISH-un)
- technologist
  (tek-NAWL-oh-jist)
- terminal (TER-mih-nal)
- therapeutic
  (THAIR-ah-PYOO-tik)
- therapist (THAIR-ah-pist)
- therapy (THAIR-ah-pee)
- thoracic cavity
  (thoh-RAS-ik KAV-ih-tee)

Answer Key

Word Search

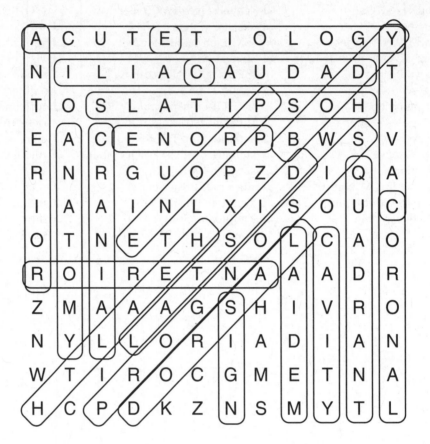

Crossword Puzzle

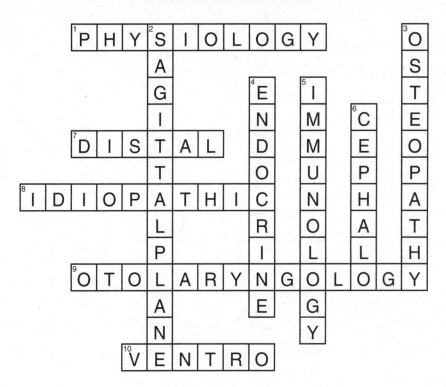

Underline the Accented Syllable

1. acute   (ah-<u>KYOOT</u>)

2. cardiovascular   (KAR-dee-oh-<u>VAS</u>- kyoo-lar)

3. congenital   (con-<u>JEN</u>-ih-tal)

4. endocrine   (<u>EN</u>-doh-krin)

5. genital   (<u>JEN</u>-ih-tal)

6. hypochondriac   (HY-poh-<u>CON</u>-dree-ak)

7. iatrogenic   (eye-AT-roh-<u>JEN</u>-ik)

8. integumentary   (in-TEG-yoo-<u>MEN</u>-tair-ee)

9. neonatology   (NEE-oh-nay-<u>TAWL</u>-oh-jee)

10. neoplastic   (NEE-oh-<u>PLAS</u>-tik)

11. ophthalmology   (OFF-thal-<u>MAWL</u>-oh-jee)

12. orthopedics   (OR-thoh-<u>PEE</u>-diks)

13. physiology   (FIZ-ee-<u>AWL</u>-oh-jee)

14. psychiatry   (sy-<u>KY</u>-ah-tree)

15. pulmonology   (PUL-moh-<u>NAWL</u>-oh-jee)

Word Surgery

1. physiology

   Suffix and its meaning: -logy *the study of*

   Prefix and its meaning: none

   Combining form and its meaning: physi/o- *physical function*

   Medical word definition: The study of the physical function (of the body)

2. auscultation

   Suffix and its meaning: -ation *a process; being or having*

   Prefix and its meaning: none

   Combining form and its meaning: auscult/o- *listening*

   Medical word definition: A process of listening

3. congenital

   Suffix and its meaning: -al *pertaining to*

   Prefix and its meaning: none

   Combining form and its meaning: congenit/o- *present at birth*

   Medical word definition: Pertaining to a (disease that is) present at birth

4. dermatology

   Suffix and its meaning: -logy *the study of*

   Prefix and its meaning: none

   Combining form and its meaning: dermat/o- *skin*

   Medical word definition: The study of the skin

5. dorsal

   Suffix and its meaning: -al *pertaining to*

   Prefix and its meaning: none

   Combining form and its meaning: dors/o- *back; dorsum*

   Medical word definition: Pertaining to the back

6. geriatrics

   Suffix and its meaning: -ics *knowledge; practice*

   Prefix and its meaning: none

   Combining form and its meaning: ger/o- *old age*

   Combining form and its meaning: iatr/o- *physician; medical treatment*

   Medical word definition: The knowledge and practice of medical treatment of old
   age

7. idiopathic

   Suffix and its meaning: -ic *pertaining to*

   Prefix and its meaning: none

   Combining form and its meaning: idi/o- *unknown; individual*

   Combining form and its meaning: path/o- *disease; suffering*

   Medical word definition: Pertaining to an unknown disease

8. microscopic

   Suffix and its meaning: -ic *pertaining to*

   Prefix and its meaning: none

   Combining form and its meaning: micr/o- *one millionth; small*

   Combining form and its meaning: scop/o- *examine with an instrument*

   Medical word definition: Pertaining to small (things) examined with an instrument

9. obstetrics

   Suffix and its meaning: -ics *knowledge; practice*

   Prefix and its meaning: none

   Combining form and its meaning: obstetr/o- *pregnancy and childbirth*

   Medical word definition: The knowledge and practice of pregnancy and childbirth

10. ophthalmology

   Suffix and its meaning: -logy *the study of*

   Prefix and its meaning: none

   Combining form and its meaning: ophthalm/o- *eye*

   Medical word definition: The study of the eye

11. palpation

    Suffix and its meaning: -ation *a process; being or having*

    Prefix and its meaning: none

    Combining form and its meaning: palpat/o- *touching; feeling*

    Medical word definition: A process of touching and feeling

12. prognosis

    Suffix and its meaning: -osis *condition; abnormal condition; process*

    Prefix and its meaning: pro- *before*

    Combining form and its meaning: gnos/o- *knowledge*

    Medical word definition: Process of (having) before knowledge

13. sagittal

    Suffix and its meaning: -al *pertaining to*

    Prefix and its meaning: none

    Combining form and its meaning: sagitt/o- *going from front to back*

    Medical word definition: Pertaining to going from front to back

14. therapist

    Suffix and its meaning: -ist *one who specializes in*

    Prefix and its meaning: none

    Combining form and its meaning: therap/o- *treatment*

    Medical word definition: One who specializes in treatment

15. urology

    Suffix and its meaning: -logy *the study of*

    Prefix and its meaning: none

    Combining form and its meaning: ur/o- *urine; urinary system*

    Medical word definition: The study of urine and the urinary system

Chapter Quiz

MULTIPLE CHOICE

1. B	4. A	7. D	10. A
2. C	5. A	8. D	
3. B	6. D	9. A	

FILL IN THE BLANK

1. asymptomatic

2. physician's assistant

3. palpation

4. above

5. navel

6. mediastinum

7. gastrointestinal

8. coronal

9. anatomical

10. dorsal

TRUE/FALSE

1. True

2. True

3. False (prognosis)

4. True

5. False (may be cancer or benign)

6. False (pharmacology)

7. False (otolaryngology)

8. False (thoracic)

9. True

10. True

CHAPTER 3

Gastroenterology

Measure Your Progress: Learning Objectives

After reading this chapter, the student should be able to

- Identify the structures of the gastrointestinal system.
- Describe the process of digestion.
- Describe common gastrointestinal diseases and conditions, laboratory and diagnostic procedures, medical and surgical procedures, and drug categories.
- Give the medical meaning of word parts related to the gastrointestinal system.
- Build gastrointestinal words from word parts and divide and define gastrointestinal words.
- Spell and pronounce gastrointestinal words.
- Analyze the medical content and meaning of a gastroenterology report.
- Dive deeper into gastroenterology by reviewing the activities at the end of this chapter and online at Medical Terminology Interactive.

It All Starts with Word Building

Medical language is all about medical words and their word parts. Jump right into this chapter by learning some of the common combining forms and their definitions that you will encounter in this chapter.

abdomin/o-	abdomen	hemat/o-	blood
aliment/o-	food; nourishment	hemorrhoid/o-	hemorrhoid
an/o-	anus	hepat/o-	liver
appendic/o-	appendix	ile/o-	ileum
append/o-	small structure hanging from a larger structure	intestin/o-	intestine
		jejun/o-	jejunum
		lapar/o-	abdomen
bili/o-	bile; gall	lingu/o-	tongue
cec/o-	cecum	lith/o-	stone
celi/o-	abdomen	mastic/o-	chewing
cheil/o-	lip	nause/o-	nausea
chez/o-	to pass feces	omphal/o-	umbilicus; navel
cholangi/o-	bile duct	orex/o-	appetite
chol/e-	bile; gall	or/o-	mouth
cholecyst/o-	gallbladder	pancreat/o-	pancreas
choledoch/o-	common bile duct	peps/o-	digestion
col/o-	colon	pept/o-	digestion
colon/o-	colon	peritone/o-	peritoneum
constip/o-	compacted feces	phag/o-	eating; swallowing
degluti/o-	swallowing	pharyng/o-	pharynx (throat)
digest/o-	break down food; digest	polyp/o-	polyp
		rect/o-	rectum
diverticul/o-	diverticulum	regurgitat/o-	flow backward
duoden/o-	duodenum	saliv/o-	saliva; salivary gland
enter/o-	intestine		
esophag/o-	esophagus	sial/o-	saliva; salivary gland
fec/a-	feces; stool		
fec/o-	feces; stool	sigmoid/o-	sigmoid colon
gastr/o-	stomach	stomat/o-	mouth
gloss/o-	tongue	umbilic/o-	umbilicus; navel
gustat/o-	the sense of taste		

Chapter Spelling Test

Dictate and spell (or photocopy a handout that contains) this list of 20 spelling words. Give this list to students to study for the week. At the beginning of next week's class, dictate 10 of these words as the spelling test. The spelling test is included with the chapter test that is given on the previous week's material.

1. anorexia
2. ascites
3. biliary
4. cholangiography
5. choledocholithiasis
6. cirrhosis
7. dysphagia
8. emesis
9. esophagus
10. hematochezia
11. hemorrhoidectomy
12. ileum
13. ileus
14. intussusception
15. jaundice
16. melena
17. pharynx
18. sialolithiasis
19. steatorrhea
20. umbilicus

Chapter Pronunciation Test

Photocopy a handout that contains this list of 20 pronunciation words. Give this list to students to study for the week. Sometime at the beginning of the next week, each student should call your office or home answering machine and pronounce each word.

1. anastomosis (ah-NAS-toh-MOH-sis)

2. ascites (ah-SY-teez)

3. bilirubin (BIL-ih-ROO-bin)

4. cholecystectomy (KOH-lee-sis-TEK-toh-mee)

5. cholelithiasis (KOH-lee-lih-THY-ah-sis)

6. peritoneal (PAIR-ih-toh-NEE-al)

7. colonscopy (KOH-lon-AWS-koh-pee)

8. diverticulosis (DY-ver-TIK-yoo-LOH-sis)

9. emesis (EM-eh-sis)

10. gastroenterologist (GAS-troh-EN-ter-AWL-oh-jist)

11. hematochezia (hee-MAH-toh-KEE-zee-ah)

12. hemorrhoidectomy (HEM-oh-roy-DEK-toh-mee)

13. ileostomy (IL-ee-AWS-toh-mee)

14. jaundice (JAWN-dis)

15. jejunostomy (JEH-joo-NAWS-toh-mee)

16. laparotomy (LAP-ah-RAW-toh-mee)

17. mesenteric (MEZ-en-TAIR-ik)

18. pancreatitis (PAN-kree-ah-TY-tis)

19. pharynx (FAIR-ingks)

20. steatorrhea (stee-AT-oh-REE-ah)

Word Search

Complete this word search puzzle that contains Chapter 3 words. Look for the following words as given in the list below. The number in parentheses indicates how many times the word appears in the puzzle.

alimentary	duct	liver	rugae
anal (2)	emesis	lumen	RUQ
anus	esophageal	mucosa	saliva
appendectomy	gastric	omentum	stoma
bile (2)	gustatory	oral (2)	stool
bowel	hernia	pepsin	UGI
CBD	ileum (2)	polyp	villi
cecum	intestine	rectum	vomit
digestion	LFTs	RLQ	uvula

```
V  B  F  M  U  C  E  C  I  A  N  O
D  I  G  E  S  T  I  O  N  N  E  R
U  L  L  T  M  R  E  C  T  U  M  A
C  E  O  L  T  U  A  H  E  S  U  L
T  O  K  S  I  N  E  O  S  S  L  Y
L  U  A  A  A  R  R  L  T  O  A  M
I  G  G  L  N  A  O  F  I  M  E  O
V  C  B  I  L  E  L  A  N  A  G  T
E  O  A  V  O  M  I  T  E  U  A  C
R  M  P  A  M  U  C  O  S  A  H  E
U  E  E  T  L  B  J  T  T  B  P  D
G  N  P  S  D  U  A  R  O  M  O  N
A  T  S  Q  I  T  V  W  M  U  S  E
E  U  I  U  O  S  E  U  A  E  E  P
J  M  N  R  R  L  Q  P  Y  L  O  P
S  A  Y  R  A  T  N  E  M  I  L  A
```

Crossword Puzzle

ACROSS

1. Heartburn, or temporary inflammation of the esophagus due to reflux of the stomach, is also called _____.

4. A _____ is a cancerous tumor in the liver.

7. _____ is the vomiting of blood.

8. Drugs used to treat heartburn and peptic ulcer disease by neutralizing stomach acids are known as _____.

9. A condition where the intestines bulge through a defect in the diaphragm or abdominal wall is referred to as a/an _____.

DOWN

1. The combining form "_____" refers to eating or swallowing.

2. The process of swallowing food is called _____.

3. The cardia, fundus, body, and pylorus comprise the four areas of the _____.

5. _____ is a semisolid mixture of partially digested food, saliva, and digestive juices in the stomach.

6. The digestive enzyme _____ breaks down carbohydrates and starches into sugars and food fibers.

Underline the Accented Syllable

Read the medical word. Then review the syllables in the pronunciation. Underline the primary (main) accented syllable in the pronunciation.

1. adenocarcinoma (ad-eh-noh-kar-sih-noh-mah)

2. anastomosis (ah-nas-toh-moh-sis)

3. bilirubin (bil-ih-roo-bin)

4. cecal (see-kal)

5. cholecystectomy (koh-lee-sis-tek-toh-mee)

6. colonic (koh-lawn-ik)

7. diarrhea (dy-ah-ree-ah)

8. diverticulosis (dy-ver-tik-yoo-loh-sis)

9. dysphagia (dis-fay-jee-ah)

10. esophagogastroduodenoscopy

    (ee-sawf-ah-goh-gas-troh-doo-oh-den-aws-koh pee)

11. gastroenteritis (gas-troh-en-ter-eye-tis)

12. guaiac (gwy-ak)

13. nausea (naw-see-ah)

14. omphalocele (om-fal-oh-seel)

15. steatorrhea (stee-at-oh-ree-ah)

Word Surgery

Read the medical word. Break the medical word into its word parts and give the meaning of each word part. Then give the definition of the medical word.

1. adenocarcinoma

   Suffix and its meaning: _____

   Prefix and its meaning: _____

   Combining form and its meaning: _____

   Combining form and its meaning: _____

   Medical word definition: _____

2. anorexia

   Suffix and its meaning: _____

   Prefix and its meaning: _____

   Combining form and its meaning: _____

   Medical word definition: _____

3. antiemetic

   Suffix and its meaning: _____

   Prefix and its meaning: _____

   Combining form and its meaning: _____

   Medical word definition: _____

4. peritonitis

   Suffix and its meaning: _____

   Prefix and its meaning: _____

   Combining form and its meaning: _____

   Medical word definition: _____

5. cholangiography

   Suffix and its meaning: _____

   Prefix and its meaning: _____

   Combining form and its meaning: _____

   Medical word definition: _____

6. cholelithiasis

Suffix and its meaning: _____

Prefix and its meaning: _____

Combining form and its meaning: _____

Combining form and its meaning: _____

Medical word definition: _____

7. gastroesophageal

Suffix and its meaning: _____

Prefix and its meaning: _____

Combining form and its meaning: _____

Combining form and its meaning: _____

Medical word definition: _____

8. hematochezia

Suffix and its meaning: _____

Prefix and its meaning: _____

Combining form and its meaning: _____

Combining form and its meaning: _____

Medical word definition: _____

9. hemorrhoidectomy

Suffix and its meaning: _____

Prefix and its meaning: _____

Combining form and its meaning: _____

Medical word definition: _____

10. hepatosplenomegaly

Suffix and its meaning: _____

Prefix and its meaning: _____

Combining form and its meaning: _____

Combining form and its meaning: _____

Medical word definition: _____

11. endoscopic

Suffix and its meaning: _____

Prefix and its meaning: _____

Combining form and its meaning: _____

Medical word definition: _____

12. herniorrhaphy

Suffix and its meaning: _____

Prefix and its meaning: _____

Combining form and its meaning: _____

Medical word definition: _____

13. sialolithiasis

Suffix and its meaning: _____

Prefix and its meaning: _____

Combining form and its meaning: _____

Combining form and its meaning: _____

Medical word definition: _____

14. postoperative

Suffix and its meaning: _____

Prefix and its meaning: _____

Combining form and its meaning: _____

Medical word definition: _____

15. hematemesis

Suffix and its meaning: _____

Prefix and its meaning: _____

Combining form and its meaning: _____

Medical word definition: _____

Chapter Quiz

MULTIPLE CHOICE

1. The teeth and tongue begin digestion in a process known as:

    A. chemical digestion.

    B. deglutination.

    C. mastication.

    D. emulsification.

2. A product of the stomach that kills microorganisms, breaks down fibers, and converts pepsinogen to the digestive enzyme pepsin is:

    A. gastrin.

    B. hydrochloric acid.

    C. cholecystokinin.

    D. amylase.

3. Food mixed with digestive enzymes in the stomach is known as:

    A. flatus.

    B. gastrin.

    C. lipase.

    D. chyme.

4. Anorexia is:

    A. hiatal hernia.

    B. a decrease in appetite.

    C. also known as sialolithiasis.

    D. regurgitation.

5. Crohn's disease:

    A. affects the ileum and colon.

    B. mostly affects the stomach.

    C. is also known as celiac disease.

    D. is treated with antibiotics.

6. The accumulation of fluid in the abdominopelvic cavity due to underlying liver disease is known as:

   A. spastic colon.

   B. ascities.

   C. hiatal hernia.

   D. inflammatory bowel disease.

7. The accumulation of bilirubin in the blood is a result of:

   A. liver disease or gallstones.

   B. an allergic reaction to gluten.

   C. diverticulosis.

   D. pancreatic cancer.

8. A cholangiography is used to:

   A. view the colon.

   B. examine the jejunum.

   C. outline the bile ducts.

   D. test for parasites.

9. A colostomy bag is used to allow the collection of:

   A. feces.

   B. blood.

   C. urine.

   D. mucus.

10. GERD is an abbreviation for:

   A. a test for the presence of *Helicobacter pylori*.

   B. a highly trained gastroenterologist.

   C. a surgical procedure for inserting a feeding tube.

   D. a condition where the stomach contents flow back into the esophagus.

FILL IN THE BLANK

1. NG is an abbreviation for _____.

2. A surgical procedure that creates a permanent opening from the abdominal wall to the stomach is a _____.

3. A radiologic procedure that uses x-rays to create an image of many thin, successive slices of the abdomen is known as _____.

4. The presence of one or more gallstones in the gallbladder is known as

   _____.

5. _____ is a yellowish discoloration of the skin and whites of the eyes.

6. Swollen, protruding veins in the rectum or on the perianal skin are known as

   _____.

7. _____ is a common disorder in babies that includes symptoms of crampy abdominal pain after eating.

8. Indigestion or epigastric pain that may be accompanied by gas or nausea is known as _____.

9. The first 10 inches of the small intestine is known as the _____.

10. _____ is the rhythmic contraction of the gastrointestinal tract that propels food through it.

TRUE/FALSE

_____ 1. Ova and parasites are eggs and parasitic worms.

_____ 2. The cecum is the first part of the large intestine.

_____ 3. The function of the intestinal villi is to increase the surface area needed for absorption of nutrients.

_____ 4. Polyphagia is excessive overeating.

_____ 5. A rectocele is a tube.

_____ 6. Hematochezia is blood found in the stomach.

_____ 7. An enlarged liver is known as hepatomegaly.

_____ 8. The term "regurgitation" means having a stone in the gallbladder.

_____ 9. Proton pump inhibitor drugs treat cancer.

_____ 10. The abbreviation PEG refers to a feeding tube placed into the stomach.

Pronunciation Checklist

Read each word and its pronunciation. Practice pronouncing each word. Verify your pronunciation by listening to the Pronunciation List on Medical Terminology Interactive. Check the box next to the word after you master its pronunciation.

❑ abdominopelvic cavity
(ab-DAWM-ih-noh-PEL-vik
KAV-ih-tee)

❑ absorption (ab-SORP-shun)

❑ adenocarcinoma
(AD-eh-noh-KAR-sih-NOH-mah)

❑ adhesion (ad-HEE-zhun)

❑ albumin (al-BYOO-min)

❑ alimentary canal
(AL-ih-MEN-tair-ee kah-NAL)

❑ alkaline phosphatase
(AL-kah-line FAWS-fah-tays)

❑ amylase (AM-il-ace)

❑ anal (AA-nal)

❑ anastomosis
(ah-NAS-toh-MOH-sis)

❑ anorexia (AN-oh-REK-see-ah)

❑ anorexic (AN-oh-REK-sik)

❑ antacid drug
(ant-AS-id DRUHG)

❑ antibiotic drug
(AN-tee-by-AWT-ik DRUHG)
(AN-tih-by-AWT-ik)

❑ antidiarrheal drug
(AN-tee-DY-ah-REE-al DRUHG)

❑ antiemetic drug
(AN-tee-eh-MET-ik DRUHG)

❑ anus (AA-nus)

❑ aphthous ulcer
(AF-thus UL-ser)

❑ appendectomy
(AP-pen-DEK-toh-mee)

❑ appendiceal (AP-pen-DIS-ee-al)

❑ appendicitis (ah-PEN-dih-SY-tis)

❑ appendix (ah-PEN-diks)

❑ ascites (ah-SY-teez)

❑ ascitic (ah-SIT-ik)

❑ barium (BAIR-ee-um)

❑ benign (bee-NINE)

❑ bile (BILE)

❑ biliary (BIL-ee-AIR-ee)

❑ bilirubin (BIL-ih-ROO-bin)

❑ biliverdin (BIL-ih-VER-din)

❑ biopsy (BY-awp-see)

❑ cancer (KAN-ser)

❑ carcinoma (KAR-sih-NOH-mah)

❑ cardia (KAR-dee-ah)

❑ cavity (KAV-ih-tee)

❑ cecal (SEE-kal)

❑ cecum (SEE-kum)

❑ celiac (SEE-lee-ak)

❑ cheilitis (ky-LY-tis)

❑ chemotherapy drug (KEE-moh-
THAIR-ah-pee DRUHG)

❑ cholangiogram
(koh-LAN-jee-oh-gram)

❑ cholangiography
(koh-LAN-jee-AWG-rah-fee)

❑ cholangiopancreatography
(koh-LAN-jee-oh-PAN-kree-ah-
TAWG-rah-fee)

❑ cholangitis (KOH-lan-JY-tis)

❑ cholecystectomy
(KOH-lee-sis-TEK-toh-mee)

❑ cholecystitis (KOH-lee-sis-TY-tis)

❑ cholecystogram
(KOH-lee-SIS-toh-gram)

❑ cholecystography
(KOH-lee-sis-TAWG-rah-fee)

❑ cholecystokinin
(KOH-lee-SIS-toh-KY-nin)

❑ choledocholithiasis (koh-LED-
oh-koh-lith-EYE-ah-sis)

❑ choledocholithotomy (koh-LED-
oh-koh-lih-THAW-toh-mee)

❑ cholelithiasis
(KOH-lee-lih-THY-ah-sis)

❑ chyme (KIME)

❑ cirrhosis (sih-ROH-sis)

❑ colic (KAWL-ik)

❑ colitis (koh-LY-tis)

❑ colon (KOH-lon)

❑ colonic (koh-LAWN-ik)

❑ colonoscope
(koh-LAWN-oh-skohp)

❑ colonoscopy
(KOH-lon-AWS-koh-pee)

❑ colorectal (KOH-loh-REK-tal)

❑ colostomy
(koh-LAWS-toh-mee)

❑ constipation
(CON-stih-PAY-shun)

❑ Crohn's disease
(KROHNZ dih-ZEEZ)

❑ cystic duct (SIS-tik DUKT)

❑ defecation (DEF-eh-KAY-shun)

❑ deglutition (DEE-gloo-TISH-un)
(DEG-loo-TISH-un)

❑ diarrhea (DY-ah-REE-ah)

❑ digestion (dy-JES-chun)
(dih-JES-chun)

❑ digestive system
(dy-JES-tiv SIS-tem)

❑ diverticula (DY-ver-TIK-yoo-lah)

❑ diverticular
(DY-ver-TIK-yoo-lar)

❑ diverticulitis
(DY-ver-TIK-yoo-LY-tis)

❑ diverticulosis
(DY-ver-TIK-yoo-LOH-sis)

❑ diverticulum
(DY-ver-TIK-yoo-lum)

❑ donor (DOH-nor)

❑ duct (DUKT)

❑ duodenal (DOO-oh-DEE-nal)
(doo-AWD-ah-nal)

❑ duodenum (DOO-oh-DEE-num)
(doo-AWD-ah-num)

❑ dysentery (DIS-en-TAIR-ee)

❑ dyspepsia (dis-PEP-see-ah)

❑ dysphagia (dis-FAY-jee-ah)

❑ elimination
(ee-LIM-ih-NAY-shun)

❑ emesis (EM-eh-sis)

❑ emulsification
(ee-MUL-sih-fih-KAY-shun)

❑ endoscope (EN-doh-skohp)

❑ endoscopic
(EN-doh-SKAWP-ik)

❑ endoscopic retrograde
cholangiopancreatography
(EN-doh-SKAWP-ik
RET-roh-grayd koh-LAN-jee-oh-
PAN-kree-ah-TAWG-rah-fee)

❑ endoscopy
(en-DAWS-koh-pee)

❑ enema (EN-eh-mah)

❑ enteritis (EN-ter-EYE-tis)

❑ enteropathy
(EN-ter-AWP-ah-thee)

❑ enzyme (EN-zime)

❑ esophageal
(eh-SAWF-ah-JEE-al)

❑ esophagitis (ee-SAWF-ah-JY-tis)

❑ esophagogastroduodenoscopy
(ee-SAWF-ah-goh-GAS-troh-DOO-
oh-den-AWS-koh-pee)

- esophagoscopy (ee-SAWF-ah-GAWS-koh-pee)
- esophagus (eh-SAWF-ah-gus)
- fecal (FEE-kal)
- fecalith (FEE-kah-lith)
- feces (FEE-seez)
- flatulence (FLAT-yoo-lens)
- flatus (FLAY-tus)
- fundus (FUN-dus)
- gallbladder (GAWL-blad-er)
- gastrectomy (gas-TREK-toh-mee)
- gastric (GAS-trik)
- gastrin (GAS-trin)
- gastritis (gas-TRY-tis)
- gastroenteritis (GAS-troh-EN-ter-EYE-tis)
- gastroenterologist (GAS-troh-EN-ter-AWL-oh-jist)
- gastroenterology (GAS-troh-EN-ter-AWL-oh-jee)
- gastroesophageal (GAS-troh-ee-SAWF-ah-JEE-al)
- gastrointestinal system (GAS-troh-in-TES-tih-nal SIS-tem)
- gastroplasty (GAS-troh-PLAS-tee)
- gastroscope (GAS-troh-skohp)
- gastroscopy (gas-TRAWS-koh-pee)
- gastrostomy (gas-TRAWS-toh-mee)
- gland (GLAND)
- glossal (GLAWS-al)
- gluten (GLOO-ten)
- gluten enteropathy (GLOO-ten EN-ter-AWP-ah-thee)
- guaiac (GWY-ak)
- haustra (HAW-strah)
- hematemesis (HEE-mah-TEM-ah-sis)
- hematochezia (hee-MAH-toh-KEE-zee-ah)
- hemorrhoid (HEM-oh-royd)
- hemorrhoidectomy (HEM-oh-roy-DEK-toh-mee)
- hepatic (heh-PAT-ik)
- hepatitis (HEP-ah-TY-tis)
- hepatocellular (HEP-ah-toh-SEL-yoo-lar)
- hepatocyte (HEP-ah-toh-SITE)
- hepatoma (HEP-ah-TOH-mah)
- hepatomegaly (HEP-ah-toh-MEG-ah-lee)
- hernia (HER-nee-ah)
- herniorrhaphy (HER-nee-OR-ah-fee)
- hiatal hernia (hy-AA-tal HER-nee-ah)
- hydrochloric acid (HY-droh-KLOR-ik AS-id)
- hyperemesis gravidarum (HY-per-EM-eh-sis GRAV-ih-DAIR-um)
- hypochondriac (HY-poh-CON-dree-ak)
- hypogastric (HY-poh-GAS-trik)
- ileal (IL-ee-al)
- ileostomy (IL-ee-AWS-toh-mee)
- ileum (IL-ee-um)
- ileus (IL-ee-us)
- imperforate anus (im-PER-for-ate AA-nus)
- incarcerated hernia (in-KAR-seh-ray-ted HER-nee-ah)
- incisional hernia (in-SIH-shun-al HER-nee-ah)
- incontinence (in-CON-tih-nens)
- indigestion (IN-dy-JES-chun)
- inguinal (ING-gwih-nal)
- intestinal (in-TES-tih-nal)
- intestine (in-TES-tin)
- intravenous (IN-trah-VEE-nus)
- intussusception (IN-tus-suh-SEP-shun)
- jaundice (JAWN-dis)
- jejunal (jeh-JOO-nal)
- jejunostomy (JEH-joo-NAWS-toh-mee)
- jejunum (jeh-JOO-num)
- lactase (LAK-tace)
- laparoscope (LAP-ah-roh-skohp)
- laparoscopic (LAP-ah-roh-SKAWP-ik)
- laparoscopy (LAP-ah-RAWS-koh-pee)
- laparotomy (LAP-ah-RAW-toh-mee)
- laxative (LAK-sah-tiv)
- lingual (LING-gwal)
- lipase (LIP-ace)
- liver (LIV-er)
- liver transplantation (LIV-er TRANS-plan-TAY-shun)
- lumen (LOO-men)
- malrotation (MAL-roh-TAY-shun)
- mastication (MAS-tih-KAY-shun)
- meconium (meh-KOH-nee-um)
- melena (meh-LEE-nah)
- mesenteric (MEZ-en-TAIR-ik)
- mesentery (MEZ-en-TAIR-ee)
- mucosa (myoo-KOH-sah)
- mucosal (myoo-KOH-sal)
- mucous (MYOO-kus)
- nasogastric (NAY-zoh-GAS-trik)
- nausea (NAW-see-ah) (NAW-zha)
- obstipation (AWB-stih-PAY-shun)
- obstructive (awb-STRUK-tiv)
- occult (oh-KULT)
- omentum (oh-MEN-tum)
- omphalocele (OM-fal-oh-seel)
- oncologist (ong-KAWL-oh-jist)
- oral (OR-al)
- ova and parasites (OH-vah and PAIR-ah-sites)
- palate (PAL-at)
- pancreas (PAN-kree-as)
- pancreatic (PAN-kree-AT-ik)
- pancreatitis (PAN-kree-ah-TY-tis)
- parotid (pah-RAWT-id)
- patent (PAY-tent)
- pedunculated (peh-DUNG-kyoo-lay-ted)
- pepsin (PEP-sin)
- pepsinogen (pep-SIN-oh-jen)
- peptic (PEP-tik)
- peptic ulcer (PEP-ik UL-ser)
- peptidase (PEP-tih-dace)
- percutaneous transhepatic cholangiography (PER-kyoo-TAY-nee-us TRANS-heh-PAT-ik KOH-lan-jee-AWG-rah-fee)
- peristalsis (PAIR-ih-STAL-sis)
- peritoneal (PAIR-ih-toh-NEE-al)
- peritoneum (PAIR-ih-toh-NEE-um)
- peritonitis (PAIR-ih-toh-NY-tis)
- pharyngeal (fah-RIN-jee-al)
- pharynx (FAIR-ingks)
- polyp (PAW-lip)
- polypectomy (PAWL-ih-PEK-toh-mee)
- polyphagia (PAWL-ee-FAY-jee-ah)
- polyposis (PAWL-ee-POH-sis)
- portal (POR-tal)
- postoperative (post-AWP-er-ah-tiv)

- protease (PROH-tee-ace)
- pyloric (py-LOR-ik)
- pyloric sphincter
  (py-LOR-ik SFINGK-ter)
- pylorus (py-LOR-us)
- pyrosis (py-ROH-sis)
- rectal (REK-tal)
- rectum (REK-tum)
- rectocele (REK-toh-seel)
- reflux (REE-fluks)
- regurgitation
  (ree-GER-jih-TAY-shun)
- resection (ree-SEK-shun)
- retroperitoneal
  (REH-troh-PAIR-ih-toh-NEE-al)
- rugae (ROO-gee)
- saliva (sah-LY-vah)
- salivary (SAL-ih-VAIR-ee)
- sessile (SES-il)
- sialolith (sy-AL-oh-lith)
- sialolithiasis
  (sy-AL-oh-lih-THY-ah-sis)

- sigmoid colon
  (SIG-moyd KOH-lon)
- sigmoidoscopy
  (SIG-moy-DAWS-koh-pee)
- sonogram (SAWN-oh-gram)
- spasm (SPAZM)
- spastic (SPAS-tik)
- sphincter (SFINGK-ter)
- steatorrhea
  (stee-AT-oh-REE-ah)
- stoma (STOH-mah)
- stomach (STUM-uk)
- stomatitis (STOH-mah-TY-tis)
- stool (STOOL)
- strangulated hernia
  (STRANG-gyoo-lay-ted
  HER-nee-ah)
- sublingual (sub-LING-gwal)
- submandibular
  (SUB-man-DIB-yoo-lar)
- suppository
  (soo-PAWZ-ih-TOR-ee)

- surgeon (SER-jun)
- syndrome (SIN-drohm)
- tomography
  (toh-MAWG-rah-fee)
- tract (TRAKT)
- transplantation
  (TRANS-plan-TAY-shun)
- ulcer (UL-ser)
- varix (VAR-iks)
- ventral (VEN-tral)
- villi (VIL-eye)
- volvulus (VAWL-vyoo-lus)
- vomit (VAWM-it)
- vomitus (VAWM-ih-tus)
- ulcerative (UL-sir-ah-tiv)
- ultrasound (UL-trah-sound)
- umbilical (um-BIL-ih-kal)
- umbilicus (um-BIL-ih-kus)
  (um-bih-LIE-kus)
- uvula (YOO-vyoo-lah)
- varices (VAIR-ih-seez)

Answer Key

Word Search

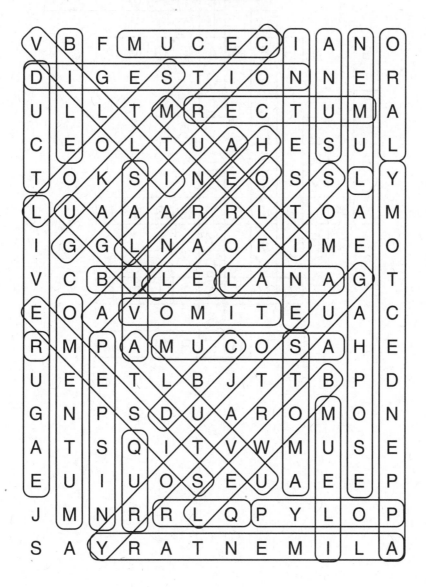

Crossword Puzzle

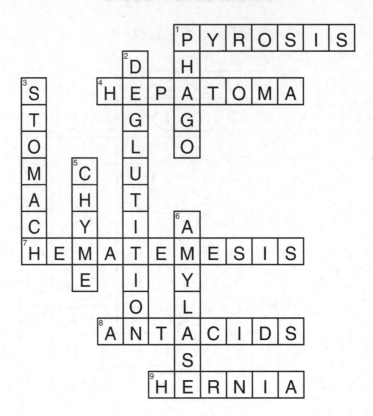

Underline the Accented Syllable

1. adenocarcinoma   (AD-eh-noh-KAR-sih-<u>NOH</u>-mah)

2. anastomosis   (ah-NAS-toh-<u>MOH</u>-sis)

3. bilirubin   (BIL-ih-<u>ROO</u>-bin)

4. cecal   (<u>SEE</u>-kal)

5. cholecystectomy   (KOH-lee-sis-<u>TEK</u>-toh-mee)

6. colonic   (koh-<u>LAWN</u>-ik)

7. diarrhea   (DY-ah-<u>REE</u>-ah)

8. diverticulosis   (DY-ver-TIK-yoo-<u>LOH</u>-sis)

9. dysphagia   (dis-<u>FAY</u>-jee-ah)

10. esophagogastroduodenoscopy

    (ee-SAWF-ah-goh-GAS-troh-DOO-oh-den-<u>AWS</u>-koh-pee)

11. gastroenteritis   (GAS-troh-EN-ter-<u>EYE</u>-tis)

12. guaiac   (<u>GWY</u>-ak)

13. nausea   (<u>NAW</u>-see-ah)

14. omphalocele   (<u>OM</u>-fal-oh-seel)

15. steatorrhea   (stee-AT-oh-<u>REE</u>-ah)

Word Surgery

1. adenocarcinoma

   Suffix and its meaning: -oma *tumor; mass*

   Prefix and its meaning: none

   Combining form and its meaning: aden/o- *gland*

   Combining form and its meaning: carcin/o- *cancer*

   Medical word definition: Tumor in a gland that is a cancer

2. anorexia

   Suffix and its meaning: -ia *condition; state; thing*

   Prefix and its meaning: an- *without; not*

   Combining form and its meaning: orex/o- *appetite*

   Medical word definition: Condition (of being) without an appetite

3. antiemetic

   Suffix and its meaning: -ic *pertaining to*

   Prefix and its meaning: anti- *against*

   Combining form and its meaning: emet/o- *to vomit*

   Medical word definition: Pertaining to (being) against (the urge) to vomit

4. peritonitis

   Suffix and its meaning: -itis *inflammation of; infection of*

   Prefix and its meaning: none

   Combining form and its meaning: peritone/o- *peritoneum*

   Medical word definition: Inflammation or infection of the peritoneum

5. cholangiography

   Suffix and its meaning: -graphy *process of recording*

   Prefix and its meaning: none

   Combining form and its meaning: cholangi/o- *bile duct*

   Medical word definition: Process of recording a bile duct

6. cholelithiasis

   Suffix and its meaning: -iasis *state of; process of*

   Prefix and its meaning: none

   Combining form and its meaning: chol/e- *bile; gall*

   Combining form and its meaning: lith/o- *stone*

   Medical word definition: State of (having) gallstones

7. gastroesophageal

   Suffix and its meaning: -al *pertaining to*

   Prefix and its meaning: none

   Combining form and its meaning: gastr/o- *stomach*

   Combining form and its meaning: esophag/o- *esophagus*

   Medical word definition: Pertaining to the stomach and esophagus

8. hematochezia

   Suffix and its meaning: -ia *condition; state; thing*

   Prefix and its meaning: none

   Combining form and its meaning: hemat/o- *blood*

   Combining form and its meaning: chez/o- *to pass feces*

   Medical word definition: A condition of blood when passing feces

9. hemorrhoidectomy

   Suffix and its meaning: -ectomy *surgical excision*

   Prefix and its meaning: none

   Combining form and its meaning: hemorrhoid/o- *hemorrhoid*

   Medical word definition: Surgical excision of hemorrhoids

10. hepatosplenomegaly

    Suffix and its meaning: -megaly *enlargement*

    Prefix and its meaning: none

    Combining form and its meaning: hepat/o- *liver*

    Combining form and its meaning: splen/o- *spleen*

    Medical word definition: Enlargement of the liver and spleen

11. endoscopic

   Suffix and its meaning: -ic *pertaining to*

   Prefix and its meaning: endo- *innermost; within*

   Combining form and its meaning: scop/o- *examine with an instrument*

   Medical word definition: Pertaining to (a structure) within (being) examined with an instrument

12. herniorrhaphy

   Suffix and its meaning: -rrhaphy *procedure of suturing*

   Prefix and its meaning: none

   Combining form and its meaning: herni/o- *hernia*

   Medical word definition: Procedure of suturing a hernia

13. sialolithiasis

   Suffix and its meaning: -iasis *state of; process of*

   Prefix and its meaning: none

   Combining form and its meaning: sial/o- *saliva; salivary gland*

   Combining form and its meaning: lith/o- *stone*

   Medical word definition: State of salivary gland stones

14. postoperative

   Suffix and its meaning: -ive *pertaining to*

   Prefix and its meaning: post- *after; behind*

   Combining form and its meaning: operat/o- *perform a procedure; surgery*

   Medical word definition: Pertaining to after surgery

15. hematemesis

   Suffix and its meaning: -emesis *vomiting*

   Prefix and its meaning: none

   Combining form and its meaning: hemat/o- *blood*

   Medical word definition: Vomiting blood

Chapter Quiz

MULTIPLE CHOICE

1. C	4. B	7. A	10. D
2. B	5. A	8. C	
3. D	6. B	9. A	

FILL IN THE BLANK

1. nasogastric

2. gastrostomy

3. computerized axial tomography (or tomography or CAT scan or CT scan)

4. cholelithiasis

5. Jaundice

6. hemorrhoids

7. Colic

8. dyspepsia

9. duodenum

10. Peristalsis

TRUE/FALSE

1. True

2. True

3. True

4. True

5. False (hernia of the rectal wall)

6. False (stool)

7. True

8. False (moving backward)

9. False (peptic ulcers or GERD)

10. True

CHAPTER 4

Pulmonology

Measure Your Progress: Learning Objectives

After reading this chapter, the student should be able to

- Identify the structures of the respiratory system.
- Describe the process of respiration.
- Describe common respiratory diseases and conditions, laboratory and diagnostic procedures, medical and surgical procedures, and drug categories.
- Give the medical meaning of word parts related to the respiratory system.
- Build respiratory words from word parts and divide and define respiratory words.
- Spell and pronounce respiratory words.
- Analyze the medical content and meaning of a pulmonology report.
- Dive deeper into pulmonology by reviewing the activities at the end of this chapter and online at Medical Terminology Interactive.

It All Starts with Word Building

Medical language is all about medical words and their word parts. Jump right into this chapter by learning some of the common combining forms and their definitions that you will encounter in this chapter.

alveol/o-	alveolus (air sac)
aspir/o-	to breathe in; to suck in
asthm/o-	asthma
auscult/o-	listening
bronchi/o-	bronchus
bronchiol/o-	bronchiole
bronch/o-	bronchus
capn/o-	carbon dioxide
cost/o-	rib
cyan/o-	blue
diaphragmat/o-	diaphragm
glott/o-	glottis (of the larynx)
hal/o-	breathe
hem/o-	blood
laryng/o-	larynx (voice box)
lob/o-	lobe of an organ
mucos/o-	mucous membrane
nas/o-	nose
ox/i-	oxygen
ox/o-	oxygen
ox/y-	oxygen; quick
pector/o-	chest
pharyng/o-	pharynx (throat)
phren/o-	diaphragm; mind
pleur/o-	pleura (lung membrane)
pne/o-	breathing
pneum/o-	lung; air
pneumon/o-	lung; air
pulmon/o-	lung
py/o-	pus
sept/o-	septum (dividing wall)
spir/o-	breathe; a coil
thorac/o-	thorax (chest)
tubercul/o-	nodule; tuberculosis
turbin/o-	scroll-like structure; turbinate
tuss/o-	cough
trache/o-	trachea (windpipe)
ventil/o-	movement of air

Chapter Spelling Test

Dictate and spell (or photocopy a handout that contains) this list of 20 spelling words. Give this list to students to study for the week. At the beginning of the next week's class, dictate 10 of these words as the spelling test. The spelling test is included with the chapter test that is given on the previous week's material.

1. apnea
2. atelectasis
3. auscultation
4. bronchiectasis
5. bronchiole
6. cyanosis
7. diaphragm
8. dyspnea
9. emphysema
10. hemoptysis
11. laryngeal
12. larynx
13. mucosa
14. parenchyma
15. pleura
16. pneumonia
17. resuscitation
18. stethoscope
19. tachypneic
20. tracheostomy

Chapter Pronunciation Test

Photocopy a handout that contains this list of 20 pronunciation words. Give this list to students to study for the week. Sometime at the beginning of the next week, each student should call your office or home answering machine and pronounce each word.

1. alveoli (al-VEE-oh-lie)

2. apnea (AP-nee-ah)

3. aspiration (AS-pih-RAY-shun)

4. asthma (AZ-mah)

5. bronchiole (BRONG-kee-ohl)

6. bronchopneumonia (BRONG-koh-noo-MOH-nee-ah)

7. emphysema (EM-fih-SEE-mah)

8. empyema (EM-py-EE-mah)

9. eupnea (YOOP-nee-ah)

10. hemoptysis (hee-MAWP-tih-sis)

11. hypoxia (hy-PAWK-see-ah)

12. laryngeal (lah-RIN-jee-al)

13. oxyhemoglobin (AWK-see-HEE-moh-GLOH-bin)

14. paroxysmal (PAIR-awk-SIZ-mal)

15. pharynx (FAIR-ingks)

16. pleurisy (PLOOR-ih-see)

17. purulent (PYOOR-yoo-lent)

18. rhonchi (RONG-kigh)

19. spirometry (spih-RAWM-eh-tree)

20. tachypnea (TAK-ip-NEE-ah)

Word Search

Complete this word search puzzle that contains Chapter 4 words. Look for the following words as given in the list below.

apex	nasal
apnea	nose
asthma	oxygen
breathe	pharynx
bronchus	pulmonary
cilia	rales
hilar	ribs
intubation	SARS
lumen	thorax
lungs	URI
mucus	

```
A  M  A  I  L  I  C  F  J  E  E
P  U  L  M  O  N  A  R  Y  H  S
N  C  Z  K  E  T  T  A  X  T  O
E  U  R  M  W  U  H  L  T  A  N
A  S  U  C  R  B  O  I  S  E  A
M  L  A  A  I  A  R  H  G  R  S
H  E  L  R  B  T  A  Y  N  B  A
T  E  U  E  S  I  X  O  U  K  L
S  U  H  C  N  O  R  B  L  C  X
A  P  E  X  X  N  Y  R  A  H  P
```

Crossword Puzzle

ACROSS

4. The rounded tip of each lung is called the _____.

5. Shortness of breath or _____ is difficult, labored, or painful respirations due to lung disease.

6. The combining form "_____" means blue.

8. A/an _____ is a drug used for productive coughs to reduce the thickness of sputum so that the sputum can be coughed up.

9. The _____ is a central opening through which air flows insides the trachea, bronchi, and bronchioles.

10. The windpipe or _____ is inferior to the larynx and is a passageway for inhaled and exhaled air.

DOWN

1. Irregular crackling or bubbling sounds during inspiration are known as _____.

2. The bronchioles branch into _____, which are hollow spheres of cells that expand and contract with each breath.

3. _____ is characterized by a very low level of oxygen in the arterial blood.

7. _____ is a condition caused by hyperreactivity of the bronchi and bronchioles with bronchospasm.

Underline the Accented Syllable

Read the medical word. Then review the syllables in the pronunciation. Underline the primary (main) accented syllable in the pronunciation.

1. apnea   (ap-nee-ah)

2. asphyxia   (as-fik-see-ah)

3. auscultation   (aws-kul-tay-shun)

4. bradypnea   (brad-ip-nee-ah)

5. bronchoscopy   (brong-kaws-koh-pee)

6. carboxyhemoglobin   (kar-bawk-see-hee-moh-gloh-bin)

7. dyspnea   (disp-nee-ah)

8. hemoptysis   (hee-mawp-tih-sis)

9. hypoxic   (hy-pawk-sik)

10. laryngeal   (lah-rin-jee-al)

11. Mantoux   (man-too)

12. parenchyma   (pah-reng-kih-mah)

13. phrenic   (fren-ik)

14. rhonchi   (rong-kigh)

15. tachypnea   (tak-ip-nee-ah)

Word Surgery

Read the medical word. Break the medical word into its word parts and give the meaning of each word part. Then give the definition of the medical word.

1. apneic

   Suffix and its meaning: _____

   Prefix and its meaning: _____

   Combining form and its meaning: _____

   Medical word definition: _____

2. bronchopneumonia

   Suffix and its meaning: _____

   Prefix and its meaning: _____

   Combining form and its meaning: _____

   Combining form and its meaning: _____

   Medical word definition: _____

3. bronchospasm

   Suffix and its meaning: _____

   Prefix and its meaning: _____

   Combining form and its meaning: _____

   Medical word definition: _____

4. carboxyhemoglobin

   Suffix and its meaning: _____

   Prefix and its meaning: _____

   Combining form and its meaning: _____

   Combining form and its meaning: _____

   Combining form and its meaning: _____

   Medical word definition: _____

5. cardiopulmonary

   Suffix and its meaning: _____

   Prefix and its meaning: _____

   Combining form and its meaning: _____

   Combining form and its meaning: _____

   Medical word definition: _____

6. circumoral

   Suffix and its meaning: _____

   Prefix and its meaning: _____

   Combining form and its meaning: _____

   Medical word definition: _____

7. oximeter

   Suffix and its meaning: _____

   Prefix and its meaning: _____

   Combining form and its meaning: _____

   Medical word definition: _____

8. emphysema

   Suffix and its meaning: _____

   Prefix and its meaning: _____

   Combining form and its meaning: _____

   Medical word definition: _____

9. endotracheal

   Suffix and its meaning: _____

   Prefix and its meaning: _____

   Combining form and its meaning: _____

   Medical word definition: _____

10. epiglottic

   Suffix and its meaning: _____

   Prefix and its meaning: _____

   Combining form and its meaning: _____

   Medical word definition: _____

11. expectorant

   Suffix and its meaning: _____

   Prefix and its meaning: _____

   Combining form and its meaning: _____

   Medical word definition: _____

12. hypoxemia

   Suffix and its meaning: _____

   Prefix and its meaning: _____

   Combining form and its meaning: _____

   Medical word definition: _____

13. orthopnea

   Suffix and its meaning: _____

   Prefix and its meaning: _____

   Combining form and its meaning: _____

   Medical word definition: _____

14. pneumococcal

   Suffix and its meaning: _____

   Prefix and its meaning: _____

   Combining form and its meaning: _____

   Combining form and its meaning: _____

   Medical word definition: _____

15. spirometry

   Suffix and its meaning: _____

   Prefix and its meaning: _____

   Combining form and its meaning: _____

   Medical word definition: _____

Chapter Quiz

MULTIPLE CHOICE

1. The combining form that means lung or air is:

   A. pleur/o-.

   B. pneum/o.

   C. py/o-.

   D. aer/o-.

2. The muscles that control expansion of the thoracic cavity by pulling the ribs up and out are the:

   A. intercostal muscles.

   B. pleural membrane.

   C. costal muscles.

   D. diaphragm.

3. Chronic, permanent enlargement and loss of flexibility of the bronchioles is:

   A. bronchitis.

   B. bronchospasm.

   C. rhonchi.

   D. bronchiectasis.

4. Pneumonia is:

   A. a form of lung cancer.

   B. infection of some or all of the lobes of the lung.

   C. blockage of the pulmonary artery.

   D. a type of SARS.

5. Anoxia refers to the lack of _____, whereas hypercapnia refers to an abnormally high level of _____.

   A. oxygen, carbon dioxide

   B. carbon dioxide, oxygen

   C. nitrogen, oxygen

   D. oxygen, carbon monoxide

6. Intubation is:

    A. a procedure to insert a tube into the chest cavity.

    B. a method used to deliver medication to the pharynx.

    C. placement of a tube between the vocal cords and into the trachea.

    D. a method used to visualize the alveoli.

7. Antitussive drugs are used to:

    A. dilate the bronchi.

    B. constrict blood vessels.

    C. lower blood pressure.

    D. suppress the cough center of the brain.

8. There are four syllables in the word "pulmonary (pul-moh-nair-ee)." Which is the primary (main) accented syllable?

    A. "pul"

    B. "moh"

    C. "nair"

    D. "ee"

9. The larynx is open during inhalation and exhalation but is covered by the
   _____ during swallowing.

    A. epiglottis

    B. bronchus

    C. pharynx

    D. pleura

10. A pneumonectomy might be performed:

    A. to relieve the symptoms of carbon monoxide poisoning.

    B. to treat pneumonia.

    C. as a treatment for lung cancer.

    D. to treat cystic fibrosis.

FILL IN THE BLANK

1. The combining form for "listening" is "_____."

2. The pleural cavity is surrounded by a double-layered serous membrane known as the _____.

3. The combining form for "rib" is "_____."

4. _____ disease was first discovered in Philadelphia in 1976.

5. _____ is a bluish-gray discoloration of the skin because of very low levels of oxygen and very high levels of carbon dioxide in the tissue.

6. An arterial blood gases test measures the partial _____ of oxygen and carbon dioxide in the blood.

7. A _____ is an instrument used to visualize the larynx.

8. Drugs used to relax constricted smooth muscles of the bronchi are

   _____.

9. The medical specialty that studies lungs and breathing is

   _____.

10. The abbreviation for shortness of breath is _____.

TRUE/FALSE

_____ 1. Antibiotic drugs can be used to treat respiratory infections caused by bacteria.

_____ 2. A lung resection removes part or all of a lung.

_____ 3. A sphygmomanometer is used to listen to sounds that indicate if the lungs are clear or if there is fluid or a tumor present.

_____ 4. Paroxysmal nocturnal dyspnea (PND) is shortness of breath at night due to fluid accumulation in the lungs.

_____ 5. Acid-fast bacteria are associated with a lung infection called apnea.

_____ 6. Pneumococcal pneumonia is caused by a fungus.

_____ 7. Emphysema is characterized by the accumulation of purulent material in the thoracic cavity.

_____ 8. Chronic obstructive pulmonary disease is often associated with smoking and pollution.

_____ 9. The combining form "spir/o-" means "lung."

_____ 10. The right lung is smaller than the left lung.

Pronunciation Checklist

Read each word and its pronunciation. Practice pronouncing each word. Verify your pronunciation by listening to the Pronunciation List on Medical Terminology Interactive. Check the box next to the word after you master its pronunciation.

❏ adenocarcinoma
(AD-eh-noh-KAR-sih-NOH-mah)
❏ alveolar (al-VEE-oh-lar)
❏ alveoli (al-VEE-oh-lie)
❏ alveolus (al-VEE-oh-lus)
❏ Ambu bag (AM-boo BAG)
❏ anoxia (an-AWK-see-ah)
❏ anoxic (an-AWK-sik)
❏ anthracosis (AN-thrah-KOH-sis)
❏ antibiotic drug
(AN-tee-by-AWT-ik DRUHG)
(AN-tih-by-AWT-ik DRUHG)
❏ antitubercular drug
(AN-tee-too-BER-kyoo-lar
DRUHG)
❏ antitussive drug
(AN-tee-TUS-iv DRUHG)
❏ apex (AA-peks)
❏ apices (AA-pih-sees)
❏ apnea (AP-nee-ah)
❏ apneic (AP-nee-ik)
❏ arterial blood gases
(ar-TEER-ee-al BLUD GAS-ez)
❏ asbestosis (AS-bes-TOH-sis)
❏ asphyxia (as-FIK-see-ah)
❏ aspiration pneumonia
(AS-pih-RAY-shun
noo-MOH-nee-ah)
❏ asthma (AZ-mah)
❏ asthmatic (az-MAT-ik)
❏ atelectasis (AT-eh-LEK-tah-sis)
❏ atelectatic (AT-eh-lek-TAT-ik)
❏ auscultation
(AWS-kul-TAY-shun)
❏ bacterial pneumonia
(bak-TEER-ee-al
noo-MOH-nee-ah)
❏ bradypnea (BRAD-ip-NEE-ah)
❏ bronchi (BRONG-kigh)
❏ bronchial (BRONG-kee-al)
❏ bronchiectasis
(BRONG-kee-EK-tah-sis)
❏ bronchiolar
(BRONG-kee-OH-lar)
❏ bronchiole (BRONG-kee-ohl)
❏ bronchitis (brong-KY-tis)
❏ bronchodilator drug
(BRONG-koh-DY-lay-ter
DRUHG)

❏ bronchopneumonia
(BRONG-koh-noo-MOH-nee-ah)
❏ bronchopulmonary
(BRONG-koh-PUL-moh-NAIR-ee)
❏ bronchoscope
(BRONG-koh-skohp)
❏ bronchoscopy
(brong-KAWS-koh-pee)
❏ bronchospasm
(BRONG-koh-spazm)
❏ bronchus (BRONG-kus)
❏ cancer (KAN-ser)
❏ cannula (KAN-yoo-lah)
❏ carbon dioxide
(KAR-bon dy-AWK-side)
❏ carboxyhemoglobin
(kar-BAWK-see-HEE-moh-gloh-
bin)
❏ carcinoma (KAR-sih-NOH-mah)
❏ cardiopulmonary
(KAR-dee-oh-PUL-moh-NAIR-ee)
❏ cardiopulmonary resuscitation
(KAR-dee-oh-PUL-moh-NAIR-ee
ree-SUS-ih-TAY-shun)
❏ cardiothoracic surgeon
(KAR-dee-oh-thoh-RAS-ik
SER-jun)
❏ chronic obstructive pulmonary
disease
(KRAW-nik awb-STRUK-tiv
PUL-moh-NAIR-ee dih-ZEEZ)
❏ cilia (SIL-ee-ah)
❏ circumoral cyanosis
(SIR-kum-OR-al SY-ah-NOH-sis)
❏ concha (CON-kah)
❏ conchae (CON-kee)
❏ corticosteroid drug
(KOR-tih-koh-STAIR-oyd
DRUHG)
❏ costal (KAWS-tal)
❏ cough (KAWF)
❏ culture and sensitivity
(KUL-chur and
SEN-sih-TIV-ih-tee)
❏ cyanosis (SY-ah-NOH-sis)
❏ cyanotic (SY-ah-NAWT-ik)
❏ cystic fibrosis (SIS-tik
fy-BROH-sis)
❏ diaphragm (DY-ah-fram)

❏ diaphragmatic
(DY-ah-frag-MAT-ik)
❏ dyspnea (DISP-nee-ah)
❏ dyspneic (DISP-nee-ik)
❏ effusion (ee-FYOO-zhun)
❏ emphysema (EM-fih-SEE-mah)
❏ empyema (EM-py-EE-mah)
❏ endotracheal intubation
(EN-doh-TRAY-kee-al
IN-too-BAY-shun)
❏ epiglottic (EP-ih-GLAWT-ik)
❏ epiglottis (EP-ih-GLAWT-is)
❏ eupnea (YOOP-nee-ah)
❏ eupneic (YOOP-nik)
❏ exhalation (EKS-hah-LAY-shun)
❏ expectorant
(ek-SPEK-toh-rant)
❏ expectoration
(ek-SPEK-toh-RAY-shun)
❏ expiration (EKS-pih-RAY-shun)
❏ external (eks-TER-nal)
❏ Heimlich maneuver
(HYM-lik mah-NOO-ver)
❏ hemoptysis
(hee-MAWP-tih-sis)
❏ hemothorax
(HEE-moh-THOR-aks)
❏ hila (HY-lah)
❏ hilar (HY-lar)
❏ hilum (HY-lum)
❏ histamine (HIS-tah-meen)
❏ hypercapnia
(HY-per-KAP-nee-ah)
❏ hypoxemia
(HY-pawk-SEE-mee-ah)
❏ hypoxia (hy-PAWK-see-ah)
❏ hypoxic (hy-PAWK-sik)
❏ influenza (IN-floo-EN-zah)
❏ inhalation (IN-hah-LAY-shun)
❏ inspiration (IN-spih-RAY-shun)
❏ intercostal retraction
(IN-ter-KAWS-tal
ree-TRAK-shun)
❏ internal (in-TER-nal)
❏ intubation (IN-too-BAY-shun)
❏ laryngeal (lah-RIN-jee-al)
❏ laryngoscope
(lah-RING-goh-skohp)
❏ larynx (LAIR-ingks)

- *Legionella pneumophilia* (LEE-jeh-NEL-ah NOO-moh-FIL-ee-ah)
- Legionnaires' disease (lee-jen-AIRS dih-ZEEZ)
- leukotriene (LOO-koh-TRY-een)
- lobar (LOH-bar)
- lobe (LOHB)
- lobar pneumonia (LOH-bar noo-MOH-nee-ah)
- lobectomy (loh-BEK-toh-mee)
- lumen (LOO-men)
- malignant (mah-LIG-nant)
- Mantoux test (man-TOO TEST)
- mediastinal (MEE-dee-as-TY-nal)
- mediastinum (MEE-dee-as-TY-num)
- metabolic (MET-ah-BAWL-ik)
- metabolism (meh-TAB-oh-lizm)
- mucosa (myoo-KOH-sah)
- mucosal (myoo-KOH-sal)
- mucous (MYOO-kus)
- mucus (MYOO-kus)
- nasal cavity (NAY-zal KAV-ih-tee)
- obstructive apnea (awb-STRUK-tiv AP-nee-ah)
- opportunistic infection (AWP-or-too-NIS-tik in-FEK-shun)
- orthopnea (or-THAWP-nee-ah)
- orthopneic (or-THAWP-nee-ik)
- oximeter (awk-SIM-eh-ter)
- oximetry (awk-SIM-eh-tree)
- oxygen (AWK-seh-jen)
- oxygenated (AWK-see-jen-AA-ted)
- oxyhemoglobin (AWK-see-HEE-moh-GLOH-bin)
- panlobar pneumonia (pan-LOH-bar noo-MOH-nee-ah)
- parenchyma (pah-RENG-kih-mah)
- parietal (pah-RY-eh-tal)
- paroxysmal nocturnal dyspnea (PAIR-awk-SIZ-mal nawk-TER-nal DISP-nee-ah)
- pectus excavatum (PEK-tus EKS-kah-VAH-tum)
- perfusion (per-FYOO-zhun)
- pharyngeal (fah-RIN-jee-al)
- pharynx (FAIR-ingks)
- phrenic nerve (FREN-ik NERV)
- pleura (PLOOR-ah)
- pleural (PLOOR-al)
- pleural effusion (PLOOR-al ee-FYOO-zhun)
- pleurisy (PLOOR-ih-see)
- pleuritic (ploo-RIT-ik)
- pleuritis (ploo-RY-tis)
- pneumococcal pneumonia (NOO-moh-KAW-kal noo-MOH-nee-ah)
- pneumoconiosis (NOO-moh-KOH-nee-OH-sis)
- *Pneumocystis jiroveci* (NOO-moh-SIS-tis YEE-roh-VET-zee)
- pneumonectomy (NOO-moh-NEK-toh-mee)
- pneumonia (noo-MOH-nee-ah)
- pneumothorax (NOO-moh-THOR-aks)
- pulmonary (PUL-moh-NAIR-ee)
- pulmonary edema (PUL-moh-NAIR-ee eh-DEE-mah)
- pulmonary embolism (PUL-moh-NAIR-ee EM-boh-lizm)
- pulmonary embolus (PUL-moh-NAIR-ee EM-boh-lus)
- pulmonologist (PUL-moh-NAWL-oh-jist)
- pulmonology (PUL-moh-NAWL-oh-jee)
- purulent (PYOOR-yoo-lent)
- pyothorax (PY-oh-THOR-aks)
- radiography (RAY-dee-AWG-rah-fee)
- rales (RAWLZ)
- resection (ree-SEK-shun)
- respiration (RES-pih-RAY-shun)
- respirator (RES-pih-RAY-tor)
- respiratory system (RES-pih-rah-TOR-ee SIS-tem) (reh-SPYR-ah-TOR-ee)
- respiratory therapist (RES-pih-rah-TOR-ee THAIR-ah-pist)
- resuscitation (ree-SUS-ih-TAY-shun)
- retraction (re-TRAK-shun)
- Reye's syndrome (RYZ SIN-drohm)
- rhonchi (RONG-kigh)
- septal (SEP-tal)
- septum (SEP-tum)
- spirometer (spih-RAWM-eh-ter)
- spirometry (spih-RAWM-eh-tree)
- sputum (SPYOO-tum)
- status asthmaticus (STAT-us az-MAT-ih-kus)
- sternal (STER-nal)
- sternal retraction (STER-nal ree-TRAK-shun)
- sternum (STER-num)
- stethoscope (STETH-oh-skohp)
- stridor (STRY-dor)
- surfactant (ser-FAK-tant)
- tachypnea (TAK-ip-NEE-ah)
- tachypneic (TAK-ip-NEE-ik)
- therapist (THAIR-ah-pist)
- thoracentesis (THOR-ah-sen-TEE-sis)
- thoracic (thoh-RAS-ik)
- thoracic cavity (thoh-RAS-ik KAV-ih-tee)
- thoracotomy (THOR-ah-KAWT-oh-mee)
- thorax (THOR-aks)
- tomography (toh-MAWG-rah-fee)
- trachea (TRAY-kee-ah)
- tracheal (TRAY-kee-al)
- tracheobronchial (TRAY-kee-oh-BRONG-kee-al)
- tracheostomy (TRAY-kee-AWS-toh-mee)
- tracheotomy (TRAY-kee-AW-toh-mee)
- tubercle (TOO-ber-kl)
- tuberculosis (too-BER-kyoo-LOH-sis)
- turbinate (TER-bih-nayt)
- ventilation (VEN-tih-LAY-shun)
- ventilator (VEN-tih-LAY-tor)
- viral pneumonia (VY-ral noo-MOH-nee-ah)
- visceral (VIS-eh-ral)
- wheezes (WHEE-zes)

Answer Key

Word Search

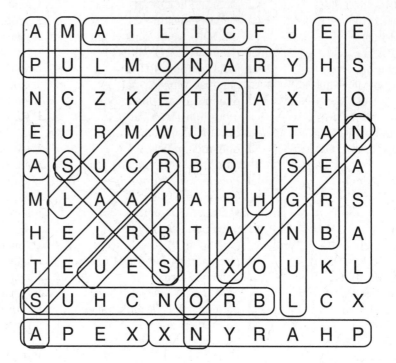

Crossword Puzzle

```
                    ¹R                        ²A
      ³H      ⁴A  P  E  X                      L
⁵D  Y  S  P  N  E  A                           V
      O       L            ⁶C  Y  A  ⁷N  O      E
      X       S                      S          O
⁸E  X  P  E  C  T  O  R  A  N  T     T          L
      M                              H          I
      I                   ⁹L  U  M  E  N
¹⁰T  R  A  C  H  E  A           A
```

Underline the Accented Syllable

1. apnea   (<u>AP</u>-nee-ah)

2. asphyxia   (as-<u>FIK</u>-see-ah)

3. auscultation   (AWS-kul-<u>TAY</u>-shun)

4. bradypnea   (BRAD-ip-<u>NEE</u>-ah)

5. bronchoscopy   (brong-<u>KAWS</u>-koh-pee)

6. carboxyhemoglobin   (kar-BAWK-see-<u>HEE</u>-moh-GLOH-bin)

7. dyspnea   (<u>DISP</u>-nee-ah)

8. hemoptysis   (hee-<u>MAWP</u>-tih-sis)

9. hypoxic   (hy-<u>PAWK</u>-sik)

10. laryngeal   (lah-<u>RIN</u>-jee-al)

11. Mantoux   (man-<u>TOO</u>)

12. parenchyma   (pah-<u>RENG</u>-kih-mah)

13. phrenic   (<u>FREN</u>-ik)

14. rhonchi   (<u>RONG</u>-kigh)

15. tachypnea   (TAK-ip-<u>NEE</u>-ah)

Word Surgery

1. apneic

   Suffix and its meaning: -ic *pertaining to*

   Prefix and its meaning: a- *away from; without*

   Combining form and its meaning: -pne/o- *breathing*

   Medical word definition: Pertaining to without breathing

2. bronchopneumonia

   Suffix and its meaning: -ia *condition; state; thing*

   Prefix and its meaning: none

   Combining form and its meaning: bronch/o- *bronchus*

   Combinign form and its meaning: pneumon/o- *lung; air*

   Medical word definition: Condition of the bronchus and lung

3. bronchospasm

   Suffix and its meaning: -spasm *sudden, involuntary muscle contraction*

   Prefix and its meaning: none

   Combining form and its meaning: bronch/o- *bronchus*

   Medical word definition: Sudden, involuntary (smooth) muscle contraction of the bronchus

4. carboxyhemoglobin

   Suffix and its meaning: -in *a substance*

   Prefix and its meaning: none

   Combining form and its meaning: carbox/y- *carbon monoxide*

   Combining form and its meaning: hem/o- *blood*

   Combining form and its meaning: glob/o- *shaped like a globe; comprehensive*

   Medical word definition: A substance of carbon monoxide (combined with a substance in the) blood that is shaped like a globe

5. cardiopulmonary

   Suffix and its meaning: -ary *pertaining to*

   Prefix and its meaning: none

   Combining form and its meaning: cardi/o- *heart*

   Combining form and its meaning: pulmon/o- *lung*

   Medical word definition: Pertaining to the heart and lung

6. circumoral

    Suffix and its meaning: -al *pertaining to*

    Prefix and its meaning: circum- *around*

    Combining form and its meaning: or/o- *mouth*

    Medical word definition: Pertaining to around the mouth

7. oximeter

    Suffix and its meaning: -meter *instrument used to measure*

    Prefix and its meaning: none

    Combining form and its meaning: ox/i- *oxygen*

    Medical word definition: Instrument used to measure oxygen

8. emphysema

    Suffix and its meaning: -ema *condition*

    Prefix and its meaning: em- *in*

    Combining form and its meaning: phys/o- *inflate; distend; grow*

    Medical word definition: Condition in (which the lungs are excessively) inflated and
       distended

9. endotracheal

    Suffix and its meaning: -al *pertaining to*

    Prefix and its meaning: endo- *innermost; within*

    Combining form and its meaning: trache/o- *trachea (windpipe)*

    Medical word definition: Pertaining to within the trachea

10. epiglottic

    Suffix and its meaning: -ic *pertaining to*

    Prefix and its meaning: epi- *upon; above*

    Combining form and its meaning: glott/o- *glottis (of the larynx)*

    Medical word definition: Pertaining to above the glottis

11. expectorant

    Suffix and its meaning: -ant *pertaining to*

    Prefix and its meaning: ex- *out; away from*

    Combining form and its meaning: pector/o- *chest*

    Medical word definition: Pertaining to (a drug that takes sputum) away from the chest

12. hypoxemia

    Suffix and its meaning: -emia *condition of the blood; substance in the blood*

    Prefix and its meaning: hypo- *below; deficient*

    Combining form and its meaning: ox/o- *oxygen*

    Medical word definition: Condition of the blood (being) deficient in oxygen

13. orthopnea

    Suffix and its meaning: -pnea *breathing*

    Prefix and its meaning: none

    Combining form and its meaning: orth/o- *straight*

    Medical word definition: Breathing (in a) straight (up position)

14. pneumococcal

    Suffix and its meaning: -al *pertaining to*

    Prefix and its meaning: none

    Combining form and its meaning: pneum/o- *lung; air*

    Combining form and its meaning: cocc/o- *spherical bacterium*

    Medical word definition: Pertaining to (there being in the) lung a spherical
      bacterium

15. spirometry

    Suffix and its meaning: -metry *process of measuring*

    Prefix and its meaning: none

    Combining form and its meaning: spir/o- *breathe; a coil*

    Medical word definition: Process of measuring the breathing

Chapter Quiz

MULTIPLE CHOICE

1. B	4. B	7. D	10. C
2. A	5. A	8. A	
3. D	6. C	9. A	

FILL IN THE BLANK

1. auscult/o-
2. pleura
3. cost/o-
4. Legionnaire's
5. Cyanosis
6. pressure
7. laryngoscope
8. bronchodilators
9. pulmonology
10. SOB

TRUE/FALSE

1. True
2. True
3. False (stethoscope)
4. True
5. False (tuberculosis)
6. False (bacteria)
7. False (empyema)
8. True
9. False (breathe)
10. False (the left lung is smaller)

CHAPTER 5

Cardiology

Measure Your Progress: Learning Objectives

After reading this chapter, the student should be able to

- Identify the structures of the cardiovascular system.
- Describe the process of circulation.
- Describe common cardiovascular diseases and conditions, laboratory and diagnostic procedures, medical and surgical procedures, and drug categories.
- Give the medical meaning of word parts related to the cardiovascular system.
- Build cardiovascular words from word parts and divide and define cardiovascular words.
- Spell and pronounce cardiovascular words.
- Analyze the medical content and meaning of a cardiology report.
- Dive deeper into cardiology by reviewing the activities at the end of this chapter and online at Medical Terminology Interactive.

It All Starts with Word Building

Medical language is all about medical words and their word parts. Jump right into this chapter by learning some of the common combining forms and their definitions you will encounter in this chapter.

aneurysm/o-	aneurysm
angi/o-	blood vessel; lymphatic vessel
aort/o-	aorta
arteri/o-	artery
arteriol/o-	arteriole
ather/o-	soft, fatty substance
atri/o-	atrium
auscult/o-	listening
capill/o-	hairlike structure; capillary
card/i-	heart
cardi/o-	heart
circulat/o-	movement in a circular route
coron/o-	structure that encircles like a crown
cusp/o-	projection; point
diastol/o-	dilating
infarct/o-	area of dead tissue
isch/o-	keep back; block
lipid/o-	lipid (fat)
my/o-	muscle
phleb/o-	vein
rrhythm/o-	rhythm
scler/o-	hard; sclera (white of the eye)
sphygm/o-	pulse
steth/o-	chest
systol/o-	contracting
tens/o-	pressure; tension
valv/o-	valve
valvul/o-	valve
vascul/o-	blood vessel
ven/o-	vein
ventricul/o-	ventricle

Chapter Spelling Test

Dictate and spell (or photocopy a handout that contains) this list of 20 spelling words. Give this list to students to study for the week. At the beginning of next week's class, dictate 10 of these words as the spelling test. The spelling test is included with the chapter test that is given on the previous week's material.

1. aneurysm
2. arrhythmia
3. arteriosclerosis
4. bradycardia
5. cardiopulmonary
6. defibrillator
7. diastolic
8. epinephrine
9. hypertriglyceridemia
10. lipoprotein
11. mediastinum
12. paroxysmal tachycardia
13. pericardiocentesis
14. peroneal artery
15. phlebitis
16. sphygmomanometer
17. systolic
18. telemetry
19. thrombophlebitis
20. trigeminy

Chapter Pronunciation Test

Photocopy a handout that contains this list of 20 pronunciation words. Give this list to students to study for the week. Sometime at the beginning of the next week, each student should call your office or home answering machine and pronounce each word.

1. aneurysm (AN-yoo-rizm)

2. angina pectoris (AN-jih-nah PEK-toh-ris)

3. angioplasty (AN-jee-oh-PLAS-tee)

4. arrhythmia (aa-RITH-mee-ah)

5. arteriosclerosis (ar-TEER-ee-oh-skleh-ROH-sis)

6. atheromatous (ATH-eh-ROH-mah-tus)

7. cardiomyopathy (KAR-dee-oh-my-AWP-ah-thee)

8. diastole (dy-AS-toh-lee)

9. diastolic (DY-ah-STAWL-ik)

10. hypertrophy (hy-PER-troh-fee)

11. orthostatic (OR-thoh-STAT-ik)

12. pericarditis (PAIR-ee-kar-DY-tis)

13. plaque (PLAK)

14. prosthetic valve (praws-THET-ik VALV)

15. rheumatic heart disease (roo-MAT-ik HART dih-ZEEZ)

16. sphygmomanometer (SFIG-moh-mah-NAWM-eh-ter)

17. systole (SIS-toh-lee)

18. telemetry (teh-LEM-eh-tree)

19. thrombophlebitis (THRAWM-boh-fleh-BY-tis)

20. varicose veins (VAIR-ih-kohs VAYNZ)

Word Search

Complete this word search puzzle that contains Chapter 5 words. Look for the following words as given in the list below. The number in parentheses indicates how many times the word appears in the puzzle.

angina	LBBB
aorta	LVH
apex	murmur
arrhythmia	node
artery	pulse
atrium	telemetry
bruit	troponin
heart (2)	valve
ions	

```
R  U  M  R  U  M  L  C  X  A
X  J  E  S  L  U  P  V  I  Y
E  L  B  B  B  I  O  M  H  R
P  N  A  B  U  R  H  F  E  T
A  O  R  T  A  T  U  E  A  E
N  D  T  J  Y  A  H  I  R  M
I  E  E  H  H  E  A  R  T  E
G  T  R  O  P  O  N  I  N  L
N  R  Y  L  F  V  A  L  V  E
A  K  G  S  N  O  I  Q  F  T
```

Crossword Puzzle

ACROSS

1. The center wall of the heart, the _____, divides the heart into left and right halves.

4. A _____ is a harsh, rushing sound made by blood passing through an artery that is narrowed and roughened by atherosclerosis.

6. The abbreviation _____ stands for hypertension.

7. The _____ _____ _____ is the major vein that carries blood from the head, neck, arms, and chest to the right atrium.

10. The contraction of the atria or ventricles is known as _____.

DOWN

2. The _____ valve is between the right atrium and right ventricle.

3. Blood vessels are lined with _____, a smooth layer that promotes the flow of blood.

5. _____ is a diagnostic procedure used in the hospital to continuously monitor a patient's heart rate and rhythm.

8. The largest artery in the body is the _____.

9. The combining form "_____" refers to muscle.

Underline the Accented Syllable

Read the medical word. Then review the syllables in the pronunciation. Underline the primary (main) accented syllable in the pronunciation.

1. aneurysm   (an-yoo-rizm)

2. atherosclerosis   (ath-eh-roh-skleh-roh-sis)

3. bruit   (broo-ee)

4. claudication   (klaw-dih-kay-shun)

5. diastole   (dy-as-toh-lee)

6. dysrhythmia   (dis-rith-mee-ah)

7. hypercholesterolemia (hy-per-koh-les-ter-awl-ee-mee-ah)

8. ischemia   (is-kee-mee-ah)

9. paroxysmal   (pair-awk-siz-mal)

10. Purkinje   (per-kin-jee)

11. saphenous   (sah-fee-nus)

12. sphygmomanometer   (sfig-moh-mah-nawm-eh-ter)

13. thrombophlebitis   (thrawm-boh-fleh-by-tis)

14. valvuloplasty   (val-vyoo-loh-plas-tee)

15. xenograft   (zen-oh-graft)

Word Surgery

Read the medical word. Break the medical word into its word parts and give the meaning of each word part. Then give the definition of the medical word.

1. antiarrhythmic

   Suffix and its meaning: _____

   Prefix and its meaning: _____

   Prefix and its meaning: _____

   Combining form and its meaning: _____

   Medical word definition: _____

2. arrhythmia

   Suffix and its meaning: _____

   Prefix and its meaning: _____

   Combining form and its meaning: _____

   Medical word definition: _____

3. arteriosclerotic

   Suffix and its meaning: _____

   Prefix and its meaning: _____

   Combining form and its meaning: _____

   Combining form and its meaning: _____

   Medical word definition: _____

4. cardiomyopathy

   Suffix and its meaning: _____

   Prefix and its meaning: _____

   Combining form and its meaning: _____

   Combining form and its meaning: _____

   Medical word definition: _____

5. cardiopulmonary

   Suffix and its meaning: _____

   Prefix and its meaning: _____

   Combining form and its meaning: _____

   Combining form and its meaning: _____

   Medical word definition: _____

6. defibrillator

Suffix and its meaning: _____

Prefix and its meaning: _____

Combining form and its meaning: _____

Medical word definition: _____

7. hypertension

Suffix and its meaning: _____

Prefix and its meaning: _____

Combining form and its meaning: _____

Medical word definition: _____

8. echocardiography

Suffix and its meaning: _____

Prefix and its meaning: _____

Combining form and its meaning: _____

Combining form and its meaning: _____

Medical word definition: _____

9. endocardial

Suffix and its meaning: _____

Prefix and its meaning: _____

Combining form and its meaning: _____

Medical word definition: _____

10. hyperlipidemia

Suffix and its meaning: _____

Prefix and its meaning: _____

Combining form and its meaning: _____

Medical word definition: _____

11. pericardiocentesis

Suffix and its meaning: _____

Prefix and its meaning: _____

Combining form and its meaning: _____

Medical word definition: _____

12. anastomosis

  Suffix and its meaning: _____

  Prefix and its meaning: _____

  Combining form and its meaning: _____

  Medical word definition: _____

13. phlebitis

  Suffix and its meaning: _____

  Prefix and its meaning: _____

  Combining form and its meaning: _____

  Medical word definition: _____

14. sinoatrial

  Suffix and its meaning: _____

  Prefix and its meaning: _____

  Combining form and its meaning: _____

  Combining form and its meaning: _____

  Medical word definition: _____

15. ultrasonography

  Suffix and its meaning: _____

  Prefix and its meaning: _____

  Combining form and its meaning: _____

  Medical word definition: _____

Chapter Quiz

MULTIPLE CHOICE

1. The function of the valves of the heart is to:

   A. prevent regurgitation (backflow of blood).

   B. assist in the electrical control of the normal sinus rhythm.

   C. seal the left ventricle from the right ventricle.

   D. prevent blood loss.

2. Blood vessels that carry blood back to the heart from the body tissues and lungs are:

   A. arteries.

   B. lymph vessels.

   C. nodes.

   D. veins.

3. The arteries, blood, capillaries, and veins that go in and out of the lungs but not to the rest of the body comprise the:

   A. lymph circulation.

   B. aortic flow.

   C. pulmonary circulation.

   D. ejection fraction.

4. Idiopathic cardiomyopathy is:

   A. a problem with the heart muscle with an unknown cause.

   B. a heart attack.

   C. an infection that leads to heart block.

   D. congestive heart failure.

5. Bradycardia is defined as:

   A. a tachycardia.

   B. a myocardial infarction.

   C. an arrhythmia in which the heart fibrillates.

   D. an arrhythmia in which the heart beats too slowly.

6. A hypotensive patient is one who has:

    A. difficulty clotting blood.

    B. high blood pressure.

    C. low blood pressure.

    D. low platelet count.

7. A Holter monitor is a diagnostic recorder used to measure the:

    A. blood pressure.

    B. heart rate and rhythm continuously.

    C. electrolyte balance.

    D. prothrombin time.

8. A balloon angioplasty is used to:

    A. compress atheromatous plaque.

    B. test for heart block.

    C. repair varicose veins.

    D. convert ventricular fibrillation.

9. Which of the following abbreviations refers to a heart attack?

    A. LA

    B. MI

    C. LDL

    D. MVP

10. Beta-blocker drugs, such as propranolol and metoprolol, are used to:

    A. increase blood volume and the blood pressure.

    B. treat angina pectoris and hypertension.

    C. prevent and treat a cardiac arrhythmia.

    D. Lower the level of lipids in the blood.

FILL IN THE BLANK

1. _____ is the combining form for "hard."

2. The _____ node is sometimes referred to as the pacemaker of the heart.

3. The _____ vena cava returns blood to the right atrium from the head, neck, arms, and chest.

4. The combining form "path/o-" means "_____."

5. In the condition known as _____ of Fallot, there are four specific congenital heart defects.

6. Soft, fatty deposits and hardening of the arteries is known as _____.

7. A necrotic tissue is a tissue that is _____.

8. A diagnostic radiologic procedure that uses a transducer to produce ultra high-frequency sound waves to image the heart is _____.

9. The radial pulse can be found at the _____.

10. An ACE inhibitor is a category of drug used to treat congestive heart failure and _____.

TRUE/FALSE

_____ 1. Thrombolytic drugs are used to treat blood clots.

_____ 2. The combining form "angi/o-" refers to a stent inserted in a vein.

_____ 3. The suffix "-graphy" is an image or record.

_____ 4. Hyperlipidemia refers to elevated levels of lipids in the blood including cholesterol and triglycerides.

_____ 5. An aneurysm is an area of dilation and weakness in the wall of an artery.

_____ 6. When the valve between the left atrium and left ventricle does not close tightly, this condition is known as mitral valve prolapse.

_____ 7. An aneurysm can produce angina pectoris.

_____ 8. The opposite of vasoconstriction is fibrillation.

_____ 9. The bundle branches are part of the system that controls the heart rate.

_____ 10. The carotid arteries carry blood to the lungs.

Pronunciation Checklist

Read each word and its pronunciation. Practice pronouncing each word. Verify your pronunciation by listening to the Pronunciation List on Medical Terminology Interactive. Check the box next to the word after you master its pronunciation.

❏ anastomosis
(ah-NAS-toh-MOH-sis)
❏ aneurysm (AN-yoo-rizm)
❏ aneurysmal (AN-yoo-RIZ-mal)
❏ aneurysmectomy
(AN-yoo-riz-MEK-toh-mee)
❏ angina (AN-jih-nah)
(an-JY-nah)
❏ anginal (AN-jih-nal) (an-JY-nal)
❏ angina pectoris
(AN-jih-nah PEK-toh-ris)
❏ angiogram (AN-jee-oh-gram)
❏ angiography
(AN-jee-AWG-rah-fee)
❏ angioplasty
(AN-jee-oh-PLAS-tee)
❏ angiotensin (AN-jee-oh-TEN-sin)
❏ antiarrhythmic drug
(AN-tee-aa-RITH-mik DRUHG)
❏ antibiotic drug
(AN-tee-by-AWT-ik DRUHG)
(AN-tih-by-AWT-ik)
❏ antihypertensive drug
(AN-tee-HY-per-TEN-siv DRUHG)
❏ aorta (aa-OR-tah)
❏ aortic valve (aa-OR-tik VALV)
❏ aortogram (aa-OR-toh-gram)
❏ aortography
(AA-or-TAWG-rah-fee)
❏ apex (AA-peks)
❏ apical (AP-ih-kal)
❏ arrhythmia (aa-RITH-mee-ah)
❏ arterial (ar-TEER-ee-al)
❏ arteriogram
(ar-TEER-ee-oh-gram)
❏ arteriography
(ar-TEER-ee-AWG-rah-fee)
❏ arteriolar (ar-TEER-ee-OH-lar)
❏ arteriole (ar-TEER-ee-ohl)
❏ arteriosclerosis
(ar-TEER-ee-oh-skleh-ROH-sis)
❏ arteriosclerotic
(ar-TEER-ee-oh-skleh-RAW-tik)
❏ artery (AR-ter-ee)
❏ asystole (aa-SIS-toh-lee)
❏ atheroma (ATH-eh-ROH-mah)
❏ atheromatous
(ATH-eh-ROH-mah-tus)
❏ atherosclerosis
(ATH-eh-roh-skleh-ROH-sis)

❏ atria (AA-tree-ah)
❏ atrial (AA-tree-al)
❏ atrioventricular
(AA-tree-oh-ven-TRIK-yoo-lar)
❏ atrium (AA-tree-um)
❏ auscultation
(AWS-kul-TAY-shun)
❏ axillary artery
(AK-zih-LAIR-ee AR-ter-ee)
❏ bicuspid valve
(by-KUS-pid VALV)
❏ bigeminal rhythm
(by-JEM-ih-nal RITH-um)
❏ bigeminy (by-JEM-ih-nee)
❏ brachial artery
(BRAY-kee-al AR-ter-ee)
❏ bradycardia
(BRAD-ee-KAR-ee-ah)
❏ bradycardic (BRAD-ee-KAR-dik)
❏ bruit (BROO-ee)
❏ bundle of His (BUN-dl of HISS)
❏ capillary (KAP-ih-LAIR-ee)
❏ cardiac (KAR-dee-ak)
❏ cardiac catheterization
(KAR-dee-ak
KATH-eh-TER-ih-ZAY-shun)
❏ cardiac enzymes
(KAR-dee-ak EN-zimez)
❏ cardiologist
(KAR-dee-AWL-oh-jist)
❏ cardiology
(KAR-dee-AWL-oh-jee)
❏ cardiomegaly
(KAR-dee-oh-MEG-ah-lee)
❏ cardiomyopathy
(KAR-dee-oh-my-AWP-ah-thee)
❏ cardiopulmonary
(KAR-dee-oh-PUL-moh-NAIR-ee)
❏ cardiopulmonary resuscitation
(KAR-dee-oh-PUL-moh-NAIR-ee
ree-SUS-ih-TAY-shun)
❏ cardiothoracic
(KAR-dee-oh-thoh-RAS-ik)
❏ cardiovascular system
(KAR-dee-oh-VAS-kyoo-lar
SIS-tem)
❏ cardioversion
(KAR-dee-oh-VER-zhun)
❏ carotid artery
(kah-ROT-id AR-ter-ee)

❏ cavity (KAV-ih-tee)
❏ chordae tendineae
(KOHR-dee TEN-dih-nee-ee)
❏ circulation (SIR-kyoo-LAY-shun)
❏ circulatory
(SIR-kyoo-lah-TOH-ree)
❏ claudication
(KLAW-dih-KAY-shun)
❏ coarctation (KOH-ark-TAY-shun)
❏ compensated heart failure
(KAWM-pen-SAY-ted HART
FAYL-yer)
❏ conduction (con-DUK-shun)
❏ congestive (con-JES-tiv)
❏ contraction (con-TRAK-shun)
❏ cor pulmonale
(KOR PUL-moh-NAL-ee)
❏ coronary artery (KOR-oh-NAIR-
ee AR-ter-ee)
❏ creatine phosphokinase
(KREE-ah-teen
FAWS-foh-KY-nays)
❏ decompensated heart failure
(dee-KAWM-pen-SAY-ted
HART FAYL-yer)
❏ defibrillator
(dee-FIB-rih-LAY-tor)
❏ depolarization
(dee-POH-lar-ih-ZAY-shun)
❏ diastole (dy-AS-toh-lee)
❏ diastolic (DY-ah-STAWL-ik)
❏ digitalis (DIJ-ih-TAL-is)
❏ dissecting aneurysm
(dy-SEK-ting AN-yoo-rizm)
❏ Doppler ultrasonography
(DAWP-ler
UL-trah-soh-NAWG-rah-fee)
❏ dorsalis pedis
(dohr-SAL-is PEE-dis)
❏ ductus arteriosus
(DUK-tus ar-TEER-ee-OH-sus)
❏ duplex ultrasonography
(DOO-pleks
UL-trah-soh-NAWG-rah-fee)
❏ dysrhythmia
(dis-RITH-mee-ah)
❏ echocardiogram
(EK-oh-KAR-dee-oh-gram)
❏ echocardiography
(EK-oh-KAR-dee-AWG-rah-fee)

- ❏ ectopic (ek-TOP-ik)
- ❏ edema (eh-DEE-mah)
- ❏ electrocardiogram (ee-LEK-troh-KAR-dee-oh-gram)
- ❏ electrocardiographic technician (ee-LEK-troh-KAR-dee-oh-GRAF-ik tek-NISH-un)
- ❏ electrocardiography (ee-LEK-troh-KAR-dee-AWG-rah-fee)
- ❏ electrophysiologic (ee-LEK-troh-FIZ-ee-oh-LAW-jik)
- ❏ endarterectomy (END-ar-ter-EK-toh-mee)
- ❏ endocarditis (EN-doh-kar-DY-tis)
- ❏ endocardium (EN-doh-KAR-dee-um)
- ❏ endothelium (EN-doh-THEE-lee-um)
- ❏ epicardium (EP-ih-KAR-dee-um)
- ❏ epinephrine (EP-ih-NEF-rin)
- ❏ extrasystole (EKS-trah-SIS-toh-lee)
- ❏ femoral artery (FEM-oh-ral AR-ter-ee)
- ❏ fibrillation (FIB-rih-LAY-shun)
- ❏ foramen ovale (foh-RAY-men oh-VAH-lee)
- ❏ heart transplantation (HART TRANS-plan-TAY-shun)
- ❏ hypercholesterolemia (HY-per-koh-LES-ter-awl-EE-mee-ah)
- ❏ hyperlipidemia (HY-per-LIP-ih-DEE-mee-ah)
- ❏ hypertension (HY-per-TEN-shun)
- ❏ hypertensive (HY-per-TEN-siv)
- ❏ hypertriglyceridemia (HY-per-try-GLIS-eh-ry-DEE-mee-ah)
- ❏ hypertrophic (HY-per-TROH-fik)
- ❏ hypertrophy (hy-PER-troh-fee)
- ❏ hypotension (HY-poh-TEN-shun)
- ❏ hypotensive (HY-poh-TEN-siv)
- ❏ idiopathic (ID-ee-oh-PATH-ik)
- ❏ iliac artery (IL-ee-ak AR-ter-ee)
- ❏ infarction (in-FARK-shun)
- ❏ interatrial septum (IN-ter-AA-tree-al SEP-tum)
- ❏ interventricular septum (IN-ter-ven-TRIK-yoo-lar SEP-tum)
- ❏ intima (IN-tih-mah)
- ❏ intra-atrial (IN-trah-AA-tree-al)
- ❏ intraventricular (IN-trah-ven-TRIK-yoo-lar)
- ❏ ischemia (is-KEE-mee-ah)
- ❏ jugular vein (JUG-yoo-lar VAYN)
- ❏ lactate dehydrogenase (LAK-tayt dee-HY-droh-jeh-nays)
- ❏ lipid (LIP-id)
- ❏ lipoprotein (LIP-oh-PROH-teen)
- ❏ lumen (LOO-men)
- ❏ mediastinal (MEE-dee-as-TY-nal)
- ❏ mediastinum (MEE-dee-as-TY-num)
- ❏ mitral valve (MY-tral VALV)
- ❏ mitral regurgitation (MY-tral ree-GER-jih-TAY-shun)
- ❏ murmur (MER-mer)
- ❏ myocardial (MY-oh-KAR-dee-al)
- ❏ myocardial infarction (MY-oh-KAR-dee-al in-FARK-shun)
- ❏ myocardial perfusion scan (MY-oh-KAR-dee-al per-FYOO-zhun SKAN)
- ❏ myocardium (MY-oh-KAR-dee-um)
- ❏ necrosis (neh-KROH-sis)
- ❏ necrotic (neh-KRAWT-ik)
- ❏ nitrate drug (NY-trayt DRUHG)
- ❏ occlusion (oh-KLOO-zhun)
- ❏ orthostatic hypotension (OR-thoh-STAT-ik HY-poh-TEN-shun)
- ❏ palpitation (PAL-pih-TAY-shun)
- ❏ paroxysmal tachycardia (PAIR-awk-SIZ-mal TAK-ih-KAR-dee-ah)
- ❏ patent (PAY-tent)
- ❏ percutaneous transluminal angioplasty (PER-kyoo-TAY-nee-us trans-LOO-mih-nal AN-jee-oh-PLAS-tee)
- ❏ perfusion (per-FYOO-zhun)
- ❏ pericardial sac (PAIR-ih-KAR-dee-al SAK)
- ❏ pericardiocentesis (PAIR-ih-KAR-dee-oh-sen-TEE-sis)
- ❏ pericarditis (PAIR-ee-kar-DY-tis)
- ❏ pericardium (PAIR-ih-KAR-dee-um)
- ❏ peripheral (peh-RIF-eh-ral)
- ❏ peroneal artery (PAIR-oh-NEE-al AR-ter-ee)
- ❏ phlebitis (fleh-BY-tis)
- ❏ plaque (PLAK)
- ❏ popliteal artery (pop-LIT-ee-al AR-ter-ee) (POP-lih-TEE-al)
- ❏ portal vein (POR-tal VAYN)
- ❏ prehypertension (pree-HY-per-TEN-shun)
- ❏ prosthetic valve (praws-THET-ik VALV)
- ❏ pulmonary artery (PUL-moh-NAIR-ee AR-ter-ee)
- ❏ pulmonary valve (PUL-moh-NAIR-ee VALV)
- ❏ pulmonary vein (PUL-moh-NAIR-ee VAYN)
- ❏ pulse (PUHLS)
- ❏ Purkinje fiber (per-KIN-jee FY-ber)
- ❏ radial artery (RAY-dee-al AR-ter-ee)
- ❏ radiofrequency catheter ablation (RAY-dee-oh-FREE-kwen-see KATH-eh-ter ah-BLAY-shun)
- ❏ radionuclide ventriculography (RAY-dee-oh-NOO-klide ven-TRIK-yoo-LAWG-rah-fee)
- ❏ Raynaud's disease (ray-NOZ dih-ZEEZ)
- ❏ refractory (ree-FRAK-tor-ee)
- ❏ renal artery (REE-nal AR-ter-ee)
- ❏ repolarization (ree-POH-lar-ih-ZAY-shun)
- ❏ rheumatic heart disease (roo-MAT-ik HART dih-ZEEZ)
- ❏ saphenous vein (sah-FEE-nus VAYN)
- ❏ sclerotherapy (SKLAIR-oh-THAIR-ah-pee)
- ❏ septal (SEP-tal)
- ❏ septum (SEP-tum)
- ❏ sinoatrial node (SY-noh-AA-tree-al NOHD)
- ❏ sinus rhythm (SY-nus RITH-um)
- ❏ sphygmomanometer (SFIG-moh-mah-NAWM-eh-ter)
- ❏ stenosis (steh-NOH-sis)
- ❏ stethoscope (STETH-oh-skohp)
- ❏ subacute (SUB-ah-KYOOT)
- ❏ subclavian artery (sub-KLAY-vee-an AR-ter-ee)

- supraventricular tachycardia (SOO-prah-ven-TRIK-yoo-lar TAK-ih-KAR-dee-ah)
- systemic (sis-TEM-ik)
- systole (SIS-toh-lee)
- systolic (sis-TAWL-ik)
- tachycardia (TAK-ih-KAR-dee-ah)
- tachycardic (TAK-ih-KAR-dik)
- tamponade (tam-poh-NAYD)
- telemetry (teh-LEM-eh-tree)
- tetralogy of Fallot (tet-RAL-oh-jee of fah-LOH)
- thallium stress test (THAL-ee-um STRES TEST)
- thoracic cavity (thoh-RAS-ik KAV-ih-tee)
- thrombolytic drug (THRAWM-boh-LIT-ik DRUHG)
- thrombophlebitis (THRAWM-boh-fleh-BY-tis)
- tibial artery (TIB-ee-al AR-ter-ee)
- tomography (toh-MAWG-rah-fee)
- transesophageal echocardio-gram (TRANS-ee-SAWF-ah-JEE-al EK-oh-KAR-dee-oh-gram)
- tricuspid valve (try-KUS-pid VALV)
- trigeminal rhythm (try-JEM-ih-nal RITH-um)
- trigeminy (try-JEM-ih-nee)
- troponin (troh-POH-nin)
- ulnar artery (UL-nar AR-ter-ee)
- ultrasonography (UL-trah-soh-NAWG-rah-fee)
- valve (VALV)
- valve prolapse (VALV PROH-laps)
- valvoplasty (VAL-voh-PLAS-tee)
- valvular (VAL-vyoo-lar)
- valvuloplasty (VAL-vyoo-loh-PLAS-tee)
- valvulotome (VAL-vyoo-loh-TOHM)
- varicose vein (VAR-ih-kohs VAYN)
- vascular (VAS-kyoo-lar)
- vasculature (VAS-kyoo-lah-CHUR)
- venous (VEE-nus)
- ventricle (VEN-trih-kl)
- ventricular (ven-TRIK-yoo-lar)
- ventriculography (ven-TRIK-yoo-LAWG-rah-fee)
- venule (VEN-yool)
- xenograft (ZEN-oh-graft)
- vasoconstriction (VAY-soh-con-STRIK-shun)
- vasodilation (VAY-soh-dy-LAY-shun)
- vegetation (VEJ-eh-TAY-shun)
- vein (VAYN)
- vena cava (VEE-nah KAY-vah)
- venogram (VEE-noh-gram)
- venography (vee-NAWG-rah-fee)

Answer Key

Word Search

Crossword Puzzle

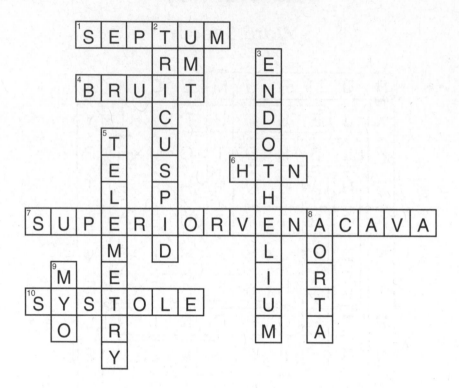

Underline the Accented Syllable

1. aneurysm   (<u>AN</u>-yoo-rizm)

2. atherosclerosis   (ATH-eh-roh-skleh-<u>ROH</u>-sis)

3. bruit   (<u>BROO</u>-ee)

4. claudication   (KLAW-dih-<u>KAY</u>-shun)

5. diastole   (dy-<u>AS</u>-toh-lee)

6. dysrhythmia   (dis-<u>RITH</u>-mee-ah)

7. hypercholesterolemia (HY-per-koh-LES-ter-awl-<u>EE</u>-mee-ah)

8. ischemia   (is-<u>KEE</u>-mee-ah)

9. paroxysmal   (PAIR-awk-<u>SIZ</u>-mal)

10. Purkinje   (per-<u>KIN</u>-jee)

11. saphenous   (sah-<u>FEE</u>-nus)

12. sphygmomanometer   (SFIG-moh-mah-<u>NAWM</u>-eh-ter)

13. thrombophlebitis   (THRAWM-boh-fleh-<u>BY</u>-tis)

14. valvuloplasty   (<u>VAL</u>-vyoo-loh-PLAS-tee)

15. xenograft   (<u>ZEN</u>-oh-graft)

Word Surgery

1. antiarrhythmic

   Suffix and its meaning: -ic *pertaining to*

   Prefix and its meaning: anti- *against*

   Prefix and its meaning: a- *away from; without*

   Combining form and its meaning: rrhythm/o- *rhythm*

   Medical word definition: Pertaining to (a drug that is) against (a heart that is) without a rhythm

2. arrhythmia

   Suffix and its meaning: -ia *condition; state; thing*

   Prefix and its meaning: a- *away from; without*

   Combining form and its meaning: rrhythm/o- *rhythm*

   Medical word definition: Condition of without rhythm

3. arteriosclerotic

   Suffix and its meaning: -tic *pertaining to*

   Prefix and its meaning: none

   Combining form and its meaning: arteri/o- *artery*

   Combining form and its meaning: scler/o- *hard; sclera*

   Medical word definition: Pertaining to an artery that is hard

4. cardiomyopathy

   Suffix and its meaning: -pathy *disease; suffering*

   Prefix and its meaning: none

   Combining form and its meaning: cardi/o- *heart*

   Combining form and its meaning: my/o- *muscle*

   Medical word definition: Disease of the heart muscle

5. cardiopulmonary

   Suffix and its meaning: -ary *pertaining to*

   Prefix and its meaning: none

   Combining form and its meaning: cardi/o- *heart*

   Combining form and its meaning: pulmon/o- *lung*

   Medical word definition: Pertaining to the heart and lung

6. defibrillator

Suffix and its meaning: -ator *person or thing that produces or does*

Prefix and its meaning: de- *reversal of; without*

Combining form and its meaning: fibrill/o- *muscle fiber; nerve fiber*

Medical word definition: Thing that produces or does a reversal of (abnormal contracting of a) muscle fiber

7. hypertension

Suffix and its meaning: -ion *action; condition*

Prefix and its meaning: hyper- *above; more than normal*

Combining form and its meaning: tens/o- *pressure; tension*

Medical word definition: Condition of more than normal (blood) pressure

8. echocardiography

Suffix and its meaning: -graphy *process of recording*

Prefix and its meaning: none

Combining form and its meaning: ech/o- *echo (sound wave)*

Combining form and its meaning: cardi/o- *heart*

Medical word definition: Process of recording an echo (sound wave) of the heart

9. endocardial

Suffix and its meaning: -ial *pertaining to*

Prefix and its meaning: endo- *innermost; within*

Combining form and its meaning: cardi/o- *heart*

Medical word definition: Pertaining to within the heart

10. hyperlipidemia

Suffix and its meaning: -emia *condition of the blood; substance in the blood*

Prefix and its meaning: hyper- *above; more than normal*

Combining form and its meaning: lipid/o- *lipid (fat)*

Medical word definition: Substance in the blood of more than normal lipid (fat)

11. pericardiocentesis

Suffix and its meaning: -centesis *procedure to puncture*

Prefix and its meaning: peri- *around*

Combining form and its meaning: cardi/o- *heart*

Medical word definition: Procedure to puncture (the membrane) around the heart

12. anastomosis

    Suffix and its meaning: -osis *condition; abnormal condition; process*

    Prefix and its meaning: none

    Combining form and its meaning: anastom/o- *create an opening between two structures*

    Medical word definition: Process to create an opening between two structures

13. phlebitis

    Suffix and its meaning: -itis *inflammation of; infection of*

    Prefix and its meaning: none

    Combining form and its meaning: phleb/o- *vein*

    Medical word definition: Inflammation of a vein

14. sinoatrial

    Suffix and its meaning: -al *pertaining to*

    Prefix and its meaning: none

    Combining form and its meaning: sin/o- *hollow cavity; channel*

    Combining form and its meaning: atri/o- *atrium*

    Medical word definition: Pertaining to the hollow cavity of the atrium

15. ultrasonography

    Suffix and its meaning: -graphy *process of recording*

    Prefix and its meaning: ultra- *beyond; higher*

    Combining form and its meaning: son/o- *sound*

    Medical word definition: Process of recording (using) higher sound (waves)

Chapter Quiz

MULTIPLE CHOICE

1. A   4. A   7. B   10. B
2. D   5. D   8. A
3. C   6. C   9. B

FILL IN THE BLANK

1. Scler/o-

2. sinoatrial

3. superior

4. disease; suffering

5. tetrology

6. atherosclerosis

7. dead

8. echocardiography

9. wrist

10. hypertension

TRUE/FALSE

1. True

2. False (a blood or lymph vessel)

3. False (-graph)

4. True

5. True

6. True

7. False (coronary artery disease)

8. False (vasodilation)

9. True

10. False (neck, head, face, and brain)

CHAPTER 6

Hematology and Immunology

Measure Your Progress: Learning Objectives

After reading this chapter, the student should be able to

- Identify the structures of the blood and the lymphatic system.
- Describe the processes of blood clotting and the immune response.
- Describe common blood, lymphatic, and immune diseases and conditions, laboratory and diagnostic procedures, medical and surgical procedures, and drug categories.
- Give the medical meaning of word parts related to the blood and immune system.
- Build blood, lymph system, and immune response words from word parts and divide and define those words.
- Spell and pronounce blood, lymph system, and immune response words.
- Analyze the medical content and meaning of an immunology report.
- Dive deeper into hematology and immunology by reviewing the activities at the end of this chapter and online at Medical Terminology Interactive.

It All Starts with Word Building

Medical language is all about medical words and their word parts. Jump right into this chapter by learning some of the common combining forms and their definitions that you will encounter in this chapter.

aden/o-	gland
bas/o-	base of a structure; basic (alkaline)
cellul/o-	cell
coagul/o-	clotting
cyt/o-	cell
embol/o-	embolus (occluding plug)
eosin/o-	eosin (red acidic dye)
erythr/o-	red
glob/o-	shaped like a globe; comprehensive
granul/o-	granule
hemat/o-	blood
hem/o-	blood
immun/o-	immune response
kary/o-	nucleus
leuk/o-	white
lymph/o-	lymph; lymphatic system
macr/o-	large
meg/a-	large
megal/o-	large
micr/o-	one millionth; small
mon/o-	one; single
morph/o-	shape
myel/o-	bone marrow; spinal cord; myelin
neutr/o-	not taking part
norm/o-	normal; usual
nucle/o-	nucleus
ox/y-	oxygen; quick
path/o-	disease; suffering
phag/o-	eating; swallowing
phil/o-	attraction to; fondness for
plasm/o-	plasma
reticul/o-	small network
splen/o-	spleen
thromb/o-	thrombus (blood clot)
thym/o-	thymus; rage

Chapter Spelling Test

Dictate and spell (or photocopy a handout that contains) this list of 20 spelling words. Give this list to students to study for the week. At the beginning of next week's class, dictate 10 of these words as the spelling test. The spelling test is included with the chapter test that is given on the previous week's material.

1. anemia
2. coagulopathy
3. dyscrasia
4. electrophoresis
5. embolism
6. eosinophil
7. erythropoietin
8. hemolysis
9. hemophiliac
10. immunoglobulin
11. leukemia
12. lymphadenopathy
13. lymphocyte
14. macrophage
15. phlebotomy
16. purpura
17. splenectomy
18. thrombocytopenia
19. vaccination
20. venipuncture

Chapter Pronunciation Test

Photocopy a handout that contains this list of 20 pronunciation words. Give this list to students to study for the week. Sometime at the beginning of the next week, each student should call your office or home answering machine and pronounce each word.

1. agglutination (ah-GLOO-tih-NAY-shun)

2. autoimmune (AW-toh-im-MYOON)

3. coagulopathy (koh-AG-yoo-LAWP-ah-thee)

4. ecchymoses (EK-ih-MOH-seez)

5. fibrinogen (fy-BRIN-oh-jen)

6. hemostasis (HEE-moh-STAY-sis)

7. idiopathic (ID-ee-oh-PATH-ik)

8. immunocompromised (IM-myoo-noh-COM-proh-myzed)

9. lymphangiography (lim-FAN-jee-AWG-rah-fee)

10. lymphoid (LIM-foyd)

11. mononucleosis (MAWN-oh-NOO-klee-OH-sis)

12. morphology (mor-FAWL-oh-jee)

13. myeloblast (MY-eh-loh-BLAST)

14. pancytopenia (PAN-sy-toh-PEE-nee-ah)

15. pernicious anemia (per-NISH-us ah-NEE-mee-ah)

16. phlebotomy (fleh-BAW-toh-mee)

17. plasmapheresis (PLAZ-mah-feh-REE-sis)

18. polymorphonuclear leukocyte (PAWL-ee-MOR-foh-NOO-klee-ar LOO-koh-site)

19. reticulocyte (reh-TIK-yoo-loh-SITE)

20. splenomegaly (SPLEH-noh-MEG-ah-lee)

Word Search

Complete this word search puzzle that contains Chapter 6 words. Look for the following words as given in the list below. The number in parentheses indicates how many times the word is found in the puzzle.

anemia
baso
blood
cell
cells
clot
coagulation
erythrocyte
fibrin
heme

hemoglobin
immune
leukemia
lymphoma
mono
node (2)
plasma
seg (2)
serum
transfusion

```
C  D  K  R  C  H  S  L  V  A  T  E
E  O  D  C  U  E  Y  W  M  I  Y  R
L  O  A  F  J  M  L  S  S  M  L  Y
L  L  O  G  P  O  E  L  E  E  E  T
S  B  N  H  U  G  P  C  R  N  U  H
E  D  O  N  C  L  L  H  U  A  K  R
B  M  M  B  A  O  A  M  M  Q  E  O
A  G  E  S  T  B  M  T  B  J  M  C
S  V  M  H  N  I  R  B  I  F  I  Y
O  A  Q  K  S  N  O  D  E  O  A  T
T  R  A  N  S  F  U  S  I  O  N  E
```

Crossword Puzzle

ACROSS

3. The protein molecules released by damaged tissues that are responsible for calling in leukocytes to the area are called _____.

6. _____ is a clear, straw-colored liquid that makes up 55% of the blood.

8. The medical procedure for drawing a sample of venous blood into a vacuum tube is known as

_____.

9. _____ anemia is a condition in which the bone marrow fails to produce erythrocytes.

10. A white blood cell (WBC) is also known as a/an _____.

DOWN

1. Each blood group is named for its _____, the protein on the cell membrane of the erythrocyte.

2. An inherited genetic abnormality that causes a lack or deficiency of a specific clotting factor is known as

_____.

4. A blood clot is referred to as a/an _____.

5. The abbreviation HCT stands for _____.

7. The combining form "_____" means red.

Underline the Accented Syllable

Read the medical word. Then review the syllables in the pronunciation. Underline the primary (main) accented syllable in the pronunciation.

1. agglutination   (ah-gloo-tih-nay-shun)

2. anisocytosis   (an-eye-soh-sy-toh-sis)

3. autoimmune   (aw-toh-im-myoon)

4. dyscrasia   (dis-kray-zee-ah)

5. ecchymosis   (ek-ih-moh-sis)

6. erythropoietin   (eh-rith-roh-poy-eh-tin)

7. hemolysis   (hee-mawl-ih-sis)

8. idiopathic   (id-ee-oh-path-ik)

9. lymphangiography   (lim-fan-jee-awg-rah-fee)

10. macrophage   (mak-roh-fayj)

11. myelogenous   (my-eh-lawj-eh-nus)

12. pancytopenia   (pan-sy-toh-pee-nee-ah)

13. phagocytosis   (fag-oh-sy-toh-sis)

14. phlebotomist   (fleh-bawt-oh-mist)

15. splenectomy   (spleh-nek-toh-mee)

Word Surgery

Read the medical word. Break the medical word into its word parts and give the meaning of each word part. Then give the definition of the medical word.

1. agranulocyte

   Suffix and its meaning: _____

   Prefix and its meaning: _____

   Combining form and its meaning: _____

   Medical word definition: _____

2. autologous

   Suffix and its meaning: _____

   Prefix and its meaning: _____

   Combining form and its meaning: _____

   Combining form and its meaning: _____

   Medical word definition: _____

3. corticosteroid

   Suffix and its meaning: _____

   Prefix and its meaning: _____

   Combining form and its meaning: _____

   Medical word definition: _____

4. electrophoresis

   Suffix and its meaning: _____

   Prefix and its meaning: _____

   Combining form and its meaning: _____

   Combining form and its meaning: _____

   Medical word definition: _____

5. lymphangiogram

   Suffix and its meaning: _____

   Prefix and its meaning: _____

   Combining form and its meaning: _____

   Combining form and its meaning: _____

   Medical word definition: _____

6. microcytic

Suffix and its meaning: _____

Prefix and its meaning: _____

Combining form and its meaning: _____

Combining form and its meaning: _____

Medical word definition: _____

7. mononucleosis

Suffix and its meaning: _____

Prefix and its meaning: _____

Combining form and its meaning: _____

Combining form and its meaning: _____

Medical word definition: _____

8. hypochromic

Suffix and its meaning: _____

Prefix and its meaning: _____

Combining form and its meaning: _____

Medical word definition: _____

9. pancytopenia

Suffix and its meaning: _____

Prefix and its meaning: _____

Combining form and its meaning: _____

Medical word definition: _____

10. plasmapheresis

Suffix and its meaning: _____

Prefix and its meaning: _____

Combining form and its meaning: _____

Combining form and its meaning: _____

Medical word definition: _____

11. polycythemia

   Suffix and its meaning: _____

   Prefix and its meaning: _____

   Combining form and its meaning: _____

   Combining form and its meaning: _____

   Medical word definition: _____

12. prothrombin

   Suffix and its meaning: _____

   Prefix and its meaning: _____

   Combining form and its meaning: _____

   Medical word definition: _____

13. septicemia

   Suffix and its meaning: _____

   Prefix and its meaning: _____

   Combining form and its meaning: _____

   Medical word definition: _____

14. thrombolytic

   Suffix and its meaning: _____

   Prefix and its meaning: _____

   Combining form and its meaning: _____

   Combining form and its meaning: _____

   Medical word definition: _____

15. transfusion

   Suffix and its meaning: _____

   Prefix and its meaning: _____

   Combining form and its meaning: _____

   Medical word definition: _____

Chapter Quiz

MULTIPLE CHOICE

1. The medical specialty that studies the anatomy and physiology of blood is:

    A. cardiology.

    B. immunology.

    C. hematology.

    D. pediatrics.

2. The combining form that means "large" is:

    A. meg/a-.

    B. micr/o-.

    C. mon/o-.

    D. morph/o-.

3. Another name for a thrombocyte is a/an:

    A. eosinophil.

    B. platelet.

    C. neutrophil.

    D. basophil.

4. B cells are a type of:

    A. immunoglobulin.

    B. plasma protein.

    C. erythrocyte.

    D. lymphocyte.

5. The most abundant plasma protein is:

    A. IgG.

    B. albumin.

    C. IgE.

    D. complement.

6. Microorganisms that cause disease are known as:

   A. pathogens.

   B. immunoglobulins.

   C. macrophages.

   D. antibodies.

7. The failure of the bone marrow to produce sufficient numbers of erythrocytes is:

   A. vitamin deficiency.

   B. thrombocytopenia.

   C. aplastic anemia.

   D. mononucleosis.

8. Small pinpoint hemorrhages of the skin are:

   A. ecchymoses.

   B. petechiae.

   C. purpura.

   D. thrombi.

9. The blood test that measures the percentage of RBC in a blood sample is the:

   A. complete blood count.

   B. hemoglobin.

   C. hematocrit.

   D. red blood cell indices.

10. The abbreviation that refers to leukocytes is:

    A. AIDS.

    B. ALL.

    C. RBC.

    D. WBC.

FILL IN THE BLANK

1. _____ is the process by which all blood cells are formed in the bone marrow.

2. _____ are chemical structures that carry a positive or negative charge.

3. The largest leukocyte that has a nucleus shaped like a kidney bean is a/an _____.

4. A lymphoid gland in the thoracic cavity that causes lymphoblasts to mature to T cells is the _____.

5. Decreased numbers of all blood cell types is known as _____.

6. _____ is an inherited abnormality that causes a deficiency of a specific clotting factor resulting in a reduced ability to clot blood.

7. _____ is an abbreviation for the first blood, urine, or saliva screening test done to detect the presence of HIV.

8. The procedure to remove red bone marrow from the posterior iliac crest of the hip is called bone marrow _____.

9. The combining form _____ means "other or strange."

10. A _____ blood count with differential includes RBC count and the percentage of the various types of WBCs.

TRUE/FALSE

_____ 1. The combining form "retr/o-" means "behind or backward."

_____ 2. The clear, straw-colored liquid portion of the blood is known as serum.

_____ 3. Neutrophils belong to a category of leukocytes that have large granules in the cytoplasm.

_____ 4. The category of antibodies known as immunoglobulins includes IgN.

_____ 5. A phagocyte is a cell that helps clot blood.

_____ 6. Iron deficiency anemia is characterized by microcytic and hypochromic erythrocytes.

_____ 7. Mononucleosis is caused by the human immunodeficiency virus.

_____ 8. Electrophoresis is a serum test used to determine the amount of immunoglobulin present in the blood.

_____ 9. An autologous blood transfusion comes from the patient's own blood.

_____ 10. The prefix "morph/o-" means "many; much."

Pronunciation Checklist

Read each word and its pronunciation. Practice pronouncing each word. Verify your pronunciation by listening to the Pronunciation List on Medical Terminology Interactive. Check the box next to the word after you master its pronunciation.

❏ agglutination
(ah-GLOO-tih-NAY-shun)
❏ aggregation
(AG-reh-GAY-shun)
❏ agranulocyte
(aa-GRAN-yoo-loh-SITE)
❏ albumin (al-BYOO-min)
❏ allogeneic (AL-oh-jeh-NEE-ik)
❏ anemia (ah-NEE-mee-ah)
❏ anemic (ah-NEE-mik)
❏ anisocytosis
(an-EYE-soh-sy-TOH-sis)
❏ antibody (AN-tih-BAWD-ee)
❏ anticoagulant drug
(AN-tee-koh-AG-yoo-lant
DRUHG)
(AN-tih-koh-AG-yoo-lant
DRUHG)
❏ antigen (AN-tih-jen)
❏ aplastic (aa-PLAS-tik)
❏ attenuated vaccine
(ah-TEN-yoo-AA-ted
vak-SEEN)
❏ autoimmune
(AW-toh-im-MYOON)
❏ basophil (BAY-soh-fil)
❏ biopsy (BY-awp-see)
❏ blood donation
(BLUD doh-NAY-shun)
❏ bone marrow aspiration
(BOHN MAIR-oh
AS-pih-RAY-shun)
❏ bone marrow transplantation
(BOHN MAIR-oh
TRANS-plan-TAY-shun)
❏ cancer (KAN-ser)
❏ coagulation
(koh-AG-yoo-LAY-shun)
❏ coagulopathy
(koh-AG-yoo-LAWP-ah-thee)
❏ complement protein
(COM-pleh-ment PRO-teen)
❏ corticosteroid drug
(KOR-tih-koh-STAIR-oyd
DRUHG)
❏ cytokine (SY-toh-kine)
❏ cytotoxic (SY-toh-TAWK-sik)
❏ differential (DIF-er-EN-shal)

❏ disseminated intravascular coagulation (dih-SEM-ih-NAYT-ed
IN-trah-VAS-kyoo-lar
koh-AG-yoo-LAY-shun)
❏ dyscrasia (dis-KRAY-zee-ah)
❏ ecchymoses (EK-ih-MOH-seez)
❏ electrolyte (ee-LEK-troh-lite)
❏ electrophoresis
(ee-LEK-troh-foh-REE-sis)
❏ embolism (EM-boh-LIZ-em)
❏ embolus (EM-boh-lus)
❏ endotoxin (EN-doh-TAWK-sin)
❏ eosinophil (EE-oh-SIN-oh-fil)
❏ erythroblast
(eh-RITH-roh-blast)
❏ erythrocyte (eh-RITH-roh-site)
❏ erythropoietin
(eh-RITH-roh-POY-eh-tin)
❏ excisional biopsy
(ek-SIH-shun-al BY-awp-see)
❏ ferritin (FAIR-ih-tin)
❏ fibrin (FY-brin)
❏ fibrinogen (fy-BRIN-oh-jen)
❏ globin (GLOH-bin)
❏ granulocyte
(GRAN-yoo-loh-SITE)
❏ hematocrit (hee-MAT-oh-krit)
❏ hematologist
(HEE-mah-TAWL-oh-jist)
❏ hematology
(HEE-mah-TAWL-oh-jee)
❏ hematopoiesis
(HEE-mah-toh-poy-EE-sis)
❏ heme (HEEM)
❏ hemoglobin
(HEE-moh-GLOH-bin)
(HEE-moh-GLOH-bin)
❏ hemolysis
(hee-MAWL-ih-sis)
❏ hemolytic anemia
(HEE-moh-LIT-ik
ah-NEE-mee-ah)
❏ hemophilia
(HEE-moh-FIL-ee-ah)
❏ hemophiliac
(HEE-moh-FIL-ee-ak)
❏ hemorrhage (HEM-oh-rij)
❏ hemostasis (HEE-moh-STAY-sis)

❏ heterophil antibody
(HET-er-oh-fil AN-tih-BAWD-ee)
❏ Hodgkin disease
(HAWJ-kin dih-ZEEZ)
❏ hypochromic
(HY-poh-KROH-mik)
❏ idiopathic (ID-ee-oh-PATH-ik)
❏ immune (im-MYOON)
❏ immunity (im-MYOO-nih-tee)
❏ immunocompromised
(IM-myoo-noh-COM-proh-
myzed)
❏ immunodeficiency
(IM-myoo-noh-deh-FISH-en-see)
❏ immunoglobulin
(IM-myoo-noh-GLAWB-yoo-lin)
❏ immunologist
(IM-myoo-NAWL-oh-jist)
❏ immunology
(IM-myoo-NAWL-oh-jee)
❏ immunosuppressant drug
(IM-myoo-noh-soo-PRES-ant
DRUHG)
❏ immunization
(IM-myoo-nih-ZAY-shun)
❏ indices (IN-dih-seez)
❏ inhibitor (in-HIB-ih-tor)
❏ interferon (IN-ter-FEER-on)
❏ interleukin (IN-ter-LOO-kin)
❏ intravascular
(IN-trah-VAS-kyoo-lar)
❏ leukemia (loo-KEE-mee-ah)
❏ leukocyte (LOO-koh-site)
❏ lymph (LIMF)
❏ lymph node (LIMF NOHD)
❏ lymph node dissection
(LIMF NOHD dy-SEK-shun)
❏ lymphadenopathy
(lim-FAD-eh-NAWP-eh-thee)
❏ lymphangiogram
(lim-FAN-jee-oh-gram)
❏ lymphangiography
(lim-FAN-jee-AWG-rah-fee)
❏ lymphatic system
(lim-FAT-ik SIS-tem)
❏ lymphedema
(LIM-fah-DEE-mah)
❏ lymphoblast (LIM-foh-blast)

- lymphocyte (LIM-foh-site)
- lymphocytic leukemia (LIM-foh-SIT-ik loo-KEE-mee-ah)
- lymphoid (LIM-foyd)
- lymphoma (lim-FOH-mah)
- macrocyte (MAK-roh-site)
- macrophage (MAK-roh-fayj)
- megakaryoblast (MEG-ah-KAIR-ee-oh-BLAST)
- megakaryocyte (MEG-ah-KAIR-ee-oh-SITE)
- microcyte (MY-kroh-site)
- microcytic (MY-kroh-SIT-ik)
- monoblast (MAWN-oh-blast)
- monocyte (MAWN-oh-site)
- mononucleosis (MAWN-oh-NOO-klee-OH-sis)
- morphology (mor-FAWL-oh-jee)
- myeloblast (MY-eh-loh-BLAST)
- myelocyte (MY-eh-loh-SITE)
- myelogenous leukemia (MY-eh-LAWJ-eh-nus loo-KEE-mee-ah)
- myeloma (MY-eh-LOH-mah)
- neutrophil (NOO-troh-fil)
- normoblast (NOR-moh-blast)
- normochromic (NOR-moh-KROH-mik)
- normocytic (NOR-moh-SIT-ik)
- opportunistic infection (AWP-or-too-NIS-tik in-FEK-shun)
- oxyhemoglobin (AWK-see-HEE-moh-GLOH-bin)
- pancytopenia (PAN-sy-toh-PEE-nee-ah)
- pathogen (PATH-oh-jen)
- peripheral (peh-RIF-eh-ral)
- pernicious anemia (per-NISH-us ah-NEE-mee-ah)
- petechiae (peh-TEE-kee-ee)
- phagocyte (FAG-oh-site)
- phagocytosis (FAG-oh-sy-TOH-sis)
- phlebotomist (fleh-BAW-toh-mist)
- phlebotomy (fleh-BAW-toh-mee)
- plasma (PLAZ-mah)
- plasmapheresis (PLAZ-mah-feh-REE-sis)
- plasminogen (plaz-MIN-oh-jen)
- platelet (PLAYT-let)
- poikilocytosis (POY-kih-loh-sy-TOH-sis)
- polycythemia vera (PAWL-ee-sy-THEE-mee-ah VER-ah)
- polymorphonuclear leukocyte (PAWL-ee-MOR-foh-NOO-klee-ar LOO-koh-site)
- protease inhibitor drug (PROH-tee-ace in-HIB-ih-tor DRUHG)
- prothrombin (proh-THRAWM-bin)
- purpura (PER-peh-rah)
- reticulocyte (reh-TIK-yoo-loh-SITE)
- reverse transcriptase inhibitor drug (ree-VERS trans-KRIP-tays in-HIB-ih-tor DRUHG)
- septic (SEP-tic)
- septicemia (SEP-tih-SEE-mee-ah)
- serum (SEER-um)
- spleen (SPLEEN)
- splenectomy (spleh-NEK-toh-mee)
- splenic (SPLEH-nik)
- splenomegaly (SPLEH-noh-MEG-ah-lee)
- suppressor (soo-PRES-or)
- thalassemia (THAL-ah-SEE-mee-ah)
- thrombocyte (THRAWM-boh-site)
- thrombocytopenia (THRAWM-boh-sy-toh-PEE-nee-ah)
- thrombolytic drug (THRAWM-boh-LIT-ik DRUHG)
- thromboplastin (THRAWM-boh-PLAS-tin)
- thrombosis (thrawm-BOH-sis)
- thrombus (THRAWM-bus)
- thymectomy (thy-MEK-toh-mee)
- thymic (THY-mik)
- thymoma (thy-MOH-mah)
- thymosin (thy-MOH-sin)
- thymus (THY-mus)
- transferrin (trans-FAIR-in)
- transfusion (trans-FYOO-shun)
- ultrasonography (UL-trah-soh-NAWG-rah-fee)
- vaccination (VAK-sih-NAY-shun)
- vaccine (vak-SEEN)
- venipuncture (VEE-nih-PUNK-chur)
- viscosity (vis-KAWS-ih-tee)

Answer Key

Word Search

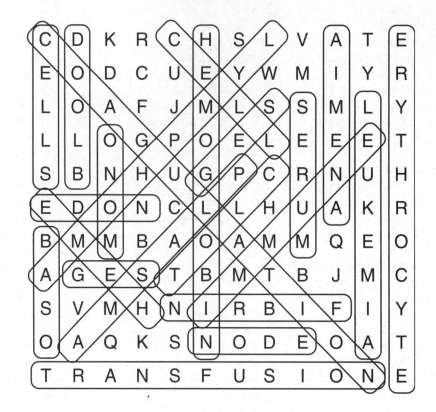

Crossword Puzzle

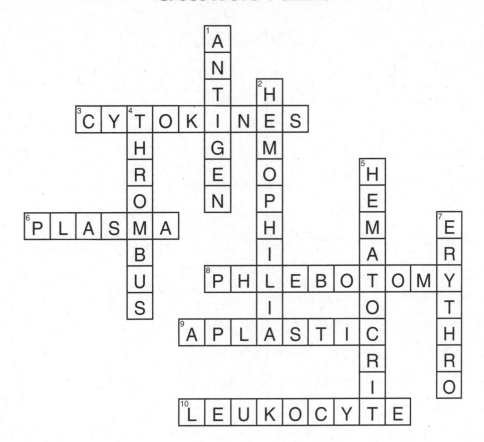

Underline the Accented Syllable

1. agglutination   (ah-GLOO-tih-<u>NAY</u>-shun)

2. anisocytosis   (an-EYE-soh-sy-<u>TOH</u>-sis)

3. autoimmune   (AW-toh-im-<u>MYOON</u>)

4. dyscrasia   (dis-<u>KRAY</u>-zee-ah)

5. ecchymosis   (EK-ih-<u>MOH</u>-sis)

6. erythropoietin   (eh-RITH-roh-<u>POY</u>-eh-tin)

7. hemolysis   (hee-<u>MAWL</u>-ih-sis)

8. idiopathic   (ID-ee-oh-<u>PATH</u>-ik)

9. lymphangiography   (lim-FAN- jee-<u>AWG</u>-rah-fee)

10. macrophage   (<u>MAK</u>-roh-fayj)

11. myelogenous   (MY-eh-<u>LAWJ</u>-eh-nus)

12. pancytopenia   (PAN-sy-toh-<u>PEE</u>-nee-ah)

13. phagocytosis   (FAG-oh-sy-<u>TOH</u>-sis)

14. phlebotomist   (fleh-<u>BAWT</u>-oh-mist)

15. splenectomy   (spleh-<u>NEK</u>-toh-mee)

Word Surgery

1. agranulocyte

   Suffix and its meaning: -cyte *cell*

   Prefix and its meaning: a- *away from; without*

   Combining form and its meaning: granul/o- *granule*

   Medical word definition: A cell without granules (in its cytoplasm)

2. autologous

   Suffix and its meaning: -ous *pertaining to*

   Prefix and its meaning: none

   Combining form and its meaning: auto- *self*

   Combining form and its meaning: log/o- *word; the study of*

   Medical word definition: Pertaining to self word

3. corticosteroid

   Suffix and its meaning: -steroid *steroid*

   Prefix and its meaning: none

   Combining form and its meaning: cortic/o- *cortex (outer region)*

   Medical word definition: Steroid from the cortex (outer region of the adrenal
     gland)

4. electrophoresis

   Suffix and its meaning: -esis *a process*

   Prefix and its meaning: none

   Combining form and its meaning: electr/o- *electricity*

   Combining form and its meaning: phor/o- *to bear; to carry*

   Medical word definition: Process of electricity (being used) to carry (substances)

5. lymphangiogram

   Suffix and its meaning: -graphy *process of recording*

   Prefix and its meaning: none

   Combining form and its meaning: lymph/o- *lymph; lymphatic system*

   Combining form and its meaning: angi/o- *blood vessel; lymphatic vessel*

   Medical word definition: Process of recording the lymph, lymphatic system, and
     lymphatic vessels

6. microcytic

   Suffix and its meaning: -ic *pertaining to*

   Prefix and its meaning: none

   Combining form and its meaning: micr/o- *one millionth; small*

   Combining form and its meaning: cyt/o- *cell*

   Medical word definition: Pertaining to a small (red blood) cell

7. mononucleosis

   Suffix and its meaning: -osis *condition; abnormal condition; process*

   Prefix and its meaning: none

   Combining form and its meaning: mon/o- *one; single*

   Combining form and its meaning: nucle/o- *nucleus*

   Medical word definition: Abnormal condition (of white blood cells that have a) single nucleus

8. hypochromic

   Suffix and its meaning: -ic *pertaining to*

   Prefix and its meaning: hypo- *below; deficient*

   Combining form and its meaning: chrom/o- *color*

   Medical word definition: Pertaining to deficient color (in a red blood cell)

9. pancytopenia

   Suffix and its meaning: -penia *condition of deficiency*

   Prefix and its meaning: pan- *all*

   Combining form and its meaning: cyt/o- *cell*

   Medical word definition: Condition of deficiency of all (types of blood) cells

10. plasmapheresis

   Suffix and its meaning: -esis *a process*

   Prefix and its meaning: none

   Combining form and its meaning: plasm/o- *plasma*

   Combinign form and its meaning: apher/o- *withdrawal*

   Medical word definition: A process of plasma withdrawal (from the blood)

11. polycythemia

Suffix and its meaning: -ia *condition; state; thing*

Prefix and its meaning: poly- *many; much*

Combining form and its meaning: cyt/o- *cell*

Combining form and its meaning: hem/o- *blood*

Medical word definition: Condition of many (red) cells in the blood

12. prothrombin

Suffix and its meaning: -in *a substance*

Prefix and its meaning: pro- *before*

Combining form and its meaning: thromb/o- *thrombus (blood clot)*

Medical word definition: A substance (that is present) before a thrombus (is formed)

13. septicemia

Suffix and its meaning: -emia *condition of the blood; substance in the blood*

Prefix and its meaning: none

Combining form and its meaning: septic/o- *infection*

Medical word definition: Condition of the blood (of having) infection

14. thrombolytic

Suffix and its meaning: -tic *pertaining to*

Prefix and its meaning: none

Combining form and its meaning: thromb/o- *thrombus (blood clot)*

Combining form and its meaning: ly/o- *break down; destroy*

Medical word definition: Pertaining to a thrombus being broken down and destroyed

15. transfusion

Suffix and its meaning: -ion *action; condition*

Prefix and its meaning: trans- *across; through*

Combining form and its meaning: fus/o- *pouring*

Medical word definition: Action (of adding blood) through pouring (it into a vein)

Chapter Quiz

MULTIPLE CHOICE

1. C	4. D	7. C	10. D
2. A	5. B	8. B	
3. B	6. A	9. C	

FILL IN THE BLANK

1. Hematopoiesis

2. Electrolytes

3. monocyte

4. thymus

5. pancytopenia

6. Hemophilia

7. ELISA

8. aspiration

9. all/o-

10. complete

TRUE/FALSE

1. True

2. False (plasma)

3. True

4. False (IgA, IgD, IgE, IgG, or IgM)

5. False (engulfs foreign cells and cellular debris)

6. True

7. False (Epstein–Barr virus)

8. True

9. True

10. False (the prefix poly-)

CHAPTER 7

Dermatology

Measure Your Progress: Learning Objectives

After reading this chapter, the student should be able to

- Identify the structures of the integumentary system.
- Describe the process of an allergic reaction.
- Describe common integumentary diseases and conditions, laboratory and diagnostic procedures, medical and surgical procedures, and drug categories.
- Give the medical meaning of word parts related to the integumentary system.
- Build integumentary words from word parts and divide and define integumentary words.
- Spell and pronounce integumentary words.
- Analyze the medical content and meaning of a dermatology report.
- Dive deeper into dermatology by reviewing the activities at the end of this chapter and online at Medical Terminology Interactive.

It All Starts with Word Building

Medical language is all about medical words and their word parts. Jump right into this chapter by learning some of the common combining forms and their definitions that you will encounter in the chapter.

abras/o-	scrape off	lip/o-	lipid (fat)
actin/o-	rays of the sun	malign/o-	intentionally causing harm; cancer
adip/o-	fat		
all/o-	other; strange		
blephar/o-	eyelid	melan/o-	black
carcin/o-	cancer	necr/o-	dead cells, tissue, or body
contus/o-	bruising		
cry/o-	cold	ne/o-	new
cutane/o-	skin	onych/o-	nail (fingernail or toenail)
cut/i-	skin		
cyan/o-	blue	pedicul/o-	lice
derm/a-	skin	pil/o-	hair
dermat/o-	skin	plast/o-	growth; formation
derm/o-	skin	prurit/o-	itching
ecchym/o-	blood in the tissues	psor/o-	itching
erythemat/o-	redness	rhytid/o-	wrinkle
esthes/o-	sensation; feeling	sarc/o-	connective tissue
gangren/o-	gangrene	sebace/o-	sebum (oil)
hirsut/o-	hairy	seb/o-	sebum (oil)
integument/o-	skin	sudor/i-	sweat
integu/o-	to cover	theli/o-	cellular layer
kel/o-	tumor	ungu/o-	nail (fingernail or toenail)
kerat/o-	hard, fibrous protein	vesicul/o-	bladder; fluid-filled sac
lacer/o-	a tearing	xer/o-	dry

Chapter Spelling Test

Dictate and spell (or photocopy a handout that contains) this list of 20 spelling words. Give this list to students to study for the week. At the beginning of next week's class, dictate 10 of these words as the spelling test. The spelling test is included with the chapter test that is given on the previous week's material.

1. adipose
2. anaphylaxis
3. cutaneous
4. sebaceous
5. vesicle
6. pruritus
7. xeroderma
8. cyanosis
9. erythema
10. callus
11. cicatrix
12. decubitus ulcer
13. abscess
14. tinea pedis
15. pediculosis
16. psoriasis
17. seborrhea
18. alopecia
19. onychomycosis
20. rhytidectomy

Chapter Pronunciation Test

Photocopy a handout that contains this list of 20 pronunciation words. Give this list to students to study for the week. Sometime at the beginning of the next week, each student should call your office or home answering machine and pronounce each word.

1. alopecia (AL-oh-PEE-shee-ah)

2. anaphylaxis (AN-ah-fih-LAK-sis)

3. blepharoplasty (BLEF-ah-roh-PLAS-tee)

4. cicatrix (SIK-ah-triks)

5. comedo (KOH-meh-doh) (koh-MEE-doh)

6. curettage (kyoo-reh-TAWZH)

7. debridement (deh-BREED-maw)

8. diaphoresis (DY-ah-foh-REE-sis)

9. ecchymosis (EK-ih-MOH-sis)

10. eczema (EK-zeh-mah)

11. erythematous (AIR-eh-THEM-eh-tus)

12. Kaposi's sarcoma (kah-POH-seez sar-KOH-mah)

13. onychomycosis (ON-ih-KOH-my-KOH-sis)

14. paronychia (PAR-oh-NIK-ee-ah)

15. psoralen drug (SOR-ah-len DRUHG)

16. rhytidectomy (RIT-ih-DEK-toh-mee)

17. seborrhea (SEB-oh-REE-ah)

18. urticaria (ER-tih-KAIR-ee-ah)

19. xanthelasma (ZAN-theh-LAZ-mah)

20. xeroderma (ZEER-oh-DER-mah)

Word Search

Complete this word search puzzle that contains Chapter 7 words. Look for the following words as given in the list below.

adipose	nail
burn	necrosis
callus	nevus
collagen	rash
cuticles	sebum
cyst	skin
dermis	subcutaneous
hair	tinea
herpes	tissues
integument	ulcer
itch	wheal
keloids	wound

```
S  U  O  E  N  A  T  U  C  B  U  S
I  K  X  R  W  D  T  N  U  H  F  U
T  K  I  M  N  I  I  R  N  A  I  L
C  A  Q  N  S  P  N  Z  A  T  S  L
H  K  P  S  N  O  E  S  N  S  W  A
D  C  U  E  R  S  A  E  E  D  H  C
B  E  V  L  E  E  M  B  C  I  E  U
S  U  R  P  C  U  D  U  R  O  A  T
S  F  R  M  G  E  G  M  O  L  L  I
U  E  L  E  I  T  R  Z  S  E  D  C
H  B  T  L  J  S  F  D  I  K  B  L
D  N  U  O  W  N  E  T  S  Y  C  E
I  S  K  N  E  G  A  L  L  O  C  S
```

Crossword Puzzle

ACROSS

3. _____ is a firm, white protein consisting of connective tissue fibers found in the dermis.

6. The abbreviation for biopsy is

_____.

7. Itching is also called

_____.

8. The combining form

"_____" means hairy.

DOWN

1. A skin infection caused by a fungus that feeds on epidermal cells is known as _____.

2. Yellowish discoloration of the skin and the whites of the eyes caused by liver disease is known as

_____.

3. A/an _____ is a medical procedure that uses a curet to scrape off superficial skin lesions.

4. Any benign or malignant new growth that occurs on or in the skin is referred to as a/an

_____.

5. The _____ is a whitish half-moon that is visible under the proximal portion of the nail plate.

6. The combining form

"_____" means eyelid.

Underline the Accented Syllable

Read the medical word. Then review the syllables in the pronunciation. Underline the primary (main) accented syllable in the pronunciation.

1. alopecia   (al-oh-pee-shee-ah)

2. anaphylaxis   (an-ah-fih-lak-sis)

3. blepharoplasty   (blef-ah-roh-plas-tee)

4. cicatrix   (sik-ah-triks)

5. curettage   (kyoo-reh-tawzh)

6. debridement   (deh-breed-maw)

7. decubitus   (dee-kyoo-bih-tus)

8. erythema   (air-eh-thee-mah)

9. fulguration   (ful-gyoo-ray-shun)

10. icterus   (ik-ter-us)

11. Kaposi   (kah-poh-see)

12. papilloma   (pap-ih-loh-mah)

13. pediculosis   (peh-dik-yoo-loh-sis)

14. rhytidectomy   (rit-ih-dek-toh-mee)

15. urticaria   (er-tih-kair-ee-ah)

Word Surgery

Read the medical word. Break the medical word into its word parts and give the meaning of each word part. Then give the definition of the medical word.

1. anesthetic

   Suffix and its meaning: _____

   Prefix and its meaning: _____

   Combining form and its meaning: _____

   Medical word definition: _____

2. anhidrosis

   Suffix and its meaning: _____

   Prefix and its meaning: _____

   Combining form and its meaning: _____

   Medical word definition: _____

3. antifungal

   Suffix and its meaning: _____

   Prefix and its meaning: _____

   Combining form and its meaning: _____

   Medical word definition: _____

4. cryosurgery

   Suffix and its meaning: _____

   Prefix and its meaning: _____

   Combining form and its meaning: _____

   Medical word definition: _____

5. dermatoplasty

   Suffix and its meaning: _____

   Prefix and its meaning: _____

   Combining form and its meaning: _____

   Medical word definition: _____

6. epidermal

   Suffix and its meaning: _____

   Prefix and its meaning: _____

   Combining form and its meaning: _____

   Medical word definition: _____

7. hypersensitivity

   Suffix and its meaning: _____

   Prefix and its meaning: _____

   Combining form and its meaning: _____

   Medical word definition: _____

8. hypodermic

   Suffix and its meaning: _____

   Prefix and its meaning: _____

   Combining form and its meaning: _____

   Medical word definition: _____

9. melanocyte

   Suffix and its meaning: _____

   Prefix and its meaning: _____

   Combining form and its meaning: _____

   Medical word definition: _____

10. microdermabrasion

   Suffix and its meaning: _____

   Prefix and its meaning: _____

   Combining form and its meaning: _____

   Combining form and its meaning: _____

   Combining form and its meaning: _____

   Medical word definition: _____

11. onychomycosis

   Suffix and its meaning: _____

   Prefix and its meaning: _____

   Combining form and its meaning: _____

   Combining form and its meaning: _____

   Medical word definition: _____

12. premalignant

   Suffix and its meaning: _____

   Prefix and its meaning: _____

   Combining form and its meaning: _____

   Medical word definition: _____

13. rhytidectomy

   Suffix and its meaning: _____

   Prefix and its meaning: _____

   Combining form and its meaning: _____

   Medical word definition: _____

14. subcutaneous

   Suffix and its meaning: _____

   Prefix and its meaning: _____

   Combining form and its meaning: _____

   Medical word definition: _____

15. xeroderma

   Suffix and its meaning: _____

   Prefix and its meaning: _____

   Combining form and its meaning: _____

   Medical word definition: _____

Chapter Quiz

1. The combining form "cry/o-" means:

   A. fat.

   B. blue.

   C. cold.

   D. black.

2. Hair follicles are found in the _____ layer.

   A. epidermis

   B. subcutaneous

   C. dermis

   D. epithelium

3. The suffix "-ary" means:

   A. pertaining to.

   B. old.

   C. wrinkled.

   D. inflammation of.

4. An autoimmune disease in which the _____ are slowly destroyed in an irregular, ever-enlarging area is called vitiligo.

   A. pruritus

   B. melanocytes

   C. follicles

   D. verrucae

5. _____ is a skin infection caused by a fungus that feeds on epidermal cells.

   A. Herpes

   B. HIV

   C. Senile lentigo

   D. Tinea

6. The suffix that means "tumor or mass" is:

   A. -oma.

   B. -itis.

   C. -dactyly.

   D. -ile.

7. An autoimmune disease with deterioration of collagen in the skin and connective tissues often accompanied with a characteristic butterfly-shaped rash is:

   A. AIDS.

   B. cystic acne.

   C. psoriasis.

   D. systemic lupus erythematosus.

8. Debridement is a medical or surgical procedure:

   A. to remove necrotic tissue from a wound, burn, or ulcer.

   B. that includes the use of electrical current to remove a small malignant tumor.

   C. that uses extreme cold to remove a wart or other skin lesion.

   D. that burns away a growth.

9. Resurfacing the skin by means of a fast spinning brush or diamond to mechanically abrade the epidermis is:

   A. chemical peel.

   B. suturing.

   C. dermabrasion.

   D. excisional biopsy.

10. The abbreviation that means cutting and allowing fluid inside to drain out is:

   A. Bx.

   B. I&D.

   C. C&S.

   D. PUVA.

FILL IN THE BLANK

1. The closely related Greek combining forms "derm/a-," "derm/o-,"and _____ mean skin.

2. The skin has several proteins that contribute to the functions of skin, including collagen and _____ , which gives the skin flexibility.

3. Any area of visible damage to the skin, whether the damage is from disease or injury, is called a _____.

4. _____ is a viral infection that may cause vesicles, erythema, edema, and pain.

5. "Xanth/o-" is the combining form that means "_____."

6. Abnormally curved fingernails and stunted growth of the fingers is

   _____.

7. A/an _____ biopsy is a surgical procedure that uses a scalpel to remove an entire large lesion.

8. A type of plastic surgery of the skin such as skin grafting or removal of a keloid is known as _____.

9. _____ drugs, such as creams, lotions, or ointments are those that are absorbed through the skin and produce a local drug effect.

10. Melanocytes contain melanin which is a _____ that gives skin its color.

TRUE/FALSE

_____ 1. "Adip/o-" is the combining form for "skin."

_____ 2. Sebaceous glands are found in the dermis layer of the skin.

_____ 3. An allergen is something that causes an allergic hypersensitivity.

_____ 4. The lack of pigmentation of the skin, hair, and iris of the eye is a genetic condition known as xeroderma.

_____ 5. A localized pus-containing pocket of bacteria, often *Staphylococcus aureus*, is known as an abscess.

_____ 6. A skin cancer that begins in connective tissue and is often associated with AIDS is psoriasis.

_____ 7. A fluid that oozes from a lesion is called pruritus.

_____ 8. Botox injections are used to smooth wrinkles in the skin.

_____ 9. A skin graft from a cadaver is called a xenograft.

_____ 10. A physician's assistant is a health care professional who does not need a license.

Pronunciation Checklist

Read each word and its pronunciation. Practice pronouncing each word. Verify your pronunciation by listening to the Pronunciation List on Medical Terminology Interactive. Check the box next to the word after you master its pronunciation.

- ❑ abrasion (ah-BRAY-zhun)
- ❑ abscess (AB-ses)
- ❑ acne rosacea (AK-nee roh-ZAY-shee-ah)
- ❑ acne vulgaris (AK-nee vul-GAIR-is)
- ❑ actinic keratosis (ak-TIN-ik KAIR-ah-TOH-sis)
- ❑ adipocere (AD-ih-poh-SEER)
- ❑ adipose (AD-ih-pohs)
- ❑ albinism (AL-by-NIZ-em)
- ❑ albino (al-BY-noh)
- ❑ allergen (AL-er-jen)
- ❑ allergic (ah-LER-jik)
- ❑ allergy (AL-er-jee)
- ❑ allograft (AL-oh-graft)
- ❑ alopecia (AL-oh-PEE-shee-ah)
- ❑ anaphylactic shock (AN-ah-fih-LAK-tik SHAWK)
- ❑ anaphylaxis (AN-ah-fih-LAK-sis)
- ❑ anesthesia (AN-es-THEE-zee-ah)
- ❑ anhidrosis (AN-hy-DROH-sis)
- ❑ antibiotic drug (AN-tee-by-AWT-ik DRUHG) (AN-tih-by-AWT-ik)
- ❑ antifungal drug (AN-tee-FUN-gal DRUHG) (AN-tih-FUN-gal)
- ❑ antipruritic drug (AN-tee-proo-RIT-ik DRUHG) (AN-tih-proo-RIT-ik)
- ❑ antiviral drug (AN-tee-VY-ral DRUHG) (AN-tih-VY-ral)
- ❑ aspiration (AS-pih-RAY-shun)
- ❑ autograft (AW-toh-graft)
- ❑ basal layer (BAY-sal LAY-er)
- ❑ benign (bee-NINE)
- ❑ biopsy (BY-awp-see)
- ❑ blepharoplasty (BLEF-ah-roh-PLAS-tee)
- ❑ blister (BLIS-ter)
- ❑ Botox (BOH-tawks)
- ❑ bulla (BUL-ah)
- ❑ bullae (BUL-ee)
- ❑ callus (KAL-us)
- ❑ cancer (KAN-ser)

- ❑ carbuncle (KAR-bung-kl)
- ❑ carcinoma (KAR-sih-NOH-mah)
- ❑ cellulitis (SEL-yoo-LY-tis)
- ❑ cicatrix (SIK-ah-triks)
- ❑ chloasma (kloh-AZ-mah)
- ❑ collagen (KAWL-lah-jen)
- ❑ comedo (KOH-me-doh)
- ❑ contusion (con-TOO-zhun)
- ❑ corticosteroid drug (KOR-tih-koh-STAIR-oyd DRUHG)
- ❑ cryosurgery (KRY-oh-SER-jer-ee)
- ❑ curettage (kyoo-reh-TAWZH)
- ❑ curet (kyoo-RET)
- ❑ cutaneous (kyoo-TAY-nee-us)
- ❑ cuticle (KYOO-tih-kl)
- ❑ cyanosis (SY-ah-NOH-sis)
- ❑ cyanotic (SY-ah-NAWT-ik)
- ❑ cyst (SIST)
- ❑ debridement (deh-BREED-maw)
- ❑ decubitus ulcer (dee-KYOO-bih-tus UL-ser)
- ❑ depigmentation (dee-PIG-men-TAY-shun)
- ❑ dermabrasion (DER-mah-BRAY-zhun)
- ❑ dermal (DER-mal)
- ❑ dermatitis (DER-mah-TY-tis)
- ❑ dermatologist (DER-mah-TAWL-oh-jist)
- ❑ dermatology (DER-mah-TAWL-oh-jee)
- ❑ dermatome (DER-mah-tohm)
- ❑ dermatoplasty (DER-mah-toh-PLAS-tee)
- ❑ dermis (DER-mis)
- ❑ diaphoresis (DY-ah-foh-REE-sis)
- ❑ diaphoretic (DY-ah-foh-RET-ik)
- ❑ dysplastic nevus (dis-PLAS-tik NEE-vus)
- ❑ ecchymosis (EK-ih-MOH-sis)
- ❑ eczema (EK-zeh-mah)
- ❑ edema (eh-DEE-mah)
- ❑ elastin (ee-LAS-tin)
- ❑ electrodesiccation (ee-LEK-troh-DES-ih-KAY-shun)

- ❑ electrosection (ee-LEK-troh-SEK-shun)
- ❑ electrosurgery (ee-LEK-troh-SER-jer-ee)
- ❑ epidermal (EP-ih-DER-mal)
- ❑ epidermis (EP-ih-DER-mis)
- ❑ epithelial (EP-ih-THEE-lee-al)
- ❑ epithelium (EP-ih-THEE-lee-um)
- ❑ erythema (AIR-eh-THEE-mah)
- ❑ erythematous (AIR-eh-THEM-ah-tus)
- ❑ eschar (ES-kar)
- ❑ excisional (ek-SIH-shun-al)
- ❑ excoriation (eks-KOH-ree-AA-shun)
- ❑ exfoliation (eks-FOH-lee-AA-shun)
- ❑ exocrine gland (EK-soh-krin GLAND) (EK-soh-krine)
- ❑ exudate (EKS-yoo-dayt)
- ❑ fissure (FISH-ur)
- ❑ fistula (FIS-tyoo-lah)
- ❑ follicle (FAWL-ih-kl)
- ❑ follicular (foh-LIK-yoo-lar)
- ❑ folliculitis (foh-LIK-yoo-LY-tis)
- ❑ fulguration (FUL-gyoo-RAY-shun)
- ❑ furuncle (FYOO-rung-kl)
- ❑ gangrene (GANG-green)
- ❑ gangrenous (GANG-greh-nus)
- ❑ gland (GLAND)
- ❑ hemangioma (hee-MAN-jee-OH-mah)
- ❑ hematoma (HEE-mah-TOH-mah)
- ❑ herpes simplex (HER-peez SIM-pleks)
- ❑ herpes varicella-zoster (HER-peez VAIR-ih-SEL-ah ZAWS-ter)
- ❑ herpes whitlow (HER-peez WHIT-loh)
- ❑ hirsutism (HER-soo-tizm)
- ❑ hypersensitivity (HY-per-SEN-sih-TIV-ih-tee)
- ❑ hypodermic (HY-poh-DER-mik)
- ❑ icterus (IK-tair-us)

- icteric (ik-TAIR-ik)
- incision (in-SIH-shun)
- incisional (in-SIH-shun-al)
- integumentary (in-TEG-yoo-MEN-tair-ee)
- intradermal (IN-trah-DER-mal)
- jaundice (JAWN-dis)
- Kaposi's sarcoma (kah-POH-seez sar-KOH-mah)
- keloid (KEE-loyd)
- keratin (KAIR-ah-tin)
- keratoses (KAIR-ah-TOH-seez)
- keratosis (KAIR-ah-TOH-sis)
- laceration (LAS-er-AA-shun)
- laser (LAY-zer)
- lesion (LEE-shun)
- linea nigra (LIN-ee-ah NY-grah)
- lipocyte (LIP-oh-site)
- lipectomy (ly-PEK-toh-mee)
- lipoma (ly-POH-mah)
- liposuction (LIP-oh-SUK-shun)
- local (LOH-kal)
- lunula (LOO-nyoo-lah)
- lupus erythematosus (LOO-pus AIR-eh-THEM-ah-TOH-sus)
- macule (MAK-yool)
- malignancy (mah-LIG-nan-see)
- malignant (mah-LIG-nant)
- melanin (MEL-ah-nin)
- melanocyte (meh-LAN-oh-site) (MEL-ah-noh-SITE)
- melanoma (MEL-ah-NOH-mah)
- microdermabrasion (MY-kroh-DER-mah-BRAY-shun)
- necrosis (neh-KROH-sis)
- necrotic (neh-KRAWT-ik)
- neoplasm (NEE-oh-plazm)
- nevus (NEE-vus)
- onychomycosis (ON-ih-KOH-my-KOH-sis)
- pallor (PAL-or)
- papilloma (PAP-ih-LOH-mah)
- papule (PAP-yool)
- paronychia (PAR-oh-NIK-ee-ah)
- pediculosis (peh-DIK-yoo-LOH-sis)
- perspiration (PER-spih-RAY-shun)
- petechiae (peh-TEE-kee-ee)
- piloerection (PY-loh-ee-REK-shun)
- pilonidal sinus (PY-loh-NY-dal SY-nus)
- plastic surgeon (PLAS-tik SER-jun)
- polydactyly (PAWL-ee-DAK-tih-lee)
- premalignant (PREE-mah-LIG-nant)
- pruritic (proo-RIT-ik)
- pruritus (proo-RY-tus)
- psoralen drug (SOR-ah-len DRUHG)
- psoriasis (soh-RY-ah-sis)
- psoriatic (SOH-ree-AT-ik)
- pustule (PUS-chool)
- rhinophyma (RY-noh-FY-mah)
- rhytidectomy (RIT-ih-DEK-toh-mee)
- scabies (SKAY-beez)
- scleroderma (SKLER-oh-DER-mah)
- sebaceous (seh-BAY-shus)
- seborrhea (SEB-oh-REE-ah)
- sebum (SEE-bum)
- senile lentigo (SEE-nile len-TY-goh)
- sensitivity (SEN-sih-TIV-ih-tee)
- shingles (SHING-glz)
- squamous (SKWAY-mus)
- solar (SOH-lar)
- striae (STRY-ee)
- subcutaneous (SUB-kyoo-TAY-nee-us)
- sudoriferous (SOO-doh-RIF-er-us)
- syndactyly (sin-DAK-tih-lee)
- systemic (sis-TEM-ik)
- tinea capitis (TIN-ee-ah KAP-ih-tis)
- tinea corporis (TIN-ee-ah KOR-por-is)
- tinea cruris (TIN-ee-ah KROOR-is)
- tinea pedis (TIN-ee-ah PEE-dis)
- topical drug (TOP-ih-kal DRUHG)
- transdermal drug
- (trans-DER-mal DRUHG)
- turgor (TER-gor)
- Tzanck (TSAHNGK)
- ulcer (UL-ser)
- ungual (UNG-gwal)
- urticaria (ER-tih-KAIR-ee-ah)
- verruca (veh-ROO-kah)
- verrucae (veh-ROO-kee)
- vesicle (VES-ih-kl)
- vesicular (veh-SIK-yoo-lar)
- vitiligo (VIT-ih-LY-goh)
- wheal (HWEEL)
- xanthelasma (ZAN-theh-LAZ-mah)
- xanthoma (zan-THOH-mah)
- xenograft (ZEN-oh-graft)
- xeroderma (ZEER-oh-DER-mah)

Answer Key
Word Search

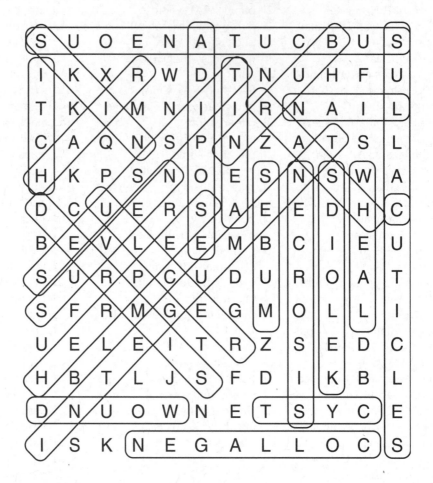

```
S  U  O  E  N  A  T  U  C  B  U  S
I  K  X  R  W  D  T  N  U  H  F  U
T  K  I  M  N  I  R  N  A  I  L  L
C  A  Q  N  S  P  N  Z  A  T  S  L
H  K  P  S  N  O  E  S  N  S  W  A
D  C  U  E  R  A  E  E  D  H  C
B  E  V  L  E  E  M  B  C  I  E  U
S  U  R  P  C  U  D  U  R  O  A  T
S  F  R  M  G  E  G  M  O  L  L  I
U  E  L  E  I  T  R  Z  S  E  D  C
H  B  T  L  J  S  F  D  I  K  B  L
D  N  U  O  W  N  E  T  S  Y  C  E
I  S  K  N  E  G  A  L  L  O  C  S
```

Crossword Puzzle

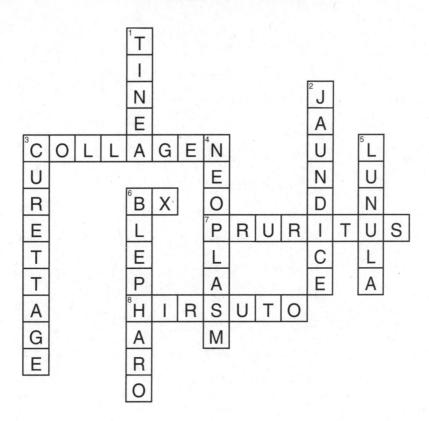

Underline the Accented Syllable

1. alopecia   (AL-oh-<u>PEE</u>-shee-ah)

2. anaphylaxis   (AN-ah-fih-<u>LAK</u>-sis)

3. blepharoplasty   (<u>BLEF</u>-ah-roh-PLAS-tee)

4. cicatrix   (<u>SIK</u>-ah-triks)

5. curettage   (kyoo-reh-<u>TAWZH</u>)

6. debridement   (deh-<u>BREED</u>-maw)

7. decubitus   (dee-<u>KYOO</u>-bih-tus)

8. erythema   (AIR-eh-<u>THEE</u>-mah)

9. fulguration   (FUL-gyoo-<u>RAY</u>-shun)

10. icterus   (<u>IK</u>-ter-us)

11. Kaposi   (kah-<u>POH</u>-see)

12. papilloma   (PAP-ih-<u>LOH</u>-mah)

13. pediculosis   (peh-DIK-yoo-<u>LOH</u>-sis)

14. rhytidectomy   (RIT-ih-<u>DEK</u>-toh-mee)

15. urticaria   (ER-tih-<u>KAIR</u>-ee-ah)

Word Surgery

1. anesthetic

   Suffix and its meaning: -ic *pertaining to*

   Prefix and its meaning: an- *without; not*

   Combining form and its meaning: esthet/o- *sensation; feeling*

   Medical word definition: Pertaining to (being) without sensation or feeling

2. anhidrosis

   Suffix and its meaning: -osis *condition; abnormal condition; process*

   Prefix and its meaning: an- *without; not*

   Combining form and its meaning: hidr/o- *sweat*

   Medical word definition: Abnormal condition (of being) without sweat

3. antifungal

   Suffix and its meaning: -al *pertaining to*

   Prefix and its meaning: anti- *against*

   Combining form and its meaning: fung/o- *fungus*

   Medical word definition: Pertaining to against fungus

4. cryosurgery

   Suffix and its meaning: -ery *process of*

   Prefix and its meaning: none

   Combining form and its meaning: cry/o- *cold*

   Combining form and its meaning: surg/o- *operative procedure*

   Medical word definition: Process of (using) cold (during an) operative procedure

5. dermatoplasty

   Suffix and its meaning: -plasty *process of reshaping by surgery*

   Prefix and its meaning: none

   Combining form and its meaning: dermat/o- *skin*

   Medical word definition: Process of reshaping by surgery (on the) skin

6. epidermal

  Suffix and its meaning: -al *pertaining to*

  Prefix and its meaning: epi- *upon; above*

  Combining form and its meaning: derm/o- *skin*

  Medical word definition: Pertaining to above the skin

7. hypersensitivity

  Suffix and its meaning: -ity *state; condition*

  Prefix and its meaning: hyper- *above; more than normal*

  Combining form and its meaning: sensitiv/o- *affected by; sensitive to*

  Medical word definition: Condition of more than normal (being) sensitive to (something)

8. hypodermic

  Suffix and its meaning: -ic *pertaining to*

  Prefix and its meaning: hypo- *below; deficient*

  Combining form and its meaning: derm/o- *skin*

  Medical word definition: Pertaining to below the skin

9. melanocyte

  Suffix and its meaning: -cyte *cell*

  Prefix and its meaning: none

  Combining form and its meaning: melan/o- *black*

  Medical word definition: Cell (that contains) black (pigment)

10. microdermabrasion

  Suffix and its meaning: -ion *action; condition*

  Prefix and its meaning: none

  Combining form and its meaning: micr/o- *one millionth; small*

  Combining form and its meaning: derm/o- *skin*

  Combining form and its meaning: abras/o- *scrape off*

  Medical word definition: Action of a small (thin layer of) skin (being) scraped off

11. onychomycosis

    Suffix and its meaning: -osis *condition; abnormal condition; process*

    Prefix and its meaning: none

    Combining form and its meaning: onych/o- *nail (fingernail or toenail)*

    Combining form and its meaning: myc/o- *fungus*

    Medical word definition: Abnormal condition of the nail (having a) fungus

12. premalignant

    Suffix and its meaning: -ant *pertaining to*

    Prefix and its meaning: pre- *before; in front of*

    Combining form and its meaning: malign/o- *intentionally causing harm; cancer*

    Medical word definition: Pertaining to before cancer

13. rhytidectomy

    Suffix and its meaning: -ectomy *surgical excision*

    Prefix and its meaning: none

    Combining form and its meaning: rhytid/o- *wrinkle*

    Medical word definition: Surgical excision of wrinkles

14. subcutaneous

    Suffix and its meaning: -ous *pertaining to*

    Prefix and its meaning: sub- *below; underneath; less than*

    Combining form and its meaning: cutane/o- *skin*

    Medical word definition: Pertaining to (a layer that is) underneath the skin

15. xeroderma

    Suffix and its meaning: -derma *skin*

    Prefix and its meaning: none

    Combining form and its meaning: xer/o- *dry*

    Medical word definition: Skin (that is) dry

Chapter Quiz

MULTIPLE CHOICE

1. C	4. B	7. D	10. B
2. C	5. D	8. A	
3. A	6. A	9. C	

FILL IN THE BLANK

1. dermat/o-
2. elastin
3. lesion
4. Herpes
5. yellow
6. clubbing
7. excisional
8. dermatoplasty
9. Topical
10. pigment

TRUE/FALSE

1. False (fat)
2. True
3. True
4. False (albinism)
5. True
6. False (Kaposi's sarcoma)
7. False (exudate)
8. True
9. False (allograft)
10. False (they are licensed)

CHAPTER **8**

Orthopedics

Measure Your Progress: Learning Objectives

After reading this chapter, the student should be able to

- Identify the structures of the skeletal system.
- Describe the process of growth.
- Describe common skeletal diseases and conditions, laboratory and diagnostic procedures, medical and surgical procedures, and drug categories.
- Give the medical meaning of word parts related to the skeletal system.
- Build skeletal words from word parts and divide and define skeletal words.
- Spell and pronounce skeletal words.
- Analyze the medical content and meaning of an orthopedic report.
- Dive deeper into orthopedics (skeletal) by reviewing the activities at the end of this chapter and online at Medical Terminology Interactive.

It All Starts with Word Building

Medical language is all about medical words and their word parts. Jump right into this chapter by learning some of the common combining forms and their definitions that you will encounter in this chapter.

ankyl/o-	fused together; stiff	orth/o-	straight
arthr/o-	joint	osse/o-	bone
articul/o-	joint	ossificat/o-	changing into bone
calcane/o-	calcaneus (heel bone)	oste/o-	bone
carp/o-	wrist	palat/o-	palate
cartilagin/o-	cartilage	pariet/o-	wall of a cavity
cervic/o-	neck; cervix	patell/o-	patella (kneecap)
chondr/o-	cartilage	pelv/i-	pelvis (hip bone; renal pelvis)
clavicul/o-	clavicle (collar bone)		
coccyg/o-	coccyx (tail bone)	pelv/o-	pelvis (hip bone; renal pelvis)
cost/o-	rib		
crani/o-	cranium (skull)	perone/o-	fibula (lower leg bone)
ethm/o-	sieve		
femor/o-	femur (thigh bone)	phalang/o-	phalanx (finger or toe)
fibul/o-	fibula (lower leg bone)		
		pub/o-	pubis (hip bone)
fract/o-	break up	radi/o-	radius (forearm bone; x-rays; radiation)
front/o-	front		
goni/o-	angle		
humer/o-	humerus (upper arm bone)	sacr/o-	sacrum
		scapul/o-	scapula (shoulder blade)
ili/o-	ilium (hip bone)		
ischi/o-	ischium (hip bone)	scoli/o-	curved; crooked
kyph/o-	bent; humpbacked	skelet/o-	skeleton
lacrim/o-	tears	sphen/o-	wedge shape
lord/o-	swayback	spin/o-	spine; backbone
lumb/o-	lower back; area between the ribs and pelvis	spondyl/o-	vertebra
		stern/o-	sternum (breast bone)
malac/o-	softening	tars/o-	ankle
mandibul/o-	mandible (lower jaw)	tempor/o-	temple (side of the head)
maxill/o-	maxilla (upper jaw)		
myel/o-	bone marrow; spinal cord; myelin	tibi/o-	tibia (shin bone)
		uln/o-	ulna (forearm bone)
occipit/o-	occiput (back of the head)	vertebr/o-	vertebra
		zygomat/o-	zygoma (cheek bone)

Orthopedic Dictation

Hand out the sheet with blanks on it to each student. Then dictate from the Instructor's Answer Sheet. Students are to fill in the missing words, spelling these words correctly.

Orthopedic Medical Dictation

1. The patient was seen by me in _____ follow-up and my tentative _____ was _____ of the left ankle. Now it would appear that a more definitive _____ would be _____ at the _____ and _____ aspects of the left ankle. She is currently having throbbing pain through the central _____. She is tender along the _____ _____ _____ and along the _____ _____ behind the _____ and _____ _____ of the left ankle.

2. The patient has a painful _____. Upon physical examination, she has a moderately severe _____ _____ of the left great toe and _____ of the midfoot. X-rays show a large deviation at the _____ joint. Otherwise, there are no signs of degenerative _____.

3. Upon exam, he has some tenderness along the _____ joint line. X-rays show a cyst in the _____.

4. Plan: Diagnostic _____ to be done in the near future.

5. Findings at this time are consistent with _____ of the right _____.

6. X-rays of the right hip show a total hip replacement _____ and no evident _____ destructive process.

7. X-ray of the right foot shows a _____ fracture of the _____ portion of the first _____. There is degenerative _____ present. There is an old _____ fracture noted.

Chapter Spelling Test

Dictate and spell (or photocopy a handout that contains) this list of 20 spelling words. Give this list to students to study for the week. At the beginning of next week's class, dictate 10 of these words as the spelling test. The spelling test is included with the chapter test that is given on the previous week's material.

1. ankylosing spondylitis
2. arthralgia
3. cancellous bone
4. cartilaginous
5. coccyx
6. diaphysis
7. hemarthrosis
8. ilium (hip bone)
9. malalignment
10. malleolus
11. meniscus
12. osseous
13. osteomyelitis
14. pectus excavatum
15. peroneal
16. phalanx
17. scoliosis
18. symphysis pubis
19. xiphoid
20. zygoma

Chapter Pronunciation Test

Photocopy a handout that contains this list of 20 pronunciation words. Give this list to students to study for the week. Sometime at the beginning of the next week, each student should call your office or home answering machine and pronounce each word.

1. ankylosing spondylitis (ANG-kih-LOH-sing SPAWN-dih-LY-tis)

2. arthralgia (ar-THRAL-jee-ah)

3. arthrocentesis (AR-throh-sen-TEE-sis)

4. cartilaginous (KAR-tih-LAJ-ih-nus)

5. chondromalacia (CON-droh-mah-LAY-shee-ah)

6. coccyx (KAWK-siks)

7. diaphysis (dy-AF-ih-sis)

8. hemarthrosis (HEE-mar-THROH-sis)

9. kyphoscoliosis (KY-foh-SKOH-lee-OH-sis)

10. malleolus (mah-LEE-oh-lus)

11. meniscus (meh-NIS-kus)

12. olecranon (oh-LEK-rah-non)

13. osseous (AW-see-us)

14. osteomyelitis (AWS-tee-oh-my-LIE-tis)

15. pectus excavatum (PEK-tus EKS-kah-VAH-tum)

16. phalangeal (fah-LAN-jee-al)

17. rongeur (rawn-ZHER)

18. symphysis pubis (SIM-fih-sis PYOO-bis)

19. xiphoid (ZY-foyd)

Word Search

Complete this word search puzzle that contains Chapter 8 words. Look for the following words as given in the list below. The number in parentheses indicates how many times the word appears in the puzzle.

axis	osteoporosis
bone	osteosarcoma
bones	pelvis
cast	rib (2)
digits	sacrum
disk	scapula
femur	skull
fracture	spinal
joint	tibia
maxilla	ulna
osteal	vertebrae
ossification	

```
J  Q  A  V  E  R  T  E  B  R  A  E
P  T  M  R  R  C  Y  M  I  A  S  R
E  N  O  B  U  D  U  B  A  N  L  U
L  I  C  S  T  R  I  L  V  A  L  M
V  O  R  B  C  W  E  G  N  Q  U  E
I  J  A  A  A  D  I  I  A  K  F
S  I  S  O  R  O  P  O  E  T  S  O
S  A  O  A  F  S  Y  U  C  A  S  T
E  X  E  I  C  V  S  K  L  T  U  Q
N  I  T  B  I  R  S  W  E  A  Y  M
O  S  S  I  F  I  C  A  T  I  O  N
B  X  O  T  D  A  L  L  I  X  A  M
```

Crossword Puzzle

ACROSS

1. The long bone in the upper arm is the _____.

3. The lower jaw bone is the _____.

5. The combining form "_____" means tears.

7. The malleus, incus, and stapes are collectively known as _____.

8. The first cervical vertebra (C1) is also known as the _____.

9. The surface of a bone is covered with a thick, fibrous membrane called the _____.

10. A deformity where the knees are rotated toward the midline and the lower legs are bent laterally is called _____.

DOWN

2. The bony projection of the distal tibia is the _____ _____.

4. The combining form "_____" means bent or humpbacked.

6. A distal radial fracture caused by falling onto an outstretched arm is referred to as a/an _____ fracture.

Underline the Accented Syllable

Read the medical word. Then review the syllables in the pronunciation. Underline the primary (main) accented syllable in the pronunciation.

1. ankylosing   (ang-kih-loh-sing)

2. calcaneus   (kal-kay-nee-us)

3. coccygeal   (kawk-sij-ee-al)

4. Colles' fracture   (koh-leez frak-chur)

5. dextroscoliosis   (deks-troh-skoh-lee-oh-sis)

6. diaphysis   (dy-af-ih-sis)

7. foramen   (foh-ray-min)

8. hemarthrosis   (hee-mar-throh-sis)

9. kyphoscoliosis   (ky-foh-skoh-lee-oh-sis)

10. osteomyelitis   (aws-tee-oh-my-lie-tis)

11. periosteum   (pair-ee-aws-tee-um)

12. rheumatoid   (roo-may-toyd)

13. scintigraphy   (sin-tig-rah-fee)

14. symphysis   (sim-fih-sis)

15. xiphoid   (zy-foyd)

Word Surgery

Read the medical word. Break the medical word into its word parts and give the meaning of each word part. Then give the definition of the medical word.

1. allograft

   Suffix and its meaning: _____

   Prefix and its meaning: _____

   Combining form and its meaning: _____

   Medical word definition: _____

2. analgesic

   Suffix and its meaning: _____

   Prefix and its meaning: _____

   Combining form and its meaning: _____

   Medical word definition: _____

3. arthrodesis

   Suffix and its meaning: _____

   Prefix and its meaning: _____

   Combining form and its meaning: _____

   Medical word definition: _____

4. chondromalacia

   Suffix and its meaning: _____

   Prefix and its meaning: _____

   Combining form and its meaning: _____

   Combining form and its meaning: _____

   Medical word definition: _____

5. demineralization

   Suffix and its meaning: _____

   Prefix and its meaning: _____

   Combining form and its meaning: _____

   Medical word definition: _____

6. dislocation

Suffix and its meaning: _____

Prefix and its meaning: _____

Combining form and its meaning: _____

Medical word definition: _____

7. extracorporeal

Suffix and its meaning: _____

Prefix and its meaning: _____

Combining form and its meaning: _____

Medical word definition: _____

8. goniometry

Suffix and its meaning: _____

Prefix and its meaning: _____

Combining form and its meaning: _____

Medical word definition: _____

9. levoscoliosis

Suffix and its meaning: _____

Prefix and its meaning: _____

Combining form and its meaning: _____

Combining form and its meaning: _____

Medical word definition: _____

10. osteoarthritis

Suffix and its meaning: _____

Prefix and its meaning: _____

Combining form and its meaning: _____

Combining form and its meaning: _____

Medical word definition: _____

11. osteoma

Suffix and its meaning: _____

Prefix and its meaning: _____

Combining form and its meaning: _____

Medical word definition: _____

12. osteomyelitis

Suffix and its meaning: _____

Prefix and its meaning: _____

Combining form and its meaning: _____

Combining form and its meaning: _____

Medical word definition: _____

13. prosthetic

Suffix and its meaning: _____

Prefix and is meaning: _____

Combining form and its meaning: _____

Medical word definition: _____

14. skeletomuscular

Suffix and its meaning: _____

Prefix and its meaning: _____

Combining form and its meaning: _____

Combining form and its meaning: _____

Medical word definition: _____

15. spondylolisthesis

Suffix and its meaning: _____

Prefix and its meaning: _____

Combining form and its meaning: _____

Medical word definition: _____

Chapter Quiz

MULTIPLE CHOICE

1. The upper arm bone is known as the:

   A. femur.

   B. humerus.

   C. tibia.

   D. carpal.

2. A joint or _____ is where two bones come together.

   A. ilium

   B. ischium

   C. articulation

   D. fusion

3. A/an _____ is a bone cell that maintains and monitors the mineral content.

   A. osteocyte

   B. osteoblast

   C. osteoclast

   D. periosteum

4. Which of the following is a type of bone fracture?

   A. hairline

   B. greenstick

   C. spiral

   D. All of the above.

5. Blood found in a joint cavity is usually from blunt force trauma or a penetrating wound and this condition is known as:

   A. gout.

   B. arthritis.

   C. a vascular necrosis.

   D. hemarthrosis.

6. _____ is a surgical procedure that uses an arthroscope inserted into a joint to visualize the structures of the joint.

   A. Arthrodesis

   B. Arthrocentesis

   C. Arthroscopy

   D. Bone graft

7. Which of the following is a *Greek* combining form for "cartilage"?

   A. oste/o-

   B. ankyl/o-

   C. chondr/o-

   D. spondyl/o-

8. An osteosarcoma is a malignant tumor of the:

   A. bone.

   B. connective tissue and bone.

   C. cartilage and connective tissue.

   D. bone and cartilage.

9. The ossicles are:

   A. tiny bones that are part of the process of hearing.

   B. cells that make new bone.

   C. bone edges that grow together in the sutures of the skull.

   D. part of the rib cage not attached to the sternum.

10. Osseous tissue is a type of:

   A. muscle tissue.

   B. bone marrow.

   C. connective tissue.

   D. nerve tissue.

FILL IN THE BLANK

1. The condition of having a humpback is known as _____.

2. The _____ process is found at the posterior tip of the sternum.

3. The anatomical name for the shoulder blade is the _____.

4. Ossification is the process by which _____ is changed into bone.

5. An osteosarcoma is a _____ or cancerous bone tumor.

6. Osteomyelitis is an infection of the bone and _____ _____.

7. _____ is an abnormal, excessive lateral curvature of the spine.

8. Gout is a _____ disorder in which the uric acid level in the blood is high.

9. The suffix "-oid" as in rheumatoid means "_____."

10. The term hallux as in hallux valgus refers to the _____ _____.

TRUE/FALSE

_____ 1. The combining form "calcane/o-" refers to the heel bone.

_____ 2. The sphenoid bone is a large, irregularly shaped bone that forms the base and side of the pelvis.

_____ 3. The metacarpal bones can be found in the foot.

_____ 4. Bone growth takes place at the diaphysis.

_____ 5. The prefix "a-" means "away from; without."

_____ 6. The suffix that means "process of making, creating, or inserting" is "-ization."

_____ 7. "Dextr/o-" refers to the "right" but "lev/o-" refers to the "left."

_____ 8. Lyme disease is caused by a virus from the bite of an infected deer tick.

_____ 9. The suffix "-itis" as in arthritis means "inflammation of."

_____ 10. A prosthetic device is a surgical tool.

Pronunciation Checklist

Read each word and its pronunciation. Practice pronouncing each word. Verify your pronunciation by listening to the Pronunciation List on Medical Terminology Interactive. Check the box next to the word after you master its pronunciation.

- ☐ acetabular (AS-eh-TAB-yoo-lar)
- ☐ acetabulum (AS-eh-TAB-yoo-lum)
- ☐ acromion (ah-KROH-mee-on)
- ☐ allograft (AL-oh-graft)
- ☐ amputation (AM-pyoo-TAY-shun)
- ☐ amputee (AM-pyoo-tee)
- ☐ analgesic drug (AN-al-JEE-zik DRUHG)
- ☐ ankylosing spondylitis (ANG-kih-LOH-sing SPAWN-dih-LY-tis)
- ☐ appendicular skeleton (AP-en-DIK-yoo-lar SKEL-eh-ton)
- ☐ arthralgia (ar-THRAL-jee-ah)
- ☐ arthritis (ar-THRY-tis)
- ☐ arthrocentesis (AR-throh-sen-TEE-sis)
- ☐ arthrodesis (AR-throh-DEE-sis)
- ☐ arthrogram (AR-throh-gram)
- ☐ arthrography (ar-THRAWG-rah-fee)
- ☐ arthropathy (ar-THRAWP-ah-thee)
- ☐ arthroplasty (AR-throh-PLAS-tee)
- ☐ arthroscope (AR-throh-skohp)
- ☐ arthroscopic (AR-throh-SKAW-pik)
- ☐ arthroscopy (ar-THRAWS-koh-pee)
- ☐ articular (ar-TIK-yoo-lar)
- ☐ articulation (ar-TIK-yoo-LAY-shun)
- ☐ atlas (AT-las)
- ☐ autograft (AW-toh-graft)
- ☐ avascular necrosis (aa-VAS-kyoo-lar neh-KROH-sis)
- ☐ axial skeleton (AK-see-al SKEL-eh-ton)
- ☐ bony (BOH-nee)
- ☐ bunion (BUN-yun)
- ☐ bunionectomy (BUN-yun-EK-toh-mee)
- ☐ calcaneal (kal-KAY-nee-al)

- ☐ calcaneus (kal-KAY-nee-us)
- ☐ cancellous bone (kan-SEL-us BOHN)
- ☐ carpal (KAR-pal)
- ☐ cartilage (KAR-tih-lij)
- ☐ cartilaginous (KAR-tih-LAJ-ih-nus)
- ☐ cast (KAST)
- ☐ cervical (SER-vih-kal)
- ☐ chondroma (con-DROH-mah)
- ☐ chondromalacia (CON-droh-mah-LAY-shee-ah)
- ☐ clavicle (KLAV-ih-kl)
- ☐ clavicular (klah-VIK-yoo-lar)
- ☐ coccygeal (kawk-SIJ-ee-al)
- ☐ coccyx (KAWK-siks)
- ☐ Colles' fracture (KOH-leez FRAK-chur)
- ☐ comminuted fracture (COM-ih-nyoo-ted FRAK-chur)
- ☐ compression fracture (com-PRESH-un FRAK-chur)
- ☐ congenital (con-JEN-ih-tal)
- ☐ coracoid (KOR-ah-koyd)
- ☐ coronal suture (kor-OH-nal SOO-chur)
- ☐ corticosteroid drug (KOR-tih-koh-STAIR-oyd DRUHG)
- ☐ costal (KAW-stal)
- ☐ costochondral (KAWS-toh-CON-dral)
- ☐ cranial (KRAY-nee-al)
- ☐ cranium (KRAY-nee-um)
- ☐ degenerative joint disease (dee-JEN-er-ah-tiv JOYNT dih-ZEEZ)
- ☐ demineralization (dee-MIN-er-al-ih-ZAY-shun)
- ☐ densitometry (DEN-sih-TAWM-eh-tree)
- ☐ depressed fracture (dee-PRESD FRAK-chur)
- ☐ DEXA scan (DEK-sah SKAN)
- ☐ dextroscoliosis (DEKS-troh-SKOH-lee-OH-sis)
- ☐ diaphyses (dy-AF-ih-seez)
- ☐ diaphysial (DY-ah-FIZ-ee-al)

- ☐ diaphysis (dy-AF-ih-sis)
- ☐ digit (DIJ-it)
- ☐ disk, disc (DISK)
- ☐ dislocation (DIS-loh-KAY-shun)
- ☐ displaced fracture (dis-PLAYSD FRAK-chur)
- ☐ epiphyses (eh-PIF-ih-seez)
- ☐ epiphysial (EP-ih-FIZ-ee-al)
- ☐ epiphysis (eh-PIF-ih-sis)
- ☐ ethmoid (ETH-moyd)
- ☐ Ewing's sarcoma (YOO-ingz sar-KOH-mah)
- ☐ external fixation (eks-TER-nal fik-SAY-shun)
- ☐ extracorporeal (EKS-trah-kor-POH-ree-al)
- ☐ extremity (eks-TREM-ah-tee)
- ☐ femora (FEM-oh-rah)
- ☐ femoral (FEM-oh-ral)
- ☐ femur (FEE-mur)
- ☐ fibula (FIB-yoo-lah)
- ☐ fibulae (FIB-yoo-lee)
- ☐ fibular (FIB-yoo-lar)
- ☐ foramen (foh-RAY-min)
- ☐ fracture (FRAK-chur)
- ☐ frontal (FRUN-tal)
- ☐ facial (FAY-shal)
- ☐ fossa (FAW-sah)
- ☐ fontanel (FAWN-tah-NEL)
- ☐ foramen magnum (foh-RAY-min MAG-num)
- ☐ genu valgum (JEE-noo VAL-gum)
- ☐ genu varum (JEE-noo VAIR-um)
- ☐ glenoid fossa (GLEH-noyd FAW-sah)
- ☐ goniometer (GOH-nee-AWM-eh-ter)
- ☐ goniometry (GOH-nee-AWM-eh-tree)
- ☐ gout (GOWT)
- ☐ gouty arthritis (GOW-tee ar-THRY-tis)
- ☐ hallux valgus (HAL-uks VAL-gus)
- ☐ hemarthrosis (HEE-mar-TROH-sis)

- humeral (HYOO-mer-al)
- humeri (HYOO-mer-eye)
- humerus (HYOO-mer-us)
- hyoid (HY-oyd)
- iliac (IL-ee-ak)
- ilium (IL-ee-um)
- injection (in-JEK-shun)
- intervertebral (IN-ter-ver-TEE-bral)
- intra-articular (IN-trah-ar-TIK-yoo-lar)
- ischial (IS-kee-al)
- ischium (IS-kee-um)
- kyphoscoliosis (KY-foh-SKOH-lee-OH-sis)
- kyphosis (ky-FOH-sis)
- kyphotic (ky-FAWT-ik)
- lacrimal (LAK-rih-mal)
- lateral (LAT-er-al)
- levoscoliosis (LEE-voh-SKOH-lee-OH-sis)
- ligament (LIG-ah-ment)
- ligamentous (LIG-ah-MEN-tus)
- lordosis (lor-DOH-sis)
- lordotic (lor-DAWT-ik)
- lumbar (LUM-bar)
- malalignment (MAL-ah-LINE-ment)
- malleolar (mah-LEE-oh-lar)
- malleoli (mah-LEE-oh-lie)
- malleolus (mah-LEE-oh-lus)
- mandible (MAN-dih-bl)
- mandibular (man-DIB-yoo-lar)
- manubrium (mah-NOO-bree-um)
- maxilla (mak-SIL-ah)
- maxillary (MAK-sih-LAIR-ee)
- medial (MEE-dee-al)
- medullary cavity (MED-yoo-LAIR-ee KAV-ih-tee)
- menisci (meh-NIS-kie)
- meniscus (meh-NIS-kus)
- metacarpal (MET-ah-KAR-pal)
- metatarsal (MET-ah-TAR-sal)
- musculoskeletal (MUS-kyoo-loh-SKEL-eh-tal)
- nasal (NAY-zal)
- nondisplaced fracture (non-dis-PLAYSD FRAK-chur)
- nonsteroidal anti-inflammatory drug (NON-stair-OY-dal AN-tee-in-FLAM-ah-TOR-ee DRUHG)
- nucleus pulposis (NOO-klee-us pul-POH-sis)
- oblique fracture (awb-LEEK FRAK-chur)
- occipital (awk-SIP-ih-tal)
- olecranon (oh-LEK-rah-non)
- orthopedics (OR-thoh-PEE-diks)
- orthopedist (OR-thoh-PEE-dist)
- orthosis (or-THOH-sis)
- osseous (AW-see-us)
- ossicle (AWS-ih-kl)
- ossicular (aw-SIK-yoo-lar)
- ossification (AWS-ih-fih-KAY-shun)
- osteoarthritis (AWS-tee-oh-ar-THRY-tis)
- osteoblast (AWS-tee-oh-BLAST)
- osteoclast (AWS-tee-oh-KLAST)
- osteocyte (AWS-tee-oh-SITE)
- osteogenic (AWS-tee-oh-JEN-ik)
- osteoma (AWS-tee-OH-mah)
- osteomalacia (AWS-tee-oh-mah-LAY-shee-ah)
- osteomyelitis (AWS-tee-oh-my-LIE-tis)
- osteophyte (AWS-tee-oh-FITE)
- osteoporosis (AWS-tee-oh-poh-ROH-sis)
- osteosarcoma (AWS-tee-oh-sar-KOH-mah)
- osteotome (AWS-tee-oh-TOHM)
- palatine (PAL-ah-tine)
- parietal (pah-RY-eh-tal)
- patella (pah-TEL-ah)
- patellae (pah-TEL-ee)
- patellar (pah-TEL-ar)
- pathologic fracture (PATH-oh-LAWJ-ik FRAK-chur)
- pectus excavatum (PEK-tus EKS-kah-VAH-tum)
- pelvic (PEL-vik)
- pelvis (PEL-vis)
- periosteal (PAIR-ee-AWS-tee-al)
- periosteum (PAIR-ee-AWS-tee-um)
- peroneal (PAIR-oh-NEE-al)
- phalangeal (fah-LAN-jee-al)
- phalanx (FAY-langks)
- physical therapy (FIZ-ih-kal THAIR-ah-pee)
- physical therapist (FIZ-ih-kal THAIR-ah-pist)
- prosthesis (praws-THEE-sis)
- prosthetic (praws-THET-ik)
- pubic (PYOO-bik)
- pubis (PYOO-bis)
- radial (RAY-dee-al)
- radii (RAY-dee-eye)
- radius (RAY-dee-us)
- reduction (ree-DUK-shun)
- resorption (ree-SORP-shun)
- rheumatoid arthritis (ROO-mah-toyd ar-THRY-tis)
- rongeur (rawn-ZHER)
- sacral (SAY-kral)
- sacrum (SAY-krum)
- sagittal suture (SAJ-ih-tal SOO-chur)
- sarcoma (sar-KOH-mah)
- scapula (SKAP-yoo-lah)
- scapulae (SKAP-yoo-lee)
- scapular (SKAP-yoo-lar)
- scintigram (SIN-tih-gram)
- scintigraphy (sin-TIG-rah-fee)
- scoliosis (SKOH-lee-OH-sis)
- scoliotic (SKOH-lee-AWT-ik)
- skeletal (SKEL-eh-tal)
- skeletomuscular system (SKEL-eh-toh-MUS-kyoo-lar SIS-tem)
- skeleton (SKEL-eh-ton)
- socket (SAWK-et)
- sphenoid (SFEE-noyd)
- spinal (SPY-nal)
- spine (SPYN)
- spinous process (SPY-nus PRAW-ses)
- spiral fracture (SPY-ral FRAK-chur)
- spondylolisthesis (SPAWN-dih-LOH-lis-THEE-sis)
- sprain (SPRAYN)
- sternal (STER-nal)
- sternum (STER-num)
- suture (SOO-chur)
- symphysis pubis (SIM-fih-sis PYOO-bis)
- synovial joint (sih-NOH-vee-al JOYNT)
- talipes equinovarus (TAY-lih-peez ee-KWY-noh-VAIR-us)
- tarsal (TAR-sal)
- temporal (TEM-poh-ral)
- thoracic (thoh-RAS-ik)
- thorax (THOH-raks)
- tibia (TIB-ee-ah)
- tibiae (TIB-ee-ee)
- tibial (TIB-ee-al)
- tomography (toh-MAWG-rah-fee)
- tophi (TOH-fie)

- tophus (TOH-fus)
- traction (TRAK-shun)
- transplant (TRANS-plant)
- transverse fracture (trans-VERS FRAK-chur)
- trochanter (troh-KAN-ter)
- ulna (UL-nah)
- ulnae (UL-nee)
- ulnar (UL-nar)
- uric acid (YOO-rik AS-id)
- vertebra (VER-teh-brah)
- vertebrae (VER-teh-bree)
- vertebral (VER-teh-bral)
- vomer (VOH-mer)
- xiphoid (ZY-foyd)
- x-ray (EKS-ray)
- zygoma (zy-GOH-mah)
- zygomatic (zy-goh-MAT-ik)

Answer Key
Orthopedic Medical Dictation

INSTRUCTOR ANSWER SHEET

1. The patient was seen by me in ORTHOPEDIC follow-up and my tentative DIAGNOSIS was SPRAIN of the left ankle. Now it would appear that a more definitive DIAGNOSIS would be TENDONITIS at the MEDIAL and LATERAL aspects of the left ankle. She is currently having throbbing pain through the central RAYS. She is tender along the POSTERIOR TIBIAL TENDON and along the PERONEAL TENDON behind the MEDIAL and LATERAL MALLEOLI of the left ankle.

2. The patient has a painful BUNION. Upon physical examination, she has a moderately severe HALLUX VALGUS of the left great toe and PRONATION of the midfoot. X-rays show a large deviation at the METATARSOPHALANGEAL joint. Otherwise, there are no signs of degenerative ARTHRITIS.

3. Upon exam, he has some tenderness along the ANTEROLATERAL joint line. X-rays show a cyst in the TALUS.

4. Plan: Diagnostic ARTHROSCOPY to be done in the near future.

5. Findings at this time are consistent with CHONDROMALACIA of the right PATELLA.

6. X-rays of the right hip show a total hip replacement PROSTHESIS and no evident OSSEOUS destructive process.

7. X-ray of the right foot shows a TRANSVERSE fracture of the PROXIMAL portion of the first PHALANX. There is degenerative OSTEOARTHRITIS present. There is an old CALCANEAL fracture noted.

Word Search

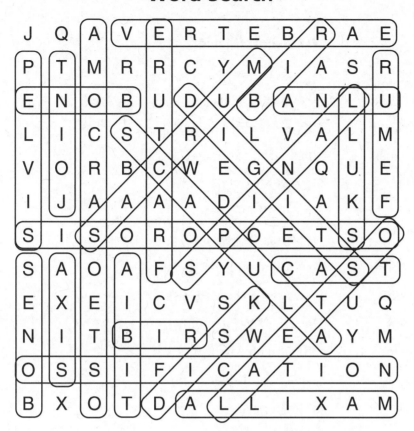

Crossword Puzzle

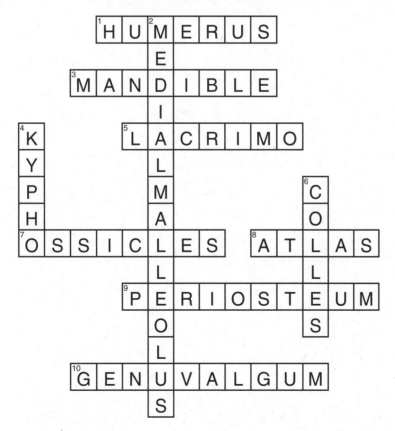

Underline the Accented Syllable

1. ankylosing   (ANG-kih-<u>LOH</u>-sing)

2. calcaneus   (kal-<u>KAY</u>-nee-us)

3. coccygeal   (kawk-<u>SIJ</u>-ee-al)

4. Colles' fracture   (<u>KOH</u>-leez <u>FRAK</u>-chur)

5. dextroscolosis   (DEKS-troh-SKOH-lee-<u>OH</u>-sis)

6. diaphysis   (dy-<u>AF</u>-ih-sis)

7. foramen   (foh-<u>RAY</u>-min)

8. hemarthrosis   (HEE-mar-<u>THROH</u>-sis)

9. kyphoscoliosis   (KY-foh-SKOH-lee-<u>OH</u>-sis)

10. osteomyelitis   (AWS-tee-oh-my-<u>LIE</u>-tis)

11. periosteum   (PAIR-ee-<u>AWS</u>-tee-um)

12. rheumatoid   (<u>ROO</u>-mah-toyd)

13. scintigraphy   (sin-<u>TIG</u>-rah-fee)

14. symphysis   (<u>SIM</u>-fih-sis)

15. xiphoid   (<u>ZY</u>-foyd)

Word Surgery

1. allograft

   Suffix and its meaning: -graft *tissue for implant or transplant*

   Prefix and its meaning: none

   Combining form and its meaning: all/o- *other; strange*

   Medical word definition: Tissue for implant or transplant from another (body)

2. analgesic

   Suffix and its meaning: -ic *pertaining to*

   Prefix and its meaning: an- *without; not*

   Combining form and its meaning: alges/o- *sensation of pain*

   Medical word definition: Pertaining to (being) without sensation of pain

3. arthrodesis

   Suffix and its meaning: -desis *procedure to fuse together*

   Prefix and its meaning: none

   Combining form and its meaning: arthr/o- *joint*

   Medical word definition: Procedure to fuse together a joint

4. chondromalacia

   Suffix and its meaning: -ia *condition; state; thing*

   Prefix and its meaning: none

   Combining form and its meaning: chondr/o- *cartilage*

   Combining form and its meaning: malac/o- *softening*

   Medical word definition: Condition of cartilage softening

5. demineralization

   Suffix and its meaning: -ization *process of making, creating, or inserting*

   Prefix and its meaning: de- *reversal of; without*

   Combining form and its meaning: mineral/o- *mineral; electrolyte*

   Medical word definition: Process of creating a reversal of mineral (content)

6. dislocation

    Suffix and its meaning: -ion *action; condition*

    Prefix and its meaning: dis- *away from*

    Combining form and its meaning: locat/o- *a place*

    Medical word definition: Action (of going) away from a place

7. extracorporeal

    Suffix and its meaning: -eal *pertaining to*

    Prefix and its meaning: extra- *outside of*

    Combining form and its meaning: corpor/o- *body*

    Medical word definition: Pertaining to outside the body

8. goniometry

    Suffix and its meaning: -metry *process of measuring*

    Prefix and its meaning: none

    Combining form and its meaning: goni/o- *angle*

    Suffix and definition: Process of measuring the angle (of a joint)

9. levoscoliosis

    Suffix and its meaning: -osis *condition; abnormal condition; process*

    Prefix and its meaning: none

    Combining form and its meaning: lev/o- *left*

    Combining form and its meaning: scoli/o- *curved; crooked*

    Medical word definition: Abnormal condition of left curved (spine)

10. osteoarthritis

    Suffix and its meaning: -itis *inflammation of; infection of*

    Prefix and its meaning: none

    Combining form and its meaning: oste/o- *bone*

    Combining form and its meaning: arthr/o- *joint*

    Medical word definition: Inflammation of the bone and joint

11. osteoma

    Suffix and its meaning: -oma *tumor; mass*

    Prefix and its meaning: none

    Combining form and its meaning: oste/o- *bone*

    Medical word definition: Tumor of the bone

12. osteomyelitis

   Suffix and its meaning: -itis *inflammation of; infection of*

   Prefix and its meaning: none

   Combining form and its meaning: oste/o- *bone*

   Combining form and its meaning: myel/o- *bone marrow; spinal cord; myelin*

   Medical word definition: Infection of the bone and bone marrow

13. prosthetic

   Suffix and its meaning: -ic *pertaining to*

   Prefix and its meaning: none

   Combining form and its meaning: prosthet/o- *artificial part*

   Medical word definition: Pertaining to an artificial part

14. skeletomuscular

   Suffix and its meaning: -ar *pertaining to*

   Prefix and its meaning: none

   Combining form and its meaning: skelet/o- *skeleton*

   Combining form and its meaning: muscul/o- *muscle*

   Medical word definition: Pertaining to the skeleton and muscles

15. spondylolisthesis

   Suffix and its meaning: -olisthesis *abnormal condition and process of slipping*

   Prefix and its meaning: none

   Combining form and its meaning: spondyl/o- *vertebra*

   Medical word definition: Abnormal condition and process of slipping of a vertebra (onto another vertebra)

Chapter Quiz

MULTIPLE CHOICE

1. B	4. D	7. C	10. C
2. C	5. D	8. B	
3. A	6. C	9. A	

FILL IN THE BLANK

1. kyphosis

2. xiphoid

3. scapula

4. cartilage

5. malignant

6. bone marrow

7. Scoliosis

8. metabolic

9. resembling

10. big toe

TRUE/FALSE

1. True

2. False (cranium)

3. False (hand)

4. False (epiphysis)

5. True

6. True

7. True

8. False (bacteria)

9. True

10. False (artificial replacement)

CHAPTER 9

Orthopedics

Measure Your Progress: Learning Objectives

After reading this chapter, the student should be able to

- Identify the structures of the muscular system.
- Describe how muscles contract and produce movement.
- Describe common muscular diseases and conditions, laboratory and diagnostic procedures, medical and surgical procedures, and drug categories.
- Give the medical meaning of word parts related to the muscular system.
- Build muscular words from word parts and divide and define muscular words.
- Spell and pronounce muscular words.
- Analyze the medical content and meaning of an orthopedic report.
- Dive deeper into orthopedics (muscular) by reviewing the activities at the end of this chapter and online at Medical Terminology Interactive.

It All Starts with Word Building

Medical language is all about medical words and their word parts. Jump right into this chapter by learning some of the common combining forms and their definitions that you will encounter in this chapter.

alg/o-	pain
brachi/o-	arm
burs/o-	bursa
chir/o-	hand
cleid/o-	clavicle (collar bone)
contract/o-	pull together
contus/o-	bruising
cost/o-	rib
delt/o-	triangle
duct/o-	bring or move; a duct
extens/o-	straightening
fasci/o-	fascia
flex/o-	bending
ganglion/o-	ganglion
habilitat/o-	give ability
kines/o-	movement
masset/o-	chewing
muscul/o-	muscle
my/o-	muscle
myos/o-	muscle
neur/o-	nerve
orbicul/o-	small circle
pector/o-	chest
pod/o-	foot
pronat/o-	face down
radi/o-	radius (forearm bone; x-rays; radiation)
relax/o-	relax
rotat/o-	rotate
stern/o-	sternum (breast bone)
sthen/o-	strength
supinat/o-	lying on the back
synov/o-	synovium (membrane)
synovi/o-	synovium (membrane)
tax/o-	coordination
tendon/o-	tendon
ten/o-	tendon
tibi/o-	tibia (shin bone)
tort/i-	twisted position
vers/o-	to travel; to turn

Chapter Spelling Test

Dictate and spell (or photocopy a handout that contains) this list of 20 spelling words. Give this list to students to study for the week. At the beginning of next week's class, dictate 10 of these words as the spelling test. The spelling test is included with the chapter test that is given on the previous week's material.

1. abduction
2. analgesic
3. biceps brachii muscle
4. chiropractor
5. dermatomyositis
6. Dupuytren's contracture
7. fascia
8. fibromyalgia
9. ganglionectomy
10. gluteus maximus muscle
11. latissimus dorsi muscle
12. musculoskeletal
13. myasthenia gravis
14. ptosis
15. rhabdomyosarcoma
16. sternocleidomastoid muscle
17. tendinous
18. tenosynovitis
19. torticollis
20. tremor

Chapter Pronunciation Test

Photocopy a handout that contains this list of 20 pronunciation words. Give this list to students to study for the week. Sometime in the beginning of the next week, each student should call your office or home answering machine and pronounce each word.

1. acetylcholine (AS-eh-til-KOH-leen)

2. atrophy (AT-roh-fee)

3. atrophic (ah-TROF-ik)

4. biceps brachii muscle (BY-seps BRAY-kee-eye MUS-el)

5. bradykinesia (BRAD-ee-kin-EE-zee-ah)

6. chiropractor (KY-roh-PRAK-tor)

7. creatine phosphokinase (KREE-ah-teen FAWS-foh-KY-nays)

8. dermatomyositis (DER-mah-toh-MY-oh-SY-tis)

9. electromyography (ee-LEK-troh-my-AWG-rah-fee)

10. fibromyalgia (FY-broh-my-AL-jee-ah)

11. ganglionectomy (GANG-glee-oh-NEK-toh-mee)

12. gluteus maximus muscle (gloo-TEE-us MAK-sih-mus MUS-el)

13. latissimus dorsi muscle (lah-TIS-ih-mus DOR-sigh MUS-el)

14. myasthenia gravis (MY-as-THEE-nee-ah GRAV-is)

15. neurotransmitter (NYOOR-oh-TRANS-mit-er) (NYOOR-oh-trans-MIT-er)

16. rectus abdominis muscle (REK-tus ab-DAWM-ih-nis MUS-el)

17. rhabdomyosarcoma (RAB-doh-MY-oh-sar-KOH-mah)

18. sternocleidomastoid muscle (STER-noh-KLY-doh-MAS-toyd MUS-el)

19. tenosynovitis (TEN-oh-SIN-oh-VY-tis)

20. trapezius muscle (trah-PEE-zee-us MUS-el)

Word Search

Complete this word search puzzle that contains Chapter 9 words. Look for the following words as given in the list below.

aponeurosis	fiber
ataxia	flexors
atrophy	gastrocnemius
belly	muscular
biceps	myalgia
bursa	NSAID
DTR	origin
dyskinesia	ptosis
EMG	strain
evertors	tendon
exercise	tremor
fascia	triceps

```
G  B  V  A  I  G  L  A  Y  M  J  F  D
F  A  S  C  I  A  F  U  H  S  V  T  Y
E  P  S  R  B  I  C  E  P  S  R  T  S
X  O  F  T  G  S  I  S  O  T  P  R  K
E  N  I  A  R  T  S  D  R  B  G  E  I
R  E  B  H  T  O  I  I  T  E  K  M  N
C  U  E  B  B  A  C  E  A  L  F  O  E
I  R  R  U  S  E  X  N  F  L  N  R  S
S  O  R  N  P  C  B  I  E  Y  I  K  I
E  S  A  S  S  D  F  X  A  M  G  G  A
A  I  T  E  N  D  O  N  R  F  I  G  W
Q  S  R  O  T  R  E  V  E  M  R  U  L
W  V  M  U  S  C  U  L  A  R  O  N  S
```

Crossword Puzzle

ACROSS

1. The combining form
   "_____" means
   coordination.

3. A fluid-filled sac that decreases
   friction where a tendon rubs against
   a bone near a synovial joint is known
   as a/an _____.

6. The turning of the palm of the hand
   posterior or downward is referred to
   as _____.

7. _____ is
   incoordination of muscles during
   movement, particularly the gait.

8. _____ muscles
   are striated, voluntary muscles that
   contract and relax in response to
   conscious thought.

9. The abbreviations ROM stands for

   _____

   _____

   _____.

DOWN

1. The _____

   _____ muscle
   bends the foot upward toward the
   leg (dorsiflexion).

2. The combining form
   "_____" means
   lying on the back.

4. The muscle of the shoulder that
   raises the arm and moves the arm
   away from the body (abduction) is
   the _____.

5. A _____ is a
   surgical procedure that cuts the
   fascia and releases pressure from
   built-up blood and tissue fluid in a
   patient with compartment syndrome.

Underline the Accented Syllable

Read the medical word. Then review the syllables in the pronunciation. Underline the primary (main) accented syllable in the pronunciation.

1. abduction   (ab-duk-shun)

2. adduction   (ad-duk-shun)

3. aponeurosis   (ap-oh-nyoo-roh-sis)

4. dyskinesia   (dis-kih-nee-zee-ah)

5. fascia   (fash-ee-ah)

6. ganglion   (gang-glee-on)

7. latissimus   (lah-tis-ih-mus)

8. myasthenia gravis   (my-as-thee-nee-ah grav-is)

9. myorrhaphy   (my-or-ah-fee)

10. peroneal   (pair-oh-nee-al)

11. ptosis   (toh-sis)

12. rhabdomyoma   (rab-doh-my-oh-mah)

13. sternocleidomastoid (ster-noh-kly-doh-mas-toyd)

14. tenosynovitis   (ten-oh-sin-oh-vy-tis)

15. thenar   (thee-nar)

16. tremor   (trem-or)

Word Surgery

Read the medical word. Break the medical word into its word parts and give the meaning of each word part. Then give the definition of the medical word.

1. ataxia

   Suffix and its meaning: _____

   Prefix and its meaning: _____

   Combining form and its meaning: _____

   Medical word definition: _____

2. atrophic

   Suffix and its meaning: _____

   Prefix and its meaning: _____

   Combining form and its meaning: _____

   Medical word definition: _____

3. avulsion

   Suffix and its meaning: _____

   Prefix and its meaning: _____

   Combining form and its meaning: _____

   Medical word definition: _____

4. bradykinesia

   Suffix and its meaning: _____

   Prefix and its meaning: _____

   Combining form and its meaning: _____

   Medical word definition: _____

5. electromyography

   Suffix and its meaning: _____

   Prefix and its meaning: _____

   Combining form and its meaning: _____

   Combining form and its meaning: _____

   Medical word definition: _____

6. eversion

   Suffix and its meaning: _____

   Prefix and its meaning: _____

   Combining form and its meaning: _____

   Medical word definition: _____

7. fasciotomy

   Suffix and its meaning: _____

   Prefix and its meaning: _____

   Combining form and its meaning: _____

   Medical word definition: _____

8. fibromyalgia

   Suffix and its meaning: _____

   Prefix and its meaning: _____

   Combining form and its meaning: _____

   Combining form and its meaning: _____

   Combining form and its meaning: _____

   Medical word definition: _____

9. hyperextension

   Suffix and its meaning: _____

   Prefix and its meaning: _____

   Combining form and its meaning: _____

   Medical word definition: _____

10. intercostal

   Suffix and its meaning: _____

   Prefix and its meaning: _____

   Combining form and its meaning: _____

   Medical word definition: _____

11. neuromuscular

Suffix and its meaning: _____

Prefix and its meaning: _____

Combining form and its meaning: _____

Combining form and its meaning: _____

Medical word definition: _____

12. nonsteroidal

Suffix and its meaning: _____

Prefix and its meaning: _____

Combining form and its meaning: _____

Medical word definition: _____

13. polymyalgia

Suffix and its meaning: _____

Prefix and its meaning: _____

Combining form and its meaning: _____

Combining form and its meaning: _____

Medical word definition: _____

14. rhabdomyoma

Suffix and its meaning: _____

Prefix and its meaning: _____

Combining form and its meaning: _____

Combining form and its meaning: _____

Medical word definition: _____

15. tenosynovitis

Suffix and its meaning: _____

Prefix and its meaning: _____

Combining form and its meaning: _____

Combining form and its meaning: _____

Medical word definition: _____

Chapter Quiz

MULTIPLE CHOICE

1. A muscle is attached to a bone by:

   A. cartilage.

   B. tendon.

   C. ligament.

   D. bursa.

2. The _____ brachii bends the arm toward the shoulder.

   A. trapezius

   B. biceps

   C. triceps

   D. pectoralis

3. The function of the bursa is to:

   A. decrease friction where a tendon rubs against a bone.

   B. surround a muscle fascicle.

   C. connect bone to bone.

   D. provide the power needed for flexion.

4. The combining form "_____" means "arm."

   A. extens/o-

   B. pector/o-

   C. radi/o-

   D. brachi/o-

5. A muscle is _____ when it loses bulk caused by lack of use or malnutrition.

   A. dehydrated

   B. relaxed

   C. contracted

   D. atrophic

6. The term "polymyalgia":

    A. has a prefix, combining form, and suffix.

    B. has only a prefix and combining form.

    C. has only a combining form and suffix.

    D. is an eponym.

7. Myopathy is a category of _____ disease.

    A. bone

    B. muscle

    C. tendon

    D. ptosis

8. When muscle coordination is diminished, especially in the gait, it is called:

    A. ataxia.

    B. bradykinesia.

    C. hyperkinesia.

    D. bursitis.

9. The word part "-rrhaphy" is:

    A. a suffix meaning to "suture."

    B. a prefix meaning "disease."

    C. a root meaning "to collapse."

    D. a combining form meaning "to establish a connection."

10. Which of the following are doctors who diagnose and treat patients with injuries involving bones, muscles, and nerves by manipulating the alignment of the vertebral column?

    A. podiatrists

    B. massage therapists

    C. chiropractors

    D. pharmacologists

FILL IN THE BLANK

1. The _____ of a muscle is where its tendon is attached to a stationary or nearly stationary bone.

2. _____ muscles are nonstriated muscles that are also called smooth muscles.

3. An extensor muscle is one that _____ the angle between two bones.

4. The junction between a nerve cell and a muscle fiber is called a _____ junction.

5. Muscle _____ is the shortening of a muscle fiber; it is the opposite of relaxation.

6. The disease that has pain located at certain trigger points in the muscles of the neck, back, or hips is known as _____.

7. In myasthenia gravis, drooping of the eyelids is known as _____.

8. OSHA educates healthcare professionals about workplace-related _____.

9. A _____ action is an involuntary, automatic response of the muscular nervous pathway.

10. A _____ blocker is a drug that blocks the action of epinephrine to treat essential familial tremor.

TRUE/FALSE

_____ 1. Each muscle is wrapped in fascia, a thin layer of connective tissue.

_____ 2. An abductor is a muscle that moves a body part to the midline of the body.

_____ 3. Supination is the turning of the palms posteriorly or downward.

_____ 4. Insertion is where a muscle begins and is attached to a stationary or nearly stationary bone.

_____ 5. Blunt force trauma to a muscle is a contusion that may be accompanied with bleeding in the muscle.

_____ 6. Rigor mortis is the normal condition of the muscles several hours after death due to the release of the muscles' stored calcium.

_____ 7. An overuse injury known as shin splints occurs when tendons anterior to the fibula become inflamed.

_____ 8. RICE is an abbreviation for a treatment that can be used to treat a sprain.

_____ 9. Muscle relaxant drugs are used to decrease inflammation.

_____ 10. Blocking the function of acetylcholine receptors to prevent muscle contraction is one use for beta-blocker drugs.

Pronunciation Checklist

Read each word and its pronunciation. Practice pronouncing each word. Verify your pronunciation by listening to the Pronunciation List on Medical Terminology Interactive. Check the box next to the word after you master its pronunciation.

- ❏ abduction (ab-DUK-shun)
- ❏ abductor (ab-DUK-tor)
- ❏ acetylcholine (AS-ee-til-KOH-leen)
- ❏ adduction (ad-DUK-shun)
- ❏ adductor (ad-DUK-tor)
- ❏ analgesic drug (AN-al-JEE-zik DRUHG)
- ❏ antibody (AN-tee-BAWD-ee) (AN-tih-BAWD-ee)
- ❏ aponeurosis (AP-oh-nyoo-ROH-sis)
- ❏ ataxia (ah-TAK-see-ah)
- ❏ ataxic (ah-TAK-sik)
- ❏ athetoid (ATH-eh-toyd)
- ❏ atrophic (aa-TROF-ik)
- ❏ atrophy (AT-roh-fee)
- ❏ avulsion (ah-VUL-shun)
- ❏ benign (bee-NINE)
- ❏ biceps brachii muscle (BY-seps BRAY-kee-eye MUS-el)
- ❏ biopsy (BY-awp-see)
- ❏ brachioradialis muscle (BRAY-kee-oh-RAY-dee-AL-is MUS-el)
- ❏ bradykinesia (BRAD-ee-kin-EE-zee-ah)
- ❏ buccinator muscle (BUK-sih-NAY-tor MUS-el)
- ❏ bursa (BER-sah)
- ❏ bursae (BER-see)
- ❏ bursal (BER-sal)
- ❏ bursitis (ber-SY-tis)
- ❏ chiropractic (KY-roh-PRAK-tic)
- ❏ chiropractor (KY-roh-PRAK-tor)
- ❏ contraction (con-TRAK-shun)
- ❏ contracture (con-TRAK-choor)
- ❏ contusion (con-TOO-shun)
- ❏ corticosteroid drug (KOR-tih-koh-STAIR-oyd DRUHG)
- ❏ creatine phosphokinase (KREE-ah-teen FAWS-foh-KY-nays)
- ❏ deltoid muscle (DEL-toyd MUS-el)
- ❏ dermatomyositis (DER-mah-toh-MY-oh-SY-tis)

- ❏ Duchenne's muscular dystrophy (doo-SHAYNZ MUS-kyoo-lar DIS-troh-fee)
- ❏ Dupuytren's contracture (DOO-pyoo-trenz con-TRAK-chur)
- ❏ dyskinesia (DIS-kih-NEE-zee-ah)
- ❏ dystrophy (DIS-troh-fee)
- ❏ electromyogram (ee-LEK-troh-MY-oh-gram)
- ❏ electromyography (ee-LEK-troh-my-AWG-rah-fee)
- ❏ eversion (ee-VER-zhun)
- ❏ evertor (ee-VER-tor)
- ❏ extension (eks-TEN-shun)
- ❏ extensor digitorum muscle (eks-TEN-sor DIJ-ih-TOR-um MUS-el)
- ❏ external oblique muscle (eks-TER-nal awb-LEEK MUS-el)
- ❏ fascia (FASH-ee-ah)
- ❏ fascial (FASH-ee-al)
- ❏ fascicle (FAS-ih-kl)
- ❏ fasciectomy (FASH-ee-EK-toh-mee)
- ❏ fasciotomy (FASH-ee-AWT-oh-mee)
- ❏ fibromyalgia (FY-broh-my-AL-jah)
- ❏ flexion (FLEK-shun)
- ❏ flexor hallucis brevis muscle (FLEK-sor HAL-yoo-sis BREV-is MUS-el)
- ❏ frontalis muscle (frun-TAY-lis MUS-el)
- ❏ ganglion (GANG-glee-on)
- ❏ ganglionectomy (GANG-glee-oh-NEK-toh-mee)
- ❏ gastrocnemius muscle (GAS-trawk-NEE-mee-us MUS-el)
- ❏ gluteus maximus muscle (gloo-TEE-us MAK-sih-mus MUS-el)
- ❏ hyperextension (HY-per-eks-TEN-shun)
- ❏ hyperflexion (HY-per-FLEK-shun)

- ❏ hyperkinesis (HY-per-kih-NEE-sis)
- ❏ hypertrophy (hy-PER-troh-fee)
- ❏ incisional (in-SIH-zhun-al)
- ❏ injection (in-JEK-shun)
- ❏ intercostal muscle (IN-ter-KAWS-tal MUS-el)
- ❏ internal oblique muscle (in-TER-nal awb-LEEK MUS-el)
- ❏ intramuscular (IN-trah-MUS-kyoo-lar)
- ❏ inversion (in-VER-zhun)
- ❏ invertor (in-VER-tor)
- ❏ latissimus dorsi muscle (lah-TIS-ih-mus DOR-sigh MUS-el)
- ❏ malignancy (mah-LIG-nan-see)
- ❏ masseter muscle (MAS-eh-ter MUS-el)
- ❏ muscle (MUS-el)
- ❏ muscle insertion (MUS-el in-SER-shun)
- ❏ muscle origin (MUS-el OR-ih-jin)
- ❏ muscular (MUS-kyoo-lar)
- ❏ musculature (MUS-kyoo-lah-CHUR)
- ❏ musculoskeletal (MUS-kyoo-loh-SKEL-eh-tal)
- ❏ myalgia (my-AL-jee-ah) (my-AL-jah)
- ❏ myasthenia gravis (MY-as-THEE-nee-ah GRAV-is)
- ❏ myoclonus (MY-oh-KLOH-nus)
- ❏ myofibril (MY-oh-FY-bril)
- ❏ myopathy (my-AWP-ah-thee)
- ❏ myorrhaphy (my-OR-ah-fee)
- ❏ myositis (MY-oh-SY-tis)
- ❏ neuromuscular (NYOOR-oh-MUS-kyoo-lar)
- ❏ neurotransmitter (NYOOR-oh-TRANS-mit-er) (NYOOR-oh-trans-MIT-er)
- ❏ nonsteroidal anti-inflammatory drug (NON-stair-OY-dal AN-tee-in-FLAM-ah-TOR-ee DRUHG)

- orbicularis oculi muscle (or-BIK-yoo-LAIR-is AWK-yoo-ligh MUS-el)
- orbicularis oris muscle (or-BIK-yoo-LAIR-is OR-is MUS-el)
- orthopedics (OR-thoh-PEE-diks)
- osteopath (AW-stee-oh-PATH)
- osteopathy (AWS-tee-AWP-ah-thee)
- pectoralis major muscle (PEK-toh-RAY-lis MAY-jur MUS-el)
- peroneal (PAIR-oh-NEE-al)
- peroneus longus muscle (PAIR-oh-NEE-us LONG-gus MUS-el)
- physiatrist (fih-ZY-ah-trist)
- physiatry (fih-ZY-ah-tree)
- platysma muscle (plah-TIZ-mah MUS-el)
- podiatric (POH-dee-AT-rik)
- podiatrist (poh-DY-ah-trist)
- podiatry (poh-DY-ah-tree)
- polymyalgia (PAWL-ee-my-AL-jee-ah) (PAWL-ee-my-AL-jah)
- polymyositis (PAWL-ee-MY-oh-SY-tis)
- pronation (proh-NAY-shun)
- pronator (proh-NAY-tor)
- ptosis (TOH-sis)
- quadriceps femoris muscles (KWAD-rih-seps FEM-oh-ris MUS-elz)
- receptor (ree-SEP-tor)
- rectus abdominis muscle (REK-tus ab-DAWM-ih-nis MUS-el)
- rectus femoris muscle (REK-tus FEM-oh-ris MUS-el)
- rehabilitation (REE-hah-BIL-ih-TAY-shun)
- relaxant drug (ree-LAK-sant DRUHG)
- retinaculum (RET-ih-NAK-yoo-lum)
- rhabdomyoma (RAB-doh-my-OH-mah)
- rhabdomyosarcoma (RAB-doh-MY-oh-sar-KOH-mah)
- rigor mortis (RIG-or MOR-tis)
- rotation (roh-TAY-shun)
- rotator (ROH-tay-tor)
- sartorius muscle (sar-TOR-ee-us MUS-el)
- spasm (SPAZM)
- sternocleidomastoid muscle (STER-noh-KLY-doh-MAS-toyd MUS-el)
- strain (STRAYN)
- striated muscle (STRY-aa-ted MUS-el)
- supination (SOO-pih-NAY-shun)
- supinator (SOO-pih-NAY-tor)
- temporalis muscle (TEM-poh-RAY-lis MUS-el)
- tendinous (TEN-dih-nus)
- tendon (TEN-dun)
- tendonitis (TEN-doh-NY-tis)
- tenorrhaphy (teh-NOR-ah-fee)
- tenosynovitis (TEN-oh-SIN-oh-VY-tis)
- Tensilon (TEN-sih-lawn)
- thenar muscle (THEE-nar MUS-el)
- therapist (THAIR-ah-pist)
- thymectomy (thy-MEK-toh-mee)
- tibialis anterior muscle (TIB-ee-AL-is an-TEER-ee-or MUS-el)
- torticollis (TOR-tih-KOL-is)
- trapezius muscle (trah-PEE-zee-us MUS-el)
- tremor (TREM-or)
- tremulous (TREM-yoo-lus)
- triceps brachii muscle (TRY-seps BRAY-kee-eye MUS-el)
- voluntary muscle (VAWL-un-TAIR-ee MUS-el)

Answer Key

Word Search

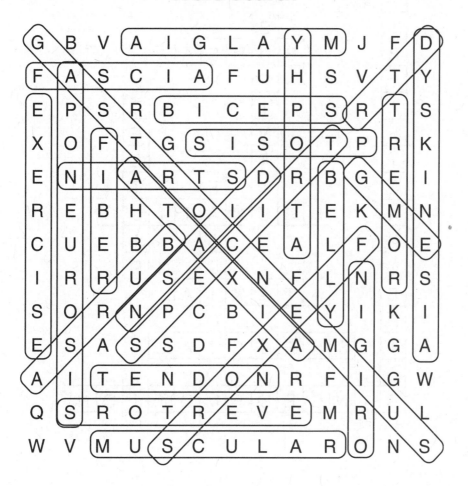

Crossword Puzzle

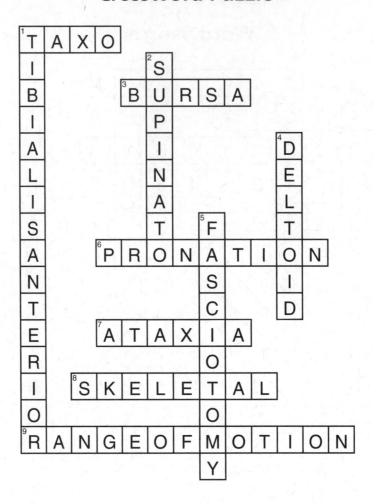

Underline the Accented Syllable

1. abduction   (ab-<u>DUK</u>-shun)

2. adduction   (ad-<u>DUK</u>-shun)

3. aponeurosis   (AP-oh-nyoo-<u>ROH</u>-sis)

4. dyskinesia   (DIS-kih-<u>NEE</u>-zee-ah)

5. fascia   (<u>FASH</u>-ee-ah)

6. ganglion   (<u>GANG</u>-glee-on)

7. latissimus   (lah-<u>TIS</u>-ih-mus)

8. myasthenia gravis   (MY-as-<u>THEE</u>-nee-ah <u>GRAV</u>-is)

9. myorrhaphy   (my-<u>OR</u>-ah-fee)

10. peroneal   (PAIR-oh-<u>NEE</u>-al)

11. ptosis   (<u>TOH</u>-sis)

12. rhabdomyoma   (RAB-doh-my-<u>OH</u>-mah)

13. sternocleidomastoid   (STER-noh-KLY-doh-<u>MAS</u>-toyd)

14. tenosynovitis   (TEN-oh-SIN-oh-<u>VY</u>-tis)

15. thenar   (<u>THEE</u>-nar)

16. tremor   (<u>TREM</u>-or)

Word Surgery

1. ataxia

   Suffix and its meaning: -ia *condition; state; thing*

   Prefix and its meaning a- *away from; without*

   Combining form and its meaning: tax/o- *coordination*

   Medical word definition: Condition of (being) without coordination

2. atrophic

   Suffix and its meaning: -ic *pertaining to*

   Prefix and its meaning: a- *away from; without*

   Combining form and its meaning: troph/o- *development*

   Medical word definition: Pertaining to without development

3. avulsion

   Suffix and its meaning: -ion *action; condition*

   Prefix and its meaning: a- *away from; without*

   Combining form and its meaning: vuls/o- *to tear*

   Medical word definition: Action of away from to tear

4. bradykinesia

   Suffix and its meaning: -ia *condition; state; thing*

   Prefix and its meaning: brady- *slow*

   Combining form and its meaning: kines/o- *movement*

   Medical word definition: Condition of slow movement

5. electromyography

   Suffix and its meaning: -graphy *process of recording*

   Prefix and its meaning: none

   Combining form and its meaning: electr/o- *electricity*

   Combining form and its meaning: my/o- *muscle*

   Medical word definition: Process of recording electricity in the muscle

6. eversion

  Suffix and its meaning: -ion *action; condition*

  Prefix and its meaning: e- *without; out*

  Combining form and its meaning: vers/o- *to travel; to turn*

  Medical word definition: Action of (going) out to turn

7. fasciotomy

  Suffix and its meaning: -tomy *process of cutting or making an incision*

  Prefix and its meaning: none

  Combining form and its meaning: fasci/o- *fascia*

  Medical word definition: Process of cutting or making an incision in the fascia

8. fibromyalgia

  Suffix and its meaning: -ia *condition; state; thing*

  Prefix and its meaning: none

  Combining form and its meaning: fibr/o- *fiber*

  Combining form and its meaning: my/o- *muscle*

  Combining form and its meaning: alg/o- *pain*

  Medical word definition: Condition of the fibers of the muscles (having) pain

9. hyperextension

  Suffix and its meaning: -ion *action; condition*

  Prefix and its meaning: hyper- *above; more than normal*

  Combining form and its meaning: extens/o- *straightening*

  Medical word definition: Action of more than normal straightening

10. intercostal

  Suffix and its meaning: -al *pertaining to*

  Prefix and its meaning: inter- *between*

  Combining form and its meaning: cost/o- *rib*

  Medical word definition: Pertaining to between the ribs

11. neuromuscular

Suffix and its meaning: -ar *pertaining to*

Prefix and its meaning: none

Combining form and its meaning: neur/o- *nerve*

Combining form and its meaning: muscul/o- *muscle*

Medical word definition: Pertaining to the nerve and muscle

12. nonsteroidal

Suffix and its meaning: -al *pertaining to*

Prefix and its meaning: non- *not*

Combining form and its meaning: steroid/o- *steroid*

Medical word definition: Pertaining to (a drug that is) not a steroid

13. polymyalgia

Suffix and its meaning: -ia *condition; state; thing*

Prefix and its meaning: poly- *many; much*

Combining form and its meaning: my/o- *muscle*

Combining form and its meaning: alg/o- *pain*

Medical word definition: Condition of many muscle pains

14. rhabdomyoma

Suffix and its meaning: -oma *tumor; mass*

Prefix and its meaning: none

Combining form and its meaning: rhabd/o- *rod shaped*

Combining form and its meaning: my/o- *muscle*

Medical word definition: Tumor with rod-shaped (cells of the) muscle

15. tenosynovitis

Suffix and its meaning: -itis *inflammation of; infection of*

Prefix and its meaning: ten/o- *tendon*

Combining form and its meaning: synov/o- *synovium (membrane)*

Medical word definition: Inflammation of the tendon and synovium

Chapter Quiz

MULTIPLE CHOICE

1. B   4. D   7. B   10. C

2. B   5. D   8. A

3. A   6. A   9. A

FILL IN THE BLANK

1. origin

2. Involuntary

3. increases

4. neuromuscular

5. contraction

6. fibromyalgia

7. ptosis

8. injuries

9. reflex

10. beta

TRUE/FALSE

1. True

2. False (adductor)

3. False (pronation)

4. False (origin)

5. True

6. True

7. False (tibia)

8. True

9. False (corticosteroid drug)

10. False (neuromuscular blocker drugs)

CHAPTER 10
Neurology

Measure Your Progress: Learning Objectives

After reading this chapter, the student should be able to

- Identify the structures of the nervous system.
- Describe the process of nerve transmission.
- Describe common nervous system diseases and conditions, laboratory and diagnostic procedures, medical and surgical procedures, and drug categories.
- Give the medical meaning of word parts related to the nervous system.
- Build nervous system words from word parts and divide and define words.
- Spell and pronounce nervous system words.
- Analyze the medical content and meaning of a neurology report.
- Dive deeper into neurology by reviewing the activities at the end of this chapter and online at Medical Terminology Interactive.

It All Starts with Word Building

Medical language is all about medical words and their word parts. Jump right into this chapter by learning some of the common combining forms and their definitions that you will encounter in this chapter.

affer/o-	bring toward the center	lumb/o-	lower back; area between the ribs and pelvis
arachn/o-	spider; spider web		
astr/o-	starlike structure	meningi/o-	meninges
autonom/o-	independent; self-governing	mening/o-	meninges
		ment/o-	mind; chin
cephal/o-	head	mot/o-	movement
cerebell/o-	cerebellum (posterior part of the brain)	myelin/o-	myelin
		myel/o-	bone marrow; spinal cord; myelin
cerebr/o-	cerebrum (largest part of the brain)	narc/o-	stupor; sleep
comat/o-	unconsciousness	nerv/o-	nerve
concuss/o-	violent shaking or jarring	neur/o-	nerve
		occipit/o-	occiput (back of the head)
crani/o-	cranium (skull)		
dendr/o-	branching structure	pariet/o-	wall of a cavity
disk/o-	disk	pleg/o-	paralyis
dors/o-	back; dorsum	radicul/o-	spinal nerve root
dur/o-	dura mater	sens/o-	sensation
effer/o-	go out from the center	somat/o-	body
		somn/o-	sleep
encephal/o-	brain	spin/o-	spine; backbone
ependym/o-	cellular lining	syncop/o-	fainting
epilept/o-	seizure	temporo/o-	temple (side of the head)
esthes/o-	sensation; feeling		
front/o-	front	thalam/o-	thalamus
gli/o-	cells that provide support	ventricul/o-	ventricle (lower heart chamber; chamber of the brain)
ict/o-	seizure		
lamin/o-	lamina (flat area on the vertebra)	ventr/o-	front; abdomen

Chapter Spelling Test

Dictate and spell (or photocopy a handout that contains) this list of 20 spelling words. Give this list to students to study for the week. At the beginning of next week's class, dictate 10 of these words as the spelling test. The spelling test is included with the chapter test that is given on the previous week's material.

1. Alzheimer's dementia
2. astrocytoma
3. cephalalgia
4. cerebrovascular accident
5. dysphasia
6. electroencephalogram
7. encephalitis
8. epilepsy
9. grand mal seizure
10. hemiparesis
11. meninges
12. neurosurgery
13. paresthesia
14. polysomnography
15. quadriplegic
16. radiculopathy
17. rhizotomy
18. sciatica
19. subdural hematoma
20. syncope

Chapter Pronunciation Test

Photocopy a handout that contains this list of 20 pronunciation words. Give this list to students to study for the week. Sometime in the beginning of the next week, each student should call your office or home answering machine and pronounce each word.

1. aphasia (ah-FAY-zee-ah)

2. cephalalgia (SEF-al-AL-jee-ah)

3. cerebrovascular (SAIR-eh-broh-VAS-kyoo-lar) (seh-REE-broh-VAS-kyoo-lar)

4. dysphasia (dis-FAY-zee-ah)

5. electroencephalogram (ee-LEK-troh-en-SEF-ah-loh-gram)

6. encephalitis (en-SEF-ah-LY-tis)

7. epilepsy (EP-ih-LEP-see)

8. hemiparesis.(HEM-ee-pah-REE-sis)

9. intraventricular (IN-trah-ven-TRIK-yoo-lar)

10. medulla oblongata (meh-DUL-ah AWB-long-GAW-tah) (meh-DOOL-ah)

11. meninges (meh-NIN-jeez)

12. meningomyelocele (meh-NING-goh-MY-loh-seel)

13. paresthesia (PAIR-es-THEE-zee-ah)

14. polysomnography (PAWL-ee-sawm-NAWG-rah-fee)

15. quadriplegic (KWAH-drih-PLEE-jik)

16. radiculopathy (rah-DIK-yoo-LAWP-oh-thee)

17. rhizotomy (ry-ZAW-toh-mee)

18. sciatica (sy-AT-ih-kah)

19. subdural hematoma (sub-DOO-ral HEE-mah-TOH-mah)

20. syncope (SIN-koh-pee)

Word Search

Complete this word search puzzle that contains Chapter 10 words. Look for the following words as given in the list below. The number in parentheses indicates how many times the word appears in the puzzle.

aphasia   glioma
auras   gyrus
axon   hemiparesis
brain (2)   lobe
cerebral   myelin
CNS   nerve
coma   nervous
cortex   pons
dementia   RIND
dural   sulcus
EEG   TENS
epilepsy

```
Y  S  P  E  L  I  P  E  L  D  H
A  Z  A  G  C  H  C  O  R  E  E
I  Q  X  J  E  O  B  N  M  M  A
S  U  O  V  R  E  N  I  S  E  M
A  B  N  T  E  Q  P  L  N  N  O
H  F  E  V  B  A  G  E  E  T  I
P  X  R  R  R  M  C  Y  T  I  L
A  E  A  E  A  O  L  M  R  A  G
N  I  S  U  L  C  U  S  R  U  F
N  I  A  R  B  K  A  U  R  A  S
S  N  O  P  J  S  D  N  I  R  W
```

Crossword Puzzle

ACROSS

2. Cranial nerve XI, the
   _____ nerve, is
   responsible for movement of muscles
   in the throat, neck, and upper back.

4. _____ is the
   condition in which there is an
   excessive amount of cerebrospinal
   fluid produced or the flow of
   cerebrospinal fluid is blocked.

7. The _____ is
   composed of the midbrain, pons, and
   the medulla oblongata.

8. The combining form
   "_____" means
   cells that provide support.

9. The _____
   division of the autonomic nervous
   system is active when the body is
   sleeping, resting, eating—the "rest
   and digest" activities.

10. The combining form
    "_____" means
    unconsiousness.

DOWN

1. A loss of the ability to communicate
   verbally or in writing is referred to
   as _____.

3. The only connection between the left
   and right hemispheres of the brain is
   the structure of the
   _____
   _____.

5. A spinal nerve and ventral nerve
   root are characterized as
   _____ nerves
   because they carry nerve impulses
   away from the spinal cord to the
   body.

6. The _____ lobe
   analyzes sensory information about
   taste.

Underline the Accented Syllable

Read the medical word. Then review the syllables in the pronunciation. Underline the primary (main) accented syllable in the pronunciation.

1. amyotrophic   (ah-my-oh-troh-fik)

2. Babinski   (bah-bin-ski)

3. cauda equine   (kaw-dah ee-kwy-nah)

4. craniotomy   (kray-nee-aw-toh-mee)

5. glioma   (gly-oh-mah)

6. hyperesthesia   (hy-per-es-thee-zee-ah)

7. meningioma   (meh-nin-jee-oh-mah)

8. meningomyelocele   (meh-ning-goh-my-loh-seel)

9. neurofibromatosis   (nyoor-oh-fy-broh-mah-toh-sis)

10. oligodendroglia   (ol-ih-goh-den-drohg-lee-ah)

11. paraplegia   (pair-ah-plee-jee-ah)

12. polysomnography   (pawl-ee-sawm-nawg-rah fee)

13. radiculopathy   (rah-dik-yoo-lawp-ah-thee)

14. sciatica   (sy-at-ih-kah)

15. sulci   (sul-sigh)

Word Surgery

Read the medical word. Break the medical word into its word parts and give the meaning of each word part. Then give the definition of the medical word.

1. antiepileptic

   Suffix and its meaning: _____

   Prefix and its meaning: _____

   Combining form and its meaning: _____

   Medical word definition: _____

2. aphasia

   Suffix and its meaning: _____

   Prefix and its meaning: _____

   Combining form and its meaning: _____

   Medical word definition: _____

3. cerebrovascular

   Suffix and its meaning: _____

   Prefix and its meaning: _____

   Combining form and its meaning: _____

   Combining form and its meaning: _____

   Medical word definition: _____

4. dementia

   Suffix and its meaning: _____

   Prefix and its meaning: _____

   Combining form and its meaning: _____

   Medical word definition: _____

5. demyelination

   Suffix and its meaning: _____

   Prefix and its meaning: _____

   Combining form and its meaning: _____

   Medical word definition: _____

6. dyslexic

Suffix and its meaning: _____

Prefix and its meaning: _____

Combining form and its meaning: _____

Medical word definition: _____

7. electroencephalography

Suffix and its meaning: _____

Prefix and its meaning: _____

Combining form and its meaning: _____

Combining form and its meaning: _____

Medical word definition: _____

8. hemiplegic

Suffix and its meaning: _____

Prefix and its meaning: _____

Combining form and its meaning: _____

Medical word definition: _____

9. hyperesthesia

Suffix and its meaning: _____

Prefix and its meaning: _____

Combining form and its meaning: _____

Medical word definition: _____

10. hypoglossal

Suffix and its meaning: _____

Prefix and its meaning: _____

Combining form and its meaning: _____

Medical word definition: _____

11. meningitis

Suffix and its meaning: _____

Prefix and its meaning: _____

Combining form and its meaning: _____

Medical word definition: _____

12. neuralgia

   Suffix and its meaning: _____

   Prefix and its meaning: _____

   Combining form and its meaning: _____

   Combining form and its meaning: _____

   Medical word definition: _____

13. paresthesia

   Suffix and its meaning: _____

   Prefix and its meaning: _____

   Combining form and its meaning: _____

   Medical word definition: _____

14. polysomnography

   Suffix and its meaning: _____

   Prefix and its meaning: _____

   Combining form and its meaning: _____

   Medical word definition: _____

15. postictal

   Suffix and its meaning: _____

   Prefix and its meaning: _____

   Combining form and its meaning: _____

   Medical word definition: _____

Chapter Quiz

MULTIPLE CHOICE

1. Which two combining forms mean "nerve"?

    A. meningi/o- and ment/o-

    B. nerv/o- and narc/o-

    C. neur/o- and nerv/o-

    D. myelin/o- and ment/o-

2. There are 12 cranial nerves; the eighth cranial nerve receives sensory information about:

    A. sounds.

    B. taste.

    C. smell.

    D. touch.

3. Which of the following is the system that controls voluntary skeletal muscles?

    A. somatic nervous system

    B. autonomic nervous system

    C. parasympathetic division

    D. sympathetic division

4. Four hollow chambers within the brain that contain cerebrospinal fluid are the:

    A. sulci.

    B. ventricles.

    C. lobes.

    D. gyri.

5. The prefix "tri-" in trigeminal means:

    A. nerve.

    B. sensation.

    C. myelin.

    D. three.

6. Which of the following is a congenital genetic defect that results in mild to severe mental retardation?

   A. Alzheimer's disease

   B. concussion

   C. dementia

   D. Down syndrome

7. The temporary loss of consciousness that may be caused by the stenosis and plaque that blocks the carotid arteries is called:

   A. Huntington's chorea.

   B. syncope.

   C. neural tube defect.

   D. subdural hematoma.

8. The prefix "quadri-," as in quadriplegia, means:

   A. four.

   B. three.

   C. below.

   D. condition of.

9. The condition of abnormal sensations such as tingling, burning, or pinpricks is:

   A. neurofibromatosis.

   B. neuroma.

   C. paresthesia.

   D. neuropathy.

10. Computed axial tomography:

   A. uses a strong magnetic field to make an image.

   B. is a radiologic procedure that uses x-rays to make closely spaced images.

   C. uses sound waves to make an image.

   D. is a treatment regimen.

FILL IN THE BLANK

1. A neurologic test in which the end of a metal handle is used to stroke the sole of the foot is known as the _____ sign.

2. A surgical procedure that removes the flat area of the arch of a vertebra is a

   _____.

3. Acetaminophen, aspirin, and ibuprofen are _____ nonsteroidal drugs.

4. Each pair of spinal nerves is named according to the _____ next to it.

5. An involuntary muscle reaction that is controlled by the _____ is a reflex.

6. A fatal neurologic disorder caused by the presence of an infectious agent known as a _____ is Creutzfeldt-Jakob disease.

7. Bell's _____ is a weakness, with drooping or paralysis of one side of the face due to viral infection of the facial nerve.

8. Neuritis is inflammation or infection of a nerve, whereas _____ is a generalized inflammation of many nerves.

9. A _____ _____ is performed to acquire a sample of cerebrospinal fluid.

10. _____ are physicians who perform surgery on the brain, spinal cord, and nerves.

TRUE/FALSE

_____ 1. The central nervous system includes the brain and spinal cord.

_____ 2. Afferent nerves carry nerve impulses away from the spinal cord.

_____ 3. The middle layer of the meninges is the dura mater.

_____ 4. The fatty sheath around a large axon is known as the myelin sheath.

_____ 5. A disease of the brain in older persons in which many neurons in the cerebrum die is mental retardation.

_____ 6. Amyotrophic lateral sclerosis is also known as Lou Gehrig's disease.

_____ 7. An astrocytoma is most likely a benign tumor.

_____ 8. Testing of the patient's concrete and abstract reasoning is done during a mini-mental status examination.

_____ 9. The *Latin* combining form for "mind" is "ment/o-" and the *Greek* form is "psych/o-."

_____ 10. Drugs used to prevent the seizures of epilepsy are known as antiepileptic or anticonvulsant drugs.

Pronunciation Checklist

Read each word and its pronunciation. Practice pronouncing each word. Verify your pronunciation by listening to the Pronunciation List on Medical Terminology Interactive. Check the box next to the word after you master its pronunciation.

- ❏ abducens nerve (ab-DOO-senz NERV)
- ❏ absence seizure (AB-sens SEE-zher)
- ❏ accessory nerve (ak-SES-oh-ree NERV)
- ❏ acetylcholine (AS-ee-til-KOH-leen)
- ❏ afferent nerve (AF-eh-rent NERV)
- ❏ alpha fetoprotein (AL-fah FEE-toh-PROH-teen)
- ❏ Alzheimer's disease (AWLZ-hy-merz dih-ZEEZ)
- ❏ amnesia (am-NEE-zee-ah)
- ❏ amyotrophic lateral sclerosis (ah-MY-oh-TROH-fik LAT-eh-ral skleh-ROH-sis)
- ❏ analgesic drug (AN-al-JEE-zik DRUHG)
- ❏ anencephaly (AN-en-SEF-ah-lee)
- ❏ anesthesia (AN-es-THEE-zee-ah)
- ❏ anesthetic drug (AN-es-THET-ik DRUHG)
- ❏ angiogram (AN-jee-oh-gram)
- ❏ angiography (AN-jee-AWG-rah-fee)
- ❏ anticonvulsant drug (AN-tee-con-VUL-sant DRUHG) (AN-tih-con-VUL-sant)
- ❏ antiepileptic drug (AN-tee-EP-ih-LEP-tik DRUHG) (AN-tih-EP-ih-LEP-tik)
- ❏ aphasia (ah-FAY-zee-ah)
- ❏ aphasic (ah-FAY-sik)
- ❏ arachnoid membrane (ah-RAK-noyd MEM-brayn)
- ❏ arteriogram (ar-TEER-ee-oh-gram)
- ❏ arteriography (ar-TEER-ee-AWG-rah-fee)
- ❏ arteriovenous malformation (ar-TEER-ee-oh-VEE-nus MAL-for-MAY-shun)
- ❏ astrocyte (AS-troh-site)
- ❏ astrocytoma (AS-troh-sy-TOH-mah)
- ❏ auditory cortex (AW-dih-TOR-ee KOR-teks)

- ❏ aura (AW-rah)
- ❏ automatism (aw-TAW-mah-tizm)
- ❏ autonomic nervous system (AW-toh-NAWM-ik NER-vus SIS-tem)
- ❏ axon (AK-sawn)
- ❏ Babinski's sign (bah-BIN-skeez SIGHN)
- ❏ benign (bee-NINE)
- ❏ biopsy (BY-awp-see)
- ❏ brain (BRAYN)
- ❏ brainstem (BRAYN-stem)
- ❏ carotid duplex scan (kah-ROT-id DOO-pleks SKAN)
- ❏ carotid endarterectomy (kah-RAWT-id END-ar-ter-EK-toh-mee)
- ❏ carpal tunnel syndrome (KAR-pal TUN-el SIN-drohm)
- ❏ cauda equina (KAW-dah ee-KWY-nah)
- ❏ causalgia (kaw-ZAL-jee-ah)
- ❏ central nervous system (SEN-tral NER-vus SIS-tem)
- ❏ cephalalgia (SEF-al-AL-jee-ah)
- ❏ cerebellar (SAIR-eh-BEL-ar)
- ❏ cerebellum (SAIR-eh-BEL-um)
- ❏ cerebral hemisphere (SAIR-eh-bral HEM-ih-sfeer) (seh-REE-bral)
- ❏ cerebral palsy (SAIR-eh-bral PAWL-zee) (seh-REE-bral)
- ❏ cerebrospinal fluid (SAIR-eh-broh-SPY-nal FLOO-id) (seh-REE-broh-SPY-nal)
- ❏ cerebrovascular accident (SAIR-eh-broh-VAS-kyoo-lar AK-sih-dent) (seh-REE-broh-VAS-kyoo-lar)
- ❏ cerebrum (SAIR-eh-brum) (seh-REE-brum)
- ❏ coma (KOH-mah)
- ❏ comatose (KOH-mah-tohs)
- ❏ computed axial tomography (com-PYOO-ted AK-see-al toh-MAWG-rah-fee)
- ❏ concussion (con-KUH-shun)
- ❏ contusion (con-TOO-shun)

- ❏ convulsion (con-VUL-shun)
- ❏ corpus callosum (KOR-pus kah-LOH-sum)
- ❏ cortex (KOR-teks)
- ❏ cortical (KOR-tih-kal)
- ❏ corticosteroid drug (KOR-tih-koh-STAIR-oyd DRUHG)
- ❏ cranial cavity (KRAY-nee-al KAV-ih-tee)
- ❏ craniotomy (KRAY-nee-AW-toh-mee)
- ❏ cranium (KRAY-nee-um)
- ❏ Creutzfeldt-Jakob disease (KROITS-felt YAH-kohp dih-ZEEZ)
- ❏ dementia (deh-MEN-shee-ah)
- ❏ dendrite (DEN-dryt)
- ❏ diabetic neuropathy (DY-ah-BET-ik nyoo-RAWP-ah-thee)
- ❏ diskectomy (dis-KEK-toh-mee)
- ❏ dopamine (DOH-pah-meen)
- ❏ dorsal (DOR-sal)
- ❏ dural membrane (DOO-ral MEM-brayn)
- ❏ dura mater (DOO-rah MAY-ter) (DOO-rah MAH-ter)
- ❏ dyslexia (dis-LEK-see-ah)
- ❏ dyslexic (dis-LEK-sik)
- ❏ dysphasia (dis-FAY-zee-ah)
- ❏ efferent nerve (EF-eh-rent NERV)
- ❏ electroencephalogram (ee-LEK-troh-en-SEF-ah-loh-gram)
- ❏ electroencephalograph (ee-LEK-troh-en-SEF-ah-loh-graf)
- ❏ electroencephalography (ee-LEK-troh-en-SEF-ah-LAWG-rah-fee)
- ❏ encephalitis (en-SEF-ah-LY-tis)
- ❏ endorphins (en-DOR-finz)
- ❏ ependymal cell (eh-PEN-dih-mal SELL)
- ❏ ependymoma (eh-PEN-dih-MOH-mah)
- ❏ epidural (EP-ih-DOO-ral)
- ❏ epilepsy (EP-ih-LEP-see)

- epileptic (EP-ih-LEP-tik)
- epinephrine (EP-ih-NEF-rin)
- evoked potential (ee-VOKED poh-TEN-shal)
- excisional biopsy (ek-SIH-shun-al BY-awp-see)
- expressive aphasia (eks-PREH-siv ah-FAY-zee-ah)
- facial nerve (FAY-shal NERV)
- fissure (FISH-ur)
- flaccid paralysis (FLAS-id pah-RAL-ih-sis) (FLAK-sid)
- focal seizure (FOH-kal SEE-zher)
- frontal lobe (FRUN-tal LOHB)
- Glasgow Coma Scale (GLAS-goh KOH-mah SKAYL)
- glioblastoma multiforme (GLY-oh-blas-TOH-mah MUL-tih-FOR-may)
- glioma (gly-OH-mah)
- global aphasia (GLOH-bal ah-FAY-zee-ah)
- glossopharyngeal nerve (GLAWS-oh-fah-RIN-jee-al NERV)
- grand mal seizure (GRAN MAWL SEE-zher)
- Guillain-Barré syndrome (GEE-yah bah-RAY SIN-drohm)
- gustatory cortex (GUS-tah-TOR-ee KOR-teks)
- gyri (JY-rye)
- gyrus (JY-rus)
- hematoma (HEE-mah-TOH-mah)
- hemiparesis (HEM-ee-pah-REE-sis) (HEM-ee-PAIR-eh-sis)
- hemiplegia (HEM-ee-PLEE-jee-ah)
- hemiplegic (HEM-ee-PLEE-jik)
- hemisphere (HEM-ih-sfeer)
- herniated nucleus pulposus (HER-nee-AA-ted NOO-klee-us pul-POH-sus)
- hippocampus (HIP-oh-KAM-pus)
- Huntington's chorea (HUN-ting-tonz kor-EE-ah)
- hydrocephalic (HY-droh-sih-FAL-ik)
- hydrocephalus (HY-droh-SEF-ah-lus)
- hyperesthesia (HY-per-es-THEE-zee-ah)
- hypoglossal nerve (HY-poh-GLAWS-al)

- hypothalamic (HY-poh-thah-LAM-ik)
- hypothalamus (HY-poh-THAL-ah-mus)
- infarct (IN-farkt)
- inhibitor (in-HIB-ih-tor)
- intracranial (IN-trah-KRAY-nee-al)
- intraventricular (IN-trah-ven-TRIK-yoo-lar)
- ischemia (is-KEE-mee-ah)
- ischemic (is-KEE-mik)
- laminectomy (LAM-ih-NEK-toh-mee)
- lobe (LOHB)
- lumbar puncture (LUM-bar PUNK-chur)
- lymphoma (lim-FOH-mah)
- magnetic resonance imaging (mag-NET-ik REZ-oh-nans IM-ah-jing)
- malignant (mah-LIG-nant)
- medulla oblongata (meh-DUL-ah AWB-long-GAW-tah) (meh-DOOL-ah)
- meningeal (meh-NIN-jee-al) (MEN-in-JEE-al)
- meninges (meh-NIN-jeez)
- meningioma (meh-NIN-jee-OH-mah)
- meningitis (MEN-in-JY-tis)
- meningocele (meh-NING-goh-seel)
- meningomyelocele (meh-NING-goh-MY-loh-seel)
- mental retardation (MEN-tal REE-tar-DAY-shun)
- mental status (MEN-tal STAT-us)
- microglia (my-KROHG-lee-ah)
- migraine (MY-grayn)
- motor nerve (MOH-tor NERV)
- multiple sclerosis (MUL-tih-pl skleh-ROH-sis)
- myelin (MY-eh-lin)
- myelinated (MY-eh-lih-NAYT-ed)
- myelogram (MY-eh-loh-gram)
- myelography (MY-eh-LAWG-rah-fee)
- myelomeningocele (MY-loh-meh-NING-goh-seel)
- narcolepsy (NAR-koh-LEP-see)
- narcotic drug (nar-KAWT-ik DRUHG)

- nerve (NERV)
- nerve conduction (NERV con-DUK-shun)
- nervous system (NER-vus SIS-tem)
- neural (NYOOR-al)
- neuralgia (nyoo-RAL-jee-ah)
- neuritis (nyoo-RY-tis)
- neurofibrillary (NYOOR-oh-FIB-rih-LAIR-ee)
- neurofibroma (NYOOR-oh-fy-BROH-mah)
- neurofibromatosis (NYOOR-oh-fy-BROH-mah-TOH-sis)
- neuroglia (nyoo-ROH-glee-ah)
- neurologic (NYOOR-oh-LAWJ-ik)
- neurologic deficit (NYOOR-oh-LAWJ-ik DEF-ih-sit)
- neurologist (nyoo-RAWL-oh-jist)
- neurology (nyoo-RAWL-oh-jee)
- neuroma (nyoo-ROH-mah)
- neuromuscular system (NYOOR-oh-MUS-kyoo-lar SIS-tem)
- neuron (NYOOR-on)
- neuropathy (nyoo-RAWP-ah-thee)
- neurosurgeon (NYOOR-oh-SER-jun)
- neurotransmitter (NYOOR-oh-TRANS-mit-er)
- norepinephrine (NOR-ep-ih-NEF-rin)
- nuchal rigidity (NOO-kal rih-GID-ih-tee)
- nucleus pulposus (NOO-klee-us pul-POH-sus)
- occipital lobe (awk-SIP-ih-tal LOHB)
- oculomotor nerve (AWK-yoo-loh-MOH-tor NERV)
- olfactory cortex (ol-FAK-toh-ree KOR-teks)
- olfactory nerve (ol-FAK-toh-ree NERV)
- oligodendroglia (OL-ih-goh-den-DROHG-lee-ah)
- oligodendroglioma (OL-ih-goh-den-DROH-gly-OH-mah)
- optic nerve (AWP-tik NERV)
- palsy (PAWL-see)
- paralysis (pah-RAL-ih-sis)
- paraplegia (PAIR-ah-PLEE-jee-ah)

- paraplegic (PAIR-ah-PLEE-jik)
- parasympathetic nervous system (PAIR-ah-SIM-pah-THET-ik NER-vus SIS-tem)
- paresthesia (PAIR-es-THEE-zee-ah)
- parietal lobe (pah-RY-eh-tal LOHB)
- Parkinson's disease (PAR-kin-sonz dih-ZEEZ)
- peripheral nervous system (peh-RIF-eh-ral NER-vus SIS-tem)
- petit mal seizure (peh-TEE MAWL SEE-zher)
- photophobia (FOH-toh-FOH-bee-ah)
- pia mater (PY-ah MAY-ter) (PEE-ah MAH-ter)
- plaque (PLAK)
- polyneuritis (PAWL-ee-nyoo-RY-tis)
- polysomnography (PAWL-ee-sawm-NAWG-rah-fee)
- pons (PAWNZ)
- positron emission tomography (PAWZ-ih-trawn ee-MISH-un toh-MAWG-rah-fee)
- postictal (post-IK-tal)
- presenile dementia (pree-SEE-nile deh-MEN-shee-ah)
- proprioception (PROH-pree-oh-SEP-shun)
- psychomotor seizure (SY-koh-MOH-tor SEE-zher)
- quadriplegia (KWAH-drih-PLEE-jee-ah)
- quadriplegic (KWAH-drih-PLEE-jik)
- radiculopathy (rah-DIK-yoo-LAWP-oh-thee)

- receptive aphasia (ree-SEP-tiv ah-FAY-zee-ah)
- receptor (ree-SEP-tor)
- reflex (REE-fleks)
- rhizotomy (ry-ZAW-toh-mee)
- Romberg test (RAWM-berg TEST)
- Schwann cell (SHVAHN SELL)
- schwannoma (shwah-NOH-mah)
- sciatica (sy-AT-ih-kah)
- seizure (SEE-zher)
- senile dementia (SEE-nile deh-MEN-shee-ah)
- sensory nerve (SEN-soh-ree NERV)
- serotonin (SAIR-oh-TOH-nin)
- somatic nervous system (soh-MAT-ik NER-vus SIS-tem)
- somatosensory (soh-MAH-toh-SEN-soh-ree)
- spastic (SPAS-tik)
- spina bifida (SPY-nah BIF-ih-dah)
- spinal canal (SPY-nal kah-NAL)
- spinal cavity (SPY-nal KAV-ih-tee)
- spinal cord (SPY-nal KORD)
- spinal nerve (SPY-nal NERV)
- spinal traction (SPY-nal TRAK-shun)
- status epilepticus (STAT-us EP-ih-LEP-tih-kus)
- stereotactic neurosurgery (STAIR-ee-oh-TAK-tik NYOOR-oh-SER-jer-ee)
- subarachnoid (SUB-ah-RAK-noyd)
- subdural hematoma (sub-DOO-ral HEE-mah-TOH-mah)

- substantia nigra (sub-STAN-shee-ah NY-grah)
- sulci (SUL-sigh)
- sulcus (SUL-kus)
- sympathetic nervous system (SIM-pah-THET-ik NER-vus SIS-tem)
- synapse (SIN-aps)
- syncopal (SIN-koh-pal)
- syncope (SIN-koh-pee)
- tardive dysinesia (TAR-dive DIS-kih-NEE-zee-ah)
- temporal lobe (TEM-poh-ral LOHB)
- thalamic (thah-LAM-ik)
- thalamus (THAL-ah-mus)
- tic douloureux (TIK doo-loo-ROO)
- tonic-clonic seizure (TAWN-ik CLAWN-ik SEE-zher)
- transcutaneous (TRANS-kyoo-TAY-nee-us)
- transection (tran-SEK-shun)
- trigeminal nerve (tri-JEM-ih-nal NERV)
- trochlear nerve (TROH-klee-ar NERV)
- vagus nerve (VAY-gus NERV)
- ventral (VEN-tral)
- ventricle (VEN-trih-kl)
- ventricular (ven-TRIK-yoo-lar)
- ventriculoperitoneal shunt (ven-TRIK-yoo-loh-PAIR-ih-toh-NEE-al SHUNT)
- vestibulocochlear nerve (ves-TIB-yoo-loh-KOH-klee-ar NERV)
- visual cortex (VIH-shoo-al KOR-teks)
- von Recklinghausen's disease (vawn REK-ling-HOW-senz dih-ZEEZ)

Answer Key

Word Search

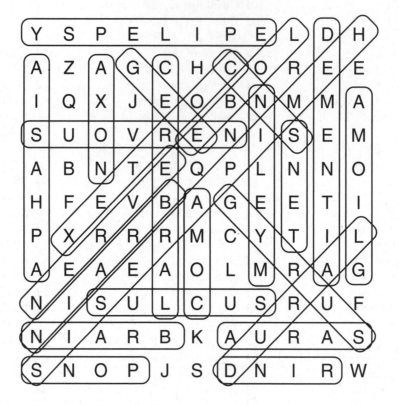

Crossword Puzzle

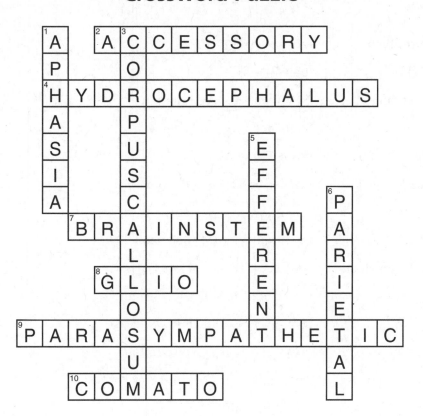

Underline the Accented Syllable

1. amyotrophic   (ah-MY-oh-<u>TROH</u>-fik)

2. Babinski   (bah-<u>BIN</u>-skee)

3. cauda equina   (<u>KAW</u>-dah ee-<u>KWY</u>-nah)

4. craniotomy   (KRAY-nee-<u>AW</u>-toh-mee)

5. glioma   (gly-<u>OH</u>-mah)

6. hyperesthesia   (HY-per-es-<u>THEE</u>-zee-ah)

7. meningioma   (meh-NIN-jee-<u>OH</u>-mah)

8. meningomyelocele   (meh-NING-goh-<u>MY</u>-loh-seel)

9. neurofibromatosis   (NYOOR-oh-fy-BROH-mah-<u>TOH</u>-sis)

10. oligodendroglia   (OL-ih-goh-den-<u>DROHG</u>-lee-ah)

11. paraplegia   (PAIR-ah-<u>PLEE</u>-jee-ah)

12. polysomnography   (PAWL-ee-sawm-<u>NAWG</u>-rah-fee)

13. radiculopathy   (rah-DIK-yoo-<u>LAWP</u>-oh-thee)

14. sciatica   (sy-<u>AT</u>-ih-kah)

15. sulci   (<u>SUL</u>-sigh)

Word Surgery

1. antiepileptic

   Suffix and its meaning: -ic *pertaining to*

   Prefix and its meaning: anti- *against*

   Combining form and its meaning: epilept/o- *seizure*

   Medical word definition: Pertaining to (being) against seizures

2. aphasia

   Suffix and its meaning: -ia *condition; state; thing*

   Prefix and its meaning: a- *without; not*

   Combining form and its meaning: phas/o- *speech*

   Medical word definition: Condition (of being) without speech

3. cerebrovascular

   Suffix and its meaning: -ar *pertaining to*

   Prefix and its meaning: none

   Combining form and its meaning: cerebr/o- *cerebrum (largest part of the brain)*

   Combining form and its meaning: vascul/o- *blood vessel*

   Medical word definition: Pertaining to the cerebrum and blood vessels

4. dementia

   Suffix and its meaning: : -ia *condition; state; thing*

   Prefix and its meaning: de- *reversal of; without*

   Combining form and its meaning: ment/o- *mind; chin*

   Medical word definition: Condition (of being) without the mind

5. demyelination

   Suffix and its meaning: -ation *a process; being or having*

   Prefix and its meaning: de- *reversal of; without*

   Combining form and its meaning: myelin/o- *myelin*

   Medical word definition: A process (of being) without myelin

6. dyslexic

   Suffix and its meaning: -ia *condition; state; thing*

   Prefix and its meaning: dys- *painful; difficult; abnormal*

   Combining form and its meaning: lex/o- *word*

   Medical word definition: Condition (of having) difficulty with words

7. electroencephalography

   Suffix and its meaning: -graphy *process of recording*

   Prefix and its meaning: none

   Combining form and its meaning: electr/o- *electricity*

   Combining form and its meaning: encephal/o- *brain*

   Medical word definition: Process of recording the electricity of the brain

8. hemiplegic

   Suffix and its meaning: -ic *pertaining to*

   Prefix and its meaning: hemi- *one half*

   Combining form and its meaning: pleg/o- *paralysis*

   Medical word definition: Pertaining to one half (of the body having) paralysis

9. hyperesthesia

   Suffix and its meaning: -ia *condition; state; thing*

   Prefix and its meaning: hyper- *above; more than normal*

   Combining form and its meaning: esthes/o- *sensation; feeling*

   Medical word definition: Condition of more than normal sensation and feeling

10. hypoglossal

   Suffix and its meaning: -al *pertaining to*

   Prefix and its meaning: hypo- *below; deficient*

   Combining form and its meaning: gloss/o- *tongue*

   Medical word definition: Pertaining to below the tongue

11. meningitis

   Suffix and its meaning: : -itis *inflammation of; infection of*

   Prefix and its meaning: none

   Combining form and its meaning: mening/o- *meninges*

   Medical word definition: Inflammation or infection of the meninges

12. neuralgia

    Suffix and its meaning: -ia *condition; state; thing*

    Prefix and its meaning: none

    Combining form and its meaning: neur/o- *nerve*

    Combining form and its meaning: alg/o- *pain*

    Medical word definition: Condition of nerve pain

13. paresthesia

    Suffix and its meaning: -ia *condition; state; thing*

    Prefix and its meaning: para- *beside; apart from; two parts of a pair; abnormal*

    Combining form and its meaning: esthes/o- *sensation; feeling*

    Medical word definition: Condition of abnormal sensation or feeling

14. polysomnography

    Suffix and its meaning: -graphy *process of recording*

    Prefix and its meaning: poly- *many; much*

    Combining form and its meaning: somn/o- *sleep*

    Medical word definition: Process of recording many (different things during) sleep

15. postictal

    Suffix and its meaning: -al *pertaining to*

    Prefix and its meaning: post- *after; behind*

    Combining form and its meaning: ict/o- *seizure*

    Medical word definition: Pertaining to after a seizure

Chapter Quiz

MULTIPLE CHOICE

1. C	4. B	7. B	10. B
2. A	5. D	8. A	
3. A	6. D	9. C	

FILL IN THE BLANK

1. Babinski's
2. laminectomy
3. analgesic
4. vertebra
5. spinal cord
6. prion
7. palsy
8. polyneuritis
9. lumbar puncture (or spinal tap)
10. Neurosurgeons

TRUE/FALSE

1. True
2. False (efferent)
3. False (arachnoid)
4. True
5. False (dementia)
6. True
7. False (malignant)
8. True
9. True
10. True

Copyright © 2011 by Pearson Education, Inc.

Urology

Measure Your Progress: Learning Objectives

After reading this chapter, the student should be able to

- Identify the structures of the urinary system.
- Describe the process of urine production and excretion.
- Describe common urinary diseases and conditions, laboratory and diagnostic procedures, medical and surgical procedures, and drug categories.
- Give the medical meaning of word parts related to the urinary system.
- Build urinary words from word parts and divide and define urinary words.
- Spell and pronounce urinary words.
- Analyze the medical content and meaning of a urology report.
- Dive deeper into urology by reviewing the activities at the end of this chapter and online at Medical Terminology Interactive.

It All Starts with Word Building

Medical language is all about medical words and their word parts. Jump right into this chapter by learning some of the common combining forms and their definitions that you will encounter in this chapter.

albumin/o-	albumin
calcul/o-	stone
calic/o-	calix
cali/o-	calix
catheter/o-	catheter
cyst/o-	bladder; fluid-filled sac; semisolid cyst
enur/o-	to urinate
excret/o-	removing from the body
glomerul/o-	glomerulus
glycos/o-	glucose (sugar)
hemat/o-	blood
keton/o-	ketones
lith/o-	stone
micturi/o-	making urine
nephr/o-	kidney; nephron
olig/o-	scanty; few
pyel/o-	renal pelvis
py/o-	pus
ren/o-	kidney
ureter/o-	ureter
urethr/o-	urethra
ur/o-	urine; urinary system
vesic/o-	bladder; fluid-filled sac

Chapter Spelling Test

Dictate and spell (or photocopy a handout that contains) this list of 20 spelling words. Give this list to students to study for the week. At the beginning of next week's class, dictate 10 of these words as the spelling test. The spelling test is included with the chapter test that is given on the previous week's material.

1. albuminuria
2. catheterization
3. creatinine
4. cystitis
5. cystoscopy
6. diuretic drug
7. glomerulonephritis
8. hemodialysis
9. hypospadias
10. incontinence
11. intravesical
12. lithotripsy
13. nephrolithiasis
14. nephroptosis
15. nocturia
16. pyelonephritis
17. retroperitoneal space
18. ureter
19. urethra
20. urinalysis

Chapter Pronunciation Test

Photocopy a handout that contains this list of 20 pronunciation words. Give this list to students to study for the week. Sometime at the beginning of the next week, each student should call your office or home answering machine and pronounce each word.

1. caliectasis (KAY-lee-EK-tah-sis)

2. catheterization (KATH-eh-TER-ih-ZAY-shun)

3. creatinine (kree-AT-ih-neen)

4. cystitis (sis-TY-tis)

5. cystocele (SIS-toh-seel)

6. dysuria (dis-YOO-ree-ah)

7. epispadias (EP-ih-SPAY-dee-as)

8. glomerulonephritis (gloh-MAIR-yoo-loh-neh-FRY-tis)

9. hemodialysis (HEE-moh-dy-AL-ih-sis)

10. hydronephrosis (HY-droh-neh-FROH-sis)

11. incontinence (in-CON-tih-nens)

12. lithotripsy (LITH-oh-TRIP-see)

13. nephrolithiasis (NEF-roh-lih-THY-ah-sis)

14. nephrologist (neh-FRAWL-oh-jist)

15. nocturia (nawk-TYOO-ree-ah)

16. pyelonephritis (PY-eh-loh-neh-FRY-tis)

17. retroperitoneal (REH-troh-PAIR-ih-toh-NEE-al)

18. ureter (YOO-ree-ter) (yoo-REE-ter)

19. urethra (yoo-REE-thrah)

20. urinalysis (YOO-rih-NAL-ih-sis)

Word Search

Complete this word search puzzle that contains Chapter 11 words. Look for the following words as given in the list below. The number in parentheses indicates how many times the word appears in the puzzle.

anuria	pyuria
bladder	renal (2)
BUN	renin
cystitis	rugae
enuresis	urea
ESRD	ureter
hilum	urinalysis
IVP	urine
kidneys	UTI

```
E  N  U  R  E  S  I  S  X  A
D  J  A  I  R  U  Y  P  N  F
E  N  I  R  U  E  V  U  U  C
U  S  T  E  N  I  R  K  B  Y
R  T  R  D  H  I  L  U  M  S
E  W  I  D  A  R  N  B  P  T
T  K  Y  A  U  E  I  E  O  I
E  V  E  L  A  N  E  R  R  T
R  R  T  B  E  A  G  U  R  I
U  R  I  N  A  L  Y  S  I  S
```

Crossword Puzzle

ACROSS

2. A _____ catheter is an indwelling tube with an expandable balloon tip that drains urine continuously.

4. The combining form "glycos/o-" means sugar or _____.

5. _____ is a condition caused by excessive amounts of the waste product urea in the blood due to renal failure.

8. Patients with uncontrolled diabetes mellitus or malnutrition or marathon runners excrete _____ in the urine because the body cannot use or does not have enough glucose and instead metabolizes fat.

9. The medical procedure that is used to get rid of wastes when the kidneys are not functioning is called _____.

DOWN

1. A decreased amount of potassium in the blood is known as _____.

3. The microscopic, functional unit of the kidney and the site of urine production is the _____.

6. The _____ is a 12-inch tube that connects the renal pelvis of the kidney to the bladder.

7. The rounded top (dome) of the bladder is known as the _____.

10. The combining form "_____" means stone.

Underline the Accented Syllable

Read the medical word. Then review the syllables in the pronunciation. Underline the primary (main) accented syllable in the pronunciation.

1. anuria   (an-yoo-ree-ah)

2. bacteriuria   (bac-teer-ee-yoo-ree-ah)

3. calices   (kal-ih-seez)

4. creatinine   (kree-at-ih-neen)

5. cystourethrography   (sis-toh-yoo-ree-thrawg-rah-fee)

6. electrolyte   (ee-lek-troh-lite)

7. epispadias   (ep-ih-spay-dee-as)

8. erythropoietin   (eh-rith-roh-poy-eh-tin)

9. glomeruli   (gloh-mair-yoo-lie)

10. ketonuria   (kee-toh-nyoo-ree-ah)

11. lithotripsy   (lith-oh-trip-see)

12. nephrolithotomy   (nef-roh-lih-thaw-toh-mee)

13. nephropexy   (nef-roh-pek-see)

14. rugae   (roo-gee)

15. vesicocele   (ves-ih-koh-seel)

Word Surgery

Read the medical word. Break the medical word into its word parts and give the meaning of each word part. Then give the definition of the medical word.

1. anuria

   Suffix and its meaning: _____

   Prefix and its meaning: _____

   Combining form and its meaning: _____

   Medical word definition: _____

2. cystoscopy

   Suffix and its meaning: _____

   Prefix and its meaning: _____

   Combining form and its meaning: _____

   Medical word definition: _____

3. epispadias

   Suffix and its meaning: _____

   Prefix and its meaning: _____

   Combining form and its meaning: _____

   Medical word definition: _____

4. glomerulonephritis

   Suffix and its meaning: _____

   Prefix and its meaning: _____

   Combining form and its meaning: _____

   Combining form and its meaning: _____

   Medical word definition: _____

5. hydronephrosis

   Suffix and its meaning: _____

   Prefix and its meaning: _____

   Combining form and its meaning: _____

   Combining form and its meaning: _____

   Medical word definition: _____

6. hypokalemia

   Suffix and its meaning: _____

   Prefix and its meaning: _____

   Combining form and its meaning: _____

   Medical word definition: _____

7. incontinence

   Suffix and its meaning: _____

   Prefix and its meaning: _____

   Combining form and its meaning: _____

   Medical word definition: _____

8. lithotripsy

   Suffix and its meaning: _____

   Prefix and its meaning: _____

   Combining form and its meaning: _____

   Medical word definition: _____

9. nephrolithotomy

   Suffix and its meaning: _____

   Prefix and its meaning: _____

   Combining form and its meaning: _____

   Combining form and its meaning: _____

   Medical word definition: _____

10. nocturia

   Suffix and its meaning: _____

   Prefix and its meaning: _____

   Combining form and its meaning: _____

   Combining form and its meaning: _____

   Medical word definition: _____

11. percutaneous

   Suffix and its meaning: _____

   Prefix and its meaning: _____

   Combining form and its meaning: _____

   Medical word definition: _____

12. polycystic

   Suffix and its meaning: _____

   Prefix and its meaning: _____

   Combining form and its meaning: _____

   Medical word definition: _____

13. pyelonephritis

   Suffix and its meaning: _____

   Prefix and its meaning: _____

   Combining form and its meaning: _____

   Combining form and its meaning: _____

   Medical word definition: _____

14. retroperitoneal

   Suffix and its meaning: _____

   Prefix and its meaning: _____

   Combining form and its meaning: _____

   Medical word definition: _____

15. urologist

   Suffix and its meaning: _____

   Prefix and its meaning: _____

   Combining form and its meaning: _____

   Combining form and its meaning: _____

   Medical word definition: _____

Chapter Quiz

MULTIPLE CHOICE

1. The combining form that refers to making urine is:

    A. ur/o-.

    B. mictur/o-.

    C. pyel/o-.

    D. urethr/o-.

2. Which of the following carries urine from the renal pelvis to the bladder?

    A. ureters

    B. urethra

    C. sphincter

    D. renal hilum

3. The renal pyramids are found in the:

    A. renal cortex.

    B. renal medulla.

    C. flank.

    D. renal calix.

4. A kidney stone is also known as a:

    A. glomerulus.

    B. ketone.

    C. fundus.

    D. calculus.

5. Cystitis is inflammation of the:

    A. bladder.

    B. ureters.

    C. urethra.

    D. prostate gland.

6. Blood found in the urine:

   A. may be caused by a kidney stone.

   B. is called hematuria.

   C. may be caused by bladder cancer.

   D. All of the above.

7. Protein found in the urine:

   A. indicates damage to the glomerulus.

   B. is not a normal finding.

   C. is in the form of albumin.

   D. All of the above.

8. The suffix "-gram" means:

   A. behind.

   B. below.

   C. a record or picture.

   D. a process.

9. A medical procedure in which a flexible tube is inserted through the urethra to drain the bladder is:

   A. catheterization.

   B. abbreviated as TURBT.

   C. a suprapubic approach.

   D. reflux.

10. An infection anywhere along the urinary tract is abbreviated as:

    A. ESRD.

    B. UA.

    C. UTI.

    D. pH.

FILL IN THE BLANK

1. _____ drugs decrease the volume of blood, increase the volume of urine, and are used to treat hypertension.

2. During _____ in the glomerular capsule, red blood cells, white blood cells, platelets, and albumin do not move through the capillary pores because these things are too large to pass through.

3. One of the functions of the nephron is to remove _____, a waste product of protein metabolism.

4. _____ is the general word for kidney disease.

5. Irreversible chronic renal failure in which there is little remaining kidney function is abbreviated as _____.

6. Involuntary release of urine in an otherwise normal person who should have developed bladder control is known as _____.

7. One of the signs of diabetes mellitus is the presence in the urine of _____, a waste product of fat metabolism.

8. A diagnostic procedure known as _____ evaluates the function of the nerves to the bladder.

9. A medical procedure used to remove waste products from the blood of a patient in renal failure is _____.

10. A _____ is an instrument used to visualize the bladder.

TRUE/FALSE

_____ 1. Lithotripsy is a medical procedure that uses sound waves to break up a kidney stone.

_____ 2. Nephropexy is a surgical procedure to correct nephroptosis by suturing the kidney back into an anatomical position.

_____ 3. The abbreviation mL refers to the acidity or alkalinity of a fluid.

_____ 4. A U-shaped tube of a nephron is known as the proximal convoluted tubule.

_____ 5. Hydronephrosis is characterized by swelling and pressure from the backup of urine in the ureter.

_____ 6. Acute renal failure occurs over a long period of time.

_____ 7. Pus in the urine indicating a UTI is known as urgency.

_____ 8. A renal scan uses a radioactive isotope to make an image of the kidney.

_____ 9. Dipsticks are used to collect a clean-catch specimen.

_____ 10. The chemical symbol for potassium is K^+.

Pronunciation Checklist

Read each word and its pronunciation. Practice pronouncing each word. Verify your pronunciation by listening to the Pronunciation List on Medical Terminology Interactive. Check the box next to the word after you master its pronunciation.

- ☐ acidic (ah-SID-ik)
- ☐ acute renal failure (ah-KYOOT REE-nal FAYL-yoor)
- ☐ acute tubular necrosis (ah-KYOOT TOO-byoo-lar neh-KROH-sis)
- ☐ albuminuria (AL-byoo-mih-NYOO-ree-ah)
- ☐ alkaline (AL-kah-line)
- ☐ ambulatory (AM-byoo-lah-TOR-ee)
- ☐ analgesic drug (AN-al-JEE-zik DRUHG)
- ☐ antibiotic drug (AN-tee-by-AWT-ik DRUHG) (AN-tih-by-AWT-ik)
- ☐ antispasmodic drug (AN-tee-spaz-MAWD-ik DRUHG)
- ☐ anuria (an-YOO-ree-ah)
- ☐ ascites (ah-SY-teez)
- ☐ bacteriuria (BAK-teer-ee-YOO-ree-ah)
- ☐ biopsy (BY-awp-see)
- ☐ bladder (BLAD-er)
- ☐ bladder neck suspension (BLAD-er NEK sus-PEN-shun)
- ☐ calculogenesis (KAL-kyoo-loh-JEN-eh-sis)
- ☐ calculus (KAL-kyoo-lus)
- ☐ caliceal (KAL-ih-SEE-al)
- ☐ calices (KAL-ih-seez)
- ☐ caliectasis (KAY-lee-EK-tah-sis)
- ☐ calix (KAY-liks)
- ☐ cancerous (KAN-ser-us)
- ☐ carcinoma (KAR-sih-NOH-mah)
- ☐ catheter (KATH-eh-ter)
- ☐ catheterization (KATH-eh-ter-ih-ZAY-shun)
- ☐ chronic renal failure (KRAWN-ic REE-nal FAYL-yoor)
- ☐ condom catheter (CON-dom KATH-eh-ter)
- ☐ congenital (con-JEN-ih-tal)
- ☐ cortex (KOR-teks)
- ☐ cortical (KOR-tih-kal)
- ☐ cortices (KOR-tih-seez)
- ☐ creatinine (kree-AT-ih-neen)
- ☐ culture and sensitivity (KUL-chur and SEN-sih-TIV-ih-tee)

- ☐ cystectomy (sis-TEK-toh-mee)
- ☐ cystitis (sis-TY-tis)
- ☐ cystocele (SIS-toh-seel)
- ☐ cystometer (sis-TAWM-eh-ter)
- ☐ cystometrogram (SIS-toh-MET-roh-gram)
- ☐ cystometry (sis-TAWM-eh-tree)
- ☐ cystoscope (SIS-toh-skohp)
- ☐ cystoscopy (sis-TAWS-koh-pee)
- ☐ diabetic nephropathy (DY-ah-BET-ik neh-FRAWP-ah-thee)
- ☐ dialysate (dy-AL-ih-sayt)
- ☐ dialysis (dy-AL-ih-sis)
- ☐ distal convoluted tubule (DIS-tal CON-voh-LOO-ted TOO-byool)
- ☐ diuretic drug (DY-yoo-RET-ik DRUHG)
- ☐ dysuria (dis-YOO-ree-ah)
- ☐ electrolyte (ee-LEK-troh-lite)
- ☐ enuresis (EN-yoo-REE-sis)
- ☐ epispadias (EP-ih-SPAY-dee-as)
- ☐ erythropoietin (eh-RITH-roh-POY-eh-tin)
- ☐ excretory system (EKS-kree-TOR-ee SIS-tem)
- ☐ excretory urogram (EKS-kree-TOR-ee YOO-roh-gram)
- ☐ excretory urography (EKS-kree-TOR-ee yoo-RAWG-rah-fee)
- ☐ extracorporeal lithotripsy (EKS-trah-kohr-POH-ree-al LITH-oh-TRIP-see)
- ☐ filtrate (FIL-trayt)
- ☐ filtration (fil-TRAY-shun)
- ☐ Foley catheter (FOH-lee KATH-eh-ter)
- ☐ fundus (FUN-dus)
- ☐ genitourinary system (JEN-ih-toh-YOO-rih-NAIR-ee SIS-tem)
- ☐ glomerular (gloh-MAIR-yoo-lar)
- ☐ glomeruli (gloh-MAIR-yoo-lie)
- ☐ glomerulonephritis (gloh-MAIR-yoo-loh-neh-FRY-tis)

- ☐ glomerulosclerosis (gloh-MAIR-yoo-loh-skleh-ROH-sis)
- ☐ glomerulus (gloh-MAIR-yoo-lus)
- ☐ glucose (GLOO-kohs)
- ☐ glycosuria (GLY-kohs-YOO-ree-ah)
- ☐ hematuria (HEE-mah-TYOO-ree-ah)
- ☐ hemodialysis (HEE-moh-dy-AL-ih-sis)
- ☐ hila (HY-lah)
- ☐ hilar (HY-lar)
- ☐ hilum (HY-lum)
- ☐ hyaline cast (HY-ah-lin KAST)
- ☐ hydronephrosis (HY-droh-neh-FROH-sis)
- ☐ hydroureter (HY-droh-YOO-ree-ter)
- ☐ hypokalemia (HY-poh-kay-LEE-mee-ah)
- ☐ hypospadias (HY-poh-SPAY-dee-as)
- ☐ incontinence (in-CON-tih-nens)
- ☐ interstitial cystitis (IN-ter-STISH-al sis-TY-tis)
- ☐ intravenous pyelogram (IN-trah-VEE-nus PY-eh-loh-GRAM)
- ☐ intravenous pyelography (IN-trah-VEE-nus PY-eh-LAWG-rah-fee)
- ☐ intravesical (IN-trah-VES-ih-kal)
- ☐ ketones (KEE-tohnz)
- ☐ ketonuria (KEE-toh-NYOO-ree-ah)
- ☐ kidney (KID-nee)
- ☐ kidney donor (KID-nee DOH-nor)
- ☐ kidney transplantation (KID-nee TRANS-plan-TAY-shun)
- ☐ leukocyte (LOO-koh-site)
- ☐ leukocyte esterase (LOO-koh-site ES-ter-ace)
- ☐ lithogenesis (LITH-oh-JEN-eh-sis)
- ☐ lithotripsy (LITH-oh-TRIP-see)
- ☐ lithotriptor (LITH-oh-TRIP-tor)
- ☐ meatus (mee-AA-tus)

- ❏ medulla (meh-DOOL-ah)
- ❏ medullae (meh-DOOL-ee)
- ❏ microscopic hematuria (MY-kroh-SKAWP-ik HEE-mah-TYOO-ree-ah)
- ❏ micturition (MIK-choo-RISH-un)
- ❏ mucosa (myoo-KOH-sah)
- ❏ mucosal (myoo-KOH-sal)
- ❏ nephrectomy (neh-FREK-toh-mee)
- ❏ nephritis (neh-FRY-tis)
- ❏ nephroblastoma (NEF-roh-blas-TOH-mah)
- ❏ nephrolithiasis (NEF-roh-lih-THY-ah-sis)
- ❏ nephrolithotomy (NEF-roh-lih-THAW-toh-mee)
- ❏ nephrologist (neh-FRAWL-oh-jist)
- ❏ nephron (NEF-rawn)
- ❏ nephropathy (neh-FRAWP-ah-thee)
- ❏ nephropexy (NEF-roh-PEK-see)
- ❏ nephroptosis (NEF-rawp-TOH-sis)
- ❏ nephrotic syndrome (nef-RAWT-ik SIN-drohm)
- ❏ nephrotomography (NEF-roh-toh-MAWG-rah-fee)
- ❏ nephrotoxic (NEF-roh-TAWK-sik)
- ❏ neurogenic bladder (NYOOR-oh-JEN-ik BLAD-er)
- ❏ nocturia (nawk-TYOO-ree-ah)
- ❏ occult blood (oh-KULT blud)
- ❏ oliguria (OL-ih-GYOO-ree-ah)
- ❏ parenchyma (pah-RENG-kih-mah)
- ❏ penile (PEE-nile)
- ❏ penis (PEE-nis)
- ❏ percutaneous nephrolithotomy (PER-kyoo-TAY-nee-us NEF-roh-lih-THAW-toh-mee)
- ❏ percutaneous ultrasonic lithotripsy (PER-kyoo-TAY-nee-us UL-trah-SAWN-ik LITH-oh-TRIP-see)
- ❏ peristalsis (PAIR-ih-STAL-sis)
- ❏ peritoneal dialysis (PAIR-ih-toh-NEE-al dy-AL-ih-sis)
- ❏ pH (pee-H)
- ❏ polycystic kidney disease (PAWL-ee-SIS-tik KID-nee dih-ZEEZ)

- ❏ polyuria (PAWL-ee-YOO-ree-ah)
- ❏ postvoid residual (POST-voyd ree-ZID-yoo-al)
- ❏ prostate gland (PRAWS-tayt GLAND)
- ❏ prostatic (praws-TAT-ik)
- ❏ proteinuria (PROH-tee-NYOO-ree-ah)
- ❏ proximal convoluted tubule (PRAWK-sih-mal CON-voh-LOO-ted TOO-byool)
- ❏ pyelonephritis (PY-eh-loh-neh-FRY-tis)
- ❏ pyuria (py-YOO-ree-ah)
- ❏ radiation cystitis (RAY-dee-AA-shun sis-TY-tis)
- ❏ radical cystectomy (RAD-ih-kal sis-TEK-toh-mee)
- ❏ reabsorption (REE-ab-SORP-shun)
- ❏ refractometer (REE-frak-TAWM-eh-ter)
- ❏ renal (REE-nal)
- ❏ renal angiogram (REE-nal AN-jee-oh-GRAM)
- ❏ renal angiography (REE-nal AN-jee-AWG-rah-fee)
- ❏ renal arteriogram (REE-nal ar-TEER-ee-oh-GRAM)
- ❏ renal arteriography (REE-nal ar-TEER-ee-AWG-rah-fee)
- ❏ renal capsule (REE-nal KAP-sool)
- ❏ renal colic (REE-nal KAWL-ik)
- ❏ renal cortex (REE-nal KOR-teks)
- ❏ renal pelves (REE-nal PEL-veez)
- ❏ renal pelvis (REE-nal PEL-vis)
- ❏ renal pyramid (REE-nal PEER-ah-mid)
- ❏ renin (REE-nin)
- ❏ resectoscope (ree-SEK-toh-skohp)
- ❏ retrograde pyelography (RET-roh-grayd PY-eh-LAWG-rah-fee)
- ❏ retroperitoneal (REH-troh-PAIR-ih-toh-NEE-al)
- ❏ rugae (ROO-gee)
- ❏ sonogram (SAWN-oh-gram)
- ❏ sphincter (SFINGK-ter)
- ❏ suprapubic catheter (soo-prah-PYOO-bik KATH-eh-ter)

- ❏ transurethral resection (TRANS-yoo-REE-thral ree-SEK-shun)
- ❏ tubular (TOO-byoo-lar)
- ❏ tubule (TOO-byool)
- ❏ turbid urine (TUR-bid YOO-rin)
- ❏ ultrasonography (UL-trah-soh-NAWG-rah-fee)
- ❏ urea (yoo-REE-ah)
- ❏ uremia (yoo-REE-mee-ah)
- ❏ uremic (yoo-REE-mik)
- ❏ ureter (YOO-ree-ter) (yoo-REE-ter)
- ❏ ureteral (yoo-REE-teh-ral)
- ❏ ureteral orifice (yoo-REE-teh-ral OR-ih-fis)
- ❏ urethra (yoo-REE-thrah)
- ❏ urethral (yoo-REE-thrawl)
- ❏ urethritis (yoo-ree-THRY-tis)
- ❏ uric acid (YOO-rik AS-id)
- ❏ urinalysis (yoo-rih-NAL-ih-sis)
- ❏ urinary retention (YOO-rih-NAIR-ee ree-TEN-shun)
- ❏ urinary system (YOO-rih-NAIR-ee SIS-tem)
- ❏ urinary tract infection (YOO-rih-NAIR-ee TRAKT in-FEK-shun)
- ❏ urination (yoo-rih-NAY-shun)
- ❏ urine (YOO-rin)
- ❏ urinometer (yoo-rih-NAWM-eh-ter)
- ❏ urogenital system (yoo-roh-JEN-ih-tal SIS-tem)
- ❏ urologist (yoo-RAWL-oh-jist)
- ❏ urology (yoo-RAWL-oh-jee)
- ❏ vesical (VES-ih-kal)
- ❏ vesicocele (VES-ih-koh-SEEL)
- ❏ vesicovaginal fistula (VES-ih-koh-VAJ-ih-nal FIS-tyoo-lah)
- ❏ void (VOYD)
- ❏ voiding cystourethrogram (VOY-ding SIS-toh-yoo-REE-throh-gram)
- ❏ voiding cystourethrography (VOY-ding SIS-toh-YOO-ree-THRAWG-rah-fee)
- ❏ Wilms' tumor (WILMZ TOO-mor)

Answer Key

Word Search

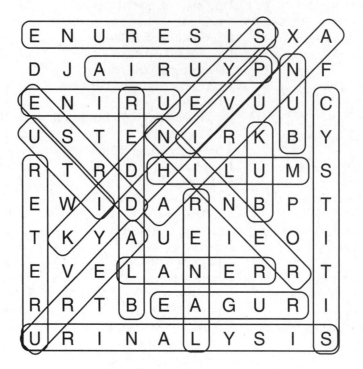

Crossword Puzzle

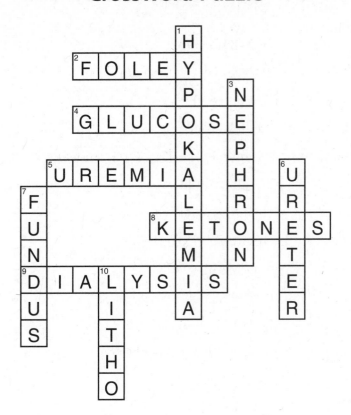

Underline the Accented Syllable

1. anuria   (an-<u>YOO</u>-ree-ah)

2. bacteriuria   (BAK-teer-ee-<u>YOO</u>-ree-ah)

3. calices   (<u>KAL</u>-ih-seez)

4. creatinine   (kree-<u>AT</u>-ih-neen)

5. cystourethrography   (SIS-toh-YOO-ree-<u>THRAWG</u>-rah-fee)

6. electrolyte   (ee-<u>LEK</u>-troh-lite)

7. epispadias   (EP-ih-<u>SPAY</u>-dee-as)

8. erythropoietin   (eh-RITH-roh-<u>POY</u>-eh-tin)

9. glomeruli   (gloh-<u>MAIR</u>-yoo-lie)

10. ketonuria   (KEE-toh-<u>NYOO</u>-ree-ah)

11. lithotripsy   (<u>LITH</u>-oh-TRIP-see)

12. nephrolithotomy   (NEF-roh-lih-<u>THAW</u>-toh-mee)

13. nephropexy   (<u>NEF</u>-roh-PEK-see)

14. rugae   (<u>ROO</u>-gee)

15. vesicocele   (<u>VES</u>-ih-koh-SEEL)

Word Surgery

1. anuria

   Suffix and its meaning: -ia *condition; state; thing*

   Prefix and its meaning: an- *without; not*

   Combining form and its meaning: ur/o- *urine; urinary system*

   Medical word definition: Condition (of being) without urine

2. cystoscopy

   Suffix and its meaning: -scopy *process of using an instrument to examine*

   Prefix and its meaning: none

   Combining form and its meaning: cyst/o- *bladder; fluid-filled sac; semisolid cyst*

   Medical word definition: Process of using an instrument to examine the bladder

3. epispadias

   Suffix and its meaning: -ias *condition*

   Prefix and its meaning: epi- *upon; above*

   Combining form and definition: spad/o- *tear; opening*

   Medical word definition: Condition upon (the upper surface of the penis of the urethral) opening

4. glomerulonephritis

   Suffix and its meaning: -itis *inflammation of; infection of*

   Prefix and its meaning: none

   Combining form and its meaning: glomerul/o- *glomerulus*

   Combining form and its meaning: nephr/o- *kidney; nephron*

   Medical word definition: Inflammation and infection of the glomerulus of the nephron

5. hydronephrosis

   Suffix and its meaning: -osis *condition; abnormal condition; process*

   Prefix and its meaning: none

   Combining form and its meaning: hydr/o- *water; fluid*

   Combining form and its meaning: nephr/o- *kidney; nephron*

   Medical word definition: Abnormal condition of fluid (urine backed up into the) kidney

6. hypokalemia

Suffix and its meaning: -emia *condition of the blood; substance in the blood*

Prefix and its meaning: hypo- *below; deficient*

Combining form and its meaning: kal/i- *potassium*

Medical word definition: Substance in the blood of deficient potassium

7. incontinence

Suffix and its meaning: -ence *state of*

Prefix and its meaning: in- *in; within; not*

Combining form and its meaning: contin/o- *hold together*

Medical word definition: State of not holding together (urine in the bladder)

8. lithotripsy

Suffix and its meaning: -tripsy *process of crushing*

Prefix and its meaning: none

Combining form and its meaning: lith/o- *stone*

Medical word definition: Process of crushing a stone

9. nephrolithotomy

Suffix and its meaning: -tomy *process of cutting or making an incision*

Prefix and its meaning: none

Combining form and its meaning: nephr/o- *kidney; nephron*

Combining form and its meaning: lith/o- *stone*

Medical word definition: Process of cutting or making an incision (into the) kidney
(to remove a) stone

10. nocturia

Suffix and its meaning: -ia *condition; state; thing*

Prefix and its meaning: none

Combining form and its meaning: noct/o- *night*

Combining form and its meaning: ur/o- *urine; urinary system*

Medical word definition: Condition of (during the) night (making) urine

11. percutaneous

   Suffix and its meaning: -ous *pertaining to*

   Prefix and its meaning: per- *through; throughout*

   Combining form and its meaning: cutane/o- *skin*

   Medical word definition: Pertaining to through the skin

12. polycystic

   Suffix and its meaning: -ic *pertaining to*

   Prefix and its meaning: poly- *many; much*

   Combining form and its meaning: cyst/o- *bladder; fluid-filled sac; semisolid cyst*

   Medical word definition: Pertaining to many semisolid cysts

13. pyelonephritis

   Suffix and its meaning: -itis *inflammation of; infection of*

   Prefix and its meaning: none

   Combining form and its meaning: pyel/o- *renal pelvis*

   Combining form and its meaning: nephr/o- *kidney; nephron*

   Medical word definition: Inflammation or infection of the renal pelvis of the kidney

14. retroperitoneal

   Suffix and its meaning: -al *pertaining to*

   Prefix and its meaning: retro- *behind; backward*

   Combining form and its meaning: peritone/o- *peritoneum*

   Medical word definition: Pertaining to behind the peritoneum

15. urologist

   Suffix and its meaning: -ist *one who specializes in*

   Prefix and its meaning: none

   Combining form and its meaning: ur/o- *urine; urinary system*

   Combining form and its meaning: log/o- *word; the study of*

   Medical word definition: One who specializes in the urinary system study of

Chapter Quiz

MULTIPLE CHOICE

1. B	4. D	7. D	10. C
2. A	5. A	8. C	
3. B	6. D	9. A	

FILL IN THE BLANK

1. Diuretic

2. filtration

3. urea

4. Nephropathy

5. ESRD

6. enuresis

7. ketones

8. cystometry

9. hemodialysis (or dialysis)

10. cystoscope

TRUE/FALSE

1. True

2. True

3. False (pH)

4. False (nephron loop)

5. True

6. False (chronic)

7. False (pyuria)

8. True

9. False (test urine)

10. True

CHAPTER 12

Male Reproductive Medicine

Measure Your Progress: Learning Objectives

After reading this chapter, the student should be able to

- Identify the structures of the male genitourinary system.
- Describe the processes of spermatogenesis and ejaculation.
- Describe common male genitourinary diseases and conditions, laboratory and diagnostic procedures, medical and surgical procedures, and drug categories.
- Give the medical meaning of word parts related to the male genitourinary system.
- Build male genitourinary words from word parts and divide and define male genitourinary words.
- Spell and pronounce male genitourinary words.
- Analyze the medical content and meaning of a male reproductive medicine report.
- Dive deeper into male reproductive medicine by reviewing the activities at the end of this chapter and online at Medical Terminology Interactive.

It All Starts with Word Building

Medical language is all about medical words and their word parts. Jump right into this chapter by learning some of the common combining forms and their definitions that you will encounter in this chapter.

adolesc/o-	the beginning of being an adult
andr/o-	male
balan/o-	glans penis
cis/o-	to cut
coit/o-	sexual intercourse
crypt/o-	hidden
didym/o-	testes (twin structures)
ejaculat/o-	to expel suddenly
erect/o-	to stand up
fer/o-	to bear
fertil/o-	able to conceive a child
genit/o-	genitalia
gon/o-	seed; ovum or spermatozoon
inguin/o-	groin
morph/o-	shape
orchi/o-	testis
orch/o-	testis
pareun/o-	sexual intercourse
pen/o-	penis
perine/o-	perineum
product/o-	produce
prostat/o-	prostate gland
puber/o-	growing up
scrot/o-	a bag; scrotum
semin/i-	spermatozoon; sperm
semin/o-	spermatozoon; sperm
spermat/o-	spermatozoon; sperm
sperm/o-	spermatozoon; sperm
testicul/o-	testis; testicle
tub/o-	tube
urethr/o-	urethra
urin/o-	urine; urinary system
vas/o-	blood vessel; vas deferens
venere/o-	sexual intercourse

Chapter Spelling Test

Dictate and spell (or photocopy a handout that contains) this list of 20 spelling words. Give this list to students to study for the week. At the beginning of next week's class, dictate 10 of these words as the spelling test. The spelling test is included with the chapter test that is given on the previous week's material.

1. adolescence
2. balanitis
3. chancre
4. chordee
5. circumcision
6. ductus deferens
7. dyspareunia
8. epididymitis
9. genitalia
10. glans penis
11. gonorrhea
12. gynecomastia
13. orchiectomy
14. perineum
15. phimosis
16. prostate gland
17. seminal vesicle
18. spermatozoon
19. testis
20. varicocele

Chapter Pronunciation Test

Photocopy a handout that contains this list of 20 pronunciation words. Give this list to students to study for the week. Sometime at the beginning of the next week, they will call your office or home answering machine and pronounce each word.

1. balanitis (BAL-ah-NY-tis)

2. chancre (SHANG-ker)

3. chordee (kor-DEE)

4. circumcision (SER-kum-SIH-shun)

5. ductus deferens (DUK-tus DEF-er-enz)

6. dyspareunia (DIS-pah-ROO-nee-ah)

7. epididymis (EP-ih-DID-ih-mis)

8. genitalia (JEN-ih-TAY-lee-ah)

9. gonorrhea (GAWN-oh-REE-ah)

10. gynecomastia (GY-neh-koh-MAS-tee-ah)

11. orchiectomy (OR-kee-EK-toh-mee)

12. perineum (PAIR-ih-NEE-um)

13. phimosis (fih-MOH-sis)

14. seminal vesicle (SEM-ih-nal VES-ih-kl)

15. spermatogenesis (SPER-mah-toh-JEN-eh-sis)

16. spermatozoon (SPER-mah-toh-ZOH-on)

17. testis (TES-tis)

18. varicocele (VAIR-ih-koh-SEEL)

19. vasectomy (vah-SEK-toh-mee)

20. venereal disease (veh-NEER-ee-al dih-ZEEZ

Word Search

Complete this word search puzzle that contains Chapter 12 words. Look for the following words as given in the list below. The number in parentheses indicates how many times the word appears in the puzzle.

AIDS	semen
biopsy	sexual
duct	sperm
genitalia	spermatozoa
glans penis	STD
gonads	syphilis
orchitis	testes (2)
penis	TURP
prostate	vasectomy
scrotum	virus

```
S  P  E  R  M  N  E  M  E  S  A  S
Y  P  S  U  R  I  V  K  E  I  I  G
P  T  E  J  L  L  A  T  D  T  S  E
H  E  X  R  A  D  S  S  I  C  T  N
I  S  N  U  M  E  E  H  R  A  C  I
L  T  X  I  T  A  C  O  T  S  U  T
I  E  W  U  S  R  T  S  B  D  D  A
S  S  R  Q  O  U  O  O  T  A  M  L
E  P  D  C  M  R  M  S  Z  N  H  I
U  B  I  O  P  S  Y  U  I  O  K  A
S  I  N  E  P  S  N  A  L  G  A  J
```

Crossword Puzzle

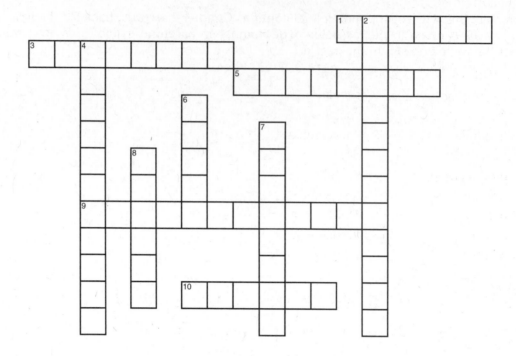

ACROSS

1. The physical union of a male and a female is known as sexual intercourse or

   _____.

3. _____ is a sexually transmitted disease caused by a spirochete bacterium that produces a painless chancre on the penis. This disease is also known as lues.

5. In a semen analysis, the forward movement of the spermatozoa is called _____.

9. The most abundant and biologically active of all the male sex hormones is

   _____.

10. The testes are the

    _____ or sex glands in a male.

DOWN

2. The most common cause of male infertility, which is characterized by fewer than the normal number of spermatozoa produced by the testes, is _____.

4. _____ is an acute or chronic infection of the prostate gland caused by a urinary tract infection or sexually transmitted disease.

6. The combining form "_____" means male.

7. The male _____ genitalia includes the scrotum, testes, epididymides, penis, and urethra.

8. The combining forms "orch/o-" and "orchi/o-" refer to the

   _____.

Underline the Accented Syllable

Read the medical word. Then review the syllables in the pronunciation. Underline the primary (main) accented syllable in the pronunciation.

1. balanitis   (bal-ah-ny-tis)

2. bulbourethral   (bul-boh-yoo-ree-thral)

3. chancre   (shang-ker)

4. chlamydia   (klah-mid-ee-ah)

5. condylomata   (con-dih-loh-mah-tah)

6. cryptorchism   (krip-tohr-kiz-em)

7. epididymitis   (ep-ih-did-ih-my-tis)

8. gonorrhea   (gawn-oh-ree-ah)

9. gynecomastia   (gy-neh-koh-mas-tee-ah)

10. impotence   (im-poh-tens)

11. luteinizing   (loo-tee-ih-ny-zing)

12. meiosis   (my-oh-sis)

13. orchitis   (or-ky-tis)

14. phimosis   (fih-moh-sis)

15. prostatectomy   (praws-tah-tek-toh-mee)

Word Surgery

Read the medical word. Break the medical word into its word parts and give the meaning of each word part. Then give the definition of the medical word.

1. antiviral

   Suffix and its meaning: _____

   Prefix and its meaning: _____

   Combining form and its meaning: _____

   Medical word definition: _____

2. aspermia

   Suffix and its meaning: _____

   Prefix and its meaning: _____

   Combining form and its meaning: _____

   Medical word definition: _____

3. balanitis

   Suffix and its meaning: _____

   Prefix and its meaning: _____

   Combining form and its meaning: _____

   Medical word definition: _____

4. circumcision

   Suffix and its meaning: _____

   Prefix and its meaning: _____

   Combining form and its meaning: _____

   Medical word definition: _____

5. cryptorchism

   Suffix and its meaning: _____

   Prefix and its meaning: _____

   Combining form and its meaning: _____

   Combining form and its meaning: _____

   Medical word definition: _____

6. dyspareunia

    Suffix and its meaning: _____

    Prefix and its meaning: _____

    Combining form and its meaning: _____

    Medical word definition: _____

7. epididymitis

    Suffix and its meaning: _____

    Prefix and its meaning: _____

    Combining form and its meaning: _____

    Medical word definition: _____

8. genitourinary

    Suffix and its meaning: _____

    Prefix and its meaning: _____

    Combining form and its meaning: _____

    Combining form and its meaning: _____

    Medical word definition: _____

9. oligospermia

    Suffix and its meaning: _____

    Prefix and its meaning: _____

    Combining form and its meaning: _____

    Combining form and its meaning: _____

    Medical word definition: _____

10. orchiectomy

    Suffix and its meaning: _____

    Prefix and its meaning: _____

    Combining form and its meaning: _____

    Medical word definition: _____

11. prostatitis

    Suffix and its meaning: _____

    Prefix and its meaning: _____

    Combining form and its meaning: _____

    Medical word definition: _____

12. spermatogenesis

Suffix and its meaning: _____

Prefix and its meaning: _____

Combining form and its meaning: _____

Medical word definition: _____

13. transurethral

Suffix and its meaning: _____

Prefix and its meaning: _____

Combining form and its meaning: _____

Medical word definition: _____

14. vasectomy

Suffix and its meaning: _____

Prefix and its meaning: _____

Combining form and its meaning: _____

Medical word definition: _____

15. varicocele

Suffix and its meaning: _____

Prefix and its meaning: _____

Combining form and its meaning: _____

Medical word definition: _____

Chapter Quiz

MULTIPLE CHOICE

1. The combining form meaning male is:

   A. male/o-.

   B. andr/o-.

   C. crypt/o-.

   D. blan/o-.

2. The prostate gland:

   A. is also called the bulbourethral gland.

   B. produces sperm.

   C. surrounds the urethra.

   D. is a rounded area at the end of the penis.

3. The fluid expelled from the penis during ejaculation:

   A. contains spermatozoa.

   B. contains seminal fluid.

   C. is called semen.

   D. All of the above.

4. Gametes:

   A. contain 23 chromosomes instead of 46 as in other body cells.

   B. include both sperm and ovum.

   C. produce semen.

   D. Both A and B are correct.

5. The suffix "-cyte" means:

   A. cell.

   B. sperm.

   C. small.

   D. having the function of.

6. Orchitis is an inflammation of the:

   A. spermatic cord.

   B. testes.

   C. urethra.

   D. prostate gland.

7. Enlargement of the male breast is known as:

   A. breast cancer.

   B. gynecomastia.

   C. varicocele.

   D. sexually transmitted disease.

8. A semen analysis is done to:

   A. determine sperm motility.

   B. count sperm.

   C. examine sperm morphology.

   D. All of the above.

9. Vasectomy is:

   A. a surgical procedure to prevent pregnancy.

   B. used to remove the prostate gland.

   C. used to resect the testes.

   D. a medical procedure to treat testicular cancer.

10. Androgen inhibitor drugs can be used to:

   A. increase muscle growth.

   B. treat BPH.

   C. prevent pregnancy.

   D. increase sperm motility.

FILL IN THE BLANK

1. The _____ is a long, coiled tube that is attached to the outer
   wall of each testis.

2. _____ is the general term that refers to an open area
   throughout the length of a tube or duct.

3. "Olig/o-," as in oligospermia, means "_____ or

_____."

4. _____ is a gram-negative coccus bacterium that causes a sexually transmitted disease characterized by painful urination with burning and itching.

5. The abbreviation _____ stands for transrectal ultrasonography.

6. A/an _____ is a surgical procedure to remove a testis because of testicular cancer.

7. The suffix "_____" means "the surgically created opening."

8. One test for syphilis is the rapid _____ _____ test.

9. Drugs such as Viagra, Cialis, and Levitra are used to treat _____

_____.

10. The newer name for a medical technologist is a _____

_____ _____.

TRUE/FALSE

_____ 1. "Cis/o-" is the combining form meaning "to cut."

_____ 2. The urogenital system includes the urinary and reproductive systems.

_____ 3. The male internal genitalia include the vas deferens, seminal vesicles, ejaculatory ducts, and prostate gland.

_____ 4. The physical union of male and female during sexual intercourse is known as cryptorchism.

_____ 5. Chordee is the inflammation and infection of the glans penis.

_____ 6. Physicians are required to report all cases of STDs to the state health department.

_____ 7. Syphilis, trichomoniasis, and gonorrhea are all sexually transmitted diseases.

_____ 8. A surgical procedure to remove tissue or fluids is known as a biopsy.

_____ 9. A PSA test is done by the physician to palpate the prostate gland.

_____ 10. In men, PAP stands for Papanicolaou smear.

Pronunciation Checklist

Read each word and its pronunciation. Practice pronouncing each word. Verify your pronunciation by listening to the Pronunciation List on Medical Terminology Interactive. Check the box next to the word after you master its pronunciation.

- ❏ acid phosphatase (AS-id FAWS-fah-tays)
- ❏ acquired immunodeficiency syndrome (ah-KWY-erd IM-myoo-noh-dee-FISH-en-see SIN-drohm)
- ❏ adolescence (AD-oh-LES-sens)
- ❏ androgen drug (AN-droh-jen DRUHG)
- ❏ antibiotic drug (AN-tee-by-AWT-ik) (AN-tih-by-AWT-ik DRUHG)
- ❏ antiviral drug (AN-tee-VY-ral DRUHG) (AN-tih-VY-ral)
- ❏ aspermia (aa-SPER-mee-ah)
- ❏ aspiration biopsy (AS-pih-RAY-shun BY-awp-see)
- ❏ balanitis (BAL-ah-NY-tis)
- ❏ benign prostatic hypertrophy (bee-NINE praws-TAT-ik hy-PER-troh-fee)
- ❏ biopsy (BY-awp-see)
- ❏ bulbourethral gland (BUL-boh-yoo-REE-thral GLAND)
- ❏ cancerous (KAN-ser-us)
- ❏ chancre (SHANG-ker)
- ❏ chlamydia (klah-MID-ee-ah)
- ❏ chordee (kor-DEE)
- ❏ circumcision (SER-kum-SIH-shun)
- ❏ clinical laboratory scientist (KLIN-ih-kal LAB-oh-rah-TOH-ree SY-en-tist)
- ❏ condylomata acuminata (CON-dih-LOH-mah-tah ah-KOO-mih-NAH-tah)
- ❏ corpora cavernosa (KOR-por-ah KAV-er-NOH-sah)
- ❏ corpus spongiosum (KOR-puhs SPUN-jee-OH-sum)
- ❏ cryptorchism (krip-TOHR-kiz-em)
- ❏ ductus deferens (DUK-tus DEF-er-enz)
- ❏ dyspareunia (DIS-pah-ROO-nee-ah)
- ❏ ejaculation (ee-JAK-yoo-LAY-shun)

- ❏ ejaculatory duct (ee-JAK-yoo-lah-TOH-ee DUKT)
- ❏ epididymides (EP-ih-dih-DIM-ih-deez)
- ❏ epididymis (EP-ih-DID-ih-mis)
- ❏ epididymitis (EP-ih-DID-ih-MY-tis)
- ❏ erectile dysfunction (ee-REK-tile dis-FUNK-shun)
- ❏ erection (ee-REK-shun)
- ❏ external genitalia (eks-TER-nal JEN-ih-TAY-lee-ah)
- ❏ flagellum (flah-JEL-um)
- ❏ follicle-stimulating hormone (FAWL-ih-kl STIM-yoo-LAY-ting HOR-mohn)
- ❏ gamete (GAM-eet)
- ❏ genitalia (JEN-ih-TAY-lee-ah)
- ❏ genital (JEN-ih-tal)
- ❏ genital herpes (JEN-ih-tal HER-peez)
- ❏ genitourinary system (JEN-ih-toh-YOO-rih-NAIR-ee SIS-tem)
- ❏ glans penis (GLANZ PEE-nis)
- ❏ gonad (GOH-nad)
- ❏ gonorrhea (GAWN-oh-REE-ah)
- ❏ gynecomastia (GY-neh-koh-MAS-tee-ah)
- ❏ hormone (HOR-mohn)
- ❏ human immunodeficiency virus (HYOO-man IM-myoo-noh-dee-FISH-en-see VY-rus)
- ❏ impotence (IM-poh-tens)
- ❏ incisional biopsy (in-SIH-shun-al BY-awp-see)
- ❏ infertility (IN-fer-TIL-ih-tee)
- ❏ inguinal canal (ING-gwih-nal kah-NAL)
- ❏ internal genitalia (in-TER-nal JEN-ih-TAY-lee-ah)
- ❏ interstitial cell (IN-ter-STISH-al SELL)
- ❏ lumen (LOO-men)
- ❏ luteinizing hormone (LOO-tee-ih-NY-zing HOR-mohn)
- ❏ malignancy (mah-LIG-nan-see)

- ❏ meiosis (my-OH-sis)
- ❏ mitosis (my-TOH-sis)
- ❏ oligospermia (OH-lih-goh-SPER-mee-ah)
- ❏ orchiectomy (OR-kee-EK-toh-mee)
- ❏ orchiopexy (OR-kee-oh-PEK-see)
- ❏ orchitis (or-KY-tis)
- ❏ pelvic cavity (PEL-vik KAV-ih-tee)
- ❏ penile (PEE-nile)
- ❏ penile implant (PEE-nile IM-plant)
- ❏ penile prosthesis (PEE-nile praws-THEE-sis)
- ❏ penis (PEE-nis)
- ❏ perineal (PAIR-ih-NEE-al)
- ❏ perineum (PAIR-ih-NEE-um)
- ❏ phimosis (fih-MOH-sis)
- ❏ postcoital (post-KOH-ih-tal)
- ❏ premature (pree-mah-CHUR)
- ❏ prepuce (PREE-poos)
- ❏ priapism (PRY-ah-pizm)
- ❏ prostate gland (PRAWS-tayt GLAND)
- ❏ prostatectomy (PRAWS-tah-TEK-toh-mee)
- ❏ prostate-specific antigen (PRAWS-tayt speh-SIF-ik AN-tih-jen)
- ❏ prostatic fluid (praws-TAT-ik FLOO-id)
- ❏ prostatitis (PRAWS-tah-TY-tis)
- ❏ puberty (PYOO-ber-tee)
- ❏ pubic (PYOO-bik)
- ❏ reproductive medicine (REE-proh-DUK-tiv MED-ih-sin)
- ❏ reproductive system (REE-proh-DUK-tiv SIS-tem)
- ❏ resectoscope (ree-SEK-toh-skohp)
- ❏ scrotal (SKROH-tal)
- ❏ scrotum (SKROH-tum)
- ❏ semen (SEE-men)
- ❏ seminal fluid (SEM-in-nal FLOO-id)
- ❏ seminal vesicle (SEM-ih-nal VES-ih-kl)

- ❏ seminiferous tubule (SEM-ih-NIF-er-us TOO-byool)
- ❏ seminoma (SEM-ih-NOH-mah)
- ❏ sperm (SPERM)
- ❏ sperm morphology (SPERM mor-FAWL-oh-jee)
- ❏ sperm motility (SPERM moh-TIL-ih-tee)
- ❏ spermatic cord (sper-MAT-ik KORD)
- ❏ spermatocyte (SPER-mah-toh-SITE)
- ❏ spermatogenesis (SPER-mah-toh-JEN-eh-sis)
- ❏ spermatozoa (SPER-mah-toh-ZOH-ah)
- ❏ spermatozoon (SPER-mah-toh-ZOH-on)
- ❏ syphilis (SIF-ih-lis)
- ❏ testes (TES-teez)
- ❏ testicle (TES-tih-kl)
- ❏ testicular (tes-TIK-yoo-lar)
- ❏ testis (TES-tis)
- ❏ testosterone (tes-TAWS-teh-rohn)
- ❏ transrectal ultrasonography (trans-REK-tal UL-trah-soh-NAWG-rah-fee)
- ❏ varicocele (VAIR-ih-koh-SEEL)
- ❏ vas deferens (VAS DEF-er-enz)
- ❏ vasectomy (vah-SEK-toh-mee)
- ❏ vasovasostomy (VAY-soh-vah-SAWS-toh-mee)
- ❏ venereal disease (veh-NEER-ee-al dih-ZEEZ)
- ❏ transurethral resection (TRANS-yoo-REE-thral ree-SEK-shun)
- ❏ tubule (TOO-byool)
- ❏ ultrasonography (UL-trah-soh-NAWG-rah-fee)
- ❏ ultrasound (UL-trah-sound)
- ❏ urogenital (YOO-roh-JEN-ih-tal)

Answer Key

Word Search

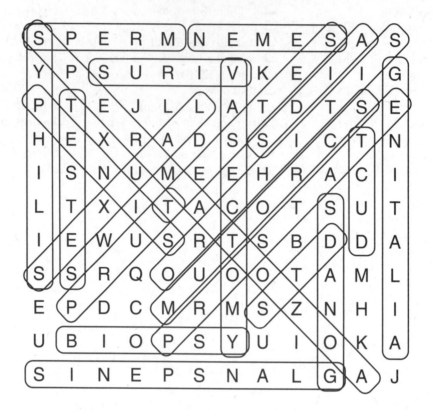

Crossword Puzzle

```
                                    ¹C O I T U S
   ³S Y P H I L I S              ²O L
      ⁴R                    ⁵M O T I L I T Y
      O        ⁶A              G
      S        N         ⁷E    O
      T    ⁸T  D         X      S
      A    E  R         T      P
   ⁹T E S T O S T E R O N E    E
      I    T         R      R
      T    I         N      M
      I   ¹⁰G O N A D S      I
      S    S         L      A
      S
```

Underline the Accented Syllable

1. balanitis   (BAL-ah-<u>NY</u>-tis)

2. bulbourethral   (BUL-boh-yoo-<u>REE</u>-thral)

3. chancre   (<u>SHANG</u>-ker)

4. chlamydia   (klah-<u>MID</u>-ee-ah)

5. condylomata   (CON-dih-<u>LOH</u>-mah-tah)

6. cryptorchism   (krip-<u>TOHR</u>-kiz-em)

7. epididymiditis   (EP-ih-DID-ih-<u>MY</u>-tis)

8. gonorrhea   (GAWN-oh-<u>REE</u>-ah)

9. gynecomastia   (GY-neh-koh-<u>MAS</u>-tee-ah)

10. impotence   (<u>IM</u>-poh-tens)

11. luteinizing   (<u>LOO</u>-tee-ih-NY-zing)

12. meiosis   (my-<u>OH</u>-sis)

13. orchitis   (or-<u>KY</u>-tis)

14. phimosis   (fih-<u>MOH</u>-sis)

15. prostatectomy   (PRAWS-tah-<u>TEK</u>-toh-mee)

Word Surgery

1. antiviral

   Suffix and its meaning: -al *pertaining to*

   Prefix and its meaning: anti- *against*

   Combining form and its meaning: vir/o- *virus*

   Medical word definition: Pertaining to (being) against a virus

2. aspermia

   Suffix and its meaning: -ia *condition; state; thing*

   Prefix and its meaning: a- *away from; without*

   Combining form and its meaning: sperm/o- *spermatozoon; sperm*

   Medical word definition: State (of being) without spermatozoa

3. balanitis

   Suffix and its meaning: -itis *inflammation of; infection of*

   Prefix and its meaning: none

   Combining form and its meaning: balan/o- *glans penis*

   Medical word definition: Inflammation and infection of the glans penis

4. circumcision

   Suffix and its meaning: -ion *action; condition*

   Prefix and its meaning: circum- *around*

   Combining form and its meaning: cis/o- *to cut*

   Medical word definition: Action around (the foreskin) to cut

5. cryptorchism

   Suffix and its meaning: -ism *process; disease from a specific cause*

   Prefix and its meaning: none

   Combining form and its meaning: crypt/o- *hidden*

   Combining form and its meaning: orch/o- *testis*

   Medical word definition: Disease from a specific cause of hidden testis

6. dyspareunia

   Suffix and its meaning: -ia *condition; state; thing*

   Prefix and its meaning: dys- *painful; difficult; abnormal*

   Combining form and its meaning: pareun/o- *sexual intercourse*

   Medical word definition: Condition of painful or difficult sexual intercourse

7. epididymitis

   Suffix and its meaning: -itis *inflammation of; infection of*

   Prefix and its meaning: epi- *upon; above*

   Combining form and its meaning: didym/o- *testes*

   Medical word definition: Inflammation or infection (of the structure) upon the testis

8. genitourinary

   Suffix and its meaning: -ary *pertaining to*

   Prefix and its meaning: none

   Combining form and its meaning: genit/o- *genitalia*

   Combining form and its meaning: urin/o- *urine; urinary system*

   Medical word definition: Pertaining to the genitalia and the urinary system

9. oligospermia

   Suffix and its meaning: -ia *condition; state; thing*

   Prefix and its meaning: none

   Combining form and its meaning: olig/o- *scanty; few*

   Combining form and its meaning: sperm/o- *spermatozoon; sperm*

   Medical word definition: Condition of few spermatozoa

10. orchiectomy

    Suffix and its meaning: -ectomy *surgical excision*

    Prefix and its meaning: none

    Combining form and its meaning: orchi/o- *testis*

    Medical word definition: Surgical excision of the testis

11. prostatitis

    Suffix and its meaning: -itis *inflammation of; infection of*

    Prefix and its meaning: none

    Combining form and its meaning: prostat/o- *prostate gland*

    Medical word definition: Inflammation or infection of the prostate gland

12. spermatogenesis

   Suffix and its meaning: -esis *a process*

   Prefix and its meaning: none

   Combining form and its meaning: spermat/o- *spermatozoon; sperm*

   Combining form and its meaning: gen/o *arising from; produced by*

   Medical word definition: A process of spermatozoon produced by (the testis)

13. transurethral

   Suffix and its meaning: -al *pertaining to*

   Prefix and its meaning: trans- *across; through*

   Combining form and its meaning: urethr/o- *urethra*

   Medical word definition: Pertaining to through the urethra

14. vasectomy

   Suffix and its meaning: -ectomy *surgical excision*

   Prefix and its meaning: none

   Combining form and its meaning: vas/o- *blood vessel; vas deferens*

   Medical word definition: Surgical excision (of part of the) vas deferens

15. varicocele

   Suffix and its meaning: -cele *hernia*

   Prefix and its meaning: none

   Combining form and its meaning: varic/o- *varix; varicose vein*

   Medical word definition: Hernia of a varicose vein (in the spermatic cord)

Chapter Quiz

MULTIPLE CHOICE

1. B	4. D	7. B	10. B
2. C	5. A	8. D	
3. D	6. B	9. A	

FILL IN THE BLANK

1. epididymis

2. Lumen

3. few or less than

4. Chlamydia

5. TRUS

6. orchiectomy

7. -stomy

8. plasma reagin

9. erectile dysfunction

10. clinical laboratory specialist

TRUE/FALSE

1. True

2. True

3. True

4. False (coitus)

5. False (balanitis)

6. True

7. True

8. True

9. False (DRE)

10. False (prostatic acid phosphatase)

CHAPTER 13

Gynecology and Obstetrics

Measure Your Progress: Learning Objectives

After reading this chapter, the student should be able to

- Identify the structures of the female genital and reproductive system.
- Describe the processes of oogenesis, menstruation, conception, and labor and delivery.
- Describe normal and abnormal findings in the neonate.
- Describe common female genital and reproductive diseases and conditions, laboratory and diagnostic procedures, medical and surgical procedures, and drug categories.
- Give the medical meaning of word parts related to the female genital and reproductive system.
- Build female genital and reproductive words from word parts and divide and define words.
- Spell and pronounce female genital and reproductive words.
- Analyze the medical content and meaning of a gynecology report.
- Dive deeper into gynecology and obstetrics by reviewing the activities at the end of this chapter and online at Medical Terminology Interactive.

It All Starts with Word Building

Medical language is all about medical words and their word parts. Jump right into this chapter by learning some of the common combining forms and their definitions that you will encounter in this chapter.

abort/o-	stop prematurely	lact/i-	milk
adnex/o-	accessory connecting parts	lact/o-	milk
		lei/o-	smooth
amni/o-	amnion (fetal membrane)	mamm/a-	breast
		mamm/o-	breast
areol/o-	small area around the nipple	mast/o-	breast; mastoid process
cephal/o-	head		
cervic/o-	neck; cervix	men/o-	month
chorion/o-	chorion (fetal membrane)	menstru/o-	monthly discharge of blood
colp/o-	vagina	metri/o-	uterus (womb)
concept/o-	to conceive or form	metr/o-	uterus (womb)
		nat/o-	birth
eclamps/o-	a seizure	null/i-	none
embryon/o-	embryo; immature form	obstetr/o-	pregnancy and childbirth
episi/o-	vulva	o/o-	ovum (egg)
estr/a-	female	oophor/o-	ovary
estr/o-	female	ovari/o-	ovary
fallopi/o-	uterine (fallopian) tube	ov/i-	ovum (egg)
		ov/o-	ovum (egg)
fertil/o-	able to conceive a child	ovul/o-	ovum (egg)
		pareun/o-	sexual intercourse
fet/o-	fetus	par/o-	birth
galact/o-	milk	parturit/o-	to be in labor
genit/o-	genitalia	placent/o-	placenta
gestat/o-	from conception to birth	pregn/o-	being with child
		prim/i-	first
gonad/o-	gonads (ovaries and testes)	salping/o-	uterine (fallopian) tube
gon/o-	seed (ovum or spermatozoon)	toc/o-	labor and childbirth
gynec/o-	female; woman	uter/o-	uterus (womb)
hyster/o-	uterus (womb)	vagin/o-	vagina
insemin/o-	plant a seed	vulv/o-	vulva
labi/o-	lip; labium		

Milestones in Embryo and Fetal Development

Month	Trimester	Designation	Description
1	1	Embryo	Heart begins to beat at 3 weeks. Lungs, trachea, liver, pancreas, and intestines form.
2	1	Embryo	Sweat glands and hair follicles form. Kidneys form and begin to produce urine. Umbilical cord forms.
3	1	Fetus	Spinal cord and brain begin to form. Gallbladder and genitalia form.
4	2	Fetus	Hair begins to grow; facial features form. The fetus swallows amniotic fluid. Eyes and ears begin to form. Mother feels first fetal movements (quickening).
5	2	Fetus	Nails begin to grow on fingers and toes. Tonsils form.
6	2	Fetus	Spleen, adrenal glands, and bone marrow form. Vernix caseosa and lanugo develop on skin.
7	3	Fetus	Eyelids open; testes begin to descend.
8	3	Fetus	All five senses are developed. The fingernails and toenails are completely formed. The hair is growing.
9	3	Fetus	At the end of 37 weeks (about midway through the ninth month, the fetus' status changes from preterm to term.

Chapter Spelling Test

Dictate and spell (or photocopy a handout that contains) this list of 20 spelling words. Give this list to students to study for the week. At the beginning of next week's class, dictate 10 of these words as the spelling test. The spelling test is included with the chapter test that is given on the previous week's material.

1. amniocentesis
2. areola
3. cerclage
4. cesarean section
5. culdoscopy
6. dysmenorrhea
7. dystocia
8. embryo
9. endometriosis
10. gamete
11. genitalia
12. gravida
13. hysterectomy
14. intrauterine
15. laparoscopy
16. lochia
17. mammography
18. menstruation
19. preeclampsia
20. salpingo-oophorectomy

Chapter Pronunciation Test

Photocopy a handout that contains this list of 20 pronunciation words. Give this list to students to study for the week. Sometime at the beginning of the next week, each student should call your office or home answering machine and pronounce each word.

1. adnexal (ad-NEK-sal)

2. amenorrhea (AH-meh-noh-REE-ah)

3. amniocentesis (AM-nee-oh-sen-TEE-sis)

4. carcinoma *in situ* (KAR-sih-NOH-mah IN SY-too)

5. cerclage (sir-CLAWJ)

6. colostrum (koh-LAWS-trum)

7. culdoscopy (kul-DAWS-koh-pee)

8. dystocia (dis-TOH-see-ah)

9. effacement (eh-FAYS-ment)

10. endometriosis (EN-doh-MEE-tree-OH-sis)

11. genitalia (JEN-ih-TAY-lee-ah)

12. hemosalpinx (HEE-moh-SAL-pinks)

13. hysterectomy (HIS-ter-EK-toh-mee)

14. intrauterine (IN-trah-YOO-ter-in)

15. laparoscopy (LAP-ah-RAWS-koh-pee)

16. lochia (LOH-kee-ah)

17. menarche (meh-NAR-kee)

18. multiparous (mul-TIP-ah-rus)

19. oxytocin (AWK-see-TOH-sin)

20. salpingo-oophorectomy (sal-PING-goh-OH-of-or-EK-toh-mee)

Word Search

Complete this word search puzzle that contains Chapter 13 words. Look for the following words as given in the list below. The number in parentheses indicates how many times the word appears in the puzzle.

amniocentesis	menses
breast	neonate
cesarean	NICU
clitoris	ovum
contraception	para
corpus	pica
CPD	placenta
EGA	PMS (3)
fetal	pregnancies
fetus	pubic
gonad	uterus
gravida	vernix
labial	zygote
LMP	

```
A  L  C  R  L  A  G  E  J  X  P  D  N
X  M  O  D  L  A  T  K  I  U  R  A  E
E  P  N  A  R  B  B  N  C  L  E  N  O
V  O  T  I  R  Z  R  I  E  R  G  O  N
C  E  R  E  O  E  N  D  A  C  N  G  A
F  W  A  T  V  C  Z  S  C  L  A  Y  T
E  S  C  P  D  Y  E  O  L  D  N  L  E
T  U  E  U  G  C  R  N  I  A  C  I  P
U  Q  P  O  T  P  Y  V  T  D  I  N  M
S  M  T  U  U  E  A  A  O  E  E  C  S
S  E  I  S  B  R  R  E  R  V  S  Q  P
L  W  O  K  G  I  T  U  U  A  U  I  J
M  E  N  S  E  S  C  B  S  W  P  M  S
```

Crossword Puzzle

ACROSS

5. The combining form "oophor/o-" means _____.

7. The female _____ _____ includes the ovaries, uterine tubes, uterus, and vagina.

9. The combining form "galact/o-" means _____.

10. The combining form "_____" means vulva.

DOWN

1. The second phase of the menstrual cycle is the _____ phase.

2. A surgical procedure that sutures a weakness in the vaginal wall is called a/an _____.

3. The outer layer of the uterus is called the _____.

4. The ovaries are held in place by the _____ ligament.

6. _____ is the most abundant and biologically active of the female hormones.

8. The combining form "_____" means seizure.

Underline the Accented Syllable

Read the medical word. Then review the syllables in the pronunciation. Underline the primary (main) accented syllable in the pronunciation.

1. amenorrhea   (ah-meh-noh-ree-ah)

2. amniocentesis   (am-nee-oh-sen-tee-sis)

3. candidiasis   (kan-dih-dy-ah-sis)

4. colposcopy   (kohl-paws-koh-pee)

5. curettage   (kyoo-reh-tawzh)

6. dysplasia   (dis-play-zee-ah)

7. dystocia   (dis-toh-see-ah)

8. endometriosis   (en-doh-mee-tree-oh-sis)

9. fibrocystic   (fy-broh-sis-tik)

10. galactorrhea   (gah-lak-toh-ree-ah)

11. gynecology   (gy-neh-kawl-oh-jee)

12. hysterosalpingography   (his-ter-oh-sal-ping-gawg-rah-fee)

13. leiomyoma   (lie-oh-my-oh-mah)

14. nuchal   (noo-kal)

15. vaginitis   (vaj-ih-ny-tis)

Word Surgery

Read the medical word. Break the medical word into its word parts and give the meaning of each word part. Then give the definition of the medical word.

1. amenorrhea

   Suffix and its meaning: _____

   Prefix and its meaning: _____

   Combining form and its meaning: _____

   Medical word definition: _____

2. anovulation

   Suffix and its meaning: _____

   Prefix and its meaning: _____

   Combining form and its meaning: _____

   Medical word definition: _____

3. bilateral

   Suffix and its meaning: _____

   Prefix and its meaning: _____

   Combining form and its meaning: _____

   Medical word definition: _____

4. colposcopy

   Suffix and its meaning: _____

   Prefix and its meaning: _____

   Combining form and its meaning: _____

   Medical word definition: _____

5. dysplasia

   Suffix and its meaning: _____

   Prefix and its meaning: _____

   Combining form and its meaning: _____

   Medical word definition: _____

6. ectopic

Suffix and its meaning: _____

Prefix and its meaning: _____

Combining form and its meaning: _____

Medical word definition: _____

7. endometriosis

Suffix and its meaning: _____

Prefix and its meaning: _____

Combining form and its meaning: _____

Medical word definition: _____

8. episiotomy

Suffix and its meaning: _____

Prefix and its meaning: _____

Combining form and its meaning: _____

Medical word definition: _____

9. hysterosalpingography

Suffix and its meaning: _____

Prefix and its meaning: _____

Combining form and its meaning: _____

Combining form and its meaning: _____

Medical word definition: _____

10. leiomyoma

Suffix and its meaning: _____

Prefix and its meaning: _____

Combining form and its meaning: _____

Combining form and its meaning: _____

Medical word definition: _____

11. mammoplasty

Suffix and its meaning: _____

Prefix and its meaning: _____

Combining form and its meaning: _____

Medical word definition: _____

12. mastectomy

Suffix and its meaning: _____

Prefix and its meaning: _____

Combining form and its meaning: _____

Medical word definition: _____

13. oligohydramnios

Suffix and its meaning: _____

Prefix and its meaning: _____

Combining form and its meaning: _____

Combining form and its meaning: _____

Medical word definition: _____

14. perimenopausal

Suffix and its meaning: _____

Prefix and its meaning: _____

Combining form and its meaning: _____

Combining form and its meaning: _____

Medical word definition: _____

15. preeclampsia

Suffix and its meaning: _____

Prefix and its meaning: _____

Combining form and its meaning: _____

Medical word definition: _____

Chapter Quiz

MULTIPLE CHOICE

1. The most abundant and biologically active female hormone is:

    A. progesterone.

    B. estradiol.

    C. testosterone.

    D. menarche.

2. "Metri/o-" is the combining form for:

    A. follicle stimulating hormone.

    B. cervix.

    C. uterine tubes.

    D. uterus.

3. The production of colostrum and milk after childbirth is:

    A. effacement.

    B. lactation.

    C. anteflexion.

    D. parturition.

4. "Poly-" as in polycystic ovary syndrome means:

    A. many.

    B. malignancy.

    C. few.

    D. ovulation.

5. Dysmenorrhea has:

    A. a prefix meaning "painful or difficult."

    B. a combining form meaning "month."

    C. a suffix meaning "flow or discharge."

    D. All of the above.

6. Complete or partial separation of the placenta from the uterine wall is:

   A. abruptio placenta.

   B. cephalopelvic disproportion.

   C. ectopic pregnancy.

   D. inflammation of the placenta.

7. The immature neonate liver is not able to conjugate sufficient amounts of bilirubin, resulting in:

   A. nuchal cord.

   B. apnea.

   C. fetal distress.

   D. jaundice.

8. Chorionic villus sampling is a:

   A. genetic test of a portion of the placenta.

   B. test to measure the fetal age.

   C. treatment using stem cells.

   D. method of contraception.

9. When a speculum is inserted into the vagina to visualize the cervix, a tissue sample can be harvested. This procedure is known as:

   A. multigravida.

   B. lithotomy.

   C. Pap smear.

   D. Tanner staging.

10. Which of the following is a surgical procedure to change the size, shape, or position of the breast?

   A. mammoplasty

   B. lumpectomy

   C. culdoscopy

   D. conization

FILL IN THE BLANK

1. The wall of the uterus is made of three layers: the perimetrium, the myometrium, and the _____.

2. The _____ period is the time after birth (from the baby's perspective).

3. The production of a mature ovum through the process of mitosis and then meiosis is known as _____.

4. _____ is the first stool passed by a newborn.

5. "_____" is a prefix that means "forward or before."

6. Uterine descensus, also known as uterine _____, is the descent of the uterus from its usual position.

7. Inflammation of the breast caused by milk engorement in the breast or infection is known as _____.

8. The suffix "-centesis," as in amniocentesis, means a "_____."

9. _____ anesthesia is a local anesthesia produced by injection to decrease labor pain.

10. A surgical procedure to prevent pregnancy where short segments of both uterine tubes are removed is called a tubal _____.

TRUE/FALSE

_____ 1. Fraternal twins arise from two separate fertilized ova, but identical twins arise from a single fertilized ovum.

_____ 2. The uterine tubes are directly connected to the ovaries.

_____ 3. The chorion is a membranous sac that produces the fluid that surrounds and cushions the developing embryo and fetus.

_____ 4. "Toc/o-" is the combining form that refers to "labor and birth."

_____ 5. Pelvic pain, excessive uterine bleeding, and painful sexual intercourse can be caused by a benign smooth muscle tumor of the myometrium known as leiomyoma.

_____ 6. Painful or difficult intercourse is known as cystocele.

_____ 7. Placenta previa describes the position of the fetus as breech.

_____ 8. A medical procedure to induce labor involves inserting a hook into the cervical os to rupture the amniotic sac.

_____ 9. BRCA is an abbreviation that refers to a gene for breast cancer.

_____ 10. The words "gynecologist" and "obstetrician" both refer to the same medical specialty.

Pronunciation Checklist

Read each word and its pronunciation. Practice pronouncing each word. Verify your pronunciation by listening to the Pronunciation List on Medical Terminology Interactive. Check the box next to the word after you master its pronunciation.

❑ abortion (ah-BOR-shun)
❑ abruptio placentae
  (ab-RUP-shee-oh plah-SEN-tee)
❑ acrocyanosis
  (AK-roh-SY-ah-NOH-sis)
❑ adenocarcinoma
  (AD-eh-noh-KAR-sih-NOH-mah)
❑ adnexa (ad-NEK-sah)
❑ adnexal (ad-NEK-sal)
❑ alpha fetoprotein
  (AL-fah FEE-toh-PROH-teen)
❑ amenorrhea
  (AH-meh-noh-REE-ah)
❑ amniocentesis
  (AM-nee-oh-sen-TEE-sis)
❑ amnion (AM-nee-on)
❑ amniotic fluid (AM-nee-AWT-ik
  FLOO-id)
❑ amniotomy
  (AM-nee-AW-toh-mee)
❑ androgen (AN-droh-jen)
❑ anovulation
  (AN-aw-vyoo-LAY-shun)
❑ anteflexion (AN-tee-FLEK-shun)
❑ antepartum (AN-tee-PAR-tum)
❑ antibiotic drug
  (AN-tee-by-AWT-ik DRUHG)
  (AN-tih-by-AWT-ik)
❑ antibody (AN-tee-BAWD-ee)
  (AN-tih-BAWD-ee)
❑ apnea (AP-nee-ah)
❑ apneic (AP-nee-ik)
❑ areola (ah-REE-oh-lah)
❑ areolae (ah-REE-oh-lee)
❑ areolar (ah-REE-oh-lar)
❑ aspiration (AS-pih-RAY-shun)
❑ assay (AS-say)
❑ augmentation mammaplasty
  (AWG-men-TAY-shun
  MAM-ah-PLAS-tee)
❑ Bartholin's glands
  (BAR-thoh-linz GLANZ)
❑ bilateral (by-LAT-er-al)
❑ bimanual examination
  (by-MAN-yoo-al
  eks-ZAM-ih-NAY-shun)
❑ biophysical profile
  (BY-oh-FIZ-ih-kal PRO-file)

❑ biopsy (BY-awp-see)
❑ biparietal diameter
  (BY-pah-RY-eh-tal dy-AM-eh-ter)
❑ Braxton Hicks contraction
  (BRAK-ston HIKS
  con-TRAK-shun)
❑ breast (BREST)
❑ breech (BREECH)
❑ cancerous (KAN-ser-us)
❑ candidiasis (KAN-dih-DY-ah-sis)
❑ carcinoma (KAR-sih-NOH-mah)
❑ carcinoma *in situ*
  (KAR-sih-NOH-mah IN SY-too)
❑ cephalic presentation
  (seh-FAL-ik PREE-sen-TAY-shun)
❑ cephalopelvic disproportion
  (SEF-ah-loh-PEL-vik
  DIS-proh-POR-shun)
❑ cerclage (sir-CLAWJ)
❑ cervical (SER-vih-kal)
❑ cervical canal
  (SER-vih-kal kah-NAL)
❑ cervical os (SER-vih-kal AWS)
❑ cervix (SER-viks)
❑ cesarean section
  (seh-ZAY-ree-an SEK-shun)
❑ chorion (KOH-ree-on)
❑ chorionic (KOH-ree-ON-ik)
❑ chorionic villus sampling
  (KOH-ree-ON-ik VIL-us
  SAM-pling)
❑ chromosome
  (KROH-moh-sohm)
❑ cilia (SIL-ee-ah)
❑ climacteric (kly-MAK-ter-ik)
❑ clitoris (KLIT-oh-ris)
❑ colostrum (koh-LAWS-trum)
❑ colporrhaphy
  (kohl-POR-ah-fee)
❑ conception (con-SEP-shun)
❑ congenital (con-JEN-ih-tal)
❑ conization
  (KOH-nih-ZAY-shun)
❑ contraception
  (CON-trah-SEP-shun)
❑ corpus (KOR-pus)
❑ corpus luteum (KOR-pus
  LOO-tee-um)

❑ crowning (KROWN-ing)
❑ cryoprobe (KRY-oh-prohb)
❑ cryosurgery
  (KRY-oh-SER-jer-ee)
❑ culdoscopy
  (kul-DAWS-koh-pee)
❑ curettage (kyoo-reh-TAWZH)
❑ curet (kyoo-RET)
❑ cystocele (SIS-toh-seel)
❑ cytology (sy-TAWL-oh-jee)
❑ descensus (dee-SEN-sus)
❑ dilation (dy-LAY-shun)
❑ dissection (dih-SEK-shun)
❑ dorsal lithotomy (DOR-sal
  lih-THAW-toh-mee)
❑ dysfunctional uterine bleeding
  (dis-FUNK-shun-al YOO-ter-in
  BLEED-ing)
❑ dysmenorrhea
  (DIS-men-oh-REE-ah)
❑ dyspareunia
  (DIS-pah-ROO-nee-ah)
❑ dysplasia (dis-PLAY-zee-ah)
❑ dysplastic (dis-PLAS-tik)
❑ dystocia (dis-TOH-see-ah)
❑ eclampsia
  (ee-KLAMP-see-ah)
❑ ectocervical
  (EK-toh-SER-vih-kal)
❑ ectopic pregnancy
  (ek-TOP-ik PREG-nan-see)
❑ effacement (eh-FAYS-ment)
❑ embolization
  (EM-bol-ih-ZAY-shun)
❑ embryo (EM-bree-oh)
❑ embryonic (EM-bree-ON-ik)
❑ endocervical
  (EN-doh-SER-vih-kal)
❑ endometrial
  (EN-doh-MEE-tree-al)
❑ endometrial ablation
  (EN-doh-MEE-tree-al
  ah-BLAY-shun)
❑ endometriosis
  (EN-doh-MEE-tree-OH-sis)
❑ endometrium
  (EN-doh-MEE-tree-um)
❑ endoscope (EN-doh-skohp)

- epidural anesthesia
  (EP-ih-DOO-ral
  AN-es-THEE-zee-ah)
- episiotomy
  (eh-PIS-ee-AW-toh-mee)
- estradiol (ES-trah-DY-awl)
- excisional biopsy
  (ek-SIH-shun-al BY-awp-see)
- exfoliative cytology
  (eks-FOH-lee-ah-tiv
  sy-TAWL-oh-jee)
- fallopian tube (fah-LOH-pee-an
  TOOB)
- fertilization
  (FER-til-ih-ZAY-shun)
- fetal (FEE-tal)
- fetus (FEE-tus)
- fibrocystic disease
  (FY-broh-SIS-tik dih-ZEEZ)
- fimbriae (FIM-bree-ee)
- follicle (FAWL-ih-kl)
- follicle-stimulating hormone
  (FAWL-ih-kl STIM-yoo-lay-ting
  HOR-mohn)
- fontanel (FAWN-tah-NEL)
- fornix (FOR-niks)
- fraternal twins (frah-TER-nal
  TWINZ)
- fundal (FUN-dal)
- fundus (FUN-dus)
- galactorrhea
  (gah-LAK-toh-REE-ah)
- gamete (GAM-eet)
- gene (JEEN)
- genetic (jeh-NET-ik)
- genital (JEN-ih-tal)
- genitalia (JEN-ih-TAY-lee-ah)
- gestation (jes-TAY-shun)
- gestational diabetes mellitus
  (jes-TAY-shun-al
  DY-ah-BEE-teez MEL-ih-tus)
- gonad (GOH-nad)
- gonadotropin
  (GOH-nah-doh-TROH-pin)
- gravida (GRAV-ih-dah)
- gynecologic
  (GY-neh-koh-LAW-jik)
- gynecologist
  (GY-neh-KAWL-oh-jist)
- gynecology
  (GY-neh-KAWL-oh-jee)
- hemosalpinx
  (HEE-moh-SAL-pinks)

- human papillomavirus
  (HYOO-man
  PAP-ih-LOH-mah-VY-rus)
- hydatidiform mole
  (HY-dah-TID-ih-form MOHL)
- hydrosalpinx
  (HY-droh-SAL-pinks)
- hymen (HY-men)
- hyperbilirubinemia
  (HY-per-BIL-ih-ROO-bih-NEE-
  mee-ah)
- hyperemesis gravidarum
  (HY-per-EM-eh-sis
  GRAV-ih-DAIR-um)
- hysterectomy
  (HIS-ter-EK-toh-mee)
- hysteropexy
  (HIS-ter-oh-PEK-see)
- hysterosalpingogram
  (HIS-ter-oh-sal-PING-goh-gram)
- hysterosalpingography
  (HIS-ter-oh-SAL-ping-GAWG-
  rah-fee)
- incisional biopsy
  (in-SIH-shun-al BY-awp-see)
- incompetent cervix
  (in-COM-peh-tent SER-viks)
- induction (in-DUK-shun)
- inframammary
  (IN-frah-MAM-ah-ree)
- infundibulum
  (IN-fun-DIB-yoo-lum)
- insemination
  (in-SEM-ih-NAY-shun)
- intracytoplasmic sperm
  injection
  (IN-trah-SY-toh-PLAS-mik
  SPERM in-JEK-shun)
- intrafallopian transfer
  (IN-trah-fah-LOH-pee-an
  TRANS-fer)
- intrauterine cavity
  (IN-trah-YOO-ter-in)
  (IN-trah-YOO-ter-ine
  KAV-ih-tee)
- introitus (in-TROH-ih-tus)
- *in vitro* fertilization
  (IN VEE-troh
  FER-til-ih-ZAY-shun)
- involution (IN-voh-LOO-shun)
- involutional melancholy
  (IN-voh-LOO-shun-al
  MEL-an-KOH-lee-ah)

- ischemic phase (is-KEE-mik
  FAYZ)
- jaundice (JAWN-dis)
- labial (LAY-bee-al)
- labia majora (LAY-bee-ah
  mah-JOR-ah)
- labia minora (LAY-bee-ah
  my-NOR-ah)
- lactation (lak-TAY-shun)
- lactiferous duct (lak-TIF-er-us
  DUHKT)
- lactiferous lobule (lak-TIF-er-us
  LAWB-yool)
- laparoscope
  (LAP-ah-roh-SKOHP)
- laparoscopy
  (LAP-ah-RAWS-koh-pee)
- lecithin (LES-ih-thin)
- leiomyoma
  (LIE-oh-my-OH-mah)
- leiomyomata
  (LIE-oh-my-OH-mah-tah)
- leiomyosarcoma
  (LIE-oh-MY-oh-sar-KOH-mah)
- leukorrhea (LOO-koh-REE-ah)
- ligament (LIG-ah-ment)
- lochia (LOH-kee-ah)
- lumen (LOO-men)
- lumpectomy
  (lum-PEK-toh-mee)
- luteinizing hormone
  (LOO-tee-ih-NY-zing
  HOR-mohn)
- malignancy (mah-LIG-nan-see)
- malpresentation
  (MAL-pree-sen-TAY-shun)
- mammaplasty
  (MAM-ah-PLAS-tee)
- mammary glands
  (MAM-ah-ree GLANZ)
- mammogram (MAM-oh-gram)
- mammography
  (mah-MAWG-rah-fee)
- mammoplasty
  (MAM-oh-PLAS-tee)
- mastectomy
  (mas-TEK-toh-mee)
- mastitis (mas-TY-tis)
- mastopexy (MAS-toh-PEK-see)
- meconium (meh-KOH-nee-um)
- meconium aspiration
  (meh-KOH-nee-um
  AS-pih-RAY-shun)

- meiosis (my-OH-sis)
- menarche (meh-NAR-kee)
- menometrorrhagia
  (MEN-oh-MEE-troh-RAY-jee-ah)
- menopausal (MEN-oh-PAW-zal)
- menopause (MEN-oh-pawz)
- menorrhagia
  (MEN-oh-RAY-jee-ah)
- menses (MEN-seez)
- menstrual (MEN-stroo-al)
- menstruate (MEN-stroo-ate)
- menstruation
  (MEN-stroo-AA-shun)
- mitosis (my-TOH-sis)
- mons pubis (MAWNZ
  PYOO-bis)
- multigravida
  (MUL-tih-GRAV-ih-dah)
- multiparous (mul-TIP-ah-rus)
- myomectomy
  (MY-oh-MEK-toh-mee)
- myometrial
  (MY-oh-MEE-tree-al)
- myometritis
  (MY-oh-mee-TRY-tis)
- myometrium
  (MY-oh-MEE-tree-um)
- Nägele's rule (NAY-gelz ROOL)
- neonatal (NEE-oh-NAY-tal)
- neonate (NEE-oh-nayt)
- neonatologist
  (NEE-oh-nay-TAWL-oh-jist)
- neonatology
  (NEE-oh-nay-TAWL-oh-jee)
- nipple (NIP-l)
- nuchal cord (NOO-kal CORD)
- nulligravida
  (NUL-ih-GRAV-ih-dah)
- nurse midwife
  (NURS MID-wyfe)
- obstetrician
  (AWB-steh-TRISH-an)
- obstetrics (awb-STET-riks)
- oligohydramnios
  (OL-ih-goh-hy-DRAM-nee-ohs)
- oligomenorrhea
  (OL-ih-goh-MEN-oh-REE-ah)
- oocyte (OH-oh-site)
- oogenesis (OH-oh-JEN-eh-sis)
- oophorectomy
  (OH-of-or-EK-toh-mee)
- ova (OH-vah)
- ovarian (oh-VAIR-ee-an)

- ovary (OH-vah-ree)
- oviduct (OH-vih-dukt)
- ovulation (AWV-yoo-LAY-shun)
- ovum (OH-vum)
- oxytocin (AWK-see-TOH-sin)
- para (PAIR-ah)
- parturition
  (PAR-tyoo-RIH-shun)
- peau d'orange
  (poh-deh-RAHNJ)
- pediatrician
  (PEE-dee-ah-TRISH-an)
- pediatrics (PEE-dee-AT-riks)
- pelvic cavity
  (PEL-vik KAV-ih-tee)
- pelvic inflammatory disease
  (PEL-vik in-FLAM-ah-TOR-ee
  dih-ZEEZ)
- pelvimetry (pel-VIM-ih-tree)
- pendulous breast
  (PEN-dyoo-lus BREST)
- perimenopausal
  (PAIR-ee-MEN-oh-PAW-zal)
- perineal (PAIR-ih-NEE-al)
- perineum (PAIR-ih-NEE-um)
- peristalsis (PAIR-ih-STAL-sis)
- phototherapy
  (FOH-toh-THAIR-ah-pee)
- pica (PY-kah) (PEE-kah)
- placenta (plah-SEN-tah)
- placenta previa (plah-SEN-tah
  PREE-vee-ah)
- placental (plah-SEN-tal)
- polycystic disease
  (PAWL-ee-SIS-tik dih-ZEEZ)
- polyhydramnios
  (PAWL-ee-hy-DRAM-nee-ohs)
- postnatal (post-NAY-tal)
- postpartum (post-PAR-tum)
- postpartum depression
  (post-PAR-tum
  dee-PRESH-un)
- postpartum hemorrhage
  (post-PAR-tum HEM-oh-rij)
- preeclampsia
  (PREE-ee-KLAMP-see-ah)
- pregnant (PREG-nant)
- premenstrual dysphoric
  disorder (pree-MEN-stroo-al
  dis-FOR-ik dis-OR-der)
- premenstrual syndrome
  (pree-MEN-stroo-al SIN-drohm)
- prenatal (pree-NAY-tal)

- primigravida
  (PRY-mih-GRAV-ih-dah)
- progesterone
  (proh-JES-teh-rohn)
- prolapse (PROH-laps)
- proliferative phase
  (proh-LIF-er-ah-tiv FAYZ)
- prophylactic (PROH-fih-LAK-tik)
- prostaglandin
  (PRAWS-tah-GLAN-din)
- prosthesis (praws-THEE-sis)
- pubic (PYOO-bik)
- pyometritis
  (PY-oh-mee-TRY-tis)
- pyosalpinx (PY-oh-SAL-pinks)
- radical mastectomy
  (RAD-ih-kal mas-TEK-toh-mee)
- receptor (ree-SEP-tor)
- reconstructive breast surgery
  (REE-con-STRUK-tiv BREST
  SER-jer-ee)
- reduction mammaplasty
  (ree-DUK-shun
  MAM-ah-PLAS-tee)
- reproductive system
  (REE-proh-DUK-tiv SIS-tem)
- retroflexion
  (RET-roh-FLEK-shun)
- retroversion
  (RET-roh-VER-shun)
- salpingectomy
  (SAL-pin-JEK-toh-mee)
- salpingitis (SAL-pin-JY-tis)
- salpingo-oophorectomy
  (sal-PING-goh-
  OH-of-or-EK-toh-mee)
- secretory phase
  (SEE-kreh-TOH-ree FAYZ)
- Skene's glands (SKEENZ
  GLANZ)
- sonogram (SAWN-oh-gram)
- speculum (SPEK-yoo-lum)
- sphingomyelin
  (SFING-goh-MY-eh-lin)
- stereotactic biopsy
  (STAIR-ee-oh-TAK-tik
  BY-awp-see)
- surfactant (ser-FAK-tant)
- tampon (TAM-pawn)
- tenaculum (teh-NAK-yoo-lum)
- therapeutic abortion
  (THAIR-ah-PYOO-tik
  ah-BOR-shun)

- ❏ tocolytic drug (TOH-koh-LIT-ik DRUHG)
- ❏ transvaginal ultrasound (trans-VAJ-ih-nal UL-trah-sound)
- ❏ transverse rectus abdominis muscle (trans-VERS REK-tus ab-DAWM-ih-nis MUS-el)
- ❏ trimester (TRY-mes-ter) (try-MES-ter)
- ❏ tubal anastomosis (TOO-bal ah-NAS-toh-MOH-sis)
- ❏ tubal ligation (TOO-bal ly-GAY-shun)
- ❏ tubal pregnancy (TOO-bal PREG-nan-see)
- ❏ ultrasonography (UL-trah-soh-NAWG-rah-fee)
- ❏ ultrasound (UL-trah-sound)
- ❏ umbilical (um-BIL-ih-kal)
- ❏ umbilicus (um-BIL-ih-kus) (UM-bih-LIE-kus)
- ❏ urethral glands (yoo-REE-thral GLANZ)
- ❏ uterine (YOO-ter-in) (YOO-ter-ine)
- ❏ uterine inertia (YOO-ter-in in-ER-shee-ah) (YOO-ter-ine)
- ❏ uterine suspension (YOO-ter-in sus-PEN-shun) (YOO-ter-ine)
- ❏ uterus (YOO-ter-us)
- ❏ vagina (vah-JY-nah)
- ❏ vaginal (VAJ-ih-nal)
- ❏ vaginitis (VAJ-ih-NY-tis)
- ❏ vaginosis (VAJ-ih-NOH-sis)
- ❏ vernix caseosa (VER-niks KAY-see-OH-sah)
- ❏ version (VER-zhun)
- ❏ vertex presentation (VER-teks PREE-sen-TAY-shun)
- ❏ vulva (VUL-vah)
- ❏ vulvar (VUL-var)
- ❏ xeromammogram (ZEER-oh-MAM-oh-gram)
- ❏ xeromammography (ZEER-oh-mah-MAWG-rah-fee)
- ❏ zygote (ZY-goht)

Answer Key

Word Search

Crossword Puzzle

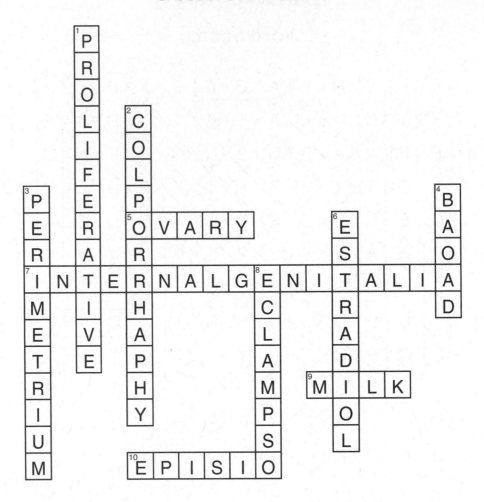

Underline the Accented Syllable

1. amenorrhea   (AH-meh-noh-<u>REE</u>-ah)

2. amniocentesis   (AM-nee-oh-sen-<u>TEE</u>-sis)

3. candidiasis   (KAN-dih-<u>DY</u>-ah-sis)

4. colposcopy   (kohl-<u>PAWS</u>-koh-pee)

5. curettage   (kyoo-reh-<u>TAWZH</u>)

6. dysplasia   (dis-<u>PLAY</u>-zee-ah)

7. dystocia   (dis-<u>TOH</u>-see-ah)

8. endometriosis   (EN-doh-MEE-tree-<u>OH</u>-sis)

9. fibrocystic   (FY-broh-<u>SIS</u>-tik)

10. galactorrhea   (gah-LAK-toh-<u>REE</u>-ah)

11. gynecology   (GY-neh-<u>KAWL</u>-oh-jee)

12. hysterosalpingography   (HIS-ter-oh-SAL-ping-<u>GAWG</u>-rah-fee)

13. leiomyoma   (LIE-oh-my-<u>OH</u>-mah)

14. nuchal   (<u>NOO</u>-kal)

15. vaginitis   (VAJ-ih-<u>NY</u>-tis)

Word Surgery

1. amenorrhea

   Suffix and its meaning: -rrhea *flow; discharge*

   Prefix and its meaning: a- *away from; without*

   Combining form and its meaning: men/o- *month*

   Medical word definition: Flow or discharge (that is) without (substance during the) month

2. anovulation

   Suffix and its meaning: -ation *a process; being or having*

   Prefix and its meaning: an- *without; not*

   Combining form and its meaning: ovul/o- *ovum (egg)*

   Medical word definition: A process of (being) without an ovum

3. bilateral

   Suffix and its meaning: -al *pertaining to*

   Prefix and its meaning: bi- *two*

   Combining form and its meaning: later/o- *side*

   Medical word definition: Pertaining to two sides

4. colposcopy

   Suffix and its meaning: -scopy *process of using an instrument to examine*

   Prefix and its meaning: none

   Combining form and its meaning: colp/o- *vagina*

   Medical word definition: Process of using an instrument to examine the vagina

5. dysplasia

   Suffix and its meaning: -ia *condition; state; thing*

   Prefix and its meaning: dys- *painful; difficult; abnormal*

   Combining form and its meaning: plas/o- *growth; formation*

   Medical word definition: Condition of abnormal growth or formation

6. ectopic

Suffix and its meaning: -ic *pertaining to*

Prefix and its meaning: none

Combining form and its meaning: ectop/o- *outside of a place*

Medical word definition: Pertaining to outside of (the usual) place

7. endometriosis

Suffix and its meaning: -osis *condition; abnormal condition; process*

Prefix and its meaning: endo- *innermost; within*

Combining form and its meaning: metri/o- *uterus (womb)*

Medical word definition: Abnormal condition (of the) innermost (lining) of the uterus

8. episiotomy

Suffix and its meaning: -tomy *process of cutting or making an incision*

Prefix and its meaning: none

Combining form and its meaning: episi/o- *vulva*

Medical word definition: Process of cutting or making an incision into the vulva

9. hysterosalpingography

Suffix and its meaning: -graphy *process of recording*

Prefix and its meaning: none

Combining form and its meaning: hyster/o- *uterus (womb)*

Combining form and its meaning: salping/o- *uterine (fallopian) tube*

Medical word definition: Process of recording (by using dye) the uterus and uterine tubes

10. leiomyoma

Suffix and its meaning: -oma *tumor; mass*

Prefix and its meaning: none

Combining form and its meaning: lei/o- *smooth*

Combining form and its meaning: my/o- *muscle*

Medical word definition: Tumor of the smooth muscle (in the uterine wall)

11. mammoplasty

   Suffix and its meaning: -plasty *process of reshaping by surgery*

   Prefix and its meaning: none

   Combining form and its meaning: mamm/a- *breast*

   Medical word definition: Process of reshaping by surgery on the breast

12. mastectomy

   Suffix and its meaning: -ectomy *surgical excision*

   Prefix and its meaning: none

   Combining form and its meaning: mast/o- *breast; mastoid process*

   Medical word definition: Surgical excision of the breast

13. oligohydramnios

   Suffix and its meaning: -amnios *amniotic fluid*

   Prefix and its meaning: none

   Combining form and its meaning: olig/o- *scanty; few*

   Combining form and its meaning: hydr/o- *water; fluid*

   Medical word definition: Amniotic fluid that (has) scanty fluid (volume)

14. perimenopausal

   Suffix and its meaning: -al *pertaining to*

   Prefix and its meaning: peri- *around*

   Combining form and its meaning: men/o- *month*

   Combining form and its meaning: paus/o- *cessation*

   Medical word definition: Pertaining to around (the time of) monthly (period) cessation

15. preeclampsia

   Suffix and its meaning: -ia *condition; state; thing*

   Prefix and its meaning: pre- *before; in front of*

   Combining form and its meaning: eclamps/o- *a seizure*

   Medical word definition: State before a seizure

Chapter Quiz

MULTIPLE CHOICE

1. B	4. A	7. D	10. A
2. D	5. D	8. A	
3. B	6. A	9. C	

FILL IN THE BLANK

1. endometrium

2. postnatal

3. oogenesis

4. Meconium

5. ante-

6. prolapse

7. mastitis

8. procedure to puncture

9. Epidural

10. ligation

TRUE/FALSE

1. True

2. False (not connected)

3. False (amnion)

4. True

5. True

6. False (dyspareunia)

7. False (incorrect position of the placenta covering the cervical canal)

8. True

9. True

10. False (gynecologists are physicians who diagnose and treat patients with diseases of the female genitalia and reproductive system, whereas obstetricians deliver babies and perform cesarean sections)

CHAPTER 14

Endocrinology

Measure Your Progress: Learning Objectives

After reading this chapter, the student should be able to

- Identify the structures of the endocrine system.
- Describe the process of hormone response and feedback.
- Describe common endocrine diseases and conditions, laboratory and diagnostic procedures, medical and surgical procedures, and drug categories.
- Give the medical meaning of word parts related to the endocrine system.
- Build endocrine words from word parts and divide and define endocrine words.
- Spell and pronounce endocrine words.
- Analyze the medical content and meaning of an endocrinology report.
- Dive deeper into endocrinology by reviewing the activities at the end of this chapter and online at Medical Terminology Interactive.

It All Starts with Word Building

Medical language is all about medical words and their word parts. Jump right into this chapter by learning some of the common combining forms and their definitions that you will encounter in the chapter.

acr/o-	extremity; highest point
aden/o-	gland
adrenal/o-	adrenal gland
andr/o-	male
antagon/o-	oppose or work against
calc/o-	calcium
cortic/o-	cortex (outer region)
diabet/o-	diabetes
estr/a-	female
estr/o-	female
genit/o-	genitalia
gigant/o-	giant
glandul/o-	gland
gluc/o-	glucose (sugar)
glyc/o-	glucose (sugar)
glycos/o-	glucose (sugar)
gonad/o-	gonads (ovaries and testes)
home/o-	same
hormon/o-	hormone
hypophys/o-	pituitary gland
inhibit/o-	block; hold back
insulin/o-	insulin
melan/o-	black
mineral/o-	mineral; electrolyte
nod/o-	node (knob of tissue)
ovari/o-	ovary
pancreat/o-	pancreas
pituitar/o-	pituitary gland
pituit/o-	pituitary gland
recept/o-	receive
secret/o-	produce; secrete
somat/o-	body
stimul/o-	exciting; strengthening
testicul/o-	testis; testicle
test/o-	testis; testicle
thyr/o-	shield-shaped structure (thyroid gland)
thym/o-	thymus
thyroid/o-	thyroid gland
trop/o-	having an affinity for; stimulating; turning

Chapter Spelling Test

Dictate and spell (or photocopy a handout that contains) this list of 20 spelling words. Give this list to students to study for the week. At the beginning of next week's class, dictate 10 of these words as the spelling test. The spelling test is included with the chapter test that is given on the previous week's material.

1. acromegaly
2. corticosteroid drug
3. diabetes insipidus
4. diabetes mellitus
5. epinephrine
6. euthyroidism
7. glucosuria
8. glycogen
9. gynecomastia
10. hirsutism
11. homeostasis
12. hyperthyroidism
13. hypothalamus
14. ketoacidosis
15. luteinizing hormone
16. pineal gland
17. pituitary gland
18. polydipsia
19. synergism
20. thyromegaly

Chapter Pronunciation Test

Photocopy a handout that contains this list of 10 pronunciation words. Give this list to students to study for the week. Sometime at the beginning of the next week, each student should call your office or home answering machine and pronounce each word.

1. acromegaly (AK-roh-MEG-ah-lee)

2. diabetes mellitus (DY-ah-BEE-teez MEL-ih-tus)

3. euthyroidism (yoo-THY-royd-izm)

4. glucosuria (GLY-kohs-YOO-ree-ah)

5. ketoacidosis (KEE-toh-AS-ih-DOH-sis)

6. hirsutism (HER-soo-tizm)

7. homeostasis (HOH-mee-oh-STAY-sis)

8. hyperpituitarism (HY-per-pih-TOO-ih-tah-rizm)

9. hyperthyroidism (HY-poh-THY-royd-izm)

10. polydipsia (PAWL-lee-DIP-see-ah)

Word Search

Complete this word search puzzle that contains Chapter 14 words. Look for the following words as given in the list below. The number in parentheses indicates how many times the word appears in the puzzle.

ACTH (2)	hormone
Addison	insulin
adenoma	ketoacidosis
Cushing	NIDDM
diabetes	nodule
dwarf	OGTT
euthyroidism	pancreas
FSH	pituitary
glands	RIA
glucose	SIADH
goiter	TSH

```
E  S  P  A  N  C  R  E  A  S  W  K
A  U  I  J  D  I  A  B  E  T  E  S
M  Q  T  A  E  K  G  U  N  T  G  T
O  O  U  H  D  L  L  P  O  M  L  T
N  B  I  S  Y  H  U  A  M  D  A  G
E  N  T  D  B  R  C  D  R  D  N  O
D  W  A  R  F  I  O  D  O  I  D  I
A  K  R  J  D  T  S  I  H  N  S  T
C  P  Y  O  S  D  E  S  D  U  A  E
T  F  S  H  Y  X  U  O  P  I  K  R
H  I  C  H  T  C  A  N  R  O  S  D
S  O  Z  J  N  I  L  U  S  N  I  M
```

Crossword Puzzle

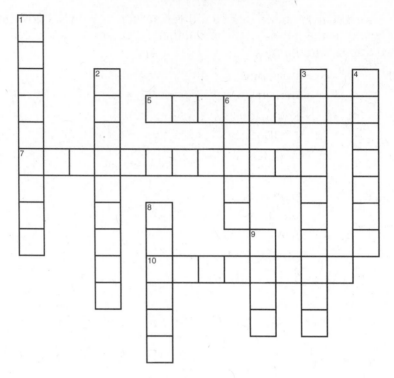

ACROSS

5. The pineal gland secretes the hormone _____, which maintains the body's internal clock and the 24-hour wake-sleep cycle.

7. _____ is a condition characterized by a low level of glucose in the blood.

10. _____ is a hormone that stimulates the pregnant uterus to contract during labor and childbirth.

DOWN

1. The Greek combining form "_____" means pituitary gland.

2. The _____ system is made up of glands in various parts of the body.

3. _____ is a process in which two hormones exert opposite effects.

4. The hormone _____ is secreted by the beta cells of the islets of Langerhans (in the pancreas) and functions to facilitate the transport of glucose.

6. The combining form for gland is "_____."

8. Hypersecretion of the _____ hormone during childhood and puberty leads to a condition known as gigantism.

9. The combining form "somat/o-" means _____.

Underline the Accented Syllable

Read the medical word. Then review the syllables in the pronunciation. Underline the primary (main) accented syllable in the pronunciation.

1. adenomata   (ad-eh-noh-mah-tah)

2. diabetes   (dy-ah-bee-teez)

3. endocrinology   (en-doh-krih-nawl-oh-jee)

4. exophthalmos   (eks-awf-thal-mohs)

5. gestational   (jes-tay-shun-al)

6. glycosuria   (gly-kohs-yoo-ree-ah)

7. gynecomastia   (gy-neh-koh-mas-tee-ah)

8. hypercalcemia   (hy-per-kal-see-mee-ah)

9. hypophysectomy   (hy-pawf-ih-sek-toh-mee)

10. hypopituitarism   (hy-poh-pih-too-ih-tah-rizm)

11. lactation   (lak-tay-shun)

12. myxedema   (mik-she-dee-mah)

13. nephropathy   (neh-frawp-ah-thee)

14. pheochromocytoma   (fee-oh-kroh-moh-sy-toh-mah)

15. polydipsia   (pawl-ee-dip-see-ah)

Word Surgery

Read the medical word. Break the medical word into its word parts and give the meaning of each word part. Then give the definition of the medical word.

1. acromegaly

   Suffix and its meaning: _____

   Prefix and its meaning: _____

   Combining form and its meaning: _____

   Medical word definition: _____

2. adrenalectomy

   Suffix and its meaning: _____

   Prefix and its meaning: _____

   Combining form and its meaning: _____

   Medical word definition: _____

3. galactorrhea

   Suffix and its meaning: _____

   Prefix and its meaning: _____

   Combining form and its meaning: _____

   Medical word definition: _____

4. glycohemoglobin

   Suffix and its meaning: _____

   Prefix and its meaning: _____

   Combining form and its meaning: _____

   Combining form and its meaning: _____

   Combining form and its meaning: _____

   Medical word definition: _____

5. infertility

   Suffix and its meaning: _____

   Prefix and its meaning: _____

   Combining form and its meaning: _____

   Medical word definition: _____

6. homeostasis

Suffix and its meaning: _____

Prefix and its meaning: _____

Combining form and its meaning: _____

Medical word definition: _____

7. hypercalcemia

Suffix and its meaning: _____

Prefix and its meaning: _____

Combining form and its meaning: _____

Medical word definition: _____

8. hyperpituitarism

Suffix and its meaning: _____

Prefix and its meaning: _____

Combining form and its meaning: _____

Medical word definition: _____

9. hypoglycemia

Suffix and its meaning: _____

Prefix and its meaning: _____

Combining form and its meaning: _____

Medical word definition: _____

10. ketoacidosis

Suffix and its meaning: _____

Prefix and its meaning: _____

Combining form and its meaning: _____

Combining form and its meaning: _____

Medical word definition: _____

11. nephropathy

Suffix and its meaning: _____

Prefix and its meaning: _____

Combining form and its meaning: _____

Medical word definition: _____

12. pheochromocytoma

Suffix and its meaning: _____

Prefix and its meaning: _____

Combining form and its meaning: _____

Combining form and its meaning: _____

Combining form and its meaning: _____

Medical word definition: _____

13. polydipsia

Suffix and its meaning: _____

Prefix and its meaning: _____

Combining form and its meaning: _____

Medical word definition: _____

14. synergism

Suffix and its meaning: _____

Prefix and its meaning: _____

Combining form and its meaning: _____

Medical word definition: _____

15. transsphenoidal

Suffix and its meaning: _____

Prefix and its meaning: _____

Combining form and its meaning: _____

Medical word definition: _____

Chapter Quiz

MULTIPLE CHOICE

1. The combining form for "gland" is:

   A. acr/o-.

   B. aden/o-.

   C. andr/o-.

   D. antagon/o-.

2. As an endocrine gland, the pancreas secretes three hormones from a group of cells called:

   A. medulla.

   B. insulin glands.

   C. islets of Langerhans.

   D. adrenal glands.

3. The endocrine gland in the brain that is connected by a stalk to the hypothalamus and is sometimes referred to as the master gland is the:

   A. pituitary gland.

   B. adrenal gland.

   C. pineal gland.

   D. thyroid gland.

4. When one hormone works to inhibit or prevent the action of an endocrine gland, the action is called:

   A. receptor failure.

   B. stimulation.

   C. synergism.

   D. inhibition.

5. Which of the following medical conditions is caused by problems with hormone secretion from the anterior pituitary?

   A. galactorrhea

   B. gigantism

   C. acromegally

   D. All of the above.

6. The suffix "-oma," as in adenoma, is a:

   A. prefix meaning "cancer."

   B. suffix meaning "tumor or mass."

   C. a combining form meaning "diabetes."

   D. a suffix meaning "secretion."

7. Which of the following can be associated with diabetes?

   A. hyperglycemia

   B. polyuria

   C. polydipsia

   D. All of the above.

8. Addison's disease is a result of:

   A. hyposecretion of cortisol.

   B. hypersecretion of luteinizing hormone.

   C. gynecomastia.

   D. All of the above.

9. The chemical symbol Na or Na^+ refers to:

   A. albumin.

   B. hemoglobin.

   C. potassium.

   D. sodium.

10. A diabetes educator:

   A. teaches patients about food, how to monitor blood sugar, and about their medications.

   B. is a physician.

   C. treats diabetes by prescribing medications.

   D. is a person who works in a medical laboratory.

FILL IN THE BLANK

1. The parathyroid glands are located on the _____ surface of the thyroid gland.

2. _____ is the state of equilibrium of the internal body environment.

3. The adrenal _____ is the outermost layer of the adrenal gland.

4. _____ of any hormone refers to excessive production.

5. The most common form of hyperthyroidism is an autoimmune disease called _____ disease.

6. Hypoglycemia refers to a _____ level of glucose in the blood.

7. A blood test that measures glucose levels after not eating for at least 12 hours is known as a _____ blood sugar test.

8. The suffix "-ectomy," as in thyroidectomy, means "_____."

9. ACTH is the abbreviation for _____.

10. "Galact/o-" is the *Greek* combining form for "milk"; the *Latin* combining form is "_____."

TRUE/FALSE

_____ 1. The prefix "endo-," as in endocrinology, means innermost or within.

_____ 2. T_3 and T_4 are hormones made in the thymus gland.

_____ 3. The pineal gland is located in the thoracic cavity.

_____ 4. The "o" in estradiol is the combining vowel.

_____ 5. Diabetes insipidus is the hyposecretion of antidiuretic hormone (ADH).

_____ 6. The suffix "-partum," as in postpartum, means childbirth.

_____ 7. One main difference between type 1 and type 2 diabetes is that type 1 usually begins in juveniles.

_____ 8. The enlargement of male breasts is known as mastectomy.

_____ 9. A high level of ketones in the blood and urine result from an excess of insulin.

_____ 10. Corticosteroid drugs mimic the action of hormones from the adrenal cortex.

Pronunciation Checklist

Read each word and its pronunciation. Practice pronouncing each word. Verify your pronunciation by listening to the Pronunciation List on Medical Terminology Interactive. Check the box next to the word after you master its pronunciation.

❑ acromegaly
(AK-roh-MEG-ah-lee)
❑ Addison's disease (AD-ih-sonz
dih-ZEEZ)
❑ adenohypophysis
(AD-eh-noh-hy-PAWF-ih-sis)
❑ adenoma (AD-eh-NOH-mah)
❑ adenomata
(AD-eh-NOH-mah-tah)
❑ adenomatous
(AD-eh-NOH-mah-tus)
❑ adrenal (ah-DREE-nal)
❑ adrenalectomy
(ah-DREE-nal-EK-toh-mee)
❑ adrenocorticotropic (ah-DREE-
noh-KOR-tih-koh-TROH-pik)
❑ adrenogenital syndrome
(ah-DREE-noh-JEN-ih-tal
SIN-drohm)
❑ aldosterone (al-DAWS-ter-ohn)
❑ androgens (AN-droh-jens)
❑ antagonism (an-TAG-on-izm)
❑ antidiabetic drug
(AN-tee-DY-ah-BET-ik DRUHG)
❑ antidiuretic hormone
(AN-tee-DY-yoo-RET-ik
HOR-mohn)
❑ antithyroglobulin antibody
(AN-tee-THY-roh-GLAWB-yoo-lin
AN-tee-BAWD-ee)
(AN-tih-BAWD-ee)
❑ antithyroid drug
(AN-tee-THY-royd DRUHG)
❑ biopsy (BY-awp-see)
❑ calcitonin (KAL-sih-TOH-nin)
❑ calcium (KAL-see-um)
❑ carcinoma (KAR-sih-NOH-mah)
❑ circadian rhythm
(ser-KAY-dee-an RITH-um)
❑ congenital (con-JEN-ih-tal)
❑ cortex (KOR-teks)
❑ cortical (KOR-tih-kal)
❑ cortices (KOR-tih-seez)
❑ corticosteroid drug
(KOR-tih-koh-STAIR-oyd
DRUHG)
❑ cortisol (KOR-tih-sawl)
❑ cretinism (KREE-tin-izm)
❑ Cushing's disease
(KOOSH-ingz dih-ZEEZ)

❑ Cushing's syndrome
(KOOSH-ingz SIN-drohm)
❑ diabetes educator
(DY-ah-BEE-teez
ED-jyoo-KAY-ter)
❑ diabetes insipidus
(DY-ah-BEE-teez in-SIP-ih-dus)
❑ diabetes mellitus
(DY-ah-BEE-teez MEL-ih-tus)
❑ diabetic (DY-ah-BET-ik)
❑ diabetic ketoacidosis
(DY-ah-BET-ik
KEE-toh-AS-ih-DOH-sis)
❑ diabetic nephropathy
(DY-ah-BET-ik
neh-FRAWP-ah-thee)
❑ diabetic neuropathy
(DY-ah-BET-ik
nyoo-RAWP-ah-thee)
❑ diabetic retinopathy
(DY-ah-BET-ik
RET-ih-NAWP-ah-thee)
❑ diabetologist
(DY-ah-beh-TAWL-oh-jist)
❑ dwarfism (DWORF-izm)
❑ endemic goiter (en-DEM-ik
GOY-ter)
❑ endocrine system (EN-doh-krin
SIS-tem) (EN-doh-krine)
❑ endocrinologist
(EN-doh-krih-NAWL-oh-jist)
❑ endocrinology
(EN-doh-krih-NAWL-oh-jee)
❑ epinephrine (EP-ih-NEF-rin)
❑ estradiol (ES-trah-DY-awl)
❑ euthyroidism
(yoo-THY-royd-izm)
❑ exophthalmos
(EKS-awf-THAL-mohs)
❑ follicle (FAWL-ih-kl)
❑ galactorrhea
(gah-LAK-toh-REE-ah)
❑ gestational diabetes
(jes-TAY-shun-al
DY-ah-BEE-teez)
❑ gigantism (jy-GAN-tizm)
(JY-gan-tizm)
❑ gland (GLAND)
❑ glandular (GLAN-dyoo-lar)
❑ glucagon (GLOO-kah-gawn)

❑ glucocorticoid
(GLOO-koh-KOR-tih-koyd)
❑ glycogen (GLY-koh-jen)
❑ glycohemoglobin
(GLY-koh-HEE-moh-GLOH-bin)
❑ glucose (GLOO-kohs)
❑ glycosuria
(GLY-kohs-YOO-ree-ah)
❑ glycosylated hemoglobin
(gly-KOH-sih-lay-ted
HEE-moh-GLOH-bin)
❑ goiter (GOY-ter)
❑ gonadotropin
(GOH-nah-doh-TROH-pin)
❑ Graves' disease
(GRAYVZ dih-ZEEZ)
❑ gynecomastia
(GY-neh-koh-MAS-tee-ah)
❑ Hashimoto's thyroiditis
(HAH-shee-MOH-tohz
THY-roy-DY-tis)
❑ hemoglobin A1c
(HEE-moh-GLOH-bin
AA-one-see)
❑ hirsutism (HER-soo-tizm)
❑ homeostasis
(HOH-mee-oh-STAY-sis)
❑ hormonal (hor-MOH-nal)
❑ hormone (HOR-mohn)
❑ hydroxycorticosteroids
(hy-DRAWK-see-KOR-tih-koh-
STAIR-oydz)
❑ hyperaldosteronism
(HY-per-al-DAWS-ter-ohn-izm)
❑ hypercalcemia
(HY-per-kal-SEE-mee-ah)
❑ hyperglycemia
(HY-per-gly-SEE-mee-ah)
❑ hyperinsulinism
(HY-per-IN-soo-lin-izm)
❑ hyperparathyroidism
(HY-per-PAIR-ah-THY-royd-izm)
❑ hyperpituitarism
(HY-per-pih-TOO-ih-tah-rizm)
❑ hypersecretion
(HY-per-seh-KREE-shun)
❑ hyperthyroidism
(HY-per-THY-royd-izm)
❑ hypoaldosteronism
(HY-poh-al-DAWS-ter-ohn-izm)

- hypocalcemia
  (HY-poh-kal-SEE-mee-ah)
- hypoglycemia
  (HY-poh-gly-SEE-mee-ah)
- hypoparathyroidism
  (HY-poh-PAIR-ah-THY-royd-izm)
- hypophysial
  (HY-poh-FIZ-ee-al)
- hypophysis (hy-PAWF-ih-sis)
- hypopituitarism
  (HY-poh-pih-TOO-ih-tah-rizm)
- hyposecretion
  (HY-poh-seh-KREE-shun)
- hypothalamic
  (HY-poh-thah-LAM-ik)
- hypothalamus
  (HY-poh-THAL-ah-mus)
- hypothyroidism
  (HY-poh-THY-royd-izm)
- infertility (IN-fer-TIL-ih-tee)
- inhibition (IN-hih-BISH-un)
- insulin (IN-soo-lin)
- insulin resistance syndrome
  (IN-soo-lin ree-ZIS-tans
  SIN-drohm)
- iodine (EYE-oh-dine)
  (EYE-oh-deen)
- islets of Langerhans (EYE-lets
  of LAHNG-er-hanz)
- isthmus (IS-mus)
- ketones (KEE-tohnz)
- lactatation (lak-TAY-shun)
- lobe (LOHB)
- lobectomy (loh-BEK-toh-mee)
- luteinizing
  (LOO-tee-in-NY-zing)
- medulla (meh-DUL-ah)
- medullae (meh-DUL-ee)
- melanocyte (meh-LAN-oh-site)
  (MEL-ah-noh-SITE)
- melatonin (MEL-ah-TOH-nin)
- menopause (MEN-oh-pawz)
- mineralocorticoid
  (MIN-er-al-oh-KOR-tih-koyd)
- multinodular goiter
  (MUL-tee-NAWD-yoo-lar
  GOY-ter)
- myxedema
  (MIK-seh-DEE-mah)
- neurohypophysis
  (NYOOR-oh-hy-PAWF-ih-sis)
- nodular (NAWD-yoo-lar)
- nodule (NAWD-yool)
- nontoxic goiter
  (non-TAWK-sik GOY-ter)
- norepinephrine
  (NOR-ep-ih-NEF-rin)
- ovarian (oh-VAIR-ee-an)
- ovary (OH-vah-ree)
- oxytocin (AWK-see-TOH-sin)
- pancreas (PAN-kree-as)
- pancreatic (PAN-kree-AT-ik)
- panhypopituitarism (pan-HY-
  poh-pih-TOO-eh-tah-rizm)
- parathyroid (PAIR-ah-THY-royd)
- parathyroidectomy (PAIR-ah-
  THY-roy-DEK-toh-mee)
- pheochromocytoma (FEE-oh-
  KROH-moh-sy-TOH-mah)
- pineal (PIN-ee-al)
- pituitary (pih-TOO-eh-TAIR-ee)
- polydipsia (PAWL-ee-DIP-see-ah)
- polyphagia
  (PAWL-ee-FAY-jee-ah)
- polyuria
  (PAWL-ee-YOO-ree-ah)
- precocious puberty
  (prih-KOH-shus PYOO-ber-tee)
- progesterone
  (proh-JES-teh-rohn)
- prolactin (proh-LAK-tin)
- radioactive iodine
  (RAY-dee-oh-AK-tiv
  EYE-oh-dine) (EYE-oh-deen)
- receptor (ree-SEP-tor)
- seasonal affective disorder
  (SEE-son-al ah-FEK-tiv
  dis-OR-der)
- sella turcica (SEL-ah
  TUR-sih-kah)
- somatostatin
  (SOH-mah-toh-STAT-in)
- stimulate (STIM-yoo-layt)
- stimulation
  (STIM-yoo-LAY-shun)
- synergism (SIN-er-jizm)
- testes (TES-teez)
- testicle (TES-tih-kl)
- testicular (tes-TIK-yoo-lar)
- testis (TES-tis)
- testosterone
  (tes-TAWS-teh-rohn)
- tetany (TET-ah-nee)
- thymectomy
  (thy-MEK-toh-mee)
- thymic (THY-mik)
- thymosin (thy-MOH-sin)
- thymus (THY-mus)
- thyroid (THY-royd)
- thyroidectomy
  (THY-roy-DEK-toh-mee)
- thyroiditis (THY-roy-DY-tis)
- thyromegaly
  (THY-roh-MEG-ah-lee)
- thyrotoxicosis
  (THY-roh-TAWK-sih-KOH-sis)
- thyroxine (thy-RAWK-seen)
  (thy-RAWK-sin)
- toxic goiter (TAWK-sik GOY-ter)
- transsphenoidal hypophysectomy (TRANS-sfee-NOY-dal
  HY-pawf-ih-SEK-toh-mee)
- triiodothyronine
  (try-EYE-oh-doh-THY-roh-neen)
- uterine inertia (YOO-ter-in)
  (YOO-ter-ine) (in-ER-shah)
  (in-ER-shee-ah)
- vanillylmandelic acid
  (VAN-ih-lil-man-DEL-ik AS-id)
- virilism (VIR-ih-lizm)

Answer Key

Word Search

E S P A N C R E A S W K
A U I J D I A B E T E S
M Q T A E K G U N T G T
O O U H D L L P O M L T
N B I S Y H U A M D A G
E N T D B R C D R D N O
D W A R F I O D O I I I
A K R J D T S I H N S T
C P Y O S D E S D U A E
T F S H Y X U O P I K R
H I C H T C A N R O S D
S O Z J N I L U S N I M

Crossword Puzzle

Across:
- 5. MELATONIN
- 7. HYPOGLYCEMIA
- 10. OXYTOCIN

Down:
- 1. HYPOPHYSO
- 2. ENDOCRINE
- 3. ANTAGONISM
- 4. INSULIN
- 5. MEDENO
- 6. ADENO
- 8. GROWTH
- 9. BODY

Underline the Accented Syllable

1. adenomata   (AD-eh-<u>NOH</u>-mah-tah)

2. diabetes   (DY-ah-<u>BEE</u>-teez)

3. endocrinology   (EN-doh-krin-<u>AWL</u>-oh-jee)

4. exophthalmos   (EKS-awf-<u>THAL</u>-mohs)

5. gestational   (jes-<u>TAY</u>-shun-al)

6. glycosuria   (GLY-kohs-<u>YOO</u>-ree-ah)

7. gynecomastia   (GY-neh-koh-<u>MAS</u>-tee-ah)

8. hypercalcemia   (HY-per-kal-<u>SEE</u>-mee-ah)

9. hypophysectomy   (HY-pawf-ih-<u>SEK</u>-toh-mee)

10. hypopituitarism   (HY-poh-pih-<u>TOO</u>-ih-tah-rizm)

11. lactation   (lak-<u>TAY</u>-shun)

12. myxedema   (MIK-seh-<u>DEE</u>-mah)

13. nephropathy   (neh-<u>FRAWP</u>-ah-thee)

14. pheochromocytoma   (FEE-oh-KROH-moh-sy-<u>TOH</u>-mah)

15. polydipsia   (PAWL-ee-<u>DIP</u>-see-ah)

Word Surgery

1. acromegaly

   Suffix and its meaning: -megaly *enlargement*

   Prefix and its meaning: none

   Combining form and its meaning: acr/o- *extremity; highest point*

   Medical word definition: Enlargement of an extremity

2. adrenalectomy

   Suffix and its meaning: -ectomy *surgical excision*

   Prefix and its meaning: none

   Combining form and its meaning: adrenal/o- *adrenal gland*

   Medical word definition: Surgical excision of the adrenal gland

3. galactorrhea

   Suffix and its meaning: -rrhea *flow; discharge*

   Prefix and its meaning: none

   Combining form and its meaning: galact/o- *milk*

   Medical word definition: Discharge of milk (from the breasts)

4. glycohemoglobin

   Suffix and its meaning: -in *a substance*

   Prefix and its meaning: none

   Combining form and its meaning: glyc/o- *glucose; sugar*

   Combining form and its meaning: hem/o- *blood*

   Combining form and its meaning: glob/o- *shaped like a globe; comprehensive*

   Medical word definition: A substance (that contains) glucose (bound to a structure
   in the) blood shaped like a globe

5. infertility

   Suffix and its meaning: -ity *state; condition*

   Prefix and its meaning: in- *in; within; not*

   Combining form and its meaning: fertil/o- *able to conceive a child*

   Medical word definition: State of not (being) able to conceive a child

6. homeostasis

Suffix and its meaning: -stasis *condition of standing still; staying in one place*

Prefix and its meaning: none

Combining form and its meaning: home/o- *same*

Medical word definition: Condition of (the internal environment of the body) staying in one place

7. hypercalcemia

Suffix and its meaning: -emia *condition of the blood; substance in the blood*

Prefix and its meaning: hyper- *above; more than normal*

Combining form and its meaning: calc/o- *calcium*

Medical word definition: Substance in the blood of more than normal calcium

8. hyperpituitarism

Suffix and its meaning: -ism *process; disease from a specific cause*

Prefix and its meaning: hyper- *above; more than normal*

Combining form and its meaning: pituitar/o- *pituitary gland*

Medical word definition: Disease from a specific cause of more than normal (hormones from) the pituitary gland

9. hypoglycemia

Suffix and its meaning: -emia *condition of the blood; substance in the blood*

Prefix and its meaning: hypo- *below; deficient*

Combining form and its meaning: glyc/o- *glucose (sugar)*

Medical word definition: Substance in the blood of deficient glucose

10. ketoacidosis

Suffix and its meaning: -osis *condition; abnormal condition; process*

Prefix and its meaning: none

Combining form and its meaning: ket/o- *ketones*

Combining form and its meaning: acid/o- *acid (low pH)*

Medical word definition: Abnormal condition of ketones (that make the blood) acid

11. nephropathy

   Suffix and its meaning: -pathy *disease; suffering*

   Prefix and its meaning: none

   Combining form and its meaning: nephr/o- *kidney; nephron*

   Medical word definition: Disease of the kidney

12. pheochromocytoma

   Suffix and its meaning: -oma *tumor; mass*

   Prefix and its meaning: none

   Combining form and its meaning: phe/o- *gray*

   Combining form and its meaning: chrom/o- *color*

   Combining form and its meaning: cyt/o- *cell*

   Medical word definition: Tumor (with a) gray color (to its) cells

13. polydipsia

   Suffix and its meaning: -ia *condition; state; thing*

   Prefix and its meaning: poly- *many; much*

   Combining form and its meaning: dips/o- *thirst*

   Medical word definition: Condition of much thirst

14. synergism

   Suffix and its meaning: -ism *process; disease from a specific cause*

   Prefix and its meaning: syn- *together*

   Combining form and its meaning: erg/o- *activity; work*

   Medical word definition: Process of together working

15. transsphenoidal

   Suffix and its meaning: -al *pertaining to*

   Prefix and its meaning: trans- *across; through*

   Combining form and its meaning: sphenoid/o- *sphenoid bone; sphenoid sinus*

   Medical word definition: Pertaining to through the sphenoid sinus

Chapter Quiz

MULTIPLE CHOICE

1. B	4. D	7. D	10. A
2. C	5. D	8. A	
3. A	6. B	9. D	

FILL IN THE BLANK

1. posterior

2. Homeostasis

3. cortex

4. Hypersecretion

5. Graves'

6. low (or below normal or deficient or decreased)

7. fasting

8. surgical excision

9. adrenocorticotropic hormone

10. lact/o-

TRUE/FALSE

1. True

2. False (thyroid)

3. False (cranial)

4. False ("a")

5. True

6. True

7. True

8. False (gynecomastia)

9. False (lack of)

10. True

CHAPTER 15

Ophthalmology

Measure Your Progress: Learning Objectives

After reading this chapter, the student should be able to

- Identify the structures of the eye.
- Describe the process of vision.
- Describe common eye diseases and conditions, laboratory and diagnostic procedures, medical and surgical procedures, and drug categories.
- Give the medical meaning of word parts related to the eye.
- Build eye words from word parts and divide and define words related to the eye.
- Spell and pronounce eye words.
- Analyze the medical content and meaning of an ophthalmology report.
- Dive deeper into ophthalmology by reviewing the activities at the end of this chapter and online at Medical Terminology Interactive.

It all Starts with Word Building

Medical language is all about medical words and their word parts. Jump right into this chapter by learning some of the common combining forms and their definitions that you will encounter in this chapter.

acu/o-	needle; sharpness	limb/o-	edge; border
ambly/o-	dimness	macul/o-	small area or spot
anis/o-	unequal	mi/o-	lessening
aque/o-	watery substance	mydr/o-	widening
blephar/o-	eyelid	myop/o-	near
capsul/o-	capsule (enveloping structure)	ocul/o-	eye
		ophthalm/o-	eye
choroid/o-	choroid	opt/o-	eye; vision
cil/o-	hairlike structure	orbit/o-	orbit (eye socket)
conjunctiv/o-	conjunctiva	phak/o-	lens
converg/o-	coming together	phot/o-	light
corne/o-	cornea	presby/o-	old age
cor/o-	pupil	pupill/o-	pupil
cycl/o-	ciliary body; cycle	retin/o-	retina
dacry/o-	lacrimal sac; tears	scler/o-	hard; sclera (white of the eye)
dipl/o-	double		
fove/o-	small, depressed area	scot/o-	darkness
		ton/o-	pressure; tone
fund/o-	fundus (part farthest from the opening)	trabecul/o-	trabecula (mesh)
		trop/o-	having an affinity for; stimulating; turning
goni/o-	angle		
irid/o-	iris	uve/o-	uvea
ir/o-	iris	vis/o-	sight; vision
kerat/o-	cornea	vitre/o-	transparent substance; vitreous humor
lacrim/o-	tears		
lenticul/o-	lens		
lent/o-	lens	xer/o-	dry

Survey

Draw these tables on the board. For each item, ask for a show of hands, and put a number in the number column. Stress that students do not need to participate if they choose not to reveal their medical history. Be sure to include yourself, the instructor, in the count.

Vision Abnormality	Number	Percentage of the Total
Myopia		
Hyperopia		
Astigmatism		
Presbyopia		
Total		100%

Corrected Vision	Number	Percentage of the Total
Glasses		
Bifocals		
Contact lens		
LASIK surgery		
Cataract surgery		
Other surgery		
Total		100%

Chapter Spelling Test

Dictate and spell (or photocopy a handout that contains) this list of 20 spelling words. Give this list to students to study for the week. At the beginning of next week's class, dictate 10 of these words as the spelling test. The spelling test is included in the chapter test that is given on the previous week's material.

1. accommodation
2. aphakia
3. astigmatism
4. blepharitis
5. cataract
6. conjunctiva
7. funduscopy
8. glaucoma
9. macular degeneration
10. mydriasis
11. myopia
12. nystagmus
13. ophthalmologist
14. papilledema
15. phacoemulsification
16. presbyopia
17. retinoblastoma
18. scotoma
19. strabismus
20. ulcerative keratitis

Chapter Pronunciation Test

Photocopy a handout that contains this list of 20 pronunciation words. Give this list to students to study for the week. Sometime at the beginning of the next week, each student should call your office or home answering machine and pronounce each word.

1. aphakia (ah-FAY-kee-ah)

2. aqueous humor (AA-kwee-us HYOO-mor)

3. blepharoptosis (BLEF-ah-rawp-TOH-sis)

4. conjunctiva (CON-junk-TY-vah) (con-JUNK-tih-vah)

5. exophthalmos (EKS-awf-THAL-mohs)

6. fluorescein angiography (floo-RES-een AN-jee-AWG-rah-fee)

7. glaucoma (glaw-KOH-mah)

8. hyphema (hy-FEE-mah)

9. laser photocoagulation (LAY-zer FOH-toh-koh-AG-yoo-LAY-shun)

10. macular degeneration (MAK-yoo-lar DEE-jen-er-AA-shun)

11. mydriasis (mih-DRY-eh-sis)

12. myopia (my-OH-pee-ah)

13. nystagmus (nis-TAG-mus)

14. ophthalmologist (AWF-thal-MAWL-oh-jist)

15. papilledema (PAP-il-eh-DEE-mah)

16. presbyopia (PREZ-bee-OH-pee-ah)

17. retinoblastoma (RET-ih-NOH-blas-TOH-mah)

18. tonometry (toh-NAWM-eh-tree)

19. vitreous humor (VIT-ree-us HYOO-mor)

20. xerophthalmia (ZEER-awf-THAL-mee-ah)

Word Search

Complete this word search puzzle that contains Chapter 15 words. Look for the following words as given in the list below. The number in parentheses indicates how many times the word appears in the puzzle.

cataract	ocular
conjunctivae	ophthalmology
cornea	optic
EOMI	PERRL
eye (3)	presbyopia
fundus	pupil
iris (2)	retina
LASIK	retinopathy
lens	rods
limbus	sclera
macular	visual
myopia	vitreous

```
Y  H  T  A  P  O  N  I  T  E  R  C  F
w  G  C  A  T  A  R  A  C  T  Y  X  U
M  Y  O  P  I  A  R  E  L  C  S  E  N
A  T  R  L  E  L  C  E  M  O  R  R  D
C  F  N  Y  O  I  O  Y  D  N  O  E  U
U  L  E  N  S  M  Y  E  S  J  D  T  S
L  C  A  D  I  B  L  L  A  U  S  I  V
A  I  H  S  I  U  E  A  L  N  W  N  R
R  R  P  R  I  S  X  A  H  C  B  A  A
M  I  I  U  L  K  F  C  I  T  P  O  L
H  S  K  Y  P  E  R  R  L  I  H  Z  U
W  E  S  U  O  E  R  T  I  V  K  P  C
P  R  E  S  B  Y  O  P  I  A  F  U  O
```

Crossword Puzzle

ACROSS

1. The combining form
   "_____" means
   small area or spot.

4. The _____ is a
   clear, flexible disk behind the pupil.

7. The _____
   _____ muscle
   turns the eye superiorly.

8. The combining form
   "_____" means
   darkness.

9. The combining form
   "_____" means
   unequal.

10. The combining form
    "_____" means
    eyelid.

DOWN

2. A medical procedure performed to
   test the ability of both eyes to turn
   medially is called

   _____.

3. The tough, fibrous, white connective
   tissue that forms a continuous outer
   layer around most of the eye is the

   _____.

5. An abnormal sensitivity to light is
   known as _____.

6. The posterior cavity of the eye is
   filled with _____
   humor, a clear, gel-like substance
   that helps maintain the shape of the
   eye.

Underline the Accented Syllable

Read the medical word. Then review the syllables in the pronunciation. Underline the primary (main) accented syllable in the pronunciation.

1. amblyopia   (am-blee-oh-pee-ah)

2. astigmatism   (ah-stig-mah-tizm)

3. blepharitis   (blef-ah-ry-tis)

4. chalazion   (kah-lay-zee-on)

5. conjunctivitis   (con-junk-tih-vy-tis)

6. entropion   (en-troh-pee-on)

7. enucleation   (ee-noo-klee-aa-shun)

8. funduscopy   (fun-duhs-koh-pee)

9. glaucoma   (glaw-koh-mah)

10. icterus   (ik-ter-us)

11. nystagmus   (nis-tag-mus)

12. ophthalmology   (awf-thal-mawl-oh-jee)

13. presbyopia   (prez-bee-oh-pee-ah)

14. retinopathy   (ret-ih-nawp-ah-thee)

15. strabismus   (strah-biz-mus)

Word Surgery

Read the medical word. Break the medical word into its word parts and give the meaning of each word part. Then give the definition of the medical word.

1. angiography

   Suffix and its meaning: _____

   Prefix and its meaning: _____

   Combining form and its meaning: _____

   Medical word definition: _____

2. aphakia

   Suffix and its meaning: _____

   Prefix and its meaning: _____

   Combining form and its meaning: _____

   Medical word definition: _____

3. blepharoptosis

   Suffix and its meaning: _____

   Prefix and its meaning: _____

   Combining form and its meaning: _____

   Medical word definition: _____

4. conjunctivitis

   Suffix and its meaning: _____

   Prefix and its meaning: _____

   Combining form and its meaning: _____

   Medical word definition: _____

5. dacryocystitis

   Suffix and its meaning: _____

   Prefix and its meaning: _____

   Combining form and its meaning: _____

   Combining form and its meaning: _____

   Medical word definition: _____

6. entropion

   Suffix and its meaning: _____

   Prefix and its meaning: _____

   Combining form and its meaning: _____

   Medical word definition: _____

7. enucleation

   Suffix and its meaning: _____

   Prefix and its meaning: _____

   Combining form and its meaning: _____

   Medical word definition: _____

8. funduscopy

   Suffix and its meaning: _____

   Prefix and its meaning: _____

   Combining form and its meaning: _____

   Medical word definition: _____

9. intraocular

   Suffix and its meaning: _____

   Prefix and its meaning: _____

   Combining form and its meaning: _____

   Medical word definition: _____

10. photophobia

   Suffix and its meaning: _____

   Prefix and its meaning: _____

   Combining form and its meaning: _____

   Combining form and its meaning: _____

   Medical word definition: _____

11. icteric

   Suffix and its meaning: _____

   Prefix and its meaning: _____

   Combining form and its meaning: _____

   Medical word definition: _____

12. oculomotor

Suffix and its meaning: _____

Prefix and its meaning: _____

Combining form and its meaning: _____

Medical word definition: _____

13. stereoscopic

Suffix and its meaning: _____

Prefix and its meaning: _____

Combining form and its meaning: _____

Combining form and its meaning: _____

Medical word definition: _____

14. trabecular

Suffix and its meaning: _____

Prefix and its meaning: _____

Combining form and its meaning: _____

Medical word definition: _____

15. xerophthalmia

Suffix and its meaning: _____

Prefix and its meaning: _____

Combining form and its meaning: _____

Combining form and its meaning: _____

Medical word definition: _____

Chapter Quiz

MULTIPLE CHOICE

1. The combining form for eyelid is:

    A. cil/o-.

    B. blephar/o-.

    C. ambly/o-.

    D. trabecul/o-.

2. The function of tears is to:

    A. moisten the eyes and fight bacterial infection.

    B. ease tension.

    C. release pressure from within the eyeball.

    D. All of the above.

3. The rods are sensitive to _____; the cones are sensitive to

    _____.

    A. tears, bacteria

    B. color, all levels of light

    C. all levels of light, color

    D. viruses, bacteria

4. A staph infection of the eyelid is commonly called:

    A. dry eye syndrome.

    B. pink eye.

    C. entropion.

    D. stye.

5. Scleral icterus is characterized by:

    A. bulging of the eye.

    B. yellow coloration of the conjunctivae.

    C. pink eye.

    D. corneal abrasion.

6. Cataracts

    A. are caused by a staph infection.

    B. result in color blindness.

    C. cause vision to blur.

    D. are more common in children than in adults.

7. Macular degeneration:

    A. can be the dry type.

    B. can be the wet type.

    C. causes a loss of flexibility of the lens.

    D. Both A and B are correct.

8. A medical procedure to test the ability of the muscles in the ciliary body to contract is:

    A. accommodation.

    B. ultrasonography.

    C. convergence.

    D. dilated funduscopy.

9. Which of the following is a plastic surgery procedure?

    A. enucleation

    B. blepharoplasty

    C. cataract surgery

    D. hyperopia surgery

10. Which of the following means left eye?

    A. OD

    B. OS

    C. LTK

    D. OU

FILL IN THE BLANK

1. A/an _____ is a physician who performs surgery on the eye.

2. _____ is a combining form that means a small area or spot.

3. The _____ muscle turns the eye upward.

4. The opposite of ectropion is _____.

5. The loss of flexibility of the lens with blurry vision and loss of accommodation caused by aging is _____.

6. _____ are clumps, dots, or strings of collagen molecules that form in the vitreous humor.

7. _____ is an involuntary motion of the eye, particularly when looking to the side.

8. A/an _____ is a handheld instrument with a light and changeable lenses of different strengths that are used to examine the eye.

9. The test of visual acuity at a _____ of 20 feet uses the Snellen chart.

10. Surgery to correct myopia using a corneal flap and a laser is known by the abbreviation of _____.

TRUE/FALSE

_____ 1. The fundus of the eye is the part farthest from the pupil.

_____ 2. The ciliary body is an extension of the retina.

_____ 3. The optic nerve (cranial nerve II) from each eye travels to the optic chiasm and parts cross over to join the optic nerve on the other side, which is why we have stereoscopic vision.

_____ 4. Conjunctivitis can be caused when a woman with gonorrhea or chlamydia transmits it to her newborn.

_____ 5. Strabismus is when one or both eyes deviate medially.

_____ 6. Photophobia is a medical procedure to test the reactivity of the pupils to light.

_____ 7. Amblyopia is commonly called lazy eye.

_____ 8. A diagnostic procedure to detect increased intraocular pressure is called tonometry.

_____ 9. The *Greek* combining form for "eye" is "ophthalm/o-"; the *Latin* combining form for "eye" is "cor/o-."

_____ 10. Opticians are allied health professionals who cut, grind, and finish lenses as well as prepare contact lenses.

Pronunciation Checklist

Read each word and its pronunciation. Practice pronouncing each word. Verify your pronunciation by listening to the Pronunciation List on Medical Terminology Interactive. Check the box next to the word after you master its pronunciation.

- ❏ accommodation (ah-KAWM-oh-DAY-shun)
- ❏ amblyopia (AM-blee-OH-pee-ah)
- ❏ anicteric sclerae (AN-ik-TAIR-ik SKLEER-ee)
- ❏ anisocoria (an-EYE-soh-KOH-ree-ah)
- ❏ anterior chamber (an-TEER-ee-or CHAYM-ber)
- ❏ antibiotic drug (AN-tee-by-AWT-ik DRUHG) (AN-tih-by-AWT-ik)
- ❏ antiviral drug (AN-tee-VY-ral DRUHG)
- ❏ aphakia (ah-FAY-kee-ah)
- ❏ aphakic (ah-FAY-kik)
- ❏ aqueous humor (AA-kwee-us HYOO-mor)
- ❏ astigmatism (ah-STIG-mah-tizm)
- ❏ blepharitis (BLEF-ah-RY-tis)
- ❏ blepharoplasty (BLEF-ah-roh-PLAS-tee)
- ❏ blepharoptosis (BLEF-ah-rawp-TOH-sis)
- ❏ capsular (KAP-soo-lar)
- ❏ capsule (KAP-sool)
- ❏ capsulotomy (KAP-soo-LAW-toh-mee)
- ❏ caruncle (KAR-ung-kl)
- ❏ cataract (KAT-ah-rakt)
- ❏ chalazion (kah-LAY-zee-on)
- ❏ choroid (KOH-royd)
- ❏ choroidal (koh-ROY-dal)
- ❏ choroiditis (KOH-roy-DY-tis)
- ❏ ciliary body (SIL-ee-AIR-ee BAW-dee)
- ❏ conductive keratoplasty (con-DUK-tiv KAIR-ah-toh-PLAS-tee)
- ❏ conjugate gaze (CON-joo-gayt GAYZ)
- ❏ conjunctiva (CON-junk-TY-vah) (con-JUNK-tih-vah)
- ❏ conjunctivae (CON-junk-TY-vee) (con-JUNK-tih-vee)
- ❏ conjunctival (CON-junk-TY-val) (con-JUNK-tih-val)

- ❏ conjunctivitis (con-JUNK-tih-VY-tis)
- ❏ convergence (con-VER-jens)
- ❏ cornea (KOR-nee-ah)
- ❏ corneae (KOR-nee-ee)
- ❏ corneal (KOR-nee-al)
- ❏ corneal abrasion (KOR-nee-al ah-BRAY-shun)
- ❏ corneal transplantation (KOR-nee-al TRANS-plan-TAY-shun)
- ❏ corneal ulcer (KOR-nee-al UL-ser)
- ❏ corticosteroid drug (KOR-tih-koh-STAIR-oyd DRUHG)
- ❏ cryotherapy (KRY-oh-THAIR-ah-pee)
- ❏ cycloplegia (SY-kloh-PLEE-jee-ah)
- ❏ dacryocystitis (DAK-ree-OH-sis-TY-tis)
- ❏ diabetic retinopathy (DY-ah-BET-ik RET-ih-NAWP-ah-thee)
- ❏ diplopia (dih-PLOH-pee-ah)
- ❏ dysconjugate gaze (dis-CON-joo-gayt GAYZ)
- ❏ ectropion (ek-TROH-pee-on)
- ❏ entropion (en-TROH-pee-on)
- ❏ enucleation (EE-noo-klee-AA-shun)
- ❏ esotropia (ES-oh-TROH-pee-ah)
- ❏ exophthalmos (EKS-awf-THAL-mohs)
- ❏ exotropia (EKS-oh-TROH-pee-ah)
- ❏ extracapsular cataract extraction (EKS-trah-KAP-soo-lar KAT-ah-rakt ek-STRAK-shun)
- ❏ extraocular muscle (EKS-trah-AWK-yoo-lar MUS-el)
- ❏ fluorescein angiogram (floo-RES-een AN-jee-oh-gram)
- ❏ fluorescein angiography (floo-RES-een AN-jee-AWG-rah-fee)
- ❏ fovea (FOH-vee-ah)
- ❏ foveae (FOH-vee-ee)

- ❏ foveal (FOH-vee-al)
- ❏ fundal (FUN-dal)
- ❏ fundi (FUN-die)
- ❏ fundus (FUN-dus)
- ❏ funduscopy (fun-DUHS-koh-pee)
- ❏ glaucoma (glaw-KOH-mah)
- ❏ gonioscopy (GOH-nee-AWS-koh-pee)
- ❏ hemianopia (HEM-ee-ah-NOH-pee-ah)
- ❏ hordeolum (hor-DEE-oh-lum)
- ❏ hyperopia (HY-per-OH-pee-ah)
- ❏ hyphema (hy-FEE-mah)
- ❏ inferior oblique muscle (in-FEER-ee-or awb-LEEK MUS-el)
- ❏ inferior rectus muscle (in-FEER-ee-or REK-tus MUS-el)
- ❏ *in situ* keratomileusis (IN SY-too KAIR-ah-toh-my-LOO-sis)
- ❏ intracapsular cataract extraction (IN-trah-KAP-soo-lar KAT-ah-rakt ek-STRAK-shun)
- ❏ intraocular (IN-trah-AWK-yoo-lar)
- ❏ iridal (IHR-ih-dal) (EYE-rih-dal)
- ❏ irides (IHR-ih-deez)
- ❏ iris (EYE-ris)
- ❏ iritis (eye-RY-tis)
- ❏ jaundice (JAWN-dis)
- ❏ keratitis (KAIR-ah-TY-tis)
- ❏ lacrimal duct (LAK-rih-mal DUHKT)
- ❏ lacrimal gland (LAK-rih-mal GLAND)
- ❏ lacrimal sac (LAK-rih-mal SAK)
- ❏ laser photocoagulation (LAY-zer FOH-toh-koh-AG-yoo-LAY-shun)
- ❏ laser thermal keratoplasty (LAY-zer THER-mal KAIR-ah-toh-PLAS-tee)
- ❏ lateral rectus muscle (LAT-er-al REK-tus MUS-el)
- ❏ lens (LENZ)
- ❏ lens capsule (LENZ KAP-sool)
- ❏ lenses (LEN-sez)

- ❏ lenticular (len-TIK-yoo-lar)
- ❏ limbic (LIM-bik)
- ❏ limbus (LIM-bus)
- ❏ macula (MAK-yoo-lah)
- ❏ maculae (MAK-yoo-lee)
- ❏ macular (MAK-yoo-lar)
- ❏ macular degeneraton (MAK-yoo-lar DEE-jen-er-AA-shun)
- ❏ medial rectus muscle (MEE-dee-al REK-tus MUS-el)
- ❏ microkeratome (MY-kroh-KAIR-ah-tohm)
- ❏ miosis (my-OH-sis)
- ❏ mydriasis (mih-DRY-eh-sis)
- ❏ mydriatic drug (MIH-dree-AT-ik DRUHG)
- ❏ myopia (my-OH-pee-ah)
- ❏ nasolacrimal duct (NAY-soh-LAK-rih-mal DUHKT)
- ❏ nystagmus (nis-TAG-mus)
- ❏ ocular (AWK-yoo-lar)
- ❏ ophthalmologist (OFF-thal-MAWL-oh-jist)
- ❏ ophthalmology (OFF-thal-MAWL-oh-jee)
- ❏ ophthalmoscope (off-THAL-moh-skohp)
- ❏ optic chiasm (AWP-tik KY-azm)
- ❏ optic disk (AWP-tik DISK)
- ❏ optic globe (AWP-tik GLOHB)
- ❏ optician (op-TISH-un)
- ❏ optic nerve (AWP-tik NERV)
- ❏ optometrist (op-TAWM-eh-trist)
- ❏ optometry (op-TAWM-eh-tree)
- ❏ orbit (OR-bit)
- ❏ papilledema (PAP-il-eh-DEE-mah)
- ❏ peripheral vision (peh-RIF-eh-ral VIH-shun)
- ❏ phacoemulsification (FAY-koh-ee-MUL-sih-fih-KAY-shun)
- ❏ phorometer (foh-RAWM-eh-ter)
- ❏ phorometry (foh-RAWM-eh-tree)
- ❏ photophobia (FOH-toh-FOH-bee-ah)
- ❏ photorefractive keratectomy (FOH-toh-ree-FRAK-tiv KAIR-ah-TEK-toh-mee)
- ❏ posterior cavity (pohs-TEER-ee-or KAV-ih-tee)
- ❏ posterior chamber (pohs-TEER-ee-or CHAYM-ber)
- ❏ presbyopia (PREZ-bee-OH-pee-ah)
- ❏ pupil (PYOO-pil)
- ❏ pupillary (PYOO-pih-LAIR-ee)
- ❏ recession (ree-SEH-shun)
- ❏ resection (ree-SEK-shun)
- ❏ retina (RET-ih-nah)
- ❏ retinae (RET-ih-nee)
- ❏ retinal (RET-ih-nal)
- ❏ retinal detachment (RET-ih-nal dee-TACH-ment)
- ❏ retinitis pigmentosa (RET-ih-NY-tis PIG-men-TOH-sah)
- ❏ retinoblastoma (RET-ih-noh-blas-TOH-mah)
- ❏ retinopathy of prematurity (RET-ih-NAWP-ah-thee of PREE-mah-TYOOR-ih-tee)
- ❏ retinopexy (RET-ih-noh-PEK-see)
- ❏ retrolental fibroplasias (REH-troh-LEN-tal FY-broh-PLAY-see-ah)
- ❏ sclera (SKLEER-ah)
- ❏ sclerae (SKLEER-ee)
- ❏ scleral (SKLEER-al)
- ❏ scleral icterus (SKLEER-al IK-ter-us)
- ❏ scotoma (skoh-TOH-mah)
- ❏ scotomata (skoh-TOH-mah-tah)
- ❏ sebaceous gland (seh-BAY-shus GLAND)
- ❏ sonogram (SAWN-oh-gram)
- ❏ stereoscopic vision (STAIR-ee-oh-SKAWP-ik VIH-shun)
- ❏ strabismus (strah-BIZ-mus)
- ❏ superior oblique muscle (soo-PEER-ee-or awb-LEEK MUS-el)
- ❏ superior rectus muscle (soo-PEER-ee-or REK-tus MUS-el)
- ❏ thalamus (THAL-ah-mus)
- ❏ tonometer (toh-NAWM-eh-ter)
- ❏ tonometry (toh-NAWM-eh-tree)
- ❏ trabecular meshwork (trah-BEK-yoo-lar MESH-wurk)
- ❏ trabeculoplasty (trah-BEK-yoo-loh-PLAS-tee)
- ❏ ulcerative keratitis (UL-ser-ah-TIV KAIR-ah-TY-tis)
- ❏ ultrasonography (UL-trah-soh-NAWG-rah-fee)
- ❏ uvea (YOO-vee-ah)
- ❏ uveal tract (YOO-vee-al TRAKT)
- ❏ uveitis (YOO-vee-EYE-tis)
- ❏ visual acuity (VIH-shoo-al ah-KYOO-ih-tee)
- ❏ visual cortex (VIH-shoo-al KOR-teks)
- ❏ visual field (VIH-shoo-al FEELD)
- ❏ vitrectomy (vih-TREK-toh-mee)
- ❏ vitreous humor (VIT-ree-us HYOO-mor)
- ❏ xerophthalmia (ZEER-off-THAL-mee-ah)

Answer Key

Word Search

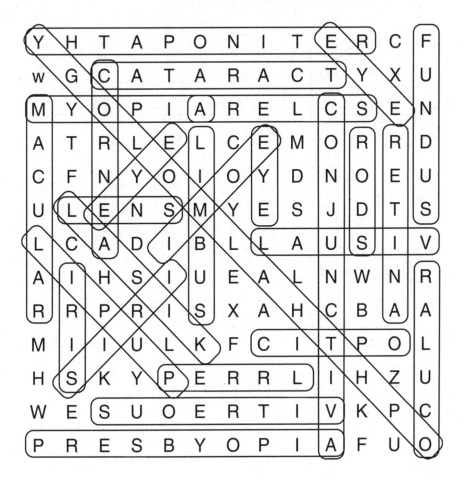

Y H T A P O N I T E R C F
w G C A T A R A C T Y X U
M Y O P I A R E L C S E N
A T R L E L C E M O R R D
C F N Y O I O Y D N O E U
U L E N S M Y E S J D T S
L C A D I B L L A U S I V
A I H S I U E A L N W N R
R R P R I S X A H C B A A
M I I U L K F C I T P O L
H S K Y P E R R L I H Z U
W E S U O E R T I V K P C
P R E S B Y O P I A F U O

Crossword Puzzle

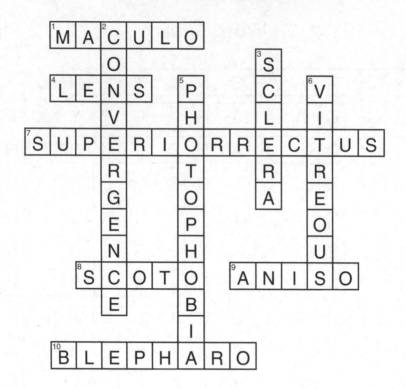

Underline the Accented Syllable

1. amblyopia   (AM-blee-<u>OH</u>-pee-ah)

2. astigmatism   (ah-<u>STIG</u>-mah-tizm)

3. blepharitis   (BLEF-ah-<u>RY</u>-tis)

4. chalazion   (kah-<u>LAY</u>-zee-on)

5. conjunctivitis   (con-JUNK-tih-<u>VY</u>-tis)

6. entropion   (en-<u>TROH</u>-pee-on)

7. enucleation   (ee-NOO-klee-<u>AA</u>-shun)

8. funduscopy   (fun-<u>DUHS</u>-koh-pee)

9. glaucoma   (glaw-<u>KOH</u>-mah)

10. icterus   (<u>IK</u>-ter-us)

11. nystagmus   (nis-<u>TAG</u>-mus)

12. ophthalmology   (AWF-thal-<u>MAWL</u>-oh-jee)

13. presbyopia   (PREZ-bee-<u>OH</u>-pee-ah)

14. retinopathy   (RET-ih-<u>NAWP</u>-ah-thee)

15. strabismus   (strah-<u>BIZ</u>-mus)

Word Surgery

1. angiography

   Suffix and its meaning: -graphy *process of recording*

   Prefix and its meaning: none

   Combining form and its meaning: angi/o- *blood vessel; lymphatic vessel*

   Medical word definition: Process of recording a blood vessel

2. aphakia

   Suffix and its meaning: -ia *condition; state; thing*

   Prefix and its meaning: a- *away from; without*

   Combining form and its meaning: phak/o- *lens (of the eye)*

   Medical word definition: Condition (of being) without the lens

3. blepharoptosis

   Suffix and its meaning: -ptosis *state of prolapse; drooping; falling*

   Prefix and its meaning: none

   Combining form and its meaning: blephar/o- *eyelid*

   Medical word definition: State of prolapse or drooping of the eyelid

4. conjunctivitis

   Suffix and its meaning: -itis *inflammation of; infection of*

   Prefix and its meaning: none

   Combining form and its meaning: conjunctiv/o- *conjunctiva*

   Medical word definition: Inflammation or infection of the conjunctiva

5. dacryocystitis

   Suffix and its meaning: -itis *inflammation of; infection of*

   Prefix and its meaning: none

   Combining form and its meaning: dacry/o- *lacrimal sac; tears*

   Combining form and its meaning: cyst/o- *bladder; fluid-filled sac; semisolid cyst*

   Medical word definition: Inflammation or infection of the lacrimal sac (that is a) fluid-filled sac

6. entropion

   Suffix and its meaning: -ion *action; condition*

   Prefix and its meaning: en- *in; within; inward*

   Combining form and its meaning: trop/o- *having an affinity for; stimulating; turning*

   Medical word definition: Action of inward turning (of the eyelid)

7. enucleation

   Suffix and its meaning: -ation *a process; being or having*

   Prefix and its meaning: none

   Combining form and its meaning: enucle/o- *to remove the main part*

   Medical word definition: A process to remove the main part (of the eye)

8. funduscopy

   Suffix and its meaning: -scopy *process of using an instrument to examine*

   Prefix and its meaning: none

   Combining form and its meaning: fundu/o- *fundus (part farthest from the opening)*

   Medical word definition: Process of using an instrument to examine the fundus

9. intraocular

   Suffix and its meaning: -ar *pertaining to*

   Prefix and its meaning: intra- *within*

   Combining form and its meaning: ocul/o- *eye*

   Medical word definition: Pertaining to within the eye

10. photophobia

    Suffix and its meaning: -ia *condition; state; thing*

    Prefix and its meaning: none

    Combining form and its meaning: phot/o- *light*

    Combining form and its meaning: phob/o- *fear or avoidance*

    Medical word definition: Condition of light (causing) fear or avoidance

11. icteric

    Suffix and its meaning: -ic *pertaining to*

    Prefix and its meaning: none

    Combining form and its meaning: icter/o- *jaundice*

    Medical word definition: Pertaining to jaundice

12. retinopathy

    Suffix and its meaning: -pathy *disease; suffering*

    Prefix and its meaning: none

    Combining form and its meaning: retin/o- *retina*

    Medical word definition: Disease of the retina

13. stereoscopic

    Suffix and its meaning: -ic *pertaining to*

    Prefix and its meaning: none

    Combining form and its meaning: stere/o- *three dimensions*

    Combining form and its meaning: scop/o- *examine with an instrument*

    Medical word definition: Pertaining to three dimensions (that can be) examined
        with an instrument (the eye)

14. trabecular

    Suffix and its meaning: -ar *pertaining to*

    Prefix and its meaning: none

    Combining form and its meaning: trabecul/o- *trabecula (mesh)*

    Medical word definition: Pertaining to the trabecula (mesh)

15. xerophthalmia

    Suffix and its meaning: -ia *condition; state; thing*

    Prefix and its meaning: none

    Combining form and its meaning: xer/o- *dry*

    Combining form and its meaning: ophthalm/o- *eye*

    Medical word definition: Condition of dry eyes

Chapter Quiz

MULTIPLE CHOICE

1. B	4. D	7. D	10. B
2. A	5. B	8. A	
3. C	6. C	9. B	

FILL IN THE BLANK

1. ophthalmologist

2. Macul/o-

3. superior rectus

4. entropion

5. presbyopia

6. Floaters

7. Nystagmus

8. ophthalmoscope

9. distance

10. LASIK

TRUE/FALSE

1. True

2. False (choroid)

3. True

4. True

5. True

6. False (pupillary response)

7. True

8. True

9. False (ocul/o-)

10. True

CHAPTER 16

Otolaryngology

Measure Your Progress: Learning Objectives

After reading this chapter, the student should be able to

- Identify the structures of the ears, nose, and throat (ENT) system.
- Describe the process of hearing.
- Describe common ENT diseases and conditions, laboratory and diagnostic procedures, medical and surgical procedures, and drug categories.
- Give the medical meaning of word parts related to the ENT system.
- Build ENT words from word parts and divide and define ENT words.
- Spell and pronounce ENT words.
- Analyze the medical content and meaning of an otolaryngology report.
- Dive deeper into otolaryngology by reviewing the activities at the end of this chapter and online at Medical Terminology Interactive.

It All Starts with Word Building

Medical language is all about medical words and their word parts. Jump right into this chapter by learning some of the common combining forms and their definitions that you will encounter in this chapter.

acous/o-	hearing; sound	nas/o-	nose
aden/o-	gland	or/o-	mouth
alg/o-	pain	osm/o-	the sense of smell
allerg/o-	allergy	ossicul/o-	ossicle (little bone)
aur/i-	ear	ot/o-	ear
auricul/o-	ear	palat/o-	palate
audi/o-	the sense of hearing	pharyng/o-	pharynx (throat)
		polyp/o-	polyp
audit/o-	the sense of hearing	presby/o-	old age
		rhin/o-	nose
bucc/o-	cheek	sensor/i-	sensory
cheil/o-	lip	sept/o-	septum (dividing wall)
cochle/o-	cochlea (of the inner ear)		
		sinus/o-	sinus
ethm/o-	sieve	sphen/o-	wedge shape
gloss/o-	tongue	staped/o-	stapes (stirrup)
glott/o-	glottis (of the larynx)	suppor/o-	pus formation
		tempor/o-	temple (side of the head)
incud/o-	incus (anvil)		
labi/o-	lip; labium	tonsill/o-	tonsil
labyrinth/o-	labyrinth (of the inner ear)	turbin/o-	scroll-like structure; turbinate
lingu/o-	tongue	tuss/o-	cough
malle/o-	malleus (hammer)	tympan/o-	tympanic membrane (eardrum)
mandibul/o-	mandible (lower jaw)		
mastoid/o-	mastoid process	vestibul/o-	vestibule (entrance)
maxill/o-	maxilla (upper jaw)	voc/o-	voice
ment/o-	mind; chin		
mucos/o-	mucous membrane		
myring/o-	tympanic membrane (eardrum)		

Chapter Spelling Test

Dictate and spell (or photocopy a handout that contains) this list of 20 spelling words. Give this list to students to study for the week. At the beginning of next week's class, dictate 10 of these words as the spelling test. The spelling test is included with the chapter test that is given on the previous week's material.

1. adenoids
2. allergic rhinitis
3. buccal mucosa
4. cerumen
5. epistaxis
6. eustachian tube
7. laryngeal
8. larynx
9. malleus
10. myringotomy
11. otitis media
12. pharynx
13. pharyngitis
14. polypectomy
15. presbyacusis
16. temporomandibular joint
17. tonsillar
18. turbinate
19. tympanoplasty
20. vertigo

Chapter Pronunciation Test

Photocopy a handout that contains this list of 20 pronunciation words. Give this list to students to study for the week. Sometime at the beginning of the next week, each student should call your office or home answering machine and pronounce each word.

1. adenoids (AD-eh-noydz)

2. audiometry (AW-dee-AWM-eh-tree)

3. buccal mucosa (BUK-al myoo-KOH-sah)

4. candidiasis (KAN-dih-DY-ah-sis)

5. cholesteatoma (koh-LES-tee-ah-TOH-mah)

6. epistaxis (EP-ih-STAK-sis)

7. larynx (LAIR-ingks)

8. laryngeal (lah-RIN-jee-al)

9. mucosal (myoo-KOH-sal)

10. myringotomy (MEER-ing-GAW-toh-mee)

11. nasolabial (NAY-zoh-LAY-bee-al)

12. otalgia (oh-TAL-jee-ah)

13. pharynx (FAIR-ingks)

14. pharyngeal (fah-RIN-jee-al)

15. polypectomy (PAWL-ih-PEK-toh-mee)

16. rhinophyma (RY-noh-FY-mah)

17. Rinne test (RIN-eh TEST)

18. sensorineural (SEN-soh-ree-NYOOR-al)

19. tonsillectomy (TAWN-sih-LEK-toh-mee)

20. vestibular (ves-TIB-yoo-lar)

Word Search

Complete this word search puzzle that contains Chapter 16 words. Look for the following words as given in the list below. The number in parentheses indicates how many times the word appears in the puzzle.

adenoids	nasopharyngeal
auditory	nose (2)
aural	oral
cerumen	pharynx
cochlea	rhinitis
ears	Rinne
ENT	sinus (2)
epistaxis	throat
ethmoid	TMJ (2)
helix	tonsil
incus	tympanoplasty
larynx	URI
malleus	vertigo
mucosa	

```
L  I  S  N  O  T  T  N  E  M  U  R  E  C
S  U  C  N  I  Y  T  B  D  U  E  M  N  O
I  Q  R  V  T  M  A  L  L  E  U  S  X  C
X  W  Q  I  J  P  E  C  X  C  L  N  E  H
A  N  A  U  R  A  L  A  O  S  Y  B  S  L
T  S  Y  G  W  N  U  S  R  R  H  K  O  E
S  D  D  R  T  O  A  D  A  S  A  G  N  A
I  I  I  I  A  P  R  H  I  N  I  T  I  S
P  O  O  N  O  L  P  N  O  T  Q  N  M  W
E  N  M  N  R  A  U  S  R  B  O  L  U  J
L  E  H  E  H  S  E  E  K  L  A  R  O  S
X  D  T  B  T  T  V  H  E  L  I  X  Y  G
L  A  E  G  N  Y  R  A  H  P  O  S  A  N
```

Crossword Puzzle

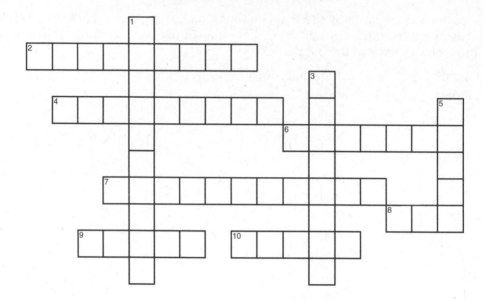

ACROSS

2. All of the structures of the inner ear are known as the

_____.

4. A surgical procedure that utilizes plastic surgery to correct deformities of the external ear is called a/an

_____.

6. The superior, middle, and inferior turbinates of the nasal cavity are known as the nasal

_____.

7. _____ is bilateral hearing loss due to aging.

8. The combining form

"_____" means mouth.

9. A _____ is a hollow cavity within a bone that is lined with a mucous membrane.

10. The _____ is the outer rim of tissue and cartilage of the ear that forms a "C" and ends at the earlobe.

DOWN

1. The middle portion of the throat is the _____.

3. A benign tumor of nerve cells of the vestibulocochlear nerve is a/an

_____ neuroma.

5. The combining form

"_____" means chin.

Underline the Accented Syllable

Read the medical word. Then review the syllables in the pronunciation. Underline the primary (main) accented syllable in the pronunciation.

1. anosmia   (an-awz-mee-ah)

2. audiometry   (aw-dee-awm-eh-tree)

3. cheiloplasty   (ky-loh-plas-tee)

4. cochlear   (kohk-lee-ar)

5. impedance   (im-pee-dans)

6. leukoplakia   (loo-koh-play-kee-ah)

7. Meniere's   (men-eh-airz)

8. otosclerosis   (oh-toh-skleh-roh-sis)

9. presbycusis   (prez-bee-koo-sis)

10. rhinitis   (ry-ny-tis)

11. sensorineural   (sen-soh-ree-nyoor-al)

12. speculum   (spek-yoo-lum)

13. stapedectomy   (stay-pee-dek-toh-mee)

14. temporomandibular   (tem-poh-roh-man-dib-yoo-lar)

15. vertigo   (ver-tih-goh)

Word Surgery

Read the medical word. Break the medical word into its word parts and give the meaning of each word part. Then give the definition of the medical word.

1. adenoidectomy

    Suffix and its meaning: _____

    Prefix and its meaning: _____

    Combining form and its meaning: _____

    Medical word definition: _____

2. anosmia

    Suffix and its meaning: _____

    Prefix and its meaning: _____

    Combining form and its meaning: _____

    Medical word definition: _____

3. antibiotic

    Suffix and its meaning: _____

    Prefix and its meaning: _____

    Combining form and its meaning: _____

    Medical word definition: _____

4. antitussive

    Suffix and its meaning: _____

    Prefix and its meaning: _____

    Combining form and its meaning: _____

    Medical word definition: _____

5. audiometry

    Suffix and its meaning: _____

    Prefix and its meaning: _____

    Combining form and its meaning: _____

    Medical word definition: _____

6. cheiloplasty

   Suffix and its meaning: _____

   Prefix and its meaning: _____

   Combining form and its meaning: _____

   Medical word definition: _____

7. labyrinthitis

   Suffix and its meaning: _____

   Prefix and its meaning: _____

   Combining form and its meaning: _____

   Medical word definition: _____

8. leukoplakia

   Suffix and its meaning: _____

   Prefix and its meaning: _____

   Combining form and its meaning: _____

   Combining form and its meaning: _____

   Medical word definition: _____

9. myringotomy

   Suffix and its meaning: _____

   Prefix and its meaning: _____

   Combining form and its meaning: _____

   Medical word definition: _____

10. otosclerosis

   Suffix and its meaning: _____

   Prefix and its meaning: _____

   Combining form and its meaning: _____

   Combining form and its meaning: _____

   Medical word definition: _____

11. pansinusitis

   Suffix and its meaning: _____

   Prefix and its meaning: _____

   Combining form and its meaning: _____

   Medical word definition: _____

12. rhinorrhea

    Suffix and its meaning: _____

    Prefix and its meaning: _____

    Combining form and its meaning: _____

    Medical word definition: _____

13. temporomandibular

    Suffix and its meaning: _____

    Prefix and its meaning: _____

    Combining form and its meaning: _____

    Combining form and its meaning: _____

    Medical word definition: _____

14. tympanometry

    Suffix and its meaning: _____

    Prefix and its meaning: _____

    Combining form and its meaning: _____

    Medical word definition: _____

15. unilateral

    Suffix and its meaning: _____

    Prefix and its meaning: _____

    Combining form and its meaning: _____

    Medical word definition: _____

Chapter Quiz

MULTIPLE CHOICE

1. "Myring/o-" is the combining form for:

   A. mouth.

   B. middle ear.

   C. mastoid process.

   D. tympanic membrane.

2. Which of the following is a structure of the inner ear?

   A. cochlea

   B. vestibule

   C. semicircular canals

   D. All of the above.

3. Which of the following connects the middle ear to the nasopharynx?

   A. eustachian tube

   B. lacrimal ducts

   C. external auditory meatus

   D. All of the above.

4. Impacted cerumen:

   A. is a malignant tumor.

   B. is a cause of presbycusis.

   C. occludes the external auditory meatus.

   D. results in high-frequency sensorineural hearing loss.

5. Tinnitus:

   A. includes buzzing, ringing, hissing, or roaring that can be heard.

   B. is an infection of the middle ear.

   C. may cause a rupture of the eardrum.

   D. is a form of anosmia.

6. Thrush is:

    A. an oral yeast-like fungal infection.

    B. a form of tonsillitis.

    C. difficulty swallowing.

    D. All of the above.

7. A laboratory test that detects the bacteria in mucus or pus and is done in a Petri plate is:

    A. culture.

    B. tympanogram.

    C. impedance.

    D. Rinne test.

8. A rhinoplasty is a surgical procedure to:

    A. connect the inner and middle ears.

    B. change the shape of the nose.

    C. remove the mastoid process.

    D. place tubes in the ears.

9. Antitussive drugs:

    A. inhibit the growth of bacteria.

    B. reduce inflammation.

    C. suppress the cough center in the brain.

    D. block histamine.

10. Allied health professionals who perform hearing tests, diagnose hearing loss, and determine how patients can best use their remaining hearing are:

    A. otolaryngologists.

    B. oral and maxillofacial surgeons.

    C. audiologists.

    D. ENT specialists.

FILL IN THE BLANK

1. The combining form "glott/o-" refers to the _____.

2. A sinus cavity is a hollow space within a bone that is lined with a _____ membrane.

3. _____ are lymphoid tissues found in the nasopharynx.

4. A benign tumor found on the vestibulocochlear nerve (cranial nerve VIII) is known as an acoustic _____.

5. The suffix "-rrhea," as in otorrhea, means "_____."

6. Cold sores are recurring, painful clusters of blisters caused by the _____ _____ virus type 1.

7. Tympanometry is a hearing test that measures the ability of the tympanic membrane and the _____ of the middle ear to move back and forth.

8. A/an _____ implant is a surgical procedure to insert a small battery-powered implant that sends electrical signals to the brain to simulate hearing.

9. The *Greek* combining form for "ear" is "_____" and the *Latin* form is "aur/o-" or "auricul/o-."

10. _____ drugs constrict blood vessels and decrease swelling of mucous membranes.

TRUE/FALSE

_____ 1. Otolaryngology is a medical specialty that studies the ears, nose, and throat.

_____ 2. The nasolabial fold is the external openings or nostrils.

_____ 3. Two combining forms that both mean tongue are "gloss/o-" and "glott/o-."

_____ 4. Conductive hearing loss affects the external or middle ear.

_____ 5. Having the sensation of motion when the body is not moving is known as vertigo.

_____ 6. A sudden, sometimes severe bleeding from the nose is anosmia.

_____ 7. Sound intensity is measured in hertz.

_____ 8. "Sept/o-," as in septoplasty, refers to a dividing wall.

_____ 9. TMJ refers to the joint between the temporal bone and the maxilla.

_____ 10. Otorhinolaryngologists are also known as ENT specialists.

Pronunciation Checklist

Read each word and its pronunciation. Practice pronouncing each word. Verify your pronunciation by listening to the Pronunciation List on Medical Terminology Interactive. Check the box next to the word after you master its pronunciation.

- ❏ acoustic neuroma
  (ah-KOOS-tik nyoo-ROH-mah)
- ❏ adenoidectomy
  (AD-eh-noy-DEK-toh-mee)
- ❏ adenoids (AD-eh-noydz)
- ❏ ala (AA-lah)
- ❏ alae (AA-lee)
- ❏ allergic rhinitis (ah-LER-jik
  ry-NY-tis)
- ❏ anacusis (AN-ah-KOO-sis)
- ❏ anosmia (an-AWZ-mee-ah)
- ❏ antibiotic drug
  (AN-tee-by-AWT-ik DRUHG)
  (AN-tih-by-AWT-ik)
- ❏ antihistamine drug
  (AN-tee-HIS-tah-meen DRUHG)
- ❏ antitussive drug
  (AN-tee-TUS-iv DRUHG)
- ❏ antiyeast drug
  (AN-tee-YEEST DRUHG)
- ❏ audiogram (AW-dee-oh-GRAM)
- ❏ audiologist
  (AW-dee-AWL-oh-jist)
- ❏ audiometer
  (AW-dee-AWM-eh-ter)
- ❏ audiometry
  (AW-dee-AWM-eh-tree)
- ❏ auditory (AW-dih-TOH-ree)
- ❏ auricle (AW-rih-kl)
- ❏ auricular (aw-RIK-yoo-lar)
- ❏ benign (bee-NINE)
- ❏ bilateral (by-LAT-eh-ral)
- ❏ buccal mucosa
  (BUK-al myoo-KOH-sah)
- ❏ *Candida albicans*
  (KAN-dih-dah AL-bih-kanz)
- ❏ candidiasis (KAN-dih-DY-ah-sis)
- ❏ carcinoma (KAR-sih-NOH-mah)
- ❏ cerumen (seh-ROO-men)
- ❏ cerumen impaction
  (seh-ROO-men im-PAK-shun)
- ❏ cervical lymphadenopathy
  (SER-vih-kal lim-FAD-eh-
  NAWP-eh-thee)
- ❏ cheiloplasty (KY-loh-PLAS-tee)
- ❏ cholesteatoma
  (koh-LES-tee-ah-TOH-mah)
- ❏ cochlea (KOH-klee-ah)
- ❏ cochleae (KOH-klee-ee)

- ❏ concha (CON-kah)
- ❏ conductive (con-DUK-tiv)
- ❏ corticosteroid drug
  (KOR-tih-koh-STAIR-oyd
  DRUHG)
- ❏ culture and sensitivity
  (KUL-chur and
  SEN-sih-TIV-ih-tee)
- ❏ decibel (DES-ih-bel)
- ❏ decongestant drug
  (DEE-con-JES-tant DRUHG)
- ❏ dorsal (DOR-sal)
- ❏ dorsum (DOR-sum)
- ❏ dysequilibrium
  (DIS-ee-kwih-LIB-ree-um)
- ❏ effusion (ee-FYOO-shun)
- ❏ endoscope (EN-doh-skohp)
- ❏ endoscopic
  (EN-doh-SKAWP-ik)
- ❏ endoscopy
  (en-DAWS-koh-pee)
- ❏ epiglottis (EP-ih-GLAWT-is)
- ❏ epistaxis (EP-ih-STAK-sis)
- ❏ ethmoid sinus
  (ETH-moyd SY-nus)
- ❏ eustachian (yoo-STAY-shun)
- ❏ external auditory canal
  (eks-TER-nal AW-dih-TOH-ree
  kah-NAL)
- ❏ external auditory meatus
  (eks-TER-nal AW-dih-TOH-ree
  mee-AA-tus)
- ❏ frontal sinus (FRUN-tal SY-nus)
- ❏ glossal (GLAWS-al)
- ❏ glossectomy
  (glaw-SEK-toh-mee)
- ❏ glossitis (glaw-SY-tis)
- ❏ glottis (GLAWT-is)
- ❏ helix (HEE-liks)
- ❏ hemotympanum
  (HEE-moh-TIM-pah-num)
- ❏ herpes simplex virus
  (HER-peez SIM-pleks VY-rus)
- ❏ hertz (HERTS)
- ❏ impedance (im-PEE-dans)
- ❏ incudal (IN-kyoo-dal)
- ❏ incudes (in-KYOO-deez)
- ❏ incus (ING-kus)
- ❏ labyrinthitis (LAB-ih-rin-THY-tis)

- ❏ laryngeal (lah-RIN-jee-al)
- ❏ laryngectomy
  (LAIR-in-JEK-toh-mee)
- ❏ laryngitis (LAIR-in-JY-tis)
- ❏ laryngopharynx
  (lah-RING-goh-FAIR-inks)
- ❏ larynx (LAIR-ingks)
- ❏ leukoplakia
  (LOO-koh-PLAY-kee-ah)
- ❏ lingual (LING-gwal)
- ❏ lingual tonsil
  (LING-gwal TAWN-sil)
- ❏ malignant (mah-LIG-nant)
- ❏ mallear (MAL-ee-ar)
- ❏ mallei (MAL-ee-eye)
- ❏ malleus (MAL-ee-us)
- ❏ mastoid (MAS-toyd)
- ❏ mastoidectomy
  (MAS-toy-DEK-toh-mee)
- ❏ mastoiditis (MAS-toy-DY-tis)
- ❏ maxillary sinus
  (MAK-sih-LAIR-ee SY-nus)
- ❏ maxillofacial surgeon
  (MAK-sil-oh-FAY-shal SER-jun)
- ❏ meati (mee-AA-tie)
- ❏ meatus (mee-AA-tus)
- ❏ Meniere's disease
  (MEN-eh-AIRZ dih-ZEEZ)
- ❏ mentum (MEN-tum)
- ❏ mucosa (myoo-KOH-sah)
- ❏ mucosal (myoo-KOH-al)
- ❏ mucosal hypertrophy
  (myoo-KOH-sal
  hy-PER-troh-fee)
- ❏ mucus (MYOO-kus)
- ❏ myringitis (MEER-in-JY-tis)
- ❏ myringotome
  (mih-RING-goh-tohm)
- ❏ myringotomy
  (MEER-ing-GAWT-oh-mee)
- ❏ nares (NAY-reez)
- ❏ naris (NAY-ris)
- ❏ nasal (NAY-zal)
- ❏ nasal cavity (NAY-zal
  KAV-ih-tee)
- ❏ nasolabial (NAY-zoh-LAY-bee-al)
- ❏ nasopharynx
  (NAY-zoh-FAIR-ingks)
- ❏ nodule (NAWD-yool)

- oral cavity (OR-al KAV-ih-tee)
- oral mucosa (OR-al myoo-KOH-sah)
- oropharynx (OR-oh-FAIR-ingks)
- ossicle (AWS-ih-kl)
- ossicular (aw-SIK-yoo-lar)
- otalgia (oh-TAL-jee-ah)
- otitis externa (oh-TY-tis eks-TER-nah)
- otitis media (oh-TY-tis MEE-dee-ah)
- otolaryngologist (OH-toh-LAIR-ing-GAWL-oh-jist)
- otolaryngology (OH-toh-LAIR-ing-GAWL-oh-jee)
- otorhinolaryngologist (OH-toh-RY-noh-LAIR-ing-GAWL-oh-jist)
- otoplasty (OH-toh-PLAS-tee)
- otorrhea (OH-toh-REE-ah)
- otosclerosis (OH-toh-skleh-ROH-sis)
- otoscope (OH-toh-skohp)
- otoscopy (oh-TAWS-koh-pee)
- palatal (PAL-ah-tal)
- palate (PAL-at)
- palatine tonsil (PAL-ah-teen TAWN-sil)
- pansinusitis (PAN-sy-nyoo-SY-tis)
- paranasal sinus (PAIR-ah-NAY-zal SY-nus)
- pharyngeal (fah-RIN-jee-al)
- pharyngitis (FAIR-in-JY-tis)
- pharynx (FAIR-ingks)

- philtrum (FIL-trum)
- pinna (PIN-ah)
- pinnae (PIN-ee)
- polyp (PAWL-ip)
- polypectomy (PAWL-ih-PEK-toh-mee)
- postnasal (post-NAY-zal)
- presbycusis (PREZ-bee-KOO-sis)
- radical neck dissection (RAD-ih-kal NEK dy-SEK-shun)
- rhinophyma (RY-noh-FY-mah)
- rhinoplasty (RY-noh-PLAS-tee)
- rhinorrhea (RY-noh-REE-ah)
- Rinne test (RIN-eh TEST)
- Romberg's sign (RAWM-bergz sine)
- sensorineural (SEN-soh-ree-NYOOR-al)
- septal (SEP-tal)
- septum (SEP-tum)
- serous (SEER-us)
- sinus (SY-nus)
- sinusitis (SY-nyoo-SY-tis)
- speculum (SPEK-yoo-lum)
- sphenoid sinus (SFEE-noyd SY-nus)
- stapedectomy (STAY-pee-DEK-toh-mee)
- stapedes (STAY-pee-deez)
- stapedial (stay-PEE-dee-al)
- stapes (STAY-peez)
- streptococcus (STREP-toh-KAWK-uhs)
- submandibular (SUB-man-DIB-yoo-lar)

- submental (sub-MEN-tal)
- suppurative (SUP-uh-rah-TIV)
- temporomandibular joint (TEM-poh-roh-man-DIB-yoo-lar JOYNT)
- tinnitus (TIN-ih-tus) (tih-NY-tus)
- tonsil (TAWN-sil)
- tonsillar (TAWN-sih-lar)
- tonsillectomy (TAWN-sih-LEK-toh-mee)
- tonsillitis (TAWN-sih-LY-tis)
- tragi (TRAY-jeye)
- tragus (TRAY-gus)
- turbinate (TER-bih-nayt)
- tympanic membrane (tim-PAN-ik MEM-brayn)
- tympanogram (tim-PAN-oh-gram)
- tympanometry (TIM-pah-NAWM-eh-tree)
- tympanoplasty (TIM-pah-noh-PLAS-tee) (TIM-pah-noh-PLAS-tee)
- tympanostomy (TIM-pan-AWS-toh-mee)
- unilateral (YOO-nih-LAT-eh-ral)
- vertigo (VER-tih-goh)
- vestibulocochlear nerve (ves-TIB-yoo-loh-KOH-klee-ar NERV)
- vestibular (ves-TIB-yoo-lar)
- vestibule (VES-tih-byool)
- vocal cord (VOH-kal KORD)
- Weber test (VAH-ber TEST)

Answer Key

Word Search

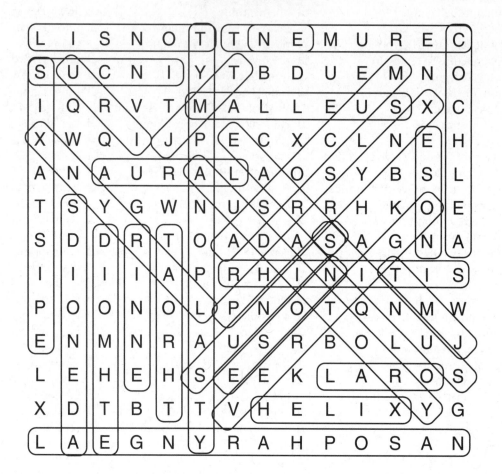

Crossword Puzzle

```
                    1O
    2L A B Y R I N T H
                     O
    4O T O P L A S T Y          3A              5M
                     H      6C O N C H A E     E
                     A           U            N
    7P R E S B Y C U S I S        S            T
                     Y           T        8O R O
    9S I N U S     10H E L I X    I
                     X           C
```

Underline the Accented Syllable

1. anosmia   (an-<u>AWZ</u>-mee-ah)

2. audiometry   (AW-dee-<u>AWM</u>-eh-tree)

3. cheiloplasty   (KY-loh-<u>PLAS</u>-tee)

4. cochlear   (<u>KOH</u>-klee-ar)

5. impedance   (im-<u>PEE</u>-dans)

6. leukoplakia   (LOO-koh-<u>PLAY</u>-kee-ah)

7. Ménière's   (men-eh-<u>AIRZ</u>)

8. otosclerosis   (OH-toh-skleh-<u>ROH</u>-sis)

9. presbycusis   (PREZ-bee-<u>KOO</u>-sis)

10. rhinitis   (ry-<u>NY</u>-tis)

11. sensorineural   (SEN-soh-ree-<u>NYOOR</u>-al)

12. speculum   (<u>SPEK</u>-yoo-lum)

13. stapedectomy   (STAY-pee-<u>DEK</u>-toh-mee)

14. temporomandibular   (TEM-poh-ROH-man-<u>DIB</u>-yoo-lar)

15. vertigo   (<u>VER</u>-ti-goh)

Word Surgery

1. adenoidectomy

   Suffix and its meaning: –ectomy *surgical excision*

   Prefix and its meaning: none

   Combining form and its meaning: adenoid/o- *adenoids*

   Medical word definition: Surgical excision of the adenoids

2. anosmia

   Suffix and its meaning: -ia *condition; state; thing*

   Prefix and its meaning: an- *without; not*

   Combining form and its meaning: osm/o- *the sense of smell*

   Medical word definition: Condition (of being) without the sense of smell

3. antibiotic

   Suffix and its meaning: -tic *pertaining to*

   Prefix and its meaning: anti- *against*

   Combining form and its meaning: bi/o- *life; living organisms; living tissue*

   Medical word definition: Pertaining to (a drug that is) against living organisms
   (bacteria)

4. antitussive

   Suffix and its meaning: -ive *pertaining to*

   Prefix and its meaning: anti- *against*

   Combining form and its meaning: tuss/o- *cough*

   Medical word definition: Pertaining to (a drug that is) against coughing

5. audiometry

   Suffix and its meaning: -metry *process of measuring*

   Prefix and its meaning: none

   Combining form and its meaning: audi/o- *the sense of hearing*

   Medical word definition: Process of measuring the sense of hearing

6. cheiloplasty

   Suffix and its meaning: -plasty *process of reshaping by surgery*

   Prefix and its meaning: none

   Combining form and its meaning: cheil/o- *lip*

   Medical word definition: Process of reshaping by surgery on the lip

7. labyrinthitis

Suffix and its meaning: -itis *inflammation or infection of*

Prefix and its meaning: none

Combining form and its meaning: labyrinth/o- *labyrinth (of the inner ear)*

Medical word definition: Inflammation or infection of the labyrinth

8. leukoplakia

Suffix and its meaning: -ia *condition; state; thing*

Prefix and its meaning: none

Combining form and its meaning: leuk/o- *white*

Combining form and its meaning: plak/o- *plaque*

Medical word definition: Condition of white plaque

9. myringotomy

Suffix and its meaning: -tomy *process of cutting or making an incision*

Prefix and its meaning: none

Combining form and its meaning: myring/o- *tympanic membrane (eardrum)*

Medical word definition: Process of cutting or making an incision in the tympanic membrane

10. otosclerosis

Suffix and its meaning: -osis *condition; abnormal condition; process*

Prefix and its meaning: none

Combining form and its meaning: ot/o- *ear*

Combining form and its meaning: scler/o- *hard; sclera (white of the eye)*

Medical word definition: Abnormal condition in the ear of hardness

11. pansinusitis

Suffix and its meaning: -itis *inflammation of; infection of*

Prefix and its meaning: pan- *all*

Combining form and its meaning: sinus/o- *sinus*

Medical word definition: Inflammation or infection of all of the sinuses

12. rhinorrhea

   Suffix and its meaning: -rrhea *flow; discharge*

   Prefix and its meaning: none

   Combining form and its meaning: rhin/o- *nose*

   Medical word definition: Flow or discharge from the nose

13. temporomandibular

   Suffix and its meaning: -ar *pertaining to*

   Prefix and its meaning: none

   Combining form and its meaning: tempor/o- *temple (side of the head)*

   Combining form and its meaning: mandibul/o- *mandible (lower jaw)*

   Suffix and definition: Pertaining to the temple and the mandible

14. tympanometry

   Suffix and its meaning: -metry *process of measuring*

   Prefix and its meaning: none

   Combining form and its meaning: tympan/o- *tympanic membrane (eardrum)*

   Medical word definition: Process of measuring the tympanic membrane

15. unilateral

   Suffix and its meaning: -al *pertaining to*

   Prefix and its meaning: uni- *single; not paired*

   Combining form and its meaning: *later/o- side*

   Medical word definition: Pertaining to a single side

Chapter Quiz

MULTIPLE CHOICE

1. D	4. C	7. A	10. C
2. D	5. A	8. B	
3. A	6. A	9. C	

FILL IN THE BLANK

1. glottis (of the larynx)
2. mucous
3. Adenoids
4. neuroma
5. flow or discharge
6. herpes simplex
7. ossicles (or stapes)
8. cochlear
9. ot/o-
10. Decongestant

TRUE/FALSE

1. True
2. False (nares)
3. False ("gloss/o-" and "lingu/o-")
4. True
5. True
6. False (epistaxis)
7. False (decibels)
8. True
9. False (mandible)
10. True

CHAPTER 17

Psychiatry

Measure Your Progress: Learning Objectives

After reading this chapter, the student should be able to

- Identify the structures of the brain that are related to psychiatry.
- Describe the process of an emotional response.
- Describe common psychiatric diseases and conditions, laboratory and diagnostic procedures, medical and psychiatric procedures and therapies, and drug categories.
- Give the medical meaning of word parts related to psychiatry.
- Build psychiatric words from word parts and divide and define psychiatric words.
- Spell and pronounce psychiatric words.
- Analyze the medical content and meaning of a psychiatric report.
- Dive deeper into psychiatry by reviewing the activities at the end of this chapter and online at Medical Terminology Interactive.

It All Starts with Word Building

Medical language is all about medical words and their word parts. Jump right into this chapter by learning these common combining forms and their definitions that you will encounter in this chapter.

acr/o-	extremity; highest point	neur/o-	nerve
addict/o-	surrender to; be controlled by	obsess/o-	besieged by thoughts
affect/o-	state of mind; mood; to have an influence on	ophidi/o-	snake
		oppos/o-	forceful resistance
		path/o-	disease; suffering
agor/a-	open area or space	ped/o-	child
amnes/o-	forgetfulness	phil/o-	attraction to; fondness for
anxi/o-	fear; worry		
arachn/o-	spider; spider web	phob/o-	fear; avoidance
aut/o-	self	phren/o-	mind
behav/o-	activity; manner of acting	psych/o-	mind
		pyr/o-	fire
cid/o-	killing	rap/o-	to seize and drag away
claustr/o-	enclosed space		
cognit/o-	thinking	schiz/o-	split
compuls/o-	drive or compel	sex/o-	sex
copr/o-	feces; stool	soci/o-	human beings; community
delus/o-	false belief		
depend/o-	to hang onto	somat/o-	body
depress/o-	press down	stress/o-	disturbing stimulus
emot/o-	emotion	su/i-	self
factiti/o-	artificial; contrived	thanat/o-	death
hallucin/o-	imagined perception	therapeut/o-	treatment
		thym/o-	thymus; rage
hedon/o-	pleasure	toler/o-	to become accustomed to
hom/i-	man		
hypn/o-	sleep	toxic/o-	poison; toxin
klept/o-	to steal	xen/o-	foreign
ment/o-	mind		

Chapter Spelling Test

Dictate and spell (or photocopy a handout that contains) this list of 15 spelling words. Give this list to students to study for the week. At the beginning of next week's class, dictate 10 of these words as the spelling test. The spelling test is included with the chapter test that is given on the previous week's material.

1. amnesia
2. anorexia nervosa
3. delirium tremens
4. delusion
5. dementia
6. euphoria
7. hallucination
8. homicidal ideation
9. hypnosis
10. paranoia
11. phobia
12. psychiatry
13. psychosis
14. schizophrenia
15. suicide

Chapter Pronunciation Test

Photocopy a handout that contains this list of 15 pronunciation words. Gives this list to students to study for the week. Sometime at the beginning of the next week, each student should call your office or home answering machine and pronounce each word.

1. anorexia nervosa (AN-oh-REK-see-ah ner-VOH-sah)

2. autism (AW-tizm)

3. bulimia (buh-LIM-ee-ah)

4. delirium tremens (dee-LEER-ee-um TREM-enz)

5. delusional (dee-LOO-shun-al)

6. dementia (dee-MEN-shee-ah)

7. detoxication (dee-TAWKS-ih-KAY-shun)

8. electroconvulsive therapy (ee-LEK-troh-con-VUL-siv THAIR-ah-pee)

9. euphoria (yoo-FOR-ee-ah)

10. homicidal ideation (HOH-mih-SY-dal EYE-dee-AA-shun)

11. milieu (meel-YOO)

12. obsessive–compulsive disorder (awb-SEH-siv com-PAWL-sive dis-OR-der)

13. psychiatry (sy-KY-ah-tree)

14. psychosis (sy-KOH-sis)

15. schizophrenia (SKIZ-oh-FREE-nee-ah)

Word Search

Complete this word search puzzle that contains Chapter 17 words. Look for the following words as given in the list below. The number in parentheses indicates how many times the word appears in the puzzle.

addict
ADHD
affect
anger
anorexia
anxiety
autism
CNS (2)
delusions
dementia
depression
drugs
ETOH
help
insane
limbic

LSD
manic
milieu
mood
OCD
panic
personality
phobia
SAD
sadism
sane
sanity
schizophrenia
suicide
therapy

```
N  J  P  E  R  S  O  N  A  L  I  T  Y
O  A  F  F  E  C  T  P  K  D  S  T  P
I  C  I  N  A  M  C  M  A  C  E  D  A
S  N  A  L  C  A  I  S  I  I  P  N  R
S  S  U  I  C  I  D  E  X  L  G  B  E
E  B  N  M  L  B  D  N  E  E  I  Y  H
R  A  D  B  J  O  A  H  R  Q  T  E  T
P  C  O  I  V  H  U  O  O  I  K  C  U
E  W  O  C  D  P  T  I  N  S  A  N  E
D  E  M  E  N  T  I  A  A  U  J  S  T
H  K  S  N  O  I  S  U  L  E  D  W  O
D  R  U  G  S  B  M  S  I  D  A  S  H
A  I  N  E  R  H  P  O  Z  I  H  C  S
```

Crossword Puzzle

ACROSS

1. A disorder in which the patient exhibits factitious medical or psychiatric symptoms to gain assistance, attention, or pity is called _____ syndrome.

3. The _____ stores long-term memories and helps to compare present and past emotions and experiences.

4. The combining form that means false belief is "_____".

6. The combining form "_____" means open area or space.

7. Chronic, mild-to-moderate depression is called _____.

8. A sudden attack of severe, overwhelming anxiety without an identifiable cause is referred to as a _____ disorder.

9. The _____ relays sensory information from the five senses to the midbrain.

DOWN

1. A fear of germs is known as _____.

2. A decreased level of _____, a neurotransmitter found in the brain and spinal cord, can cause depression.

5. The combining form "phren/o-" means diaphragm or_____.

Underline the Accented Syllable

Read the medical word. Then review the syllables in the pronunciation. Underline the primary (main) accented syllable in the pronunciation.

1. acrophobia   (ak-roh-foh-bee-ah)

2. anhedonia   (an-hee-doh-nee-ah)

3. bulimia   (buh-lim-ee-ah)

4. dysthymia   (dis-thy-mee-ah)

5. encopresis   (en-koh-pree-sis)

6. euphoria   (yoo-for-ee-ah)

7. kleptomania   (klep-toh-may-nee-ah)

8. malingering   (mah-ling-ger-ing)

9. pedophilia   (pee-doh-fil-ee-ah)

10. psychiatric   (sy-kee-at-rik)

11. Rorschach   (rohr-shak)

12. schizophrenia   (skiz-oh-free-nee-ah) (skit-soh-free-nee-ah)

13. Tourette   (toor-et)

14. trichotillomania   (trik-oh-til-oh-may-nee-ah)

15. xenophobia   (zen-oh-foh-bee-ah)

Word Surgery

Read the medical word. Break the medical word into its word parts and give the meaning of each word part. Then give the definition of the medical word.

1. anhedonia

   Suffix and its meaning: _____

   Prefix and its meaning: _____

   Combining form and its meaning: _____

   Medical word definition: _____

2. anorexia

   Suffix and its meaning: _____

   Prefix and its meaning: _____

   Combining form and its meaning: _____

   Medical word definition: _____

3. bipolar

   Suffix and its meaning: _____

   Prefix and its meaning: _____

   Combining form and its meaning: _____

   Medical word definition: _____

4. dissociative

   Suffix and its meaning: _____

   Prefix and its meaning: _____

   Combining form and its meaning: _____

   Medical word definition: _____

5. dysmorphic

   Suffix and its meaning: _____

   Prefix and its meaning: _____

   Combining form and its meaning: _____

   Medical word definition: _____

6. echolialia

Suffix and its meaning: _____

Prefix and its meaning: _____

Combining form and its meaning: _____

Medical word definition: _____

7. homicidal

Suffix and its meaning: _____

Prefix and its meaning: _____

Combining form and its meaning: _____

Combining form and its meaning: _____

Medical word definition: _____

8. pedophilia

Suffix and its meaning: _____

Prefix and its meaning: _____

Combining form and its meaning: _____

Combining form and its meaning: _____

Medical word definition: _____

9. phobia

Suffix and its meaning: _____

Prefix and its meaning: _____

Combining form and its meaning: _____

Medical word definition: _____

10. psychoanalysis

Suffix and its meaning: _____

Prefix and its meaning: _____

Combining form and its meaning: _____

Combining form and its meaning: _____

Medical word definition: _____

11. rapist

Suffix and its meaning: _____

Prefix and its meaning: _____

Combining form and its meaning: _____

Medical word definition: _____

12. schizophrenia

Suffix and its meaning: _____

Prefix and its meaning: _____

Combining form and its meaning: _____

Combining form and its meaning: _____

Medical word definition: _____

13. thanatophobia

Suffix and its meaning: _____

Prefix and its meaning: _____

Combining form and its meaning: _____

Combining form and its meaning: _____

Medical word definition: _____

14. transvestism

Suffix and its meaning: _____

Prefix and its meaning: _____

Combining form and its meaning: _____

Medical word definition: _____

15. trichotillomania

Suffix and its meaning: _____

Prefix and its meaning: _____

Combining form and its meaning: _____

Combining form and its meaning: _____

Medical word definition: _____

Chapter Quiz

MULTIPLE CHOICE

1. The term "psychiatry" has a suffix that:

   A. refers to a medical treatment.

   B. is an eponym.

   C. has a prefix that means acting out.

   D. means the study of.

2. Which of the following are neurotransmitters?

   A. epinephrine and norepinephrine

   B. dopamine and affect

   C. cocaine and alcohol

   D. serotonin and fornix

3. Constant, persistent, uncontrollable thoughts are part of a condition known as:

   A. phobia.

   B. obsessive–compulsive disorder.

   C. tremor.

   D. dementia.

4. Anorexia nervosa and bulimia:

   A. include chronic pulling out or twisting of the hair.

   B. involve abnormal eating habits.

   C. are caused by addiction to narcotics.

   D. include hallucinations.

5. Patients with schizophrenia:

   A. have lost touch with reality.

   B. have bizarre behavior.

   C. hear voices telling them to do things.

   D. All of the above.

6. Distractibility, short attention span, inability to follow directions, restlessness, and hyperactivity describe which of the following?

   A. ADHD

   B. conduct disorder

   C. exhibitionism

   D. fetishism

7. Partial or total memory loss due to trauma or disease is:

   A. anorexia.

   B. catatonia.

   C. Tourette's syndrome.

   D. amnesia.

8. Which of the following is an exaggerated sense of self-worth and importance?

   A. obsessive–compulsive disorder

   B. attention-deficit hyperactivity disorder

   C. narcissism

   D. kleptomania

9. A radiologic procedure that shows areas of abnormal metabolism in the brain related to Alzheimer's disease and dementia is:

   A. MME.

   B. PET.

   C. CT.

   D. BDI.

10. The difference between a psychologist and a psychiatrist is:

   A. psychiatrists are physicians.

   B. psychologists cannot prescribe drug therapy.

   C. There is no difference.

   D. Both A and B are correct.

FILL IN THE BLANK

1. The _____ system processes memories and controls emotion, mood, motivation, and behavior.

2. A _____ is an intense, unreasonable fear of a specific thing, situation or thought.

3. The extreme chronic fear of being fat and obsession to become thinner is known as _____ _____.

4. "Su/i-," as in suicidal, means "_____."

5. _____ is the inability to communicate or form significant relationships with others and a lack of interest in doing so.

6. Obtaining sexual arousal by wearing clothes belonging to the opposite sex or posing as someone of the opposite sex is _____.

7. The _____ test uses a set of cards with abstract shapes.

8. A therapy that places the patient in a sleep-like trance is _____.

9. Psychoanalysis was developed by (name of the person) _____.

10. Antipsychotic drugs are also known as major _____.

TRUE/FALSE

_____ 1. The thalamus is part of the limbic system.

_____ 2. The hypothalamus is located above the thalamus.

_____ 3. Acrophobia is the fear of heights.

_____ 4. Hallucinogens include LSD, PCP, and opioids.

_____ 5. PMDD stands for premenstrual syndrome.

_____ 6. Echolalia is the condition in which the patient automatically repeats what someone else has said.

_____ 7. A patient with dementia exhibits symptoms of acute confusion, disorientation, and agitation due to toxic levels of body chemicals, drugs, or alcohol.

_____ 8. A patient who exhibits false medical or psychiatric symptoms to get a reward is malingering.

_____ 9. A patient who continually is concerned with minor defects in body appearance has hypochondriasis.

_____ 10. Detoxication is a therapy that uses an electrical current to treat severe depression and schizophrenia.

Pronunciation Checklist

Read each word and its pronunciation. Practice pronouncing each word. Verify your pronunciation by listening to the Pronunciation List on Medical Terminology Interactive. Check the box next to the word after you master its pronunciation.

❑ acrophobia
(AK-roh-FOH-bee-ah)
❑ addiction (ah-DIK-shun)
❑ affect (AF-fekt)
❑ affective (ah-FEK-tiv)
❑ agoraphobia
(AG-or-ah-FOH-bee-ah)
❑ amnesia (am-NEE-zee-ah)
❑ amnestic (am-NES-tik)
❑ amygdaloid (ah-MIG-dah-loyd)
❑ anhedonia
(AN-hee-DOH-nee-ah)
❑ anorexia nervosa (AN-oh-REK-see-ah ner-VOH-sah)
❑ anterograde amnesia
(AN-ter-oh-grayd
am-NEE-zee-ah)
❑ antianxiety drug
(AN-tee-ang-ZY-eh-tee DRUHG)
❑ antidepressant drug
(AN-tee-dee-PRES-ant DRUHG)
❑ antipsychotic drug
(AN-tee-sy-KAWT-ik DRUHG)
❑ antisocial personality
(AN-tee-SOH-shal
PER-son-AL-ih-tee)
❑ anxiety (ang-ZY-eh-tee)
❑ apathy (AP-ah-thee)
❑ arachnophobia
(ah-RAK-noh-FOH-bee-ah)
❑ autism (AW-tizm)
❑ aversion therapy (ah-VER-shun
THAIR-ah-pee)
❑ behavioral (bee-HAY-vyoor-al)
❑ bipolar disorder (by-POH-lar
dis-OR-der)
❑ bulimia (buh-LIM-ee-ah)
❑ catalepsy (KAT-ah-LEP-see)
❑ catatonia (KAT-ah-TOH-nee-ah)
❑ catatonic (KAT-ah-TAWN-ik)
❑ cingulate gyrus (SIN-gyoo-layt
JY-rus)
❑ claustrophobia
(KLAW-stroh-FOH-bee-ah)
❑ cognitive (KAWG-nih-tiv)
❑ compulsion (com-PAWL-shun)
❑ compulsive (com-PAWL-siv)
❑ conversion (con-VER-shun)
❑ coprolalia
(KAWP-roh-LAY-lee-ah)

❑ cyclothymia
(SY-kloh-THY-mee-ah)
❑ delirium (deh-LEER-ee-um)
(dee-LEER-ee-um)
❑ delirium tremens
(dee-LEER-ee-um TREM-enz)
❑ delusional (dee-LOO-shun-al)
❑ dementia (dee-MEN-shee-ah)
❑ dependence (dee-PEN-dens)
❑ dependent personality (dee-PEN-dent PER-son-AL-ih-tee)
❑ depersonalization
(dee-PER-son-AL-ih-ZAY-shun)
❑ depression (dee-PRESH-un)
❑ depressive (dee-PRES-iv)
❑ desensitization therapy
(dee-SEN-sih-tih-ZAY-shun
THAIR-ah-pee)
❑ detoxification (dee-TAWK-sih-fih-KAY-shun)
❑ dissociative disorder (dih-SOH-see-ah-TIV dis-OR-der)
❑ dopamine (DOH-pah-meen)
❑ dysmorphic (dis-MOR-fik)
❑ dysthymia (dis-THY-mee-ah)
❑ echolalia (EK-oh-LAY-lee-ah)
❑ electroconvulsive therapy
(ee-LEK-troh-con-VUL-siv
THAIR-ah-pee)
❑ emotion (ee-MOH-shun)
❑ encopresis (EN-koh-PREE-sis)
❑ epinephrine (EP-ih-NEF-rin)
❑ euphoria (yoo-FOR-ee-ah)
❑ exhibitionism
(EK-sih-BIH-shun-izm)
❑ factitious disorder
(fak-TISH-us dis-OR-der)
❑ fetishism (FET-ish-izm)
❑ fornix (FOR-niks)
❑ fugue (FYOOG)
❑ global amnesia (GLOH-bal
am-NEE-zee-ah)
❑ hallucination
(hah-LOO-sih-NAY-shun)
❑ hallucinogen
(hah-LOO-sin-oh-JEN)
❑ hebephrenia (HEE-bah-FREE-nee-ah) (HEB-ee-FREE-nee-ah)
❑ hippocampus
(HIP-oh-KAM-pus)

❑ histrionic personality
(HIS-tree-AW-nik
PER-son-AL-ih-tee)
❑ homicidal ideation (HOH-mih-SY-dal EYE-dee-AA-shun)
❑ hypochondriasis
(HY-poh-con-DRY-ah-sis)
❑ hypnosis (hip-NOH-sis)
❑ hypothalamus
(HY-poh-THAL-ah-mus)
❑ kleptomania
(KLEP-toh-MAY-nee-ah)
❑ limbic lobe (LIM-bik LOHB)
❑ limbic system (LIM-bik SIS-tem)
❑ malingering
(mah-LING-ger-ing)
❑ mania (MAY-nee-ah)
❑ manic (MAN-ik)
❑ masochism (MAS-oh-kizm)
❑ microphobia
(MY-kroh-FOH-bee-ah)
❑ milieu (meel-YOO)
❑ Munchausen
(moon-CHOW-zen)
❑ Munchausen by proxy (moon-CHOW-zen by PRAWK-see)
❑ narcissism (NAWR-sih-sizm)
❑ narcissistic personality (NAWR-sih-SIS-tik PER-son-AL-ih-tee)
❑ neologism (nee-AWL-oh-jizm)
❑ neurotransmitter
(NYOOR-oh-trans-MIT-er)
❑ norepinephrine
(NOR-ep-ih-NEF-rin)
❑ obsession (awb-SEH-shun)
❑ obsessive-compulsive disorder
(awb-SEH-siv
com-PAWL-siv dis-OR-der)
❑ ophidiophobia
(oh-FID-ee-oh-FOH-bee-ah)
❑ oppositional defiant disorder
(AWP-ih-ZIH-shun-al dee-FY-ant
dis-OR-der)
❑ panic (PAN-ik)
❑ paranoia (PAIR-ah-NOY-ah)
❑ pathological
(PATH-oh-LAWJ-ih-kal)
❑ pedophile (PEE-doh-file)
❑ pedophilia (PEE-doh-FIL-ee-ah)
❑ personality (PER-son-AL-ih-tee)

- phobia (FOH-bee-ah)
- phobic (FOH-bik)
- posttraumatic stress disorder (POST-trah-MAT-ik STRES dis-OR-der)
- premenstrual dysphoric syndrome (pree-MEN-stroo-al dis-FOR-ik SIN-drohm)
- psychiatric (SY-kee-AT-rik)
- psychiatrist (sy-KY-ah-trist)
- psychiatry (sy-KY-ah-tree)
- psychoanalysis (SY-koh-ah-NAL-ih-sis)
- psychologist (sy-KAWL-oh-jist)
- psychology (sy-KAWL-oh-jee)
- psychosis (sy-KOH-sis)
- psychotherapy (SY-koh-THAIR-ah-pee)
- pyromania 0 (PY-roh-MAY-nee-ah)
- rape (RAYP)
- rapist (RAY-pist)
- reactive attachment disorder (ree-AK-tiv ah-TACH-ment dis-OR-der)
- repression (ree-PRESH-un)
- retrograde amnesia (RET-roh-grayd am-NEE-zee-ah)
- Rorschach test (ROHR-shahk TEST)
- sadism (SAY-dizm) (SAD-izm)
- schizophrenia (SKIZ-oh-FREE-nee-ah) (SKIT-soh-FREE-nee-ah)
- schizophrenic (SKIZ-oh-FREN-ik) (SKIT-soh-FREN-ik)
- serotonin (SAIR-oh-TOH-nin)
- social phobia (SOH-shal FOH-bee-ah)
- social worker (SOH-shal WER-ker)
- somatoform (soh-MAT-oh-form)
- suicidal ideation (SOO-ih-SY-dal EYE-dee-AA-shun)
- thalamus (THAL-ah-mus)
- thanatophobia (THAN-ah-toh-FOH-bee-ah)
- Thematic Apperception Test (thee-MAT-ik AP-er-SEP-shun TEST)
- therapeutic milieu (THAIR-ah-PYOO-tik meel-YOO)
- therapy (THAIR-ah-pee)
- tolerance (TAWL-er-ans)
- Tourette's syndrome (toor-ETZ SIN-drohm)
- transsexualism (tranz-SEK-shoo-ah-lizm)
- transvestism (trans-VES-tizm)
- trichotillomania (TRIK-oh-TIL-oh-MAY-nee-ah)
- voyeurism (VOY-yer-izm)
- xenophobia (ZEN-oh-FOH-bee-ah)

Answer Key

Word Search

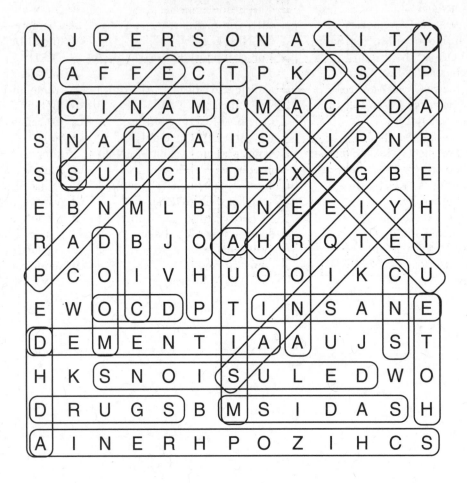

Crossword Puzzle

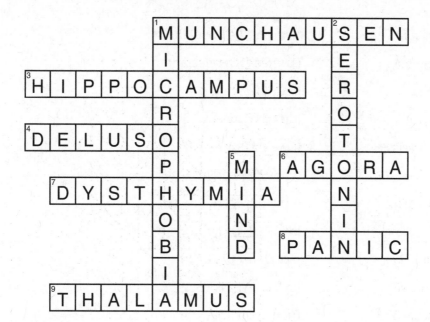

Underline the Accented Syllable

1. acrophobia   (AK-roh-<u>FOH</u>-bee-ah)

2. anhedonia   (AN-hee-<u>DOH</u>-nee-ah)

3. bulimia   (buh-<u>LIM</u>-ee-ah)

4. dysthymia   (dis-<u>THY</u>-mee-ah)

5. encopresis   (EN-koh-<u>PREE</u>-sis)

6. euphoria   (yoo-<u>FOR</u>-ee-ah)

7. kleptomania   (KLEP-toh-<u>MAY</u>-nee-ah)

8. malingering   (mah-<u>LING</u>-ger-ing)

9. pedophilia   (PEE-doh-<u>FIL</u>-ee-ah)

10. psychiatric   (SY-kee-<u>AT</u>-rik)

11. Rorschach   (<u>ROHR</u>-shahk)

12. schizophrenia   (SKIZ-oh-<u>FREE</u>-nee-ah) or (SKIT-soh-<u>FREE</u>-nee-ah)

13. Tourette   (toor-<u>ET</u>)

14. trichotillomania   (TRIK-oh-TIL-oh-<u>MAY</u>-nee-ah)

15. xenophobia   (ZEN-oh-<u>FOH</u>-bee-ah)

Word Surgery

1. anhedonia

   Suffix and its meaning: -ia *condition; state; thing*

   Prefix and its meaning: an- *without; not*

   Combining form and its meaning: hedon/o- *pleasure*

   Medical word definition: Condition (of being) without pleasure

2. anorexia

   Suffix and its meaning: -ia *condition; state; thing*

   Prefix and its meaning: an- *without; not*

   Combining form and its meaning: orex/o- *appetite*

   Medical word definition: Condition (of being) without an appetite

3. bipolar

   Suffix and its meaning: -ar *pertaining to*

   Prefix and its meaning: bi- *two*

   Combining form and its meaning: pol/o- *pole*

   Medical word definition: Pertaining to two poles

4. dissociative

   Suffix and its meaning: -ative *pertaining to*

   Prefix and its meaning: dis- *away from*

   Combining form and its meaning: soci/o- *human beings; community*

   Medical word definition: Pertaining to being away from human beings

5. dysmorphic

   Suffix and its meaning: -ic *pertaining to*

   Prefix and its meaning: dys- *painful; difficult; abnormal*

   Combining form and its meaning: morph/o- *shape*

   Medical word definition: Pertaining to an abnormal shape

6. echolalia

   Suffix and its meaning: -lalia *condition of speech*

   Prefix and its meaning: none

   Combining form and its meaning: ech/o- *echo (sound wave)*

   Medical word definition: Condition of speech that echoes (someone else)

7. homicidal

   Suffix and its meaning: -al *pertaining to*

   Prefix and its meaning: none

   Combining form and its meaning: hom/i- *man*

   Combining form and its meaning: cid/o- *killing*

   Medical word definition: Pertaining to man killing

8. pedophilia

   Suffix and its meaning: -ia *condition; state; thing*

   Prefix and its meaning: none

   Combining form and its meaning: ped/o- *child*

   Combining form and its meaning: phil/o- *attraction to; fondness for*

   Medical word definition: Condition (toward a) child (of an abnormal) attraction to or fondness (for it by an adult)

9. phobia

   Suffix and its meaning: -ia *condition; state; thing*

   Prefix and its meaning: none

   Combining form and its meaning: phob/o- *fear; avoidance*

   Medical word definition: Condition of fear

10. psychoanalysis

    Suffix and its meaning: -sis *process; condition; abnormal condition*

    Prefix and its meaning: none

    Combining form and its meaning: psych/o- *mind*

    Combining form and its meaning: analy/o- *to separate*

    Medical word definition: Process of the mind to separate (its thoughts)

11. rapist

    Suffix and its meaning: -ist *one who specializes in*

    Prefix and its meaning: none

    Combining form and its meaning: rap/o- *to seize and drag away*

    Medical word definition: One who specializes in seizing and dragging away (a person)

12. schizophrenia

    Suffix and its meaning: -ia *condition; state; thing*

    Prefix and its meaning: none

    Combining form and its meaning: schiz/o- *split*

    Combining form and its meaning: phren/o- *diaphragm; mind*

    Medical word definition: Condition of a split mind

13. thanatophobia

    Suffix and its meaning: -ia *condition; state; thing*

    Prefix and its meaning: none

    Combining form and its meaning: thanat/o- *death*

    Combining form and its meaning: phob/o- *fear; avoidance*

    Medical word definition: Condition of (thinking of) death (with) fear or avoidance

14. transvestism

    Suffix and its meaning: -ism *process; disease from a specific cause*

    Prefix and its meaning: trans- *across; through*

    Combining form and its meaning: vest/o- *to dress*

    Medical word definition: Process of (going) across (to the other sex) to dress

15. trichotillomania

    Suffix and its meaning: -mania *condition of frenzy*

    Prefix and its meaning: none

    Combining form and its meaning: trich/o- *hair*

    Combining form and its meaning: till/o- *pull out*

    Medical word definition: Condition of frenzy of hair (being) pulled out

Chapter Quiz

MULTIPLE CHOICE

1. A   4. B   7. D   10. D

2. A   5. D   8. C

3. B   6. A   9. B

FILL IN THE BLANK

1. limbic

2. phobia

3. anorexia nervosa

4. self

5. Autism

6. transvestism

7. Rorschach

8. hypnosis (or hypnotherapy)

9. Sigmund Freud (or Freud)

10. tranquilizers

TRUE/FALSE

1. True

2. False (below)

3. True

4. True

5. False (PMS)

6. True

7. False (delirium)

8. True

9. False (body dysmorphic syndrome)

10. False (electroshock therapy or electroconvulsive therapy)

CHAPTER 18

Oncology

Measure Your Progress: Learning Objectives

After reading this chapter, the student should be able to

- Identify the structures of a cell.
- Describe the process by which a normal cell divides and how a normal cell becomes a cancerous cell.
- List six characteristics of cancerous cells and tumors.
- Describe common types of cancer, laboratory and diagnostic procedures, medical and surgical procedures, and drug categories.
- Give the medical meaning of word parts related to cancer.
- Build cancer words from word parts and divide and define cancer words.
- Spell and pronounce cancer words.
- Analyze the medical content and meaning of an oncology report.
- Dive deeper into oncology by reviewing the activities at the end of this chapter and online at Medical Terminology Interactive.

It All Starts with Word Building

Medical language is all about medical words and their word parts. Jump right into this chapter by learning some of the common combining forms and their definitions that you will encounter in this chapter.

aden/o-	gland	kary/o-	nucleus
adjuv/o-	giving help or assistance	lymph/o-	lymph; lymphatic tissue
angi/o-	blood vessel; lymphatic vessel	lys/o-	break down; destroy
bas/o-	base of a structure	malign/o-	intentionally causing harm; cancer
bi/o-	life; living organisms; living tissue		
blast/o-	immature; embryonic	melan/o-	black
		mit/o-	threadlike structure
cancer/o-	cancer		
capsul/o-	capsule (enveloping structure)	mutat/o-	to change
		ne/o-	new
carcin/o-	cancer	necr/o-	dead cells, tissue, or body
cellul/o-	cell		
chem/o-	chemical; drug	nucle/o-	nucleus
chrom/o-	color	nucleol/o-	nucleolus
cry/o-	cold	onc/o-	tumor; mass
cyt/o-	cell	path/o-	disease; suffering
differentiat/o-	being distinct; specialized	plasm/o-	plasma
		plas/o-	growth; formation
dissect/o-	to cut apart	radic/o-	all parts including the root
embryon/o-	embryo; immature form		
		radi/o-	radius (forearm bone; x-rays; radiation)
excis/o-	to cut out		
explorat/o-	to search out	resect/o-	to cut out; remove
gene/o-	gene	remiss/o-	send back
gen/o-	arising from; produced by	sarc/o-	connective tissue
		squam/o-	scalelike cell
germin/o-	embryonic tissue	surg/o-	operative procedure
hered/o-	genetic inheritance		
incis/o-	to cut into	terat/o-	bizarre form
invas/o-	to go into	transit/o-	change over from one to another

Chapter Spelling Test

Dictate and spell (or photocopy a handout that contains) this list of 20 spelling words. Give this list to students to study for the week. At the beginning of next week's class, dictate 10 of these words as the spelling test. The spelling test is included with the chapter test that is given on the previous week's material.

1. adenocarcinoma
2. benign
3. biopsy
4. cancerous
5. chemotherapy
6. chondrosarcoma
7. cytology
8. dysplastic
9. excisional biopsy
10. exploratory laparotomy
11. genetic
12. heredity
13. leukemia
14. lymphadenopathy
15. lymphoma
16. metastases
17. metastatic
18. neoplasm
19. oncologist
20. squamous cell carcinoma

Chapter Pronunciation Test

Photocopy a handout that contains this list of 20 pronunciation words. Give this list to students to study for the week. Sometime at the beginning of the next week, each student should call your office or home answering machine and pronounce each word.

1. adenocarcinoma (AD-eh-noh-KAR-sih-NOH-mah)

2. benign (bee-NINE)

3. chemotherapy (KEE-moh-THAIR-ah-pee)

4. chondrosarcoma (CON-droh-sar-KOH-mah)

5. dysplastic (dis-PLAS-tik)

6. excisional biopsy (ek-SIH-shun-al BY-awp-see)

7. exfoliative cytology (eks-FOH-lee-ah-TIV sy-TAWL-oh-jee)

8. exploratory laparotomy (eks-PLOR-ah-TOR-ee LAP-ah-RAW-toh-mee)

9. genetic (jeh-NET-ik)

10. heredity (heh-RED-ih-tee)

11. Kaposi's sarcoma (KAH-poh-seez sar-KOH-mah)

12. karyotype (KAIR-ee-oh-TYPE)

13. leukemia (loo-KEE-mee-ah)

14. lymphadenopathy (LIM-fad-eh-NAWP-ah-thee)

15. lymphoma (lim-FOH-mah)

16. metastases (meh-TAS-tah-seez)

17. metastatic (MET-ah-STAT-ik)

18. neoplasm (NEE-oh-plazm)

19. oncologist (ong-KAWL-oh-jist)

20. squamous cell carcinoma (SKWAY-mus SELL KAR-sih-NOH-mah)

Word Search

Complete this word search puzzle that contains Chapter 18 words. Look for the following words as given in the list below. The number in parentheses indicates how many times the word is found in the puzzle.

adenocarcinoma	health
cancer	heredity
carcinogen	invade
cell (2)	malignant
chemotherapy	metastasis
chromosomes	mutations
debulk	neoplasm
DNA	node
excising	nucleus
gene	TNM
genetic (2)	tumor (2)

```
A  Z  J  Y  C  I  T  E  N  E  G  H  U
D  S  C  T  T  U  M  O  R  W  T  Q  C
E  R  N  W  M  I  Z  V  L  L  E  C  H
N  M  T  O  L  B  D  C  A  N  C  E  R
O  Q  R  L  I  Y  I  E  Y  A  H  D  O
C  H  E  M  O  T  H  E  R  A  P  Y  M
A  C  D  K  E  E  A  C  J  E  C  S  O
R  B  G  N  D  H  I  T  V  Z  H  U  S
C  U  E  O  C  N  Q  R  U  D  T  E  O
I  G  N  E  O  P  L  A  S  M  W  L  M
N  J  E  G  N  I  S  I  C  X  E  C  E
O  M  E  T  A  S  T  A  S  I  S  U  S
M  N  M  A  L  I  G  N  A  N  T  N  B
A  H  K  L  U  B  E  D  A  V  N  I  K
```

Crossword Puzzle

ACROSS

1. A cancer of epithelial cells in the skin or mucous membranes is called a _____.

4. The combining form "carcin/o-" means _____.

8. Bacteria and viruses that cause DNA damage are known as _____.

9. The movement of cancerous cells through the blood and lymphatic vessels to other sites in the body is called _____.

10. _____ is a condition characterized by atypical cells that are different in size, shape, or organization but have not yet become cancerous.

DOWN

2. _____ are mutated genes in the RNA of a virus.

3. The combining form "_____" means nucleus.

5. A _____ is any growing tissue that is not part of the normal body structure or function.

6. _____ are small sacs that contain powerful digestive enzymes used to destroy a bacterium or virus that invades a cell.

7. _____ is a medical or surgical procedure that classifies cancer by how far it has spread in the body.

Underline the Accented Syllable

Read the medical word. Then review the syllables in the pronunciation. Underline the primary (main) accented syllable in the pronunciation.

1. antimetabolite   (an-tee-meh-tab-oh-lite)

2. aspiration   (as-pih-ray-shun)

3. brachytherapy   (brak-ee-thair-ah-pee)

4. carcinoid   (kar-sih-noyd)

5. carcinomatosis   (kar-sih-noh-mah-toh-sis)

6. choriocarcinoma   (koh-ree-oh-kar-sih-noh-mah)

7. intraperitoneal   (in-trah-pair-ih-toh-nee-al)

8. leiomyosarcoma   (lie-oh-my-oh-sar-koh-mah)

9. lymphadenopathy   (lim-fad-eh-nawp-ah-thee)

10. mammography   (mah-mawg-rah-fee)

11. melanoma   (mel-ah-noh-mah)

12. oligodendroglioma   (oh-lih-goh-den-droh-glee-oh-mah)

13. rhabdomyosarcoma   (rab-doh-my-oh-sar-koh-mah)

14. scintigraphy   (sin-tig-rah-fee)

15. squamous   (skway-mus)

Word Surgery

Read the medical word. Break the medical word into its word parts and give the meaning of each word part. Then give the definition of the medical word.

1. adjuvant

   Suffix and its meaning: _____

   Prefix and its meaning: _____

   Combining form and its meaning: _____

   Medical word definition: _____

2. bronchogenic

   Suffix and its meaning: _____

   Prefix and its meaning: _____

   Combining form and its meaning: _____

   Combining form and its meaning: _____

   Medical word definition: _____

3. carcinoid

   Suffix and its meaning: _____

   Prefix and its meaning: _____

   Combining form and its meaning: _____

   Medical word definition: _____

4. chondrosarcoma

   Suffix and its meaning: _____

   Prefix and its meaning: _____

   Combining form and its meaning: _____

   Combining form and its meaning: _____

   Medical word definition: _____

5. dysplastic

   Suffix and its meaning: _____

   Prefix and its meaning: _____

   Combining form and its meaning: _____

   Medical word definition: _____

6. exenteration

   Suffix and its meaning: _____

   Prefix and its meaning: _____

   Combining form and its meaning: _____

   Medical word definition: _____

7. fulguration

   Suffix and its meaning: _____

   Prefix and its meaning: _____

   Combining form and its meaning: _____

   Medical word definition: _____

8. karyotype

   Suffix and its meaning: _____

   Prefix and its meaning: _____

   Combining form and its meaning: _____

   Medical word definition: _____

9. leukemia

   Suffix and its meaning: _____

   Prefix and its meaning: _____

   Combining form and its meaning: _____

   Medical word definition: _____

10. lymphangiography

   Suffix and its meaning: _____

   Prefix and its meaning: _____

   Combining form and its meaning: _____

   Combining form and its meaning: _____

   Medical word definition: _____

11. myeloma

   Suffix and its meaning: _____

   Prefix and its meaning: _____

   Combining form and its meaning: _____

   Medical word definition: _____

12. myosarcoma

   Suffix and its meaning: _____

   Prefix and its meaning: _____

   Combining form and its meaning: _____

   Combining form and its meaning: _____

   Medical word definition: _____

13. neoplasm

   Suffix and its meaning: _____

   Prefix and its meaning: _____

   Combining form and its meaning: _____

   Medical word definition: _____

14. retinoblastoma

   Suffix and its meaning: _____

   Prefix and its meaning: _____

   Combining form and its meaning: _____

   Combining form and its meaning: _____

   Medical word definition: _____

15. scintinography

   Suffix and its meaning: _____

   Prefix and its meaning: _____

   Combining form and its meaning: _____

   Medical word definition: _____

Chapter Quiz

MULTIPLE CHOICE

1. The medical words associated with cancer types:

    A. are named after the body system.

    B. often have names based on the cell type that gives rise to cancer cells.

    C. always have a prefix and suffix.

    D. are based on the tests used to diagnose the cancer.

2. Cancerous tumors are often invasive, which means that they:

    A. penetrate the normal tissue around them.

    B. are filled with fluid.

    C. are encapsulated.

    D. are benign.

3. Damaged and mutated genes that cause a cell to become cancerous are:

    A. nuclear.

    B. viruses.

    C. pathogens.

    D. oncogenes.

4. A cancer that is in remission:

    A. is in relapse.

    B. can be excised.

    C. is not showing symptoms.

    D. is growing.

5. The suffix "-oma," as in astrocytoma, means:

    A. tumor or mass.

    B. arising in the brain.

    C. secreting hormones in unusual amounts.

    D. striped.

6. Leukemia is a type of cancer that affects:

    A. plasma.

    B. platelets.

    C. red blood cells.

    D. white blood cells.

7. A BRCA1 or BRCA2 gene is associated with:

    A. Parkinson's disease.

    B. bone cancer.

    C. breast cancer.

    D. diabetes mellitus.

8. A medical treatment for leukemia and lymphoma is:

    A. bone marrow transplantation.

    B. nephrectomy.

    C. cryosurgery.

    D. fulguration.

9. A biopsy is:

    A. a treatment for malignant tumors.

    B. the removal of a tissue sample.

    C. a procedure to assist in the diagnosis of cancer.

    D. Both B and C are correct.

10. Radiotherapy:

    A. uses sound waves to treat cancer.

    B. uses x-rays, gamma rays, or particles to treat cancer.

    C. is a medical test to detect the presence of cancer.

    D. None of the above.

FILL IN THE BLANK

1. When cancerous cells move through blood vessels and lymphatic vessels to other body parts it is called _____.

2. The suffix "_____" means "that which produces."

3. A cancer of the pigment-producing cells of the skin is _____.

4. A hepatoblastoma is a cancer of the _____.

5. Blood tests, such as CA-125, detect _____ on the surface of cancer cells.

6. A medical procedure that classifies cancer by how differentiated the cells appear is called _____.

7. _____ is a surgical procedure that uses a scope to examine an internal body cavity for signs of abnormal tissues or tumors.

8. Brachytherapy uses _____ substances to treat cancerous tissues or tumors.

9. The TNM system stands for _____, _____, and metastases.

10. Drugs used to treat nausea and vomiting that are common side effects of chemotherapy are _____ drugs.

TRUE/FALSE

_____ 1. "Resect/o-," as in resection, means to cut out or remove.

_____ 2. Apoptosis is programmed cell death.

_____ 3. Differentiated cells are immature and embryonal in appearance and behavior.

_____ 4. Tumor cells that are in their primary site are referred to as *in situ*.

_____ 5. Endometrial carcinoma is cancer of the inner lining of the uterus.

_____ 6. Osteosarcoma is a cancer of the bone and connective tissue.

_____ 7. A cytologic test used to examine chromosomes is a receptor assay test.

_____ 8. The suffix "-graphy," as in scintigraphy, means process of recording.

_____ 9. Chemotherapy drugs can be delivered to the thoracic cavity by an intraperitoneal catheter.

_____ 10. A standardized written plan of treatment is fractionation.

Pronunciation Checklist

Read each word and its pronunciation. Practice pronouncing each word. Verify your pronunciation by listening to the Pronunciation List on Medical Terminology Interactive. Check the box next to the word after you master its pronunciation.

❏ adenocarcinoma
(AD-eh-noh-KAR-sih-NOH-mah)

❏ adjuvant therapy
(AD-joo-vant THAIR-ah-pee)

❏ alkylating chemotherapy drug
(AL-kih-LAY-ting KEE-moh-THAIR-ah-pee DRUHG)

❏ alpha fetoprotein (AL-fah FEE-toh-PRO-teen)

❏ anaplasia (AN-ah-PLAY-zee-ah)
(AN-ah-PLAY-zha)

❏ angiogenesis
(AN-jee-oh-JEN-eh-sis)

❏ angiosarcoma
(AN-jee-OH-sar-KOH-mah)

❏ antimetabolite chemotherapy
drug (AN-tee-meh-TAB-oh-lite KEE-moh-THAIR-ah-pee DRUHG)

❏ apoptosis (AP-awp-TOH-sis)

❏ aspiration biopsy
(AS-pih-RAY-shun BY-awp-see)

❏ astrocytoma
(AS-troh-sy-TOH-mah)

❏ basal cell carcinoma (BAY-sal SEL KAR-sih-NOH-mah)

❏ benign (bee-NINE)

❏ biopsy (BY-awp-see)

❏ bone marrow aspiration (BOHN MAIR-oh AS-pih-RAY-shun)

❏ bone marrow transplantation
(BOHN MAIR-oh TRANS-plan-TAY-shun)

❏ brachytherapy
(BRAK-ee-THAIR-ah-pee)

❏ bronchogenic carcinoma
(BRONG-koh-JEN-ik KAR-sih-NOH-mah)

❏ cancer (KAN-ser)

❏ cancerous (KAN-ser-us)

❏ carcinoembryonic antigen
(KAR-sih-noh-EM-bree-AW-nik AN-tih-jen)

❏ carcinogen (kar-SIN-oh-jen)

❏ carcinoid syndrome
(KAR-sih-noyd SIN-drohm)

❏ carcinoid tumor (KAR-sih-noyd TOO-mor)

❏ carcinoma (KAR-sih-NOH-mah)

❏ carcinomatosis
(KAR-sih-NOH-mah-TOH-sis)

❏ cell (SEL)

❏ cellular (SEL-yoo-lar)

❏ central venous catheter
(SEN-tral VEE-nus KATH-eh-ter)

❏ chemoembolization
(KEE-moh-EM-bol-ih-ZAY-shun)

❏ chemotherapy
(KEE-moh-THAIR-ah-pee)

❏ chemotherapy antibiotic drug
(KEE-moh-THAIR-ah-pee AN-tee-by-AWT-ik DRUHG)

❏ chemotherapy drug
(KEE-moh-THAIR-ah-pee DRUHG)

❏ chemotherapy protocol
(KEE-moh-THAIR-ah-pee PROH-toh-kawl)

❏ cholangiocarcinoma (koh-LAN-jee-oh-KAR-sih-NOH-mah)

❏ chondrosarcoma
(CON-droh-sar-KOH-mah)

❏ choriocarcinoma (KOH-ree-oh-KAR-sih-NOH-mah)

❏ chromosomal
(KROH-moh-SOH-mal)

❏ chromosome
(KROH-moh-sohm)

❏ conformal radiotherapy
(con-FOR-mal RAY-dee-oh-THAIR-ah-pee)

❏ cryosurgery (KRY-oh-SER-jer-ee)

❏ cystectomy (sis-TEK-toh-mee)

❏ cytoplasm (SY-toh-plazm)

❏ debulk (dee-BULK)

❏ deoxyribonucleic acid
(dee-AWK-see-RY-boh-noo-KLEE-ik AS-id)

❏ differentiation
(DIF-er-EN-shee-AA-shun)

❏ dysgerminoma
(DIS-jer-mih-NOH-mah)

❏ dysplasia (dis-PLAY-zee-ah)
(dis-PLAY-zha)

❏ dysplastic (dis-PLAS-tik)

❏ electrosurgery
(ee-LEK-troh-SER-jer-ee)

❏ embryonal cell cancer
(EM-bree-OH-nal SEL KAN-ser)

❏ encapsulated tumor
(en-KAP-soo-LAY-ted TOO-mor)

❏ endometrial carcinoma
(EN-doh-MEE-tree-al KAR-sih-NOH-mah)

❏ endoplasmic reticulum
(EN-doh-PLAS-mik reh-TIK-yoo-lum)

❏ endoscopy (en-DAWS-koh-pee)

❏ Ewing's sarcoma
(YOO-ingz sar-KOH-mah)

❏ excision (ek-SIH-shun)

❏ excisional biopsy
(ek-SIH-shun-al BY-awp-see)

❏ exenteration
(eks-EN-ter-AA-shun)

❏ exfoliative cytology
(eks-FOH-lee-ah-TIV sy-TAWL-oh-jee)

❏ exploratory laparotomy
(eks-PLOR-ah-TOR-ee LAP-ah-RAW-toh-mee)

❏ external beam radiotherapy
(eks-TER-nal BEEM RAY-dee-oh-THAIR-ah-pee)

❏ fibrosarcoma
(FY-broh-sar-KOH-mah)

❏ fractionation
(FRAK-shun-AA-shun)

❏ gene (JEEN)

❏ genetic (jeh-NET-ik)

❏ glioblastoma multiforme
(GLY-oh-blas-TOH-mah mul-tih-FOR-may)

❏ Golgi apparatus
(GOHL-jee AP-ah-RAT-us)

❏ hepatoblastoma
(HEP-ah-toh-blas-TOH-mah)

❏ hepatocellular carcinoma
(HEP-ah-to-SEL-yoo-lar KAR-sih-NOH-mah)

❏ heredity (heh-RED-ih-tee)

- Hodgkin's lymphoma (HAWJ-kinz lim-FOH-mah)
- hormonal chemotherapy drug (hor-MOH-nal KEE-moh-THAIR-ah-pee DRUHG)
- human chorionic gonadotropin (HYOO-man KOH-ree-AWN-ik GOH-nad-oh-TROH-pin)
- implantable port (im-PLANT-ah-bl PORT)
- in situ (IN SY-too)
- incisional biopsy (in-SIH-shun-al BY-awp-see)
- internal radiotherapy (in-TER-nal RAY-dee-oh-THAIR-ah-pee)
- interstitial radiotherapy (IN-ter-STISH-al RAY-dee-oh-THAIR-ah-pee)
- intra-arterial catheter (IN-trah-ar-TEER-ee-al KATH-eh-ter)
- intracavitary radiotherapy (IN-trah-KAV-ih-TAIR-ee RAY-dee-oh-THAIR-ah-pee)
- intracellular (IN-trah-SEL-yoo-lar)
- intraperitoneal catheter (IN-trah-PAIR-ih-toh-NEE-al KATH-eh-ter)
- intrathecal catheter (IN-trah-THEE-kal KATH-eh-ter)
- intrathecal chemotherapy (IN-trah-THEE-kal KEE-moh-THAIR-ah-pee)
- intravenous radiotherapy (IN-trah-VEE-nus RAY-dee-oh-THAIR-ah-pee)
- intravesical chemotherapy (IN-trah-VES-ih-kal KEE-moh-THAIR-ah-pee)
- invasive (in-VAY-siv)
- Kaposi's sarcoma (KAH-poh-seez sar-KOH-mah)
- karyotype (KAIR-ee-oh-TYPE)
- leiomyosarcoma (LIE-oh-MY-oh-sar-KOH-mah)
- leukemia (loo-KEE-mee-ah)
- liposarcoma (LIP-oh-sar-KOH-mah)
- lobectomy (loh-BEK-toh-mee)
- lumpectomy (lum-PEK-toh-mee)
- lymph node dissection (LIMF NOHD dy-SEK-shun)

- lymphadenopathy (LIM-fad-eh-NAWP-ah-thee)
- lymphangiography (lim-FAN-jee-AWG-rah-fee)
- lymphocytic leukemia (LIM-foh-SIT-ik loo-KEE-mee-ah)
- lymphoma (lim-FOH-mah)
- lysosome (LY-soh-sohm)
- malignant (mah-LIG-nant)
- malignant melanoma (mah-LIG-nant MEL-ah-NOH-mah)
- mammography (mah-MAWG-rah-fee)
- medical oncologist (MED-ih-kal ong-KAWL-oh-jist)
- metastases (meh-TAS-tah-seez)
- metastasis (meh-TAS-tah-sis)
- metastasize (meh-TAS-tah-size)
- metastatic (MET-ah-STAT-ik)
- mitochondria (MY-toh-CON-dree-ah)
- mitochondrial (MY-toh-CON-dree-al)
- mitochondrion (MY-toh-CON-dree-on)
- mitosis (my-TOH-sis)
- mitosis inhibitor drug (my-TOH-sis in-HIB-ih-tor DRUHG)
- monoclonal antibody (MAWN-oh-KLOH-nal AN-tee-BAWD-ee)
- multiple myeloma (MUL-tih-pl MY-eh-LOH-mah)
- mutation (myoo-TAY-shun)
- myelogenous leukemia (MY-eh-LAW-jeh-nus loo-KEE-mee-ah)
- myosarcoma (MY-oh-sar-KOH-mah)
- neoplasia (NEE-oh-PLAY-zee-ah)
- neoplasm (NEE-oh-plazm)
- nephroblastoma (NEF-roh-blas-TOH-mah)
- neuroblastoma (NYOOR-oh-blas-TOH-mah)
- neurofibrosarcoma (NYOOR-oh-FY-broh-sar-KOH-mah)
- nuclear (NOO-klee-ar)
- nuclei (NOO-klee-eye)
- nucleoli (noo-KLEE-oh-lie)
- nucleolus (noo-KLEE-oh-lus)
- nucleus (NOO-klee-us)

- oligodendroglioma (OH-lih-goh-DEN-droh-glee-OH-mah)
- oncogene (ONG-koh-jeen)
- oncologist (ong-KAWL-oh-jist)
- oncology (ong-KAWL-oh-jee)
- organelle (OR-gah-NEL)
- osteosarcoma (AWS-tee-oh-sar-KOH-mah)
- percutaneous radiofrequency ablation (PER-kyoo-TAY-nee-us RAY-dee-oh-FREE-kwen-see ah-BLAY-shun)
- peripheral (peh-RIF-eh-ral)
- platinum chemotherapy drug (PLAT-ih-num KEE-moh-THAIR-ah-pee DRUHG)
- radiation (RAY-dee-AA-shun)
- radiation oncologist (RAY-dee-AA-shun ong-KAWL-oh-jist)
- radical resection (RAD-ih-kal re-SEK-shun)
- radioresistant (RAY-dee-oh-ree-ZIS-tant)
- radiosensitive (RAY-dee-oh-SEN-sih-tiv)
- radiotherapy (RAY-dee-oh-THAIR-ah-pee)
- receptor assay (ree-SEP-tor AS-say)
- relapse (REE-laps)
- remission (ree-MISH-un)
- resection (ree-SEK-shun)
- retinoblastoma (RET-ih-noh-blas-TOH-mah)
- rhabdomyosarcoma (RAB-doh-MY-oh-sar-KOH-mah)
- ribonucleic acid (RY-boh-noo-KLEE-ik AS-id)
- ribosome (RY-boh-sohm)
- sarcoma (sar-KOH-mah)
- scintigraphy (sin-TIG-rah-fee)
- seminoma (SEM-ih-NOH-mah)
- sentinel lymph node (SEN-tih-nal LIMF NOHD)
- sentinel node biopsy (SEN-tih-nal NOHD BY-awp-see)
- squamous cell carcinoma (SKWAY-mus SEL KAR-sih-NOH-mah)
- stereotactic biopsy (STAIR-ee-oh-TAK-tik BY-awp-see)

- ❑ suppressor gene
  (soo-PRES-or JEEN)
- ❑ teratoma (TAIR-ah-TOH-mah)
- ❑ tomography
  (toh-MAWG-rah-fee)
- ❑ transarterial chemoembolization (TRANS-ar-TEER-ee-al
  KEE-moh-EM-bol-ih-ZAY-shun)
- ❑ transitional cell carcinoma
  (trans-ZIH-shun-al
  SEL KAR-sih-NOH-mah)
- ❑ translocation
  (TRANS-loh-KAY-shun)
- ❑ tumor (TOO-mor)
- ❑ tumor necrosis factor (TOO-
  mor neh-KROH-sis FAK-tor)
- ❑ ultrasonography
  (UL-trah-soh-NAWG-rah-fee)
- ❑ undifferentiated
  (un-DIF-er-EN-shee-AA-ted)
- ❑ urinalysis (YOO-rih-NAL-ih-sis)
- ❑ Wilms' tumor (WILMZ
  TOO-mor)

Answer Key

Word Search

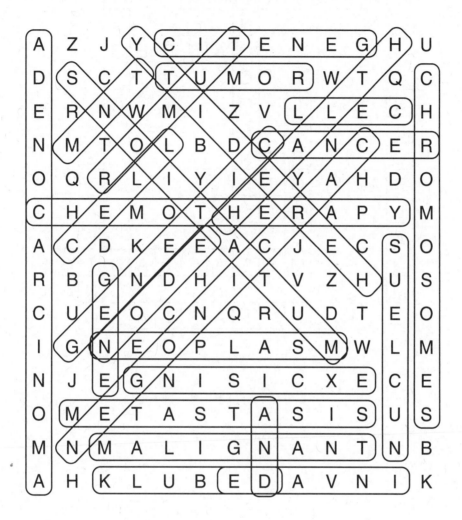

A Z J Y C I T E N E G H U
D S C T T U M O R W T Q C
E R N W M I Z V L L E C H
N M T O L B D C A N C E R
O Q R L I Y I E Y A H D O
C H E M O T H E R A P Y M
A C D K E E A C J E C S O
R B G N D H I T V Z H U S
C U E O C N Q R U D T E O
I G N E O P L A S M W L M
N J E G N I S I C X E C E
O M E T A S T A S I S U S
M N M A L I G N A N T N B
A H K L U B E D A V N I K

Crossword Puzzle

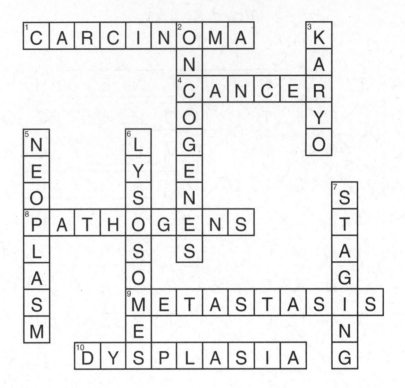

Underline the Accented Syllable

1. antimetabolite (AN-tee-meh-<u>TAB</u>-oh-lite)

2. aspiration (AS-pih-<u>RAY</u>-shun)

3. brachytherapy (BRAK-ee-<u>THAIR</u>-ah-pee)

4. carcinoid (<u>KAR</u>-sih-noyd)

5. carcinomatosis (KAR-sih-NOH-mah-<u>TOH</u>-sis)

6. choriocarcinoma (KOH-ree-oh-KAR-sih-<u>NOH</u>-mah)

7. intraperitoneal (IN-trah-PAIR-ih-toh-<u>NEE</u>-al)

8. leiomyosarcoma (LIE-oh-MY-oh-sar-<u>KOH</u>-mah)

9. lymphadenopathy (LIM-fad-eh-<u>NAWP</u>-ah-thee)

10. mammography (mah-<u>MAWG</u>-rah-fee)

11. melanoma (MEL-ah-<u>NOH</u>-mah)

12. oligodendroglioma (OH-lih-goh-DEN-droh-glee-<u>OH</u>-mah)

13. rhabdomyosarcoma (RAB-doh-MY-oh-sar-<u>KOH</u>-mah)

14. scintigraphy (sin-<u>TIG</u>-rah-fee)

15. squamous (<u>SKWAY</u>-mus)

Word Surgery

1. adjuvant

   Suffix and its meaning: -ant *pertaining to*

   Prefix and its meaning: none

   Combining form and its meaning: adjuv/o- *giving help or assistance*

   Medical word definition: Pertaining to giving help or assistance

2. bronchogenic

   Suffix and its meaning: -ic *pertaining to*

   Prefix and its meaning: none

   Combining form and its meaning: bronch/o- *bronchus*

   Combining form and its meaning: gen/o- *arising from; produced by*

   Medical word definition: Pertaining to the bronchus and (something) arising from it

3. carcinoid

   Suffix and its meaning: -oid *resembling*

   Prefix and its meaning: none

   Combining form and its meaning: carcin/o- *cancer*

   Medical word definition: Resembling cancer

4. chondrosarcoma

   Suffix and its meaning: -oma *tumor; mass*

   Prefix and its meaning: none

   Combining form and its meaning: chondr/o- *cartilage*

   Combining form and its meaning: sarc/o- *connective tissue*

   Medical word definition: Tumor of cartilage and connective tissue

5. dysplastic

   Suffix and its meaning: -tic *pertaining to*

   Prefix and its meaning: dys- *painful; difficult; abnormal*

   Combining form and its meaning: plas/o- *growth; formation*

   Medical word definition: Pertaining to abnormal growth

6. exenteration

   Suffix and its meaning: -ation *a process; being or having*

   Prefix and its meaning: ex- *out; away from*

   Combining form and its meaning: enter/o- *intestine*

   Medical word definition: A process (of taking) out (cancer), intestines, (and organs in abdominopelvic cavity)

7. fulguration

   Suffix and its meaning: -ation *a process; being or having*

   Prefix and its meaning: none

   Combining form and its meaning: fulgur/o- *spark of electricity*

   Medical word definition: A process using a spark of electricity

8. karyotype

   Suffix and its meaning: -type *particular kind of; a model of*

   Prefix and its meaning: none

   Combining form and its meaning: kary/o- *nucleus*

   Medical word definition: A model of the nucleus (and chromosomes)

9. leukemia

   Suffix and its meaning: -emia *condition of the blood; substance in the blood*

   Prefix and its meaning: none

   Combining form and its meaning: leuk/o-*white*

   Medical word definition: Substance in the blood of (too many) white (blood cells)

10. lymphangiography

    Suffix and its meaning: -graphy *process of recording*

    Prefix and its meaning: none

    Combining form and its meaning: lymph/o- *lymph; lymphatic system*

    Combining form and its meaning: angi/o- *blood vessel; lymphatic vessel*

    Medical word definition: Process of recording the lymphatic system and lymphatic vessels

11. myeloma

    Suffix and its meaning: -oma *tumor; mass*

    Prefix and its meaning: none

    Combining form and its meaning: myel/o- *bone marrow; spinal cord; myelin*

    Medical word definition: Tumor of the bone marrow

12. myosarcoma

    Suffix and its meaning: -oma *tumor; mass*

    Prefix and its meaning: none

    Combining form and its meaning: my/o- *muscle*

    Combining form and its meaning: sarc/o- *connective tissue*

    Medical word definition: Tumor of muscle and connective tissue

13. neoplasm

    Suffix and its meaning: -plasm *growth; formed substance*

    Prefix and its meaning: none

    Combining form and its meaning: ne/o- *new*

    Medical word definition: Growth that is new

14. retinoblastoma

    Suffix and its meaning: -oma *tumor; mass*

    Prefix and its meaning: none

    Combining form and its meaning: retin/o- *retina*

    Combining form and its meaning: blast/o- *immature; embryonic*

    Medical word definition: Tumor of the retina (that is) embryonic

15. scintigraphy

    Suffix and its meaning: : -graphy *process of recording*

    Prefix and its meaning: none

    Combining form and its meaning: scint/i- *point of light*

    Medical word definition: Process of recording points of light

Chapter Quiz

MULTIPLE CHOICE

1. B	4. C	7. C	10. B
2. A	5. A	8. A	
3. D	6. D	9. D	

FILL IN THE BLANK

1. metastasis
2. -gen
3. melanoma
4. liver
5. antigens
6. grading
7. Endoscopy
8. radioactive
9. tumors, nodes
10. antiemetic

TRUE/FALSE

1. True
2. True
3. False (undifferentiated)
4. True
5. True
6. True
7. False (karyotype)
8. True
9. False (abdominopelvic cavity)
10. False (protocol)

CHAPTER 19

Radiology and Nuclear Medicine

Measure Your Progress: Learning Objectives

After reading this chapter, the student should be able to

- Describe five radiology procedures that use x-rays.
- Describe common x-ray projections (views) and patient positions.
- Identify common radiology procedures that use x-rays and a contrast dye.
- Describe other radiology procedures that use a magnetic field, an electron beam, or sound waves.
- Describe nuclear medicine procedures that use gamma rays or positrons.
- Build radiology and nuclear medicine words from word parts and divide and define words.
- Spell and pronounce radiology and nuclear medicine words.
- Analyze the medical content and meaning of a radiology report.
- Dive deeper into radiology and nuclear medicine by reviewing the activities at the end of this chapter and online at Medical Terminology Interactive.

It All Starts with Word Building

Medical language is all about medical words and their word parts. Jump right into this chapter by learning some of the common combining forms and their definitions that you will encounter in this chapter.

axi/o-	axis	quantitat/o-	quantity or amount
cin/e-	movement	radi/o-	radius (forearm bone; x-rays; radiation)
cycl/o-	cycle; circle		
densit/o-	density		
dos/i-	dose	rotat/o-	rotate
ech/o-	echo (sound wave)	scint/i-	point of light
fluor/o-	fluorescence	scintill/o-	point of light
luc/o-	clear	son/o-	sound
magnet/o-	magnet	tom/o-	cut; slice; layer
pharmaceutic/o-	medicine; drug	trac/o-	visible path
project/o-	orientation		

Chapter Spelling Test

Dictate and spell (or photocopy a handout that contains) this list of 15 spelling words. Give this list to students to study for the week. At the beginning of next week's class, dictate 10 of these words as the spelling test. The spelling test is included with the chapter test that is given on the previous week's material.

1. arteriography

2. anteroposterior

3. coronary angiography

4. decubitus position

5. echocardiogram

6. fluoroscopy

7. hysterosalpingogram

8. intravenous pyelography

9. lymphangiography

10. mammography

11. positron emission tomography

12. radionuclide

13. technetium

14. thallium

15. ultrasonography

Chapter Pronunciation Test

Photocopy a handout that contains this list of 15 pronunciation words. Give this list to students to study for the week. Sometime at the beginning of the next week, each student should call your office or home answering machine and pronounce each word.

1. angiography (AN-jee-AWG-rah-fee)

2. arteriography (ar-TEER-ee-AWG-rah-fee)

3. anteroposterior (AN-ter-oh-pohs-TEER-ee-or)

4. decubitus position (dee-KYOO-bih-tus poh-SIH-shun)

5. echocardiogram (EK-oh-KAR-dee-oh-GRAM)

6. fluoroscopy (floor-AWS-koh-pee)

7. hysterosalpingogram (HIS-ter-oh-sal-PING-goh-gram)

8. intravenous pyelography (IN-trah-VEE-nus PY-eh-LAWG-rah-fee)

9. lymphangiography (lim-FAN-jee-AWG-rah-fee)

10. mammography (mah-MAWG-rah-fee)

11. positron emission tomography (PAWZ-ih-trawn ee-MIH-shun toh-MAWG-rah-fee)

12. radiopharmaceutical (RAY-dee-oh-FAR-mah-SOO-tik-al)

13. technetium (tek-NEE-shee-um)

14. thallium (THAL-ee-um)

15. ultrasonography (UL-trah-soh-NAWG-rah-fee)

Word Search

Complete this word search puzzle that contains Chapter 19 words. Look for the following words as given in the list below. The number in parentheses indicates how many times the word appears in the puzzle.

apron
artifact
barium
DEXA
Doppler
dose
echo
fluoroscopy
KUB
MUGA
nuclear

PET scan
projection
rad (2)
radiation
scan
spiral
tomography
tracer
ultrasound
x-ray

```
Y  H  P  A  R  G  O  M  O  T  Y
P  P  D  N  B  D  E  X  A  W  A
R  E  O  U  A  A  G  P  J  R  R
O  T  P  C  X  C  R  E  T  E  X
J  S  P  L  S  O  S  I  C  F  E
E  C  L  E  N  O  F  A  U  C  Q
C  A  E  A  D  A  R  G  H  M  A
T  N  R  R  C  T  Q  O  K  G  Z
I  U  L  T  R  A  S  O  U  N  D
O  S  P  I  R  A  L  M  B  L  X
N  O  I  T  A  I  D  A  R  J  F
```

Crossword Puzzle

ACROSS

5. The abbreviation _____ stands for the three structures that are being x-rayed: the kidneys, ureters, and bladder.

6. A procedure where contrast dye is injected into a joint is called _____.

7. Radioactive substances that produce _____ rays or positrons are used for nuclear medicine imaging.

8. The combining form "_____" means orientation.

10. _____ aprons are used to shield parts of the body that are not being x-rayed.

DOWN

1. When a CT scan is used to guide the insertion of a needle (for a biopsy), this is known as _____ radiology.

2. _____ is a procedure used to outline the urinary tract to show narrowing, blockage, and the presence of kidney stones in the renal pelvis and elsewhere.

3. An ultrasound image is referred to as a/an _____.

4. _____ uses continuous x-rays to capture the motion of the internal organs as it occurs.

9. The combining form "_____" means movement.

Underline the Accented Syllable

Read the medical word. Then review the syllables in the pronunciation. Underline the primary (main) accented syllable in the pronunciation.

1. cholangiography   (koh-lan-jee-awg-rah-fee)

2. decubitus   (dee-kyoo-bih-tus)

3. echocardiography   (ek-oh-kar-dee-awg-rah-fee)

4. enema   (en-eh-mah)

5. excretory   (eks-kreh-toh-ree)

6. hysterosalpingography   (his-ter-oh-sal-ping-gawg-rah-fee)

7. indium   (in-dee-um)

8. lymphangiography   (lim-fan-jee-awg-rah-fee)

9. myelography   (my-eh-lawg-rah-fee)

10. oblique   (oh-bleek)

11. quantitative   (kwan-tih-tay-tiv)

12. retrograde   (ret-roh-grayd)

13. thallium   (thal-ee-um)

14. transesophageal   (trans-ee-sawf-ah-jee-al)

15. venography   (vee-nawg-rah-fee)

Word Surgery

Read the medical word. Break the medical word into its word parts and give the meaning of each word part. Then give the definition of the medical word.

1. anteroposterior

    Suffix and its meaning: _____

    Prefix and its meaning: _____

    Combining form and its meaning: _____

    Combining form and its meaning: _____

    Medical word definition: _____

2. arthrography

    Suffix and its meaning: _____

    Prefix and its meaning: _____

    Combining form and its meaning: _____

    Medical word definition: _____

3. cineradiography

    Suffix and its meaning: _____

    Prefix and its meaning: _____

    Combining form and its meaning: _____

    Combining form and its meaning: _____

    Medical word definition: _____

4. cholangiography

    Suffix and its meaning: _____

    Prefix and its meaning: _____

    Combining form and its meaning: _____

    Combining form and its meaning: _____

    Medical word definition: _____

5. cholescintigraphy

    Suffix and its meaning: _____

    Prefix and its meaning: _____

    Combining form and its meaning: _____

    Combining form and its meaning: _____

    Medical word definition: _____

6. dosimetry

Suffix and its meaning: _____

Prefix and its meaning: _____

Combining form and its meaning: _____

Medical word definition: _____

7. echocardiography

Suffix and its meaning: _____

Prefix and its meaning: _____

Combining form and its meaning: _____

Combining form and its meaning: _____

Medical word definition: _____

8. fluoroscopy

Suffix and its meaning: _____

Prefix and its meaning: _____

Combining form and its meaning: _____

Medical word definition: _____

9. lateral

Suffix and its meaning: _____

Prefix and its meaning: _____

Combining form and its meaning: _____

Medical word definition: _____

10. myelogram

Suffix and its meaning: _____

Prefix and its meaning: _____

Combining form and its meaning: _____

Medical word definition: _____

11. posteroanterior

Suffix and its meaning: _____

Prefix and its meaning: _____

Combining form and its meaning: _____

Combining form and its meaning: _____

Medical word definition: _____

12. radiology

Suffix and its meaning: _____

Prefix and its meaning: _____

Combining form and its meaning: _____

Medical word definition: _____

13. radiolucent

Suffix and its meaning: _____

Prefix and its meaning: _____

Combining form and its meaning: _____

Combining form and its meaning: _____

Medical word definition: _____

14. transesophageal

Suffix and its meaning: _____

Prefix and its meaning: _____

Combining form and its meaning: _____

Medical word definition: _____

15. xeromammogram

Suffix and its meaning: _____

Prefix and its meaning: _____

Combining form and its meaning: _____

Combining form and its meaning: _____

Medical word definition: _____

Chapter Quiz

MULTIPLE CHOICE

1. Areas of the body that have a low density and allow x-rays to pass through are:

   A. radiolucent.

   B. microscopic.

   C. nuclear.

   D. radioactive.

2. With the patient in a standing position and the chest next to the x-ray plate, a/an _____ chest x-ray image is made.

   A. PA

   B. AP

   C. lateral

   D. oblique

3. Which of the following is used to describe the procedure in which a patient is given an injection of a contrast dye into a joint and then an x-ray is performed?

   A. barium enema

   B. arthrography

   C. aortography

   D. venography

4. Intravenous cholangiography:

   A. helps visualize the colon.

   B. produces an image of the gallbladder.

   C. uses radioactive isotopes.

   D. is usually done at autopsy.

5. Mammography:

   A. uses ultrasonography to create an image of the breast.

   B. is the surgical removal of a breast or part of a breast.

   C. is a treatment for benign breast tumors.

   D. uses x-rays to create an image of the breast.

6. Radiopharmaceuticals are drugs that:

   A. emit x-rays.

   B. are radioactive.

   C. emit gamma rays.

   D. were discovered by Einstein.

7. Thallium-201 is:

   A. used during fluoroscopy of the GI tract.

   B. radioactive.

   C. used to image the heart.

   D. All of the above.

8. Positrons are positively charged particles used in:

   A. PET scans.

   B. scintigraphy.

   C. MRI.

   D. CT scans.

9. Lying on the back as in a position for a radiograph is called:

   A. prone.

   B. densitometry.

   C. radiologic.

   D. decubitus.

10. A unit of measurement for radiation exposure is:

    A. rem.

    B. nucleotide.

    C. krypton-81.

    D. electron beams.

FILL IN THE BLANK

1. _____ aprons are extremely dense and are therefore used to shield a patient from x-rays.

2. An x-ray beam that enters the body at an angle midway between anterior and lateral is a/an _____ x-ray.

3. The x-ray procedure in which contrast dye is inserted into the vagina through a catheter that then outlines the uterus and the lumens of the uterine tubes is called _____.

4. Magnetic resonance imaging is especially useful in making images of _____ tissues.

5. _____ beam tomography is also known as a full body scan.

6. When blood flows to an organ, it is known as _____.

7. The abbreviation CAT stands for _____ _____ _____.

8. A motion _____ is a blurred image on an x-ray that occurs when a patient moves during the procedure.

9. A procedure that uses x-rays and a contrast dye to visualize the kidneys, ureters, bladder, and urethra is _____.

10. _____ are radiopharmaceutical drugs that can be followed by the gamma rays they produce.

TRUE/FALSE

_____ 1. X-rays are a form of ionizing radiation.

_____ 2. KUB describes an x-ray where the patient is lying in a supine position and the image shows the kidneys, ureters, and bladder.

_____ 3. When a contrast dye is injected to show a blockage or narrowing in a blood vessel or show an aneurysm, it is known as a barium enema.

_____ 4. "Myel/o-," as in myelography, refers to the lymphatic system.

_____ 5. Patients who undergo magnetic resonance imaging must sign a consent form that describes metal items they may be wearing or which are implanted.

_____ 6. When gamma rays enter the scintillation camera they strike a crystal structure that emits x-rays.

_____ 7. An OncoScint scan is used to detect areas of increased activity that are metastases from a cancerous tumor primary site.

_____ 8. Areas of increased uptake on a scintigram are known as "cold spots."

_____ 9. The use of CT, MRI, or ultrasonography to guide the insertion of a needle for biopsy or other procedure is interventional radiology.

_____ 10. A PET scan uses dye and x-rays to examine a vein.

Pronunciation Checklist

Read each word and its pronunciation. Practice pronouncing each word. Verify your pronunciation by listening to the Pronunciation List on Medical Terminology Interactive. Check the box next to the word after you master its pronunciation.

❑ angiogram (AN-jee-oh-GRAM)
❑ angiography
(AN-jee-AWG-rah-fee)
❑ anteroposterior position
(AN-ter-oh-pohs-TEER-ee-or
poh-SIH-shun)
❑ aortogram (aa-OR-toh-gram)
❑ aortography
(AA-or-TAWG-rah-fee)
❑ arteriogram
(ar-TEER-ee-oh-GRAM)
❑ arteriography
(ar-TEER-ee-AWG-rah-fee)
❑ arthrogram (AR-throh-gram)
❑ arthrography
(ar-THRAWG-rah-fee)
❑ artifact (AR-tih-fakt)
❑ barium enema (BAIR-ee-um
EN-eh-mah)
❑ barium swallow (BAIR-ee-um
SWAH-loh)
❑ cholangiogram
(koh-LAN-jee-oh-GRAM)
❑ cholangiography
(KOH-lan-jee-AWG-rah-fee)
❑ cholecystogram
(KOH-lee-SIS-toh-gram)
❑ cholecystography
(KOH-lee-sis-TAWG-rah-fee)
❑ cholescintigraphy
(KOH-lee-sin-TIG-rah-fee)
❑ cineradiography
(SIN-eh-RAY-dee-AWG-rah-fee)
❑ computerized axial tomography
(com-PYOO-ter-ized AK-see-al
toh-MAWG-rah-fee)
❑ decubitus position
(dee-KYOO-bih-tus
poh-SIH-shun)
❑ densitometry
(DEN-sih-TAWM-eh-tree)
❑ Doppler ultrasonography
(DAWP-ler
UL-trah-soh-NAWG-rah-fee)
❑ dosimeter (doh-SIM-eh-ter)
❑ dosimetry (doh-SIM-eh-tree)
❑ duplex ultrasonography
(DOO-pleks
UL-trah-soh-NAWG-rah-fee)

❑ echocardiogram
(EK-oh-KAR-dee-oh-GRAM)
❑ echocardiography
(EK-oh-KAR-dee-AWG-rah-fee)
❑ excretory urography
(EKS-kree-TOH-ree
yoo-RAWG-rah-fee)
❑ fluoroscopy
(floor-AWS-koh-pee)
❑ gadolinium (GAD-oh-LIN-ee-um)
❑ gallium (GAL-ee-um)
❑ hysterosalpingogram
(HIS-ter-oh-sal-PING-goh-gram)
❑ hysterosalpingography
(HIS-ter-oh-SAL-ping-GAWG-
rah-fee)
❑ interventional radiology
(IN-ter-VEN-shun-al
RAY-dee-AWL-oh-jee)
❑ intravenous cholangiography
(IN-trah-VEE-nus
KOH-lan-jee-AWG-rah-fee)
❑ intravenous pyelography
(IN-trah-VEE-nus
PY-eh-LAWG-rah-fee)
❑ iodine (EYE-oh-dine)
❑ krypton (KRIP-tawn)
❑ lateral position
(LAT-er-al poh-SIH-shun)
❑ lymphangiogram
(lim-FAN-jee-oh-GRAM)
❑ lymphangiography
(lim-FAN-jee-AWG-rah-fee)
❑ magnetic resonance imaging
(mag-NET-ik REH-soh-nans
IM-ah-jing)
❑ mammogram (MAM-oh-gram)
❑ mammography
(mah-MAWG-rah-fee)
❑ MUGA scan (MUH-gah SKAN)
❑ multidetector
(MUL-tee-dee-TEK-tor)
❑ myelogram (MY-eh-loh-GRAM)
❑ myelography
(MY-eh-LAWG-rah-fee)
❑ nuclear medicine
(NOO-klee-er MED-ih-sin)
❑ oblique position
(oh-BLEEK poh-SIH-shun)

❑ OncoScint scan
(AWN-koh-sint SKAN)
❑ perfusion scan
(per-FYOO-shun SKAN)
❑ positron emission tomography
(PAWZ-ih-trawn ee-MIH-shun
toh-MAWG-rah-fee)
❑ postcontrast image
(pohst-KAWN-trast IM-ij)
❑ posteroanterior position
(POHS-ter-oh-an-TEER-ee-or
poh-SIH-shun)
❑ precontrast image
(pree-KAWN-trast IM-ij)
❑ projection (proh-JEK-shun)
❑ ProstaScint scan
(PRAW-stah-sint SKAN)
❑ pyelogram (PY-eh-loh-GRAM)
❑ pyelography
(PY-eh-LAWG-rah-fee)
❑ radioactive (RAY-dee-oh-AK-tiv)
❑ radiograph
(RAY-dee-oh-GRAF)
❑ radiologic technologist
(RAY-dee-oh-LAWJ-ik
tek-NAWL-oh-jist)
❑ radiology
(RAY-dee-AWL-oh-jee)
❑ radiolucent
(RAY-dee-oh-LOO-sent)
❑ radiopaque (RAY-dee-oh-PAYK)
❑ radiopharmaceutical (RAY-dee-
oh-FAR-mah-SOO-tik-al)
❑ retrograde pyelography
(RET-roh-grayd
PY-eh-LAWG-rah-fee)
❑ roentgenography
(RENT-geh-NAWG-rah-fee)
❑ rotational angiography
(roh-TAY-shun-al
AN-jee-AWG-rah-fee)
❑ scintigram (SIN-tih-gram)
❑ scintigraphy (sin-TIG-rah-fee)
❑ scintillation (SIN-tih-LAY-shun)
❑ scintiscan (SIN-tih-skan)
❑ sonogram (SAWN-oh-gram)
❑ sonography
(soh-NAWG-rah-fee)
❑ SPECT scan (SPEKT SKAN)

- ❏ technetium (tek-NEE-shee-um)
- ❏ thallium (THAL-ee-um)
- ❏ tomography (toh-MAWG-rah-fee)
- ❏ tracer (TRAY-ser)
- ❏ transducer (trans-DOO-ser)
- ❏ transesophageal echocardiogram (TRANS-ee-SAWF-ah-JEE-al EK-oh-KAR-dee-oh-GRAM)
- ❏ ultrasonography (UL-trah-soh-NAWG-rah-fee)
- ❏ ultrasound (UL-trah-sound)
- ❏ upper gastrointestinal series (UH-per GAS-troh-in-TES-tin-al SEER-ez)
- ❏ urogram (YOO-roh-gram)
- ❏ urography (yoo-RAWG-rah-fee)
- ❏ venogram (VEE-noh-gram)
- ❏ venography (vee-NAWG-rah-fee)
- ❏ ventilation-perfusion scan (VEN-tih-LAY-shun per-FYOO-shun SKAN)
- ❏ xenon (ZEE-nawn)
- ❏ xeromammogram (ZEER-oh-MAM-oh-gram)
- ❏ xeromammography (ZEER-oh-mah-MAWG-rah-fee)

Answer Key
Word Search

Crossword Puzzle

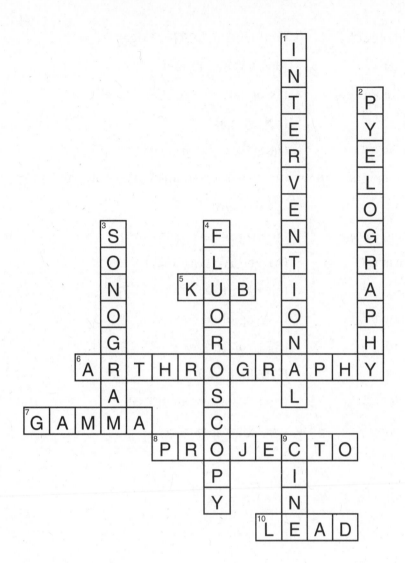

Underline the Accented Syllable

1. cholangiography   (KOH-lan-jee-<u>AWG</u>-rah-fee)

2. decubitus   (dee-<u>KYOO</u>-bih-tus)

3. echocardiography   (EK-oh-KAR-dee-<u>AWG</u>-rah-fee)

4. enema   (<u>EN</u>-eh-mah)

5. excretory   (<u>EKS</u>-kree-TOH-ree)

6. hysterosalpingography   (HIS-ter-oh-SAL-ping-<u>GAWG</u>-rah-fee)

7. indium   (<u>IN</u>-dee-um)

8. lymphangiography   (lim-FAN-jee-<u>AWG</u>-rah-fee)

9. myelography   (MY-eh-<u>LAWG</u>-rah-fee)

10. oblique   (oh-<u>BLEEK</u>)

11. quantitative   (<u>KWAN</u>-tih-TAY-tiv)

12. retrograde   (<u>RET</u>-roh-grayd)

13. thallium   (<u>THAL</u>-ee-um)

14. transesophageal   (TRANS-ee-SAWF-ah-<u>JEE</u>-al)

15. venography   (vee-<u>NAWG</u>-rah-fee)

Word Surgery

1. anteroposterior

   Suffix and its meaning: -ior *pertaining to*

   Prefix and its meaning: none

   Combining form and its meaning: anter/o- *before; front part*

   Combining form and its meaning: poster/o- *back part*

   Medical word definition: Pertaining to (going through the) front part (then the)
   back part

2. arthrography

   Suffix and its meaning: -graphy *process of recording*

   Prefix and its meaning: none

   Combining form and its meaning: arthr/o- *joint*

   Medical word definition: Process of recording a joint

3. cineradiography

   Suffix and its meaning: -graphy *process of recording*

   Prefix and its meaning: none

   Combining form and its meaning: cin/e- *movement*

   Combining form and its meaning: radi/o- *radius (forearm bone; x-rays; radiation)*

   Medical word definition: Process of recording movement with x-rays

4. cholangiography

   Suffix and its meaning: -graphy *process of recording*

   Prefix and its meaning: none

   Combining form and its meaning: cholangi/o- *bile duct*

   Medical word definition: Process of recording the bile ducts

5. cholescintigraphy

   Suffix and its meaning: -graphy *process of recording*

   Prefix and its meaning: none

   Combining form and its meaning: chol/e- *bile; gall*

   Combining form and its meaning: scint/i- *point of light*

   Medical word definition: Process of recording the bile (duct) or gall (bladder) with
   points of light (from a radiopharmaceutical drug).

6. dosimetry

   Suffix and its meaning: -metry *process of measuring*

   Prefix and its meaning: none

   Combining form and its meaning: dos/i- *dose*

   Medical word definition: Process of measuring a dose

7. echocardiography

   Suffix and its meaning: -graphy *process of recording*

   Prefix and its meaning: none

   Combining form and its meaning: ech/o- *echo (sound wave)*

   Combininig form and its meaning: cardi/o- *heart*

   Medical word definition: Process of recording using echo sound waves of the heart

8. fluoroscopy

   Suffix and its meaning: -scopy *process of using an instrument to examine*

   Prefix and its meaning: none

   Combining form and its meaning: fluor/o- *fluorescence*

   Medical word definition: Process of using an instrument to examine by
       fluorescence

9. lateral

   Suffix and its meaning: -al *pertaining to*

   Prefix and its meaning: none

   Combining form and its meaning: later/o- *side*

   Medical word definition: Pertaining to the side

10. myelogram

    Suffix and its meaning: -graphy *process of recording*

    Prefix and its meaning: none

    Combining form and its meaning: myel/o- *bone marrow; spinal cord; myelin*

    Medical word definition: Process of recording the spinal cord

11. posteroanterior

 Suffix and its meaning: -ior *pertaining to*

 Prefix and its meaning: none

 Combining form and its meaning: poster/o- *back part*

 Combining form and its meaning: anter/o- *before; front part*

 Medical word definition: Pertaining to the (going through the) back part (and then) the front part

12. radiology

 Suffix and its meaning: -logy *the study of*

 Prefix and its meaning: none

 Combining form and its meaning: radi/o- *radius (forearm bone); x-rays; radiation*

 Medical word definition: The study of x-rays and radiation

13. radiolucent

 Suffix and its meaning: -ent *pertaining to*

 Prefix and its meaning: none

 Combining form and its meaning: radi/o- *radius (forearm bone); x-rays; radiation*

 Combining form and its meaning: luc/o- *clear*

 Medical word definition: Pertaining to x-rays (passing through low density tissue and creating a) clear (area on the image)

14. transesophageal

 Suffix and its meaning: -eal *pertaining to*

 Prefix and its meaning: trans- *across; through*

 Combining form and its meaning: esophag/o- *esophagus*

 Medical word definition: Pertaining to through the esophagus

15. xeromammogram

 Suffix and its meaning: -gram *a record or picture*

 Prefix and its meaning: none

 Combining form and its meaning: xer/o- *dry*

 Combining form and its meaning: mamm/o- *breast*

 Medical word definition: A record or picture on dry (paper) of the breast

Chapter Quiz

MULTIPLE CHOICE

1. A   4. B   7. C   10. A

2. A   5. D   8. A

3. B   6. C   9. D

FILL IN THE BLANK

1. Lead

2. oblique

3. hysterosalpingography

4. soft

5. Electron

6. perfusion

7. computerized axial tomography

8. artifact

9. pyelography

10. Tracers

TRUE/FALSE

1. True

2. True

3. False (angiography)

4. False (spinal cord)

5. True

6. False (a flash of visible light or photon)

7. True

8. False ("hot spots")

9. True

10. False (venography)

FINAL EXAMINATION

THE "FINAL" FINAL EXAM

"To Boldly Go Where No One Has Gone Before"

You have been provided with surgical drapes and a scalpel. Remove your own appendix. Your work will be inspected for completeness and the neatness of the stitches in your incision.

Just kidding!!!
Congratulations! You have finished this course in medical language!

Chapter 1 Questions

1. To analyze the meaning of a medical word, begin at the _____.
   a. suffix of the word   b. prefix of the word
   c. combining form of the word   d. Any of the above
   Answer: A
   Explanation: A. Correct! B. Analysis does not begin with the prefix. C. Analysis does not begin with the combining form. D. Analysis must begin with the suffix, not any other word part.

2. Which of the following suffixes means process of cutting or making an incision?
   a. -stomy   b. -ectomy
   c. -plasty   d. -tomy
   Answer: D
   Explanation: A. The suffix -stomy means surgically created opening. B. The suffix -ectomy means surgical excision. C. The suffix -plasty means process of reshaping by surgery. D. Correct!

3. Which of the following words has a suffix that means "a record or picture"?
   a. dermatologist   b. digestion
   c. mammogram   d. psychosis
   Answer: C
   Explanation: A. The suffix -ist means one who specializes in. B. The suffix -ion means action; condition. C. Correct! D. The suffix -osis means condition; abnormal condition; process.

4. Which one of these suffixes does *not* mean "pertaining to"?
   a. -ion   b. -eal
   c. -ary   d. -ic
   Answer: A
   Explanation: A. Correct! B. This means pertaining to. C. This means pertaining to. D. This means pertaining to.

5. Which of the following medical words pertains to the liver?
   a. cholecystectomy   b. laparotomy
   c. hepatomegaly   d. hysterectomy
   Answer: C
   Explanation: A. Cholecyst/o- means gallbladder. B. Lapar/o- means abdomen. C. Correct! D. Hyster/o- means uterus.

6. Which of the following statements is *false*?
   a. A suffix is a word part at the end of a word.
   b. The suffix -scope means process of measuring.
   c. The plural of bronchus is bronchi.
   d. The combining form is the foundation of the word.
   Answer: B
   Explanation: A. This is true. B. Correct! C. This is true. D. This is true.

7. Which of the following statements is *false*?
   a. The plural form of carcinoma is carcinomata.
   b. The plural form of testis is testes.
   c. The plural form of nucleus is nuclei.
   d. The plural form of phalanges is phalanx.
   Answer: D
   Explanation: A. This is true. B. This is true. C. This is true. D. Correct!

8. Which of these adjective forms is misspelled?
   a. uterine   b. cardial
   c. digestive   d. pelvic
   Answer: B
   Explanation: A. This is spelled correctly. B. Correct! The adjective form is cardiac.
   C. This is spelled correctly. D. This is spelled correctly.

9. Which of these medical words has a prefix that means "within"?
   a. subcutaneous   b. transvaginal
   c. endotracheal   d. epidermal
   Answer: C
   Explanation: A. Sub- means below; underneath. B. Trans- means across; through.
   C. Correct! D. Epi- means upon; above.

10. Which of these words contains a prefix, combining form, and suffix?
    a. gastroenterology   b. intravenous
    c. psychotherapy   d. appendectomy
    Answer: B
    Explanation: A. This contains two combining forms and a suffix. B. Correct!
    C. This contains a combining form and a suffix. D. This contains a combining form
    and a suffix.

11. Which of these statements is *false*?
    a. A prefix modifies the medical meaning of the suffix.
    b. The medical word thorax is the same as the Greek word thorax.
    c. The plural of vertebra is vertebrae.
    d. The plural of atrium is atria.
    Answer: A
    Explanation: A. Correct! B. This is true. C. This is true. D. This is true.

12. Which of the following statements is *false*?
    a. The medical record varies in format and content from one facility to the next.
    b. Hospitals use more extensive documentation than physicians' offices.
    c. The electronic medical record is another name for the electronic patient record.
    d. The patient's medical record and his/her legal record are kept separately.
    Answer: D
    Explanation: A. This is true. B. This is true. C. This is true. D. Correct!

13. All of the following are prefixes that give information about amount or location.
    Which one is not?
    a. epi-   b. hypo-
    c. sub-   d. dys-
    Answer: D
    Explanation: A. The prefix epi- means upon; above (location). B. The prefix hypo-
    means below; deficient (amount). C. The prefix sub- means below; underneath
    (location). D. Correct!

14. All of the following abbreviations relate to a patient's record that is no longer in a paper format, *except* _____.
    a. EMR
    b. UTI
    c. CPR
    d. EPR
    Answer: B
    Explanation: A. This stands for electronic medical record. B. Correct! C. This stands for computerized patient record. D. This stands for electronic patient record.

15. The organization that has a list of abbreviations that should not be used in healthcare facilities is _____.
    a. JCAHO
    b. OSHA
    c. HIPAA
    d. CDCP
    Answer: A
    Explanation: A. Correct! B. OSHA is concerned with preventing workplace injuries. C. HIPAA is a law, not an organization. D. CDCP stands for Centers for Disease Control and Prevention.

Chapter 2 Questions

1. The cause or origin of a disease is known as its _____.
    a. prognosis
    b. etiology
    c. remission
    d. symptomatology
    Explanation: A. The prognosis is the predicted outcome of a disease. B. Correct! C. A remission is a temporary improvement in the symptoms and signs of a disease without the underlying disease being cured. D. Symptomatology is the clinical picture of all of the patient's symptoms and signs.

2. The healthcare specialty that studies the anatomy and physiology of the integumentary system is _____.
    a. immunology
    b. hematology
    c. oncology
    d. dermatology
    Answer: D
    Explanation: A. Immunology studies the immune response. B. Hematology studies the blood. C. Oncology studies cancerous tumors. D. Correct!

3. The healthy human body can be studied in all of these ways, *except* _____.
    a. planes and directions
    b. diseases and lab tests
    c. systems and medical specialties
    d. quadrants and regions
    Answer: B
    Explanation: A. This is true. B. Correct! C. This is true. D. This is true.

4. Which of the following medical specialties is correctly matched to its corresponding body system?
    a. oncology, tumors
    b. otolaryngology, respiratory
    c. hematology, blood
    d. microscopic, laboratory
    Answer: C
    Explanation: A. Oncology does not have corresponding body system.
    B. Otolaryngology has a corresponding body system of ENT, not respiratory.
    C. Correct! D. This not a medical specialty and a body system.

5. All of the following are types of diseases, *except* _____.
   a. symptomatology
   b. nosocomial
   c. degenerative
   d. neoplastic
   Answer: A
   Explanation: A. Correct! B. This is a type of disease. C. This is a type of disease.
   D. This is a type of disease.

6. All of the following are healthcare professionals, *except* _____.
   a. PCP
   b. LPN
   c. CCU
   d. CNM
   Answer: C
   Explanation: A. A primary care physician is a healthcare professional. B. A licensed practical nurse is a healthcare professional. C. Correct! D. A certified nurse midwife is a healthcare professional.

7. The thoracic cavity contains the _____.
   a. lungs and mediastinum
   b. stomach and intestines
   c. kidneys and bladder
   d. None of the above
   Answer: A
   Explanation: A. Correct! B. The stomach and intestines are in the abdominopelvic cavity. C. The kidneys are in the retroperitoneal space and the bladder is in the pelvic cavity. D. One of the answers is correct.

8. Which of the following abbreviations is related to a grid that divides the abdomen into four parts?
   a. URI
   b. KUB
   c. CXR
   d. RUQ
   Answer: D
   Explanation: A. This stands for upper respiratory infection. B. This stands for kidneys, ureters, and bladder. C. This stands for chest x-ray. D. Correct! This stands for right upper quadrant.

9. Listening to the sounds of the lungs and heart with a stethoscope is called _____.
   a. endoscopy
   b. speculum
   c. palpation
   d. auscultation
   Answer: D
   Explanation: A. This uses a scope to look inside a body cavity. B. This is an instrument, not a procedure. C. This is a procedure to feel masses or enlarged organs. D. Correct!

10. Which of the following is not a region of the abdominopelvic area?
    a. muscular
    b. hypochondriac
    c. lumbar
    d. umbilical
    Answer: A
    Explanation: A. Correct! B. This is a region of the abdominopelvic area. C. This is a region of the abdominopelvic area. D. This is a region of the abdominopelvic area.

11. The medical specialty that studies and treats persons in their old age is _____.
    a. pharmacology
    b. geriatrics
    c. pediatrics
    d. oncology

Answer: B

Explanation: A. This is the study of medicines and drugs. B. Correct! C. This is the study and treatment of children. D. This is the study of cancerous tumors.

12. A sudden worsening of the severity of symptoms is _____.

a. ambulatory
b. adjuvant
c. exacerbation
d. prosthesis

Answer: C

Explanation: A. This refers to a facility, not disease symptoms. B. This refers to a treatment, not disease symptoms. C. Correct! D. This is an orthopedic device, not disease symptoms.

13. A hospice provides _____ care.

a. inpatient
b. terminal
c. surgical
d. ancillary

Answer: B

Explanation: A. Inpatient care occurs in a hospital. B. Correct! C. Surgical care occurs in a hospital or ambulatory surgery center. D. Ancillary refers to departments within a hospital, not to care.

Chapter 3 Questions

1. Cholecystis is an inflammation or infection of the _____.

a. liver
b. bladder
c. skin
d. gallbladder

Answer: D

Explanation: A. Cholecyst/o- means gallbladder. B. Cholecyst/o- means gallbladder. C. Cholecyst/o- means gallbladder. D. Correct!

2. Bloody vomit is known as _____.

a. hemarthrosis
b. hematuria
c. hematemesis
d. hematoma

Answer: C

Explanation: A. This is a condition of blood in the joint. B. This is a condition of blood in the urine. C. Correct! D. This is a mass of blood under the skin.

3. Which structure hangs in the posterior oral cavity?

a. lunula
b. urea
c. vulva
d. uvula

Answer: D

Explanation: A. The lunula is the white half-moon of the fingernail. B. Urea is a waste product of metabolism. C. The vulva is part of the external female genitalia. D. Correct!

4. The word cardia refers to the _____.

a. heart
b. brain
c. uterus
d. stomach

Answer: D

Explanation: A. The combining form cardi/o- means heart, but cardia does not refer to the heart. B. Cardia does not refer to the brain. C. Cardia does not refer to the uterus. D. Correct!

5. All of these combining forms mean abdomen, *except* _____.
   a. enter/o-
   b. celi/o-
   c. abdomin/o-
   d. lapar/o-
   Answer: A
   Explanation: A. Correct! Enter/o- means intestine. B. Celi/o- means abdomen.
   C. Abdomin/o- means abdomen. D. Lapar/o- means abdomen.

6. Which of these abbreviations is the most closely related to the gastrointestinal system?
   a. C&S
   b. I&O
   c. N&V
   d. D&C
   Answer: C
   Explanation: A. This means culture and sensitivity. B. This means intake and output.
   C. Correct! N&V means nausea and vomiting. D. This means dilation and curettage.

7. Which of the following abbreviations does *not* pertain to the gastrointestinal system?
   a. BE
   b. BP
   c. BM
   d. BS
   Answer: B
   Explanation: A. This means barium enema. B. Correct! BP means blood pressure.
   C. This means bowel movement. D. This means bowel sounds.

8. The suffix that means "procedure of suturing" is _____.
   a. -malacia
   b. -rrhea
   c. -rrhaphy
   d. -itis
   Answer: C
   Explanation: A. This means condition of softening. B. This means flow; discharge.
   C. Correct! D. This means inflammation of; infection of.

9. Direct visual examination of the large intestine would be performed using a _____.
   a. colposcope
   b. otoscope
   c. colonoscope
   d. gastroscope
   Answer: C
   Explanation: A. This is used to examine the vagina. B. This is used to examine the ear. C. Correct! D. This is used to examine the stomach.

10. A surgically created permanent opening to bring the intestine to the outside of the body is called a _____.
    a. colostomy
    b. hysterectomy
    c. dialysis
    d. gastroenteritis
    Answer: A
    Explanation: A. Correct! B. Hysterectomy involves the uterus, not the intestine.
    C. Dialysis is a procedure that removes wastes from the blood. D. Gastroenteritis is a disease, not a surgical procedure.

11. A patient with poorly fitting dentures and pain while chewing would have _____.
    a. dysplasia
    b. dysphagia
    c. dysphasia
    d. dyspnea

Answer: B

Explanation: A. This is a condition of abnormal cell formation. B. Correct! C. This is a condition of difficulty speaking due to a stroke. D. This is a condition of difficulty breathing.

12. An hepatocyte is a cell in the _____.

    a. liver   b. stomach

    c. intestine   d. gallbladder

Answer: A

Explanation: A. Correct! B. Hepat/o- means liver, not stomach. C. Hepat/o- means liver, not intestine. D. Hepat/o- means liver, not gallbladder.

13. The act of chewing is known as _____.

    a. deglutition   b. ossification

    c. synergism   d. mastication

Answer: D

Explanation: A. This means swallowing. B. This is cartilage changing to bone. C. This is the working together of two hormones. D. Correct!

14. Intussusception is an abnormality that occurs in the _____.

    a. brain   b. intestine

    c. blood   d. mind

Answer: B

Explanation: A. Intussusception is telescoping of the intestine. B. Correct! C. Intussusception is telescoping of the intestine. D. Intussusception is telescoping of the intestine.

15. A hernia in the groin is known as a/an _____ hernia.

    a. incarcerated   b. peritoneal

    c. hiatal   d. inguinal

Answer: D

Explanation: A. This is when the intestines are trapped in the hernia sac. B. Peritoneal refers to the peritoneum of the abdomen. C. A hiatal hernia is in the diaphragm. D. Correct!

16. Ova and parasites are associated with the _____ system.

    a. respiratory   b. gastrointestinal

    c. genital   d. muscular

Answer: B

Explanation: A. Ova and parasites are not in the respiratory system. B. Correct! C. Ova and parasites are not in the genital system. D. Ova and parasites are not in the muscular system.

17. The word parts in the medical word choledocholithotomy mean _____.

    a. appendix, duct, inflammation of or infection of

    b. muscle, tendon, pain, procedure to suture

    c. uterus, uterine tube, ovary, process of recording

    d. common bile duct, stone, process of cutting or making an incision

Answer: D

Explanation: A. These are not the word part meanings for choledocholithotomy. B. These are not the word part meanings for choledocholithotomy. C. These are not the word part meanings for choledocholithotomy. D. Correct!

Chapter 4 Questions

1. _____ is a localized collection of pus in the thoracic cavity.
   a. Influenza
   b. Pneumothorax
   c. Emphysema
   d. Pyothorax

   Answer: D

   Explanation: A. Pus is caused by a bacterial infection, but influenza is a viral infection. B. Pneumothorax is an abnormal condition of air between the pleural membranes. C. Emphysema is damaged alveoli that become air spaces that trap air.
   D. Correct!

2. Coughing up blood-tinged sputum is known as _____.
   a. hematemesis
   b. hemothorax
   c. hemoptysis
   d. hematology

   Answer: C

   Explanation: A. Hematemesis is vomiting up blood. B. Hemothorax is blood in the thoracic cavity because of trauma. C. Correct! D. Hematology is the study of blood.

3. A patient who suffers from CF has _____.
   a. chronic fatigue
   b. cystic fibrosis
   c. cardiac failure
   d. compound fracture

   Answer: B

   Explanation: A. Chronic fatigue syndrome is abbreviated as CFS. B. Correct!
   C. Cardiac failure has no abbreviation. Congestive heart failure is CHF.
   D. Compound fracture has no abbreviation.

4. Which word means inflammation of the lungs?
   a. neuritis
   b. hepatitis
   c. pneumonitis
   d. laryngitis

   Answer: C

   Explanation: A. This is inflammation of a nerve. B. This is inflammation of the liver. C. Correct! D. This is inflammation of the larynx (voice box).

5. All of the following are related to the color white, *except* _____.
   a. cyanosis
   b. pallor
   c. leukocyte
   d. albinism

   Answer: A

   Explanation: A. Correct! Cyanosis is a bluish coloration of the skin. B. Pallor is a white color of the skin due to lack of blood flow. C. Leukocyte is a white blood cell.
   D. Albinism is congenital lack of skin pigment.

6. All of the following abbreviations pertain to the respiratory system, *except*
   _____.
   a. CXR
   b. CHF
   c. CPAP
   d. COPD

   Answer: B

   Explanation: A. This means chest x-ray. B. Correct! C. This means continuous positive airway pressure. D. This means chronic obstructive pulmonary disease.

7. The abbreviation RA has three different meanings that pertain to each of the following, *except* _____.

a. oxygen

b. a joint disease

c. a chamber in the heart

d. the brain

Answer: D

Explanation: A. RA means room air (21% oxygen content). B. RA means rheumatoid arthritis. C. RA means right atrium. D. Correct!

8. The larynx is open during inhalation and exhalation but is covered by the _____ during swallowing.

a. epiglottis

b. epidermis

c. pericardium

d. pleura

Answer: A

Explanation: A. Correct! B. The epidermis, the uppermost layer of skin, is not in the larynx. C. The pericardium is around the heart, not in the larynx. D. The pleural membrane is around the lungs, not in the larynx.

9. The cessation of breathing is known as _____.

a. orthopnea

b. acromegaly

c. oligomenorrhea

d. apnea

Answer: D

Explanation: A. This is sitting up straight to breathe. B. This is enlargement of the extremities. C. This is scanty menstrual flow. D. Correct!

10. A Mantoux test is used to _____.

a. encourage deep breathing

b. diagnose a heart attack

c. diagnose tuberculosis

d. test distance vision

Answer: C

Explanation: A. Incentive spirometry is used to encourage deep breathing. B. CPK-MB, LDH, and troponin are used to diagnose a heart attack. C. Correct! D. A Snellen chart is used to test distance vision.

11. A person with asthma might be given a/an _____.

a. glucose tolerance test

b. audiometry

c. spirometry

d. thallium stress test

Answer: C

Explanation: A. This is done to diagnose diabetes mellitus. B. This is a hearing test. C. Correct! D. This is a test for blood flow to the heart.

12. A patient who cannot breathe easily and has to sleep sitting up, propped up on pillows, has _____.

a. pneumothorax

b. acromegaly

c. orthopnea

d. cystitis

Answer: C

Explanation: A. Pneumothorax is air in the pleural space from a traumatic injury. B. Acromegaly is enlargement of the extremities. C. Correct! D. Cystitis is inflammation or infection of the bladder.

13. A patient who has difficulty breathing has _____.

a. dyspareunia

b. dyspepsia

c. dysuria

d. dyspnea

Answer: D

Explanation: A. This is painful sexual intercourse. B. This is painful indigestion. C. This is painful urination. D. Correct!

14. Which word means a process of expelling sputum out of the chest?
   a. epistaxis
   b. exhalation
   c. expectoration
   d. eructation
   Answer: C
   Explanation: A. This is a nosebleed. B. This is breathing out. C. Correct! D. This is belching gas through the mouth.

Chapter 5 Questions

1. The combining form for blood vessel is _____.
   a. thromb/o-
   b. angi/o-
   c. ven/o-
   d. sphygm/o-
   Answer: B
   Explanation: A. Thromb/o- means thrombus (blood clot). B. Correct! C. Ven/o- means vein. D. Sphygm/o- means pulse.

2. All of the following abbreviations pertain to the cardiovascular system, *except*
   _____.
   a. CPR
   b. CAD
   c. CNS
   d. CHF
   Answer: C
   Explanation: A. CPR means cardiopulmonary resuscitation. B. CAD means coronary artery disease. C. Correct! CNS means central nervous system. D. CHF means congestive heart failure.

3. Which of the following abbreviations means an arrhythmia of the heart?
   a. PVC
   b. NSR
   c. HCT
   d. TPR
   Answer: A
   Explanation: A. Correct! B. NSR means normal sinus rhythm, not an arrhythmia. C. HCT means hematocrit. D. TPR means temperature, pulse, and respiration.

4. All of the following laboratory tests are used to determine if the patient had an MI, *except* _____.
   a. CK-MB
   b. lipid levels
   c. LDH
   d. troponin
   Answer: B
   Explanation: A. This is used to determine if the patient had an MI. B. Correct! C. This is used to determine if the patient had an MI. D. This is used to determine if the patient had an MI.

5. The medical word that is the opposite of "fast heart rate" is _____.
   a. arrhythmia
   b. bradykinesia
   c. bradycardia
   d. hyperlipidemia
   Answer: C
   Explanation: A. There are many different kinds of arrhythmias, fast and slow. B. This means a condition of slow muscle movement. C. Correct! D. This means a condition of high levels of lipids in the blood.

6. The medical words "systolic" and "diastolic" are associated with _____.
   a. blood pressure
   b. blood cells
   c. blood clotting
   d. blood sugar

Answer: A

Explanation: A. Correct! B. They are not associated with blood cells. C. They are not associated with blood clotting. D. They are not associated with blood sugar.

7. A balloon-like enlargement of an artery that fills with blood is known as a/an
_____.

a. hernia   b. varicose vein
c. aneurysm   d. hematoma

Answer: C

Explanation: A. A hernia does not involve an artery. B. A varicose vein is in a vein, not an artery. C. Correct! D. A hematoma is a collection of blood under the skin.

8. Arthur has arteriosclerosis and experiences pain in his lower calf when he walks. This is known as _____.

a. myocardial infarction   b. claudication
c. transient ischemic attack   d. vitiligo

Answer: B

Explanation: A. Myocardial infarction does not cause pain in the calf when walking. B. Correct! C. This is associated with a stroke, not lower calf pain. D. Vitiligo is a skin disease.

9. A pacemaker would be used to treat _____.

a. bundle branch block   b. restless legs syndrome
c. Crohn's disease   d. nocturia

Answer: A

Explanation: A. Correct! B. A pacemaker is not used to treat restless legs syndrome. C. Crohn's disease involves the colon, not the heart. D. Nocturia involves the urinary system, not the heart.

10. A Holter monitor test is used to detect _____.

a. cervical dysplasia   b. urinary tract infection
c. arrhthymia   d. tuberculosis

Answer: C

Explanation: A. A Pap smear is used to detect cervical dysplasia. B. A culture is used to detect a urinary tract infection. C. Correct! D. A Mantoux test is used to detect tuberculosis.

11. The chordae tendineae are associated with the _____.

a. muscles   b. lungs
c. heart   d. eye

Answer: C

Explanation: A. Tendons, not chordae tendineae, are associated with the muscles. B. Chordae tendineae are not associated with the lungs. C. Correct! D. Chordae tendineae are not associated with the eye.

12. All of the following are heart arrhythmias, *except* _____.

a. flutter   b. nystagmus
c. bradycardia   d. fibrillation

Answer: B

Explanation: A. This is an arrhythmia. B. Correct! Nystagmus is a back-and-forth motion of the eyes. C. This is an arrhythmia. D. This is an arrhythmia.

13. Inflammation of a vein is known as _____.
    a. venitis
    b. cystitis
    c. glossitis
    d. phlebitis
    Answer: D
    Explanation: A. There is no such medical word as venitis. B. This is inflammation of the bladder. C. This is inflammation of the tongue. D. Correct!

14. The word parts of pericardiocentesis mean _____.
    a. within, heart, process of reshaping by surgery
    b. between, membrane, surgical excision
    c. around, heart, procedure to puncture
    d. valve, blood vessel, tissue for implant or transplant
    Answer: C
    Explanation: A. These are not the meanings of the word parts of pericardiocentesis. B. These are not the meanings of the word parts of pericardiocentesis. C. Correct! D. These are not the meanings of the word parts of pericardiocentesis.

15. All of the following categories of drugs are used to treat cardiovascular conditions, *except* _____.
    a. antihypertensive drugs
    b. nitrate drugs
    c. digitalis drugs
    d. antiepileptic drugs
    Answer: D
    Explanation: A. These are used to treat cardiovascular conditions. B. These are used to treat cardiovascular conditions. C. These are used to treat cardiovascular conditions. D. Correct!

16. A sphygmomanometer is an instrument that measures _____.
    a. blood pressure
    b. muscle range of motion
    c. visual acuity
    d. nerve conduction velocity
    Answer: A
    Explanation: A. Correct! B. This is measured by a goniometer. C. This is measured by a Snellen chart and other tests. D. This test does not use a sphygmomanometer.

17. Which of the following are located in the heart?
    a. cilia
    b. villi
    c. haustra
    d. valves
    Answer: D
    Explanation: A. Cilia are located in the bronchi and uterine tubes. B. Villi are located in the small intestine. C. Haustra are located in the large intestine. D. Correct!

18. The _____ arteries supply the myocardium with oxygenated blood.
    a. femoral
    b. pulmonary
    c. coronary
    d. saphenous
    Answer: C
    Explanation: A. These arteries are in the leg. B. These arteries contain deoxygenated blood. C. Correct! D. These arteries are in the leg.

19. All of the following tests record the electrical activity of an organ, *except* _____.
    a. EEG
    b. EGA
    c. ECG
    d. EMG
    Answer: B
    Explanation: A. This records the electrical activity of the brain. B. Correct! C. This records the electrical activity of the heart. D. This records the electrical activity of a muscle.

Chapter 6 Questions

1. Which of the following abbreviations refers to a disease?
   - a. polys
   - b. mono
   - c. basos
   - d. eos

   Answer: B

   Explanation: A. Polys means polymorphonucleated leukocytes. B. Correct! Mono means mononucleosis. C. Basos means basophils. D. Eos means eosinophils.

2. All of the following abbreviations are related to cells in the blood, *except* _____.
   - a. FBS
   - b. RBC
   - c. HCT
   - d. WBC

   Answer: A

   Explanation: A. Correct! B. This stands for red blood cell. C. This stands for hematocrit, a measurement of the percentage of red blood cells. D. This stands for white blood cell.

3. The leukocytes that are known as eosinophils play this role in the immune system.
   - a. Respond to lymph nodes
   - b. Respond to bacteria
   - c. Respond to allergens
   - d. Respond to viruses

   Answer: C

   Explanation: A. No type of leukocyte responds to lymph nodes. B. Neutrophils respond to bacteria. C. Correct! D. Lymphocytes respond to viruses

4. Andrew is in a severe car accident that causes injuries within in his abdominal cavity. He might need to have a _____.
   - a. splenectomy
   - b. hemorrhoidectomy
   - c. rhytidectomy
   - d. thyroidectomy

   Answer: A

   Explanation: A. Correct! B. Hemorrhoids are not within the abdominal cavity. C. This is the removal of skin wrinkles. D. The thyroid gland is not within the abdominal cavity.

5. When foreign material invades the body, the body produces _____.
   - a. hormones
   - b. enzymes
   - c. red blood cells
   - d. antibodies

   Answer: D

   Explanation: A. Hormone production is not related to foreign material invading the body. B. Enzyme production is not related to foreign material invading the body. C. Red blood cell production is not related to foreign material invading the body. D. Correct!

6. When the body attacks its own tissues, as in rheumatoid arthritis, this is known as a/an _____.
   - a. congenital defect
   - b. allergic reaction
   - c. autoimmune disease
   - d. iatrogenic disease

   Answer: C

   Explanation: A. A congenital defect is present at birth. B. An allergic reaction does not attack the body's own tissues. C. Correct! D. Iatrogenic means caused by the physician or treatment.

7. A blood clot is also known as a _____.
   a. lipid
   b. prothrombin
   c. plaque
   d. thrombus
   Answer: D
   Explanation: A. Lipids are fats in the blood. B. Prothrombin is a blood clotting factor. C. Plaque is on the artery walls. D. Correct!

8. Which medical word is closely related to platelets?
   a. aggregation
   b. alimentary
   c. amniocentesis
   d. ancillary
   Answer: A
   Explanation: A. Correct! Platelet aggregation occurs during blood clot formation. B. Alimentary refers to the gastrointestinal system. C. Amniocentesis is a test performed on pregnant women. D. Ancillary refers to departments within the hospital.

9. Thrombocytes are also known as _____.
   a. antigens
   b. osteocytes
   c. platelets
   d. oncogenes
   Answer: C
   Explanation: A. Antigens are foreign substances that cause an allergic reaction. B. Osteocytes are bone cells. C. Correct! D. Oncogenes are pathogens that cause cancer.

10. A macrophage is a type of _____.
    a. psychiatric eating disorder
    b. abnormally large red blood cell
    c. cancerous cell
    d. monocyte in the tissues
    Answer: D
    Explanation: A. The suffix -phage does not mean an eating disorder. B. The combining form macr/o- does not relate to an abnormally large red blood cell. C. This cell is not cancerous. D. Correct!

11. Each of the following is a type of pathogen, *except* _____.
    a. bacterium
    b. gene
    c. virus
    d. fungus
    Answer: B
    Explanation: A. A bacterium is a pathogen. B. Correct! C. A virus is a pathogen. D. A fungus is a pathogen.

12. All of the following are lymphoid tissues, *except* the _____.
    a. thalamus
    b. Peyer's patches
    c. thymus
    d. spleen
    Answer: A
    Explanation: A. Correct! B. Peyer's patches are lymphoid tissues in the intestine. C. The thymus is lymphoid tissue that is an organ. D. The spleen is lymphoid tissue that is an organ.

13. Immunoglobulins are also known as _____.
    a. antibodies
    b. megakaryocytes
    c. neuroglia
    d. myofibrils
    Answer: A
    Explanation: A. Correct! B. Megakaryocytes are cells that produce platelets. C. Neuroglia are supporting structures in the brain. D. Myofibrils are in the muscles.

Chapter 7 Questions

1. All of the following medical words are associated with itching, *except* _____.
   - a. urticaria
   - b. histamine
   - c. oogenesis
   - d. pruritus

   Answer: C

   Explanation: A. Urticaria is an allergic skin reaction. B. Histamine is the chemical that produces itching. C. Correct! Oogenesis is the process that creates an ovum. D. Pruritus is the medical word for itching.

2. The combining form py/o- means _____.
   - a. fire
   - b. pus
   - c. renal pelvis
   - d. infection

   Answer: B

   Explanation: A. Pyr/o- means fire. B. Correct! C. Pyel/o- means renal pelvis. D. Py/o- does not mean infection.

3. The basis of an allergic reaction is the release of _____ from basophils in the blood and mast cells in the connective tissue.
   - a. stem cells
   - b. neurotransmitters
   - c. hormones
   - d. histamine

   Answer: D

   Explanation: A. Stem cells are not released from basophils. B. Neurotransmitters are released from nerves. C. Hormones are released from endocrine glands. D. Correct!

4. Variable areas of white, depigmented skin are known as _____.
   - a. albinism
   - b. pustules
   - c. vitiligo
   - d. pallor

   Answer: C

   Explanation: A. Albinism is an overall white skin color due to a genetic defect. B. Pustules are small areas that contain white pus; they are not depigmented. C. Correct! D. Pallor is an overall white color due to a lack of blood flow.

5. All of the following are related to the color yellow, *except* _____.
   - a. xanthelasma
   - b. jaundice
   - c. scleral icterus
   - d. erythema

   Answer: D

   Explanation: A. This is a yellow plaque on the skin. B. This is yellow coloration of the skin due to liver disease. C. This is yellow coloration of the conjunctivae overlying the sclera due to liver disease. D. Correct! Erythema is a red coloration of the skin.

6. While studying for this final examination, you might have experienced sweating and a headache, which are known as _____.
   - a. hirsutism and menarche
   - b. hernia and encephalitis
   - c. diaphoresis and cephalalgia
   - d. palpitations and apnea

   Answer: C

   Explanation: A. This is excessive hairiness and the beginning of menstruation. B. This is a weakness in the abdominal wall muscle and inflammation of the brain. C. Correct! D. This is a thumping sensation of an irregular heart beat and the cessation of breathing.

7. Onychomycosis is a _____.
   - a. sexually transmitted disease
   - b. loss of touch with reality
   - c. symptom of alcohol withdrawal
   - d. fungus infection of the nails

   Answer: D

   Explanation: A. This is not a sexually transmitted disease. B. Psychosis is a loss of touch with reality. C. Delirium tremens is a symptom of alcohol withdrawal. D. Correct!

8. The blackheads and whiteheads of acne vulgaris are known as _____ and
   _____.
   - a. vesicles, bullae
   - b. calculi, cysts
   - c. comedones, pustules
   - d. fissures, decubitus ulcers

   Answer: C

   Explanation: A. Vesicles are found with herpes and chickenpox, and bullae are found with burns. B. Calculi are kidney stones. C. Correct! D. Fissures and decubitus ulcers are not associated with acne vulgaris.

9. Male pattern baldness is known as _____.
   - a. alopecia
   - b. tinea pedis
   - c. psoriasis
   - d. decubitus ulcer

   Answer: A

   Explanation: A. Correct! B. Tinea pedis is a fungal infection of the skin. C. Psoriasis is not associated with baldness. D. A decubitus ulcer is not associated with baldness.

10. Mrs. Marks decided that she wanted to look younger. She had all of these procedures done, *except* _____.
    - a. liposuction
    - b. thoracotomy
    - c. Botox injections
    - d. rhytidectomy

    Answer: B

    Explanation: A. This does help someone look younger by removing excess fat deposits. B. Correct! C. This does help someone look younger by relaxing skin wrinkles. D. This does help someone look younger by removing skin wrinkles.

11. The colors red, white, and black correspond to the combining forms of
    _____.
    - a. eosin/o-, erythemat/o-, leuk/o-
    - b. erythr/o-, leuk/o-, melan/o-
    - c. cyan/o-, hem/o-, noct/o-
    - d. alg/o-, cyan/o-, erythr/o-

    Answer: B

    Explanation: A. These mean red, redness, and white. B. Correct! C. These mean blue, blood, night. D. These mean pain, blue, red.

12. Alopecia is the opposite of _____.
    - a. jaundice
    - b. cyanosis
    - c. hirsutism
    - d. anesthesia

    Answer: C

    Explanation: A. Jaundice is a yellowish skin color; alopecia is baldness. B. Cyanosis is a bluish skin color; alopecia is baldness. C. Correct! D. Anesthesia is a lack of sensation on the skin; alopecia is baldness.

13. A dermatome is _____.
   a. a surgical instrument
   b. a skin area that sends sensory information to the spinal cord
   c. used to make a skin graft
   d. All of the above.
   Answer: D
   Explanation: A. A dermatome is a surgical instrument used to make skin grafts.
   B. A dermatome is a skin area that sends sensory information to the spinal cord.
   C. A dermatome is a surgical instrument used to make skin grafts. D. Correct!

14. A _____ is a congenital neoplasm composed of dilated blood vessels.
   a. varicose vein   b. hemarthrosis
   c. hemangioma   d. hematoma
   Answer: C
   Explanation: A. A varicose vein is not a congenital neoplasm. B. Hemarthrosis is
   blood in the joint due to trauma. C. Correct! D. A hematoma is a collection of
   blood under the skin due to trauma.

15. Which of these is a skin disease caused by lice and their eggs?
   a. pediculosis   b. myositis
   c. verruca   d. salpingitis
   Answer: A
   Explanation: A. Correct! B. Myositis is inflammation of a muscle. C. Verruca is
   warts caused by a virus. D. Salpingitis is inflammation of the uterine tubes.

16. The medical name for a scar is a/an _____.
   a. infarct   b. lymphoma
   c. bruit   d. cicatrix
   Answer: D
   Explanation: A. An infarct is an area of dead tissue. B. Lymphoma is a cancerous
   tumor of a lymph node. C. A bruit is a sound heard when blood rushes through a
   narrowed artery. D. Correct!

Chapter 8 Questions

1. The adjective peroneal refers to the _____.
   a. perineum   b. fibula
   c. peritoneum   d. skin
   Answer: B
   Explanation: A. The adjective perineal refers to the perineum. B. Correct! C. The
   adjective peritoneal refers to the peritoneum. D. The adjectives integument/o-,
   cutane/o-, or derm/o- refer to the skin.

2. An excessive anterior curvature of the lumbar spine is known as _____.
   a. lordosis   b. orthosis
   c. scoliosis   d. prosthesis
   Answer: A
   Explanation: A. Correct! B. An orthosis is a brace, splint, or collar that is used to
   immobilize or correct an orthopedic problem. C. Scoliosis is a right or left curvature of the spine. D. A prosthesis is an artificial limb (arm, leg, etc.).

3. Osteoarthritis is also known by the initials of _____.
   a. DTR
   b. DEXA
   c. DJD
   d. DVT

   Answer: C

   Explanation: A. This stands for deep tendon reflex. B. This is a bone density test.
   C. Correct! DJD stands for degenerative joint disease. D. This stands for deep
   venous thrombosis.

4. All of these abbreviations refer to the musculoskeletal system, *except* _____.
   a. ROM
   b. RUE
   c. RLL
   d. MCP

   Answer: C

   Explanation: A. ROM means range of motion. B. RUE means right upper extremity.
   C. Correct! RLL means right lower lung. D. MCP means metacarpophalangeal joint.

5. All of the following abbreviations are surgeries on the bones, *except* _____.
   a. ZIFT
   b. THR
   c. AKA
   d. ORIF

   Answer: A

   Explanation: A. Correct! ZIFT means zygote intrafallopian transfer. B. THR means
   total hip replacement. C. AKA means above-the-knee amputation. D. ORIF means
   open reduction and internal fixation.

6. The medical specialty that studies the anatomy and physiology of the skeletal and
   muscular systems is _____.
   a. orthodontics
   b. orthopedics
   c. pediatrics
   d. endocrinology

   Answer: B

   Explanation: A. Orthodontics is the medical specialty for straightening the
   teeth. B. Correct! C. Pediatrics is the medical specialty that treats children.
   D. Endocrinology is the medical specialty for the endocrine glands.

7. The combining form that means joint is _____.
   a. arteri/o-
   b. arthr/o-
   c. arachn/o-
   d. acr/o-

   Answer: B

   Explanation: A. Arteri/o- means artery. B. Correct! C. Arachn/o- means spider;
   spider web. D. Acr/o- means extremity; highest point.

8. All of the following are associated with a bone, *except* _____.
   a. ileum
   b. peroneal
   c. osseous
   d. ilium

   Answer: A

   Explanation: A. Correct! B. This is an adjective for the fibula bone. C. This is an
   adjective for bone. D. This is one of the hip bones.

9. Which disease shows marked loss of bone density and is associated with aging?
   a. osteosarcoma
   b. osteoarthritis
   c. osteomalacia
   d. osteoporosis

   Answer: D

   Explanation: A. This is a cancer of the bone. B. This is inflammation and loss of
   cartilage in the joint. C. This is softening of the bone. D. Correct!

10. The medical names for the collarbone, breastbone, and shoulder blade are
_____.

    a. fibula, scapula, symphysis pubis   b. clavicle, sternum, scapula

    c. patella, trachea, ossicles   d. humerus, tibia, calcaneus

Answer: B

Explanation: A. These are not the correct names. B. Correct! C. These are not the correct names. D. These are not the correct names.

11. The adjective costal refers to the _____.

    a. ear   b. cartilage

    c. viscera   d. rib

Answer: D

Explanation: A. The adjective for ear is otic. B. The adjective for cartilage is cartilaginous. C. Viscera are the soft, internal abdominal organs. D. Correct!

12. A patient who injured his calcaneus, tarsal, and metatarsal bones might find it painful to _____.

    a. play the piano   b. turn his head from side to side

    c. put on his shoes   d. chew his food

Answer: C

Explanation: A. The calcaneus, tarsal, and metatarsal bones are in the foot. B. The calcaneus, tarsal, and metatarsal bones are in the foot. C. Correct! D. The calcaneus, tarsal, and metatarsal bones are in the foot.

13. The acetabulum is located in the _____.

    a. ear   b. brain

    c. hip   d. uterine tube

Answer: C

Explanation: A. The acetabulum is in the hip. B. The acetabulum is in the hip. C. Correct! D. The acetabulum is in the hip.

14. The medical name for the heel bone is the _____.

    a. calculus   b. helix

    c. hallux   d. calcaneus

Answer: D

Explanation: A. A calculus is a kidney stone. B. The helix is the outer rim of the external ear. C. Hallus is the great toe. D. Correct!

Chapter 9 Questions

1. The gastrocnemius muscle is in the _____.

    a. arm   b. stomach

    c. calf   d. throat

Answer: C

Explanation: A. The gastrocnemius muscle is not in the arm. B. The gastrocnemius muscle is not in the stomach. C. Correct! D. The gastrocnemius muscle is not in the throat.

2. The combining form pod/o- means _____.

    a. child   b. straight

    c. foot   d. hand

Answer: C

Explanation: A. Ped/o- means child. B. Ortho/o- means straight. C. Correct! D. Man/o- means hand.

3. Which of the following abbreviations is related to a test on the muscles and nerves?

a. EMT   b. EEG

c. EKG   d. EMG

Answer: D

Explanation: A. EMT means emergency medical technician. B. EEG means electroencephalography. C. EKG means electrocardiography. D. Correct! EMG means electromyography.

4. Which of the following abbreviations represents an organization that is concerned with healthcare professionals and safety on the job?

a. HIPAA   b. EMR

c. OSHA   d. SPECT

Answer: C

Explanation: A. HIPAA is a law concerned with insurance and confidentiality of medical records. B. EMR means electronic medical record. C. Correct! OSHA means Occupational Safety and Health Administration. D. SPECT is a radiology test that uses tomography.

5. A contracture is _____.

a. when a muscle is used

b. a legal agreement between the patient and the doctor

c. the action of a heartbeat

d. a fixed, immovable position of a muscle

Answer: D

Explanation: A. This is a contraction. B. This is a contract. C. This is a contraction. D. Correct!

6. Moving a limb away from the body is known as _____.

a. excision   b. contraction

c. debridement   d. abduction

Answer: D

Explanation: A. Excision is a surgical procedure. B. Contraction is a shortening of a muscle to produce movement. C. Debridement is a skin procedure. D. Correct!

7. A patient who has an abnormal gait because of difficulty controlling the voluntary muscles has _____.

a. dyskinesia   b. dyspepsia

c. dyslexia   d. dysuria

Answer: A

Explanation: A. Correct! B. Dyspepsia is painful indigestion. C. Dyslexia is difficulty reading and writing. D. Dysuria is painful, difficult urination.

8. The _____ test is used to diagnose myasthenia gravis.

a. troponin   b. Tensilon

c. DEXA   d. DTR

Answer: B

Explanation: A. Troponin is used to diagnose a myocardial infarction. B. Correct! C. DEXA is used to determine bone density. D. Deep tendon reflexes test the muscular-nervous pathway.

9. A _____ is a semisolid or fluid-containing cyst that develops on a tendon.

   a. retinaculum   b. bursa

   c. ganglion   d. cul-de-sac

   Answer: C

   Explanation: A. A retinaculum is a fibrous band that holds down tendons. B. A bursa is a normal anatomic structure of a fluid-filled sac where a tendon rubs against a bone. C. Correct! D. Cul-de-sac is the area behind the cervix of the uterus.

10. The biceps femoris muscle is in the _____.

   a. arm   b. heart

   c. leg   d. abdomen

   Answer: C

   Explanation: A. The biceps brachii muscle is in the arm. B. This is not in the heart. C. Correct! D. This is not in the abdomen.

11. The orbicularis oris muscle goes around the _____.

   a. back   b. mouth

   c. eye   d. head

   Answer: B

   Explanation: A. The orbicularis oris muscle goes around the mouth. B. Correct! C. The orbicularis oculi muscle goes around the eye. D. The orbicularis oris muscle goes around the mouth.

12. Which doctor can only treat diseases of the foot?

   a. chiropractor   b. osteopath

   c. massage therapist   d. podiatrist

   Answer: D

   Explanation: A. A chiropractor can treat more than diseases of the foot. B. An osteopath can treat more than diseases of the foot. C. A massage therapist is not a doctor. D. Correct!

13. All of the following are sports-related injuries, *except* _____.

   a. concussion   b. rigor mortis

   c. lateral epicondylitis   d. shin splints

   Answer: B

   Explanation: A. This is a sports injury. B. Correct! C. This is a sports injury. D. This is a sports injury.

Chapter 10 Questions

1. Which combining form means sleep?

   a. psych/o-   b. somat/o-

   c. syncop/o-   d. somn/o-

   Answer: D

   Explanation: A. Psych/o- means mind. B. Somat/o- means body. C. Syncop/o- means fainting. D. Correct!

2. Paralysis on one side of the body following a stroke is known as _____.
   a. hemiparesis
   b. quadriplegia
   c. hemiplegia
   d. paraplegia
   Answer: C
   Explanation: A. Hemiparesis is weakness on one half of the body. B. Quadriplegia is paralysis of all four limbs following a spinal cord injury to the neck. C. Correct! D. Paraplegia is paralysis of the legs following a spinal cord injury to the lower back.

3. Epilepsy is the result of _____.
   a. traumatic injury and loss of consciousness
   b. muscle weakness following a stroke
   c. having had Down syndrome as a child
   d. uncontrolled firing of groups of neurons
   Answer: D
   Explanation: A. Epilepsy is not a result of this. B. Epilepsy is not a result of this. C. Epilepsy is not a result of this. D. Correct!

4. Parkinson's disease is due to an imbalance of _____ and _____.
   a. electrolytes and BUN
   b. dopamine and acetylcholine
   c. albumin and protein
   d. folic acid and vitamin B_{12}
   Answer: B
   Explanation: A. These are not related to Parkinson's disease. B. Correct! C. These are not related to Parkinson's disease. D. These are not related to Parkinson's disease.

5. All of the following are early signs of multiple sclerosis *except* _____.
   a. transient ischemic attack
   b. double vision
   c. large muscle weakness
   d. early fatigue after repeated muscle contractions
   Answer: A
   Explanation: A. Correct! B. This is an early sign of multiple sclerosis. C. This is an early sign of multiple sclerosis. D. This is an early sign of multiple sclerosis.

6. To prevent a neural tube defect in the fetus, the mother should take _____.
   a. folic acid
   b. vitamin B_{12}
   c. iron
   d. glucose
   Answer: A
   Explanation: A. Correct! B. Vitamin B_{12} prevents pernicious anemia. C. Iron prevents iron deficiency anemia. D. Glucose does not prevent neural tube defect.

7. A TENS unit is _____.
   a. a surgical procedure to remove plaque and prevent a stroke
   b. used to treat chronic pain
   c. a unit of measurement for the depth of a coma
   d. an electrical recording of the brain waves
   Answer: B
   Explanation: A. An endarterectomy is used to remove plaque and prevent a stroke. B. Correct! C. The Glasgow scale measures the depth of a coma. D. An EEG records the brain waves.

8. Photophobia can occur with the diseases of _____ and _____.
   a. cataract, eclampsia
   b. leukemia, strabismus
   c. migraines, meningitis
   d. cerebrovascular accident, hepatitis
   Answer: C
   Explanation: A. Photophobia is not related to these diseases. B. Photophobia is not related to these diseases. C. Correct! D. Photophobia is not related to these diseases.

9. Brief, involuntary episodes of falling asleep are known as _____.
   a. syncope
   b. hydrocephalus
   c. apnea
   d. narcolepsy
   Answer: D
   Explanation: A. Syncope is fainting. B. Hydrocephalus does not involve falling asleep. C. Apnea is an episode of not breathing. D. Correct!

10. After which procedure could a diagnosis of narcolepsy be made?
    a. polysomnography
    b. lumbar puncture
    c. blood test for drug levels
    d. craniotomy
    Answer: A
    Explanation: A. Correct! B. This does not diagnose narcolepsy. C. This does not diagnose narcolepsy. D. This does not diagnose narcolepsy.

11. All of the following are characteristic of meningitis *except* _____.
    a. fever
    b. rales and rhonchi
    c. nuchal rigidity
    d. sensitivity to light
    Answer: B
    Explanation: A. This is characteristic of meningitis. B. Correct! C. This is characteristic of meningitis. D. This is characteristic of meningitis.

12. The cause of new-variant Creutzfeldt-Jakob disease as well as mad cow disease is a _____.
    a. bacterium
    b. prion
    c. virus
    d. fungus
    Answer: B
    Explanation: A. A bacterium does not cause new-variant Creutzfeldt-Jakob disease. B. Correct! C. A virus does not cause new-variant Creutzfeldt-Jakob disease. D. A fungus does not cause new-variant Creutzfeldt-Jakob disease.

13. _____ is a white, fatty insulating layer along the axon of a nerve.
    a. Leukocyte
    b. Adipose tissue
    c. Myelin
    d. Dermatome
    Answer: C
    Explanation: A. A leukocyte is a white blood cell. B. Adipose tissue is fatty tissue in the subcutaneous layer beneath the skin. C. Correct! D. A dermatome is an area of skin that sends sensory information to a spinal nerve.

14. A spinal cord nerve receives sensory information from a specific area of the skin known as a _____.
    a. follicle
    b. dermatome
    c. sebaceous gland
    d. neuron
    Answer: B
    Explanation: A. A follicle is the source of a hair, not a specific area of the skin. B. Correct! C. A sebaceous gland does not send sensory information to a spinal nerve. D. A neuron transmits sensory information, but is not a specific area of the skin.

15. Pressure on the brain is caused by excessive amounts of cerebrospinal fluid from _____.

    a. hepatosplenomegaly   b. hydrocephalus

    c. hypertriglyceridemia   d. tetralogy of Fallot

    Answer: B

    Explanation: A. This is enlargement of the liver and spleen. B. Correct! C. This is a high level of triglycerides in the blood. D. This is a heart defect in babies.

16. _____ is pain and numbness when a herniated disk presses against a spinal nerve root.

    a. radiculopathy   b. neovascularization

    c. spondylolisthesis   d. nephrolithiasis

    Answer: A

    Explanation: A. Correct! B. This growth of new blood vessels occurs with diabetic retinopathy. C. This is slipping of one vertebra out of alignment onto another vertebra. D. This is a condition of kidney stones.

17. An aura is sometimes experienced by patients with _____.

    a. meningitis   b. glaucoma

    c. anemia   d. epilepsy

    Answer: D

    Explanation: A. Patients experience photophobia, not an aura, with meningitis. B. Patients experience pain and blurred vision with glaucoma. C. Patients experience fatigue with anemia. D. Correct!

18. A head injury that bruises the brain and causes temporary loss of consciousness is called _____.

    a. seizure   b. coma

    c. concussion   d. adenoma

    Answer: C

    Explanation: A. A seizure is not a head injury. B. A coma causes prolonged loss of consciousness. C. Correct! D. An adenoma is a tumor of a gland.

19. The loss of the ability to communicate verbally or in writing is known as _____.

    a. amnesia   b. dyslexia

    c. anemia   d. aphasia

    Answer: D

    Explanation: A. Amnesia is an inability to remember. B. Dyslexia is difficulty reading and writing. C. Anemia is a condition of too few red blood cells. D. Correct!

20. A _____ is a surgical procedure done to relieve pressure on a spinal nerve root.

    a. cholangiography   b. laminectomy

    c. thoracentesis   d. rhytidectomy

    Answer: B

    Explanation: A. Cholangiography uses dye to outline the bile ducts. B. Correct! C. Thoracentesis is done to remove blood from the thoracic cavity. D. Rhytidectomy is done to remove skin wrinkles.

21. Cerebral palsy is caused by a _____.
    a. genetic defect
    b. arteriovenous malformation
    c. concussion
    d. lack of oxygen during birth
    Answer: D
    Explanation: A. Cerebral palsy is not caused by a genetic defect. B. Cerebral palsy is not caused by an arteriovenous malformation. C. Cerebral palsy is not caused by a concussion. D. Correct!

22. Which of the following abbreviations stands for a medical procedure that removes cerebrospinal fluid?
    a. CP
    b. LP
    c. CT
    d. TB
    Answer: B
    Explanation: A. CP means cerebral palsy. B. Correct! LP means lumbar puncture. C. CT means computed tomography. D. TB means tuberculosis.

23. The combining form "myel/o-" means _____.
    a. fungus or yeast
    b. muscle or bone
    c. spinal cord or bone marrow
    d. liver, pancreas, and spleen
    Answer: C
    Explanation: A. Myc/o- means fungus. B. My/o- means muscle, and oste/o- means bone. C. Correct! D. Hepat/o- means liver, pancreat/o- means pancreas, and splen/o- means spleen.

24. Hemiplegia _____.
    a. is paralysis of one side of the body
    b. can occur when you break your neck
    c. causes paralysis of everything below the waist
    d. is caused by trauma
    Answer: A
    Explanation: A. Correct! B. This would be quadriplegia. C. This would be paraplegia. D. Trauma causes quadriplegia and paraplegia, but a stroke causes hemiplegia.

25. A cerebrovascular accident is also known as a _____.
    a. stroke or brain attack
    b. angina or myocardial infarction
    c. thrombus or arteriosclerosis
    d. None of the above.
    Answer: A
    Explanation: A. Correct! B. These are not other names for a cerebrovascular accident. C. These are not other names for a cerebrovascular accident. D. There is a correct answer.

26. People who use computers extensively are prone to develop _____.
    a. osteoporosis
    b. carpal tunnel syndrome
    c. muscular dystrophy
    d. scoliosis
    Answer: B
    Explanation: A. Osteoporosis is not related to computer use. B. Correct! C. Muscular dystrophy is a genetic disorder, not related to computer use. D. Scoliosis is a lateral bending of the spine, not related to computer use.

Chapter 11 Questions

1. Blood in the urine is known as _____.
   a. hematuria
   b. hematemesis
   c. pyuria
   d. glycosuria
   Answer: A
   Explanation: A. Correct! B. This is vomiting of blood. C. This is pus (white blood cells) in the urine. D. This is glucose in the urine.

2. A refractometer is used to _____.
   a. select a lens to correct vision
   b. test the specific gravity of urine
   c. measure the angle of joint movement
   d. measure a hormone level in the blood
   Answer: B
   Explanation: A. A phorometer is used for this. B. Correct! C. A goniometer is used for this. D. A blood test is used for this.

3. A dipstick is used to _____.
   a. check for blood in the stool
   b. take a blood pressure
   c. test for substances in the urine
   d. measure the volume of exhaled air
   Answer: C
   Explanation: A. Guaiac or Hemoccult test is for blood in the stool. B. A sphygmo-manometer takes the blood pressure. C. Correct! D. Pulmonary function tests measure this.

4. Which of the following abbreviations is related to severe kidney disease?
   a. CABG
   b. GERD
   c. ESRD
   d. ADHD
   Answer: C
   Explanation: A. CABG means coronary artery bypass graft. B. GERD means gastroesophageal reflux disease. C. Correct! ESRD means end-stage renal disease. D. ADHD means attention-deficit hyperactivity disorder.

5. A nephrectomy involves _____.
   a. removal of dead tissue
   b. incision into the nerve
   c. inflammation of a nerve
   d. excision of the kidney
   Answer: D
   Explanation: A. Debridement is removal of dead tissue. B. Neurotomy is incision into the nerve. C. Neuritis is inflammation of a nerve. D. Correct!

6. Polyuria means _____.
   a. difficult urination
   b. increased amount of urine
   c. pus in the urine
   d. protein in the urine
   Answer: B
   Explanation: A. Difficult urination is dysuria. B. Correct! C. Pus in the urine is pyuria. D. Protein in the urine is proteinuria or albuminuria.

7. The combining form that means "renal pelvis of the kidney" is _____.
   a. py/o-
   b. pyel//o-
   c. prostat/o-
   d. psych/o-
   Answer: B
   Explanation: A. Py/o- means pus. B. Correct! C. Prostat/o- means prostate gland. D. Psych/o- means mind.

8. The condition of having kidney stones is known as _____.
    a. cholecystitis
    b. cystitis
    c. hydroureter
    d. nephrolithiasis
    Answer: D
    Explanation: A. This is inflammation of the gallbladder. B. This is inflammation of the bladder. C. This is an enlarged ureter from backed-up urine. D. Correct!

9. Flank pain is a typical presenting symptom of _____.
    a. hypochondria
    b. kidney stone
    c. appendicitis
    d. emphysema
    Answer: B
    Explanation: A. Flank pain is not associated with this. B. Correct! C. Appendicitis causes pain in the right lower quadrant. D. Emphysema causes shortness of breath, not pain.

10. Producing no urine is known as _____.
    a. enuresis
    b. dysuria
    c. anosmia
    d. anuria
    Answer: D
    Explanation: A. This is urinating in the bed. B. This is painful urination. C. This is a lack of the sense of smell. D. Correct!

11. *E. coli* is the most common cause of _____.
    a. URI
    b. PMN
    c. CHF
    d. UTI
    Answer: D
    Explanation: A. This stands for upper respiratory infection. B. This stands for polymorphonuclear leukocyte. C. This stands for congestive heart failure. D. Correct! UTI means urinary tract infection.

Chapter 12 Questions

1. Which abbreviation indicates a surgical procedure on the prostate gland?
    a. TURP
    b. PUD
    c. PVD
    d. TPAL
    Answer: A
    Explanation: A. Correct! TURP means transurethral resection of the prostate. B. This stands for peptic ulcer disease. C. This stands for peripheral vascular disease. D. This stands for term (births), premature (births), abortions, and living (children).

2. Which of the following abbreviations stands for the government agency that tracks venereal diseases?
    a. VDRL
    b. STD
    c. AIDS
    d. CDCP
    Answer: D
    Explanation: A. VDRL is a laboratory test for syphilis. B. STD means sexually transmitted disease. C. AIDS means acquired immunodeficiency syndrome. D. Correct! CDCP means Centers for Disease Control and Prevention.

3. Which of the following is a condition that affects the male genitourinary system?
   a. hypospadias
   b. hydrocephalus
   c. preeclampsia
   d. pyelonephritis
   Answer: A
   Explanation: A. Correct! B. This is an excessive amount of cerebrospinal fluid in the cranial cavity. C. This is a condition of pregnant women. D. This is inflammation of the renal pelvis and the kidney.

4. Undescended testicles are known as _____.
   a. keloids
   b. cryptorchism
   c. BPH
   d. endometriosis
   Answer: B
   Explanation: A. Keloids are greatly enlarged scars on the skin. B. Correct! C. This is benign prostatic hypertrophy. D. This involves the uterus, not the testicles.

5. Surgical removal of the testis because of cancer is known as _____.
   a. orchiectomy
   b. vasectomy
   c. herniorrhaphy
   d. amniocentesis
   Answer: A
   Explanation: A. Correct! B. This removes part of the vas deferens, not the testis. C. This is the surgucal repair of a hernia. D. This procedure is only done on pregnant women.

6. All of the following are structures of the male genitourinary system, *except*
   _____.
   a. corpora cavernosa
   b. mentum
   c. epididymis
   d. vas deferens
   Answer: B
   Explanation: A. This is a column of erectile tissue in the penis. B. Correct! C. This is a coiled tubule on top of the testis. D. This is a tube from the epididymis to the prostate gland.

7. All of these medical words are related to the penis, *except* _____.
   a. prepuce
   b. priapism
   c. patella
   d. glans
   Answer: C
   Explanation: A. The prepuce is the foreskin of the penis. B. Priapism is an abnormally long-lasting erection of the penis. C. Correct! D. The glans is the head of the penis.

8. A varicocele is a hernia of the _____.
   a. abdomen
   b. spermatic cord
   c. rectum
   d. bladder
   Answer: B
   Explanation: A. A ventral hernia is in the abdomen. B. Correct! C. A rectocele is a hernia of the rectum. D. A cystocele is a hernia of the bladder.

9. All of the following are sexually transmitted diseases, *except* _____.
   a. gynecomastia
   b. gonorrhea
   c. genital warts
   d. syphilis
   Answer: A
   Explanation: A. Correct! B. This is a sexually transmitted disease. C. This is a sexually transmitted disease. D. This is a sexually transmitted disease.

Chapter 13 Questions

1. Difficult or painful intercourse is known as _____.
   a. carcinoma *in situ*   b. dyspareunia
   c. senile lentigo   d. dysmenorrhea
   Answer: B
   Explanation: A. Carcinoma *in situ* does not involve intercourse. B. Correct! C. Senile lentigo is a skin condition of age spots. D. Dysmenorrhea is painful menstruation.

2. Very light or scanty menstrual flow is known as _____.
   a. oligomenorrhea   b. oligospermia
   c. oligodendroglia   d. oliguria
   Answer: A
   Explanation: A. Correct! B. This is a low number of spermatozoa. C. This is a cell in the brain that supports the neurons. D. This is scanty urine.

3. Candidiasis is a _____ infection of the vagina.
   a. bacterial   b. viral
   c. yeast   d. sexually transmitted
   Answer: C
   Explanation: A. Candidiasis is not a bacterial infection. B. Candidiasis is not a viral infection. C. Correct! D. Candidiasis is not a sexually transmitted infection.

4. Inflammation or infection of the uterine tube is known as _____.
   a. hepatitis   b. labyrinthitis
   c. otitis   d. salpingitis
   Answer: D
   Explanation: A. Hepatitis is inflammation of the liver. B. Labyrinthitis is inflammation of the labyrinth of the inner ear. C. Otitis is an inflammation or infection of the ear. D. Correct!

5. Mammography can detect all of the following, *except* _____.
   a. cancer   b. cysts
   c. gestational age   d. microcalcifications
   Answer: C
   Explanation: A. Mammography can detect cancer. B. Mammography can detect cysts. C. Correct! D. Mammography can detect microcalcifications.

6. A/an _____ is the surgical procedure to remove the uterus.
   a. orchiectomy   b. hysterectomy
   c. lymphangiography   d. oophorectomy
   Answer: B
   Explanation: A. An orchiectomy removes a testis. B. Correct! C. Lymphangiography is not a surgical procedure. D. Oophorectomy removes an ovary.

7. Alpha fetoprotein test is done on amniotic fluid to determine if the fetus has _____.
   a. cystic fibrosis   b. multiple sclerosis
   c. concussion   d. neural tube defect
   Answer: D
   Explanation: A. Cystic fibrosis is diagnosed after birth with a sweat test. B. Multiple sclerosis does not occur in a fetus. C. A concussion is not diagnosed with alpha fetoprotein. D. Correct!

8. The abbreviation VBAC refers to _____.
   a. the heart
   b. birth
   c. breathing
   d. venereal disease
   Answer: B
   Explanation: A. VBAC means vaginal birth after cesearean section. B. Correct!
   C. VBAC means vaginal birth after cesearean section. D. VBAC means vaginal
   birth after cesarean section.

9. The hot flashes and vasodilation in menopause are caused by release of
   _____ from the anterior pituitary gland.
   a. ASCVD
   b. BRCA1
   c. Folic acid
   d. FSH
   Answer: D
   Explanation: A. This means arteriosclerotic cardiovascular disease. B. This is a
   gene that increases the risk of breast cancer. C. The anterior pituitary gland does
   not release folic acid. D. Correct! FSH means follicle-stimulating hormone.

10. Infection with HPV predisposes a woman to the later development of _____.
    a. Crohn's disease
    b. urinary tract infections
    c. breech position during birth
    d. cervical cancer
    Answer: D
    Explanation: A. Crohn's disease of the intestine is not related to HPV. B. Urinary
    tract infections are caused by bacteria; HPV is a virus. C. Breech position during
    birth has no known cause. D. Correct!

11. Postpartum hemorrhage is due to hyposecretion of _____.
    a. oxytocin
    b. sebum
    c. thyroid hormone
    d. calcium
    Answer: A
    Explanation: A. Correct! B. Sebum is oil secreted by the sebaceous glands.
    C. Hyposecretion of thyroid hormone does not cause postpartum hemorrhage.
    D. Calcium is an electrolyte; it is not secreted.

12. Diabetes mellitus in the mother can make the fetus _____.
    a. have colic
    b. be large for gestational age
    c. be born prematurely
    d. have a heart defect
    Answer: B
    Explanation: A. It does not cause colic in the fetus. B. Correct! C. It does not cause
    premature birth. D. It does not cause a heart defect in the fetus.

13. A Pap smear is a cytology test that examines cells scraped from the _____.
    a. vagina
    b. stomach
    c. breast
    d. cervix
    Answer: D
    Explanation: A. Pap smear takes cells from the cervix, not vagina. B. Pap smear
    takes cells from the cervix. C. Pap smear takes cells from the cervix. D. Correct!

14. All of the following relate to surgery on the breast, *except* _____.
    a. mastoidectomy
    b. mammoplasty
    c. mastectomy
    d. lumpectomy
    Answer: A
    Explanation: A. Correct! B. This surgery reshapes the breast. C. This surgery re-
    moves the breast. D. This surgery removes a lump from the breast.

15. Which abbreviation refers to a drug category that is used to prevent pregnancy?

    a. NSAID
    b. HRT
    c. HDL
    d. OCP

    Answer: D

    Explanation: A. NSAID means nonsteroidal anti-inflammatory drugs. B. HRT means hormone replacement therapy. C. HDL means high-density lipoproteins. D. Correct! OCP means oral contraceptive (drug).

16. The beginning of menstruation is known as _____.

    a. menarche
    b. menopause
    c. meningomyelocele
    d. meningitis

    Answer: A

    Explanation: A. Correct! B. This is the ending of menstruation. C. This is a herniation of the spinal cord to the outside of the body. D. This is an inflammation of the meninges of the brain.

17. If a couple did not want any more children in the future, the man would have a _____ or the woman would have a _____.

    a. vasovasostomy, D&C
    b. TURP, colposcopy
    c. PSA, VBAC
    d. vasectomy, tubal ligation

    Answer: D

    Explanation: A. A vasovasostomy reconnects the vas deferens so that a man can get a woman pregnant. B. Neither of these procedures is related to bearing children. C. PSA is a laboratory test, not a procedure. D. Correct!

18. A benign condition of the breasts is _____.

    a. mammography
    b. Parkinson's disease
    c. Meniere's disease
    d. fibrocystic disease

    Answer: D

    Explanation: A. This is a procedure done on the breasts, not a condition. B. This is a condition of the nerves and brain. C. This is a condition of the ear. D. Correct!

Chapter 14 Questions

1. Which of these laboratory tests is *not* associated with diabetes mellitus?

    a. oral glucose tolerance test
    b. carcinoembryonic antigen
    c. glycosylated hemoglobin
    d. fasting blood sugar

    Answer: B

    Explanation: A. This is a test to diagnose diabetes mellitus. B. Correct! C. This test is used to monitor diabetes mellitus. D. This is a test to diagnose diabetes mellitus.

2. Which of these diseases affects the thyroid gland?

    a. Ewing's sarcoma
    b. thymoma
    c. Graves' disease
    d. exophthalmos

    Answer: C

    Explanation: A. This cancer affects the bone. B. This is a tumor of the thymus, not the thyroid gland. C. Correct! D. This is a result of hyperthyroidism that affects the eye. It does not affect the thyroid gland.

3. If you want to evaluate the function of the thyroid gland, you would do a blood test to determine the level of _____.

    a. testosterone
    b. triglycerides
    c. thrombocytes
    d. T3 and T4

Answer: D

Explanation: A. Testosterone is produced by the testes. B. Triglycerides are fats in the blood. C. Thrombocytes are produced by the bone marrow. D. Correct!

4. An elevated level of sugar in the blood is known as _____.
   a. glycosuria
   b. hyperglycemia
   c. hirsutism
   d. hyperthyroidism

Answer: B

Explanation: A. This is sugar in the urine. B. Correct! C. This is excessive, dark hair in women from hypersecretion of androgens. D. This is too much thyroid hormone in the blood.

5. All of the following can be complications of diabetes mellitus, *except* _____.
   a. erectile dysfunction
   b. gangrene of the feet
   c. myasthenia gravis
   d. retinopathy

Answer: C

Explanation: A. Arteriosclerosis (from diabetes mellitus) in the arteries to the penis can cause this. B. Arteriosclerosis and diabetic neuropathy can cause this. C. Correct! D. This is a complication of diabetes mellitus.

6. Hemoglobin A1c is _____.
   a. the form of hemoglobin in sickle cell anemia
   b. the cause of microcytic red blood cells and anemia
   c. a test to monitor blood glucose over several months
   d. the compound formed when oxygen binds to hemoglobin

Answer: C

Explanation: A. This is not found in sickle cell anemia. B. This is not related to anemia. C. Correct! D. Oxyhemoglobin is oxygen bound to hemoglobin.

7. Which of the following abbreviations is *not* related to diabetes mellitus?
   a. IVP
   b. ADA
   c. IDDM
   d. DM

Answer: A

Explanation: A. Correct! IVP means intravenous pyelography. B. ADA means American Diabetes Association. C. IDDM means insulin-dependent diabetes mellitus. D. DM means diabetes mellitus.

8. Which of these is an abbreviation for a type of diabetes?
   a. COPD
   b. VBAC
   c. NIDDM
   d. CAPD

Answer: C

Explanation: A. This stands for chronic obstructive pulmonary disease. B. This stands for vaginal birth after cesarean section. C. Correct! NIDDM means non-insulin-dependent diabetes mellitus. D. This stands for continuous ambulatory peritoneal dialysis.

9. Complications from diabetes mellitus affect all of these parts of the body, *except* the _____.
   a. mouth
   b. kidneys
   c. arteries
   d. retina

Answer: A

Explanation: A. Correct! B. Diabetes mellitus causes diabetic nephropathy of the kidneys. C. Diabetes mellitus causes arteriosclerosis of the arteries. D. Diabetes mellitus causes diabetic retinopathy of the retina.

10. T3 and T4 are hormones produced by the _____.
    a. testis
    b. thymus
    c. thyroid
    d. temporal lobe
    Answer: C
    Explanation: A. The testis produces testosterone, not T3 and T4. B. The thymus produces thymosins, not T3 and T4. C. Correct! D. The temporal lobe of the brain does not produce hormones.

11. An insulin drug is used to treat _____.
    a. diabetes insipidus
    b. pancreatic cancer
    c. precocious puberty
    d. diabetes mellitus
    Answer: D
    Explanation: A. Insulin is only used to treat diabetes mellitus. B. Insulin is only used to treat diabetes mellitus. C. Insulin is only used to treat diabetes mellitus. D. Correct!

12. Enlargement of the breasts in a male is known as _____.
    a. mammography
    b. augmentation mammoplasty
    c. gynecomastia
    d. Cushing's syndrome
    Answer: C
    Explanation: A. Mammography is a radiologic procedure, not a disease. B. Augmentation mammoplasty is a surgical procedure to enlarge a woman's breasts. C. Correct! D. Cushing's syndrome is hypersecretion of cortisol from the adrenal cortex.

13. Seasonal affective disorder is due to hypersecretion of _____.
    a. epinephrine
    b. melatonin
    c. amylase
    d. sebum
    Answer: B
    Explanation: A. Epinephrine causes the "fight or flight" response. B. Correct! C. Amylase is a digestive enzyme. D. Sebum is oil secreted by oil glands in the skin.

Chapter 15 Questions

1. Increased intraocular pressure that gradually causes loss of vision is known as _____.
    a. diplopia
    b. glaucoma
    c. Kaposi's sarcoma
    d. Bell's palsy
    Answer: B
    Explanation: A. This is double vision. B. Correct! C. This is a cancerous skin disease in AIDS patients. D. This is a nerve condition that affects the face.

2. Nearsightedness is the medical condition known as _____.
    a. myasthenia gravis
    b. myopia
    c. myositis
    d. mitosis
    Answer: B
    Explanation: A. Myasthenia gravis is a muscular condition. B. Correct! C. Myositis is inflammation of the muscles. D. Mitosis is normal cellular division.

3. Loss of flexibility of the lens due to older age is _____.
    a. priapism
    b. presbyacusis
    c. presbyopia
    d. prosthesis

Answer: C

Explanation: A. Priapism is a sustained erection of the penis. B. Presbyacusis is loss of hearing in older age. C. Correct! D. Prosthesis is an artificial limb.

4. A drooping of the upper eyelid is known as _____.

a. blepharoplasty

b. blepharitis

c. rhytidectomy

d. blepharoptosis

Answer: D

Explanation: A. This is plastic surgery reshaping of the eyelid. B. This is inflammation of the eyelid. C. This is surgical removal of wrinkles. D. Correct!

5. Insufficient tears that cause dry eyes is known as _____.

a. xeroderma

b. xenograft

c. xanthelasma

d. xerophthalmia

Answer: D

Explanation: A. This is dry skin. B. This is a skin graft taken from an animal. C. This is a yellow plaque on the skin. D. Correct!

6. Which of the following is a test for color blindness?

a. Ishihara plates

b. Thematic Apperception Test

c. TNM system

d. PET scan

Answer: A

Explanation: A. Correct! B. This is a psychiatric test for emotions and attitudes. C. This is for describing cancer and metastases. D. This is a nuclear medicine scan that shows cellular metabolism.

7. Which of the following statements is *true*?

a. When the cornea is irregularly curved, this is known as astigmatism.

b. When the back is irregularly curved, this is known as pectus excavatum.

c. When the brain is irregularly curved, this is known as gyri and sulci.

d. When the epidermis is irregularly curved, this is known as a keloid.

Answer: A

Explanation: A. Correct! B. Pectus excavatum affects the anterior chest, not the back. C. Gyri and sulci are normal folds and grooves. D. A keloid is a hypertrophied scar, not an irregular curvature of the skin.

8. A phorometer is used to_____.

a. measure the diameter of a skin lesion

b. examine the chromosomes under a microscope

c. determine the lens that best corrects the vision

d. measure the volume of urine

Answer: C

Explanation: A. A ruler is used to measure the diameter of a skin lesion. B. A karyotype is used to examine chromosomes. C. Correct! D. I&O measures the intake of fluid and output of urine.

9. A/an _____ is used to treat glaucoma.

a. otoplasty

b. rhinoplasty

c. trabeculoplasty

d. mammoplasty

Answer: C

Explanation: A. This is done to reshape the ears. B. This is done to reshape the nose. C. Correct! D. This is done to reshape the breasts.

10. All of the following words pertain to the eye, *except* _____.
    a. choroid
    b. macule
    c. fovea
    d. pupil
    Answer: B
    Explanation: A. This is part of the anterior eye. B. Correct! C. This is part of the posterior eye. D. This is part of the anterior eye.

11. The medical specialist (not an M.D.) who grinds eyeglass lenses according to a prescription is an _____.
    a. ophthalmologist
    b. osteopath
    c. optician
    d. orthopedist
    Answer: C
    Explanation: A. An ophthalmologist is an M.D. B. An osteopath deals with the bones, not the eyes. C. Correct! D. An orthopedist deals with the bones, not the eyes.

12. Rebecca has an inflammation in her O.D. Which of these might be the cause of the infection?
    a. conjunctivitis
    b. appendicitis
    c. laryngitis
    d. encephalitis
    Answer: A
    Explanation: A. Correct! B. O.D. means right eye. C. O.D. means right eye. D. O.D. means right eye.

Chapter 16 Questions

1. All of the following abbreviations refer to the ear, *except* _____.
   a. OU
   b. EAC
   c. TM
   d. BOM
   Answer: A
   Explanation: A. Correct! OU means oculus unitas, which is Latin for both eyes. B. This means external auditory canal. C. This means tympanic membrane. D. This means bilateral otitis media.

2. _____ is the sensation of moving and being off balance when the body is not moving.
   a. Syncope
   b. Proprioception
   c. Ataxia
   d. Vertigo
   Answer: D
   Explanation: A. Syncope is feeling dizzy and fainting. B. Proprioception is the sense of body position. C. Ataxia is incoordination of voluntary muscle movement. D. Correct!

3. To examine the nose, the physician uses a nasal _____ and a penlight for light.
   a. otoscope
   b. endoscope
   c. speculum
   d. myringotome
   Answer: C
   Explanation: A. An otoscope is used to look in the ear. B. An endoscope is used to look far into the respiratory or gastrointestinal system. C. Correct! D. A myringotome is used to make an incision in the tympanic membrane.

4. A plastic surgery procedure to correct protruding ears is known as a/an
_____.

   a. otoplasty
   b. polypectomy
   c. blepharoplasty
   d. rhinoplasty

   Answer: A

   Explanation: A. Correct! B. This removes a polyp. C. This reshapes the eyelids.
   D. This reshapes the nose.

5. Drainage of serous fluid or pus from the external ear is known as _____.

   a. rhinorrhea
   b. epistaxis
   c. hemorrhage
   d. otorrhea

   Answer: D

   Explanation: A. This is drainage from the nose. B. This is bleeding from the nose.
   C. This is bleeding from anywhere. D. Correct!

6. All of the following are inhaled antigens that cause allergic rhinitis *except*
_____.

   a. polyp
   b. pollen
   c. animal dander
   d. mold

   Answer: A

   Explanation: A. Correct! B. This is an inhaled antigen. C. This is an inhaled antigen. D. This is an inhaled antigen.

7. A sudden severe nosebleed is known as _____.

   a. hemarthrosis
   b. otosclerosis
   c. rhinophyma
   d. epistaxis

   Answer: D

   Explanation: A. Hemarthrosis is blood in a joint. B. Otosclerosis involves the ear,
   not the nose. C. Rhinophyma does not involve bleeding. D. Correct!

8. Which of the following is a hearing test?

   a. Glasgow
   b. Rinne
   c. Babinski
   d. Holter

   Answer: B

   Explanation: A. Glasgow is a coma scale. B. Correct! C. Babinski is a neurologic
   test. D. Holter is a heart monitor test.

9. A constant ringing or buzzing sound in the ears is known as _____.

   a. tinnitus
   b. palpitation
   c. rales
   d. bruit

   Answer: A

   Explanation: A. Correct! B. Palpitation is a temporary irregular heart beat.
   C. Rales are crackling sounds heard in the lung on inspiration. D. A bruit is a
   harsh sound made by blood going through an artery with arteriosclerosis.

10. Bacterial or viral infection of the throat is known as _____.

   a. glossitis
   b. pharyngitis
   c. blepharitis
   d. gastritis

   Answer: B

   Explanation: A. This is inflammation or infection of the tongue. B. Correct! C. This
   is inflammation or infection of the eyelid. D. This is inflammation or infection of
   the stomach.

11. A sore throat is known medically as _____.
    a. pharyngitis   b. meningitis
    c. hemoptysis   d. bronchitis
    Answer: A
    Explanation: A. Correct! B. Meningitis is inflammation of the meninges of the brain. C. Hemoptysis is coughing up blood-tinged sputum. D. Bronchitis is inflammation of the bronchi in the lungs.

12. Otitis media involves _____.
    a. fluid and inflammation in the middle ear
    b. a malignant tumor of the muscle tissue
    c. spinal cord herniation
    d. degeneration of the retina
    Answer: A
    Explanation: A. Correct! B. This is a myosarcoma. C. This is a myelomeningocele. D. This is macular degeneration.

13. An incision to insert a small tube to drain fluid from the middle ear is known as a/an _____.
    a. mastoidectomy   b. myringotomy
    c. rhytidectomy   d. otoplasty
    Answer: B
    Explanation: A. This is a procedure to remove the mastoid process of the temporal bone. B. Correct! C. This is a procedure to remove skin wrinkles. D. This is a procedure to reshape the external ear.

14. A person with cancer of the throat might have to have a radical neck dissection and a _____.
    a. laryngectomy   b. tonsillectomy
    c. herniorrhaphy   d. rhinoplasty
    Answer: A
    Explanation: A. Correct! B. A tonsillectomy is not done for cancer. C. A herniorrhaphy is not done in the throat. D. A rhinoplasty is surgical reshaping of the nose.

15. Otalgia is pain in the _____.
    a. bone   b. ear
    c. mouth   d. ovary
    Answer: B
    Explanation: A. Oste/o- means bone. B. Correct! Ot/o- means ear. C. Or/o- means mouth. D. Ovari/o- means ovary.

16. Which of the following combining form pairs both mean tongue?
    a. glott/o-, lingu/o-   b. or/o-, stomat/o-
    c. pharyng/o-, trache/o-   d. gloss/o-, lingu/o-
    Answer: D
    Explanation: A. Only lingu/o- means tongue. B. Both of these mean mouth. C. Pharyng/o- means pharynx; trache/o- means trachea. D. Correct!

17. The three small bones in the middle ear are the _____.
    a. auricles
    b. ossicles
    c. atria
    d. turbinates
    Answer: B
    Explanation: A. The auricle is the external ear. B. Correct! C. The atria are the two upper chambers in the heart. D. The turbinates are in the nose.

Chapter 17 Questions

1. Which combining form means mind; chin?
   a. psych/o-
   b. phren/o-
   c. ment/o-
   d. affect/o-
   Answer: C
   Explanation: A. Psych/o- means mind, but it does not mean chin. B. Phren/o- means mind, but it also means diaphragm. C. Correct! D. Affect/o- means state of mind; mood.

2. Which pair of abbreviations is related to alcoholism?
   a. HDL, CRP
   b. FEV, PFT
   c. ETOH, DT
   d. LMP, EDC
   Answer: C
   Explanation: A. HDL and CRP are heart tests. B. FEV and PFT are lung tests. C. Correct! ETOH means ethanol (liquor), and DT means delirium tremens. D. LMP and EDC are related to pregnancy.

3. All of the following are psychiatric illnesses, *except* _____.
   a. bipolar disorder
   b. anorexia nervosa
   c. dysmenorrhea
   d. psychosis
   Answer: C
   Explanation: A. This is a psychiatric disorder. B. This is a psychiatric disorder (although anorexia is a GI disorder). C. Correct! D. This is a psychiatric disorder.

4. A loss of touch with reality is associated with _____.
   a. psychosis
   b. radiculopathy
   c. presbycusis
   d. candidiasis
   Answer: A
   Explanation: A. Correct! B. This is pain from a herniated disk pressing on a spinal nerve. C. This is hearing loss due to older age. D. This is a yeast infection of the vagina.

5. All of the following are neurotransmitters that affect emotion and behavior, *except* _____.
   a. serotonin
   b. lactase
   c. dopamine
   d. norepinephrine
   Answer: B
   Explanation: A. This is a neurotransmitter. B. Correct! C. This is a neurotransmitter. D. This is a neurotransmitter.

6. Which of the following is a phobia of snakes?
   - a. oligodendroglia
   - b. thanatophobia
   - c. anorexia nervosa
   - d. ophidophobia

   Answer: D

   Explanation: A. This is a cell that produces myelin in the brain and spinal cord. B. This is a fear of death. C. This is a psychiatric eating disorder. D. Correct!

7. Bipolar disorder swings between two poles of _____.
   - a. obsession and compulsion
   - b. fear and anxiety
   - c. mania and depression
   - d. hallucination and suicide

   Answer: C

   Explanation: A. This is obsessive-compulsive disorder, not bipolar disorder. B. This is not bipolar disorder. C. Correct! D. This is not bipolar disorder.

8. All of the following are psychiatric diseases of childhood, *except* _____.
   - a. autism
   - b. precocious puberty
   - c. reactive attachment disorder
   - d. ADHD

   Answer: B

   Explanation: A. This is a childhood psychiatric disorder. B. Correct! C. This is a childhood psychiatric disorder. D. This is a childhood psychiatric disorder.

9. Patients with body dysmorphic syndrome _____.
   - a. have repeated plastic surgeries
   - b. have endometriosis
   - c. are kleptomaniacs
   - d. have myopia

   Answer: A

   Explanation: A. Correct! B. Endometriosis is not related to body dysmorphic syndrome. C. Kleptomaniacs steal things. D. Myopia is nearsightedness.

Chapter 18 Questions

1. All of the following abbreviations are related to a type of cancer, *except* _____.
   - a. AML
   - b. NSVD
   - c. BRCA
   - d. CIS

   Answer: B

   Explanation: A. AML means acute myelogenous leukemia. B. Correct! NSVD means normal spontaneous vaginal delivery. C. BRCA means breast cancer (gene). D. CIS means carcinoma *in situ*.

2. Ralph has an abnormally elevated PSA test. This might mean that he has _____.
   - a. emphysema
   - b. prostate cancer
   - c. diverticulosis
   - d. hyperthyroidism

   Answer: B

   Explanation: A. PSA stands for prostate-specific antigen. B. Correct! C. PSA stands for prostate-specific antigen. D. PSA stands for prostate-specific antigen.

3. Growth of a cancerous tumor at a distant site is known as _____.
   - a. hemolysis
   - b. remission
   - c. oncology
   - d. metastasis

   Answer: D

   Explanation: A. This is the destruction of red blood cells. B. This is a temporary cessation of symptoms. C. This is the study of cancers. D. Correct!

4. The BRCA1 and BRCA2 genes are associated with _____.
   a. Parkinson's disease
   b. breast cancer
   c. diabetes mellitus
   d. sickle cell disease
   Answer: B
   Explanation: A. BRCA stands for breast cancer. B. Correct! C. BRCA stands for breast cancer. D. BRCA stands for breast cancer.

5. All of the following are characteristics of cancerous cells, *except* _____.
   a. mitochondria
   b. angiogenesis
   c. encapsulated
   d. undifferentiated
   Answer: A
   Explanation: A. Correct! B. This is a characteristic of cancerous cells. C. This is a characteristic of cancerous cells. D. This is a characteristic of cancerous cells.

6. Which cancer occurs in cells in the brain?
   a. squamous cell carcinoma
   b. Kaposi's sarcoma
   c. leukemia
   d. astrocytoma
   Answer: D
   Explanation: A. This is a skin cancer. B. This is a skin cancer. C. This is a cancer of the white blood cells. D. Correct!

7. A karyotype shows the _____.
   a. number of white blood cells in the blood
   b. presence of alpha fetoprotein in the amniotic fluid
   c. chromosomes in the nucleus
   d. level of oxygen in the blood
   Answer: C
   Explanation: A. This is a differential count. B. This is an amniocentesis. C. Correct! D. This is oximetry.

8. A bone marrow transplantation is done to _____.
   a. treat leukemia
   b. obtain a bone graft
   c. treat bone cancer
   d. diagnose cystic fibrosis
   Answer: A
   Explanation: A. Correct! B. Bone, not bone marrow, is used for a bone graft. C. Bone cancer is treated with chemotherapy drugs. D. Cystic fibrosis is diagnosed with a sweat test.

Chapter 19 Questions

1. All of the following abbreviations are related to radiology tests performed on the gastrointestinal system, *except* _____.
   a. KUB
   b. UGI
   c. BE
   d. IVC
   Answer: A
   Explanation: A. Correct! KUB means kidneys, ureters, and bladder. B. UGI means upper gastrointestinal (series). C. BE means barium enema. D. IVC means intravenous cholangiography.

2. The test that uses sound waves to form an image of a body part is _____.
   a. pyelography   b. x-ray
   c. MRI   d. ultrasound
   Answer: D
   Explanation: A. Pyelography uses x-rays and contrast dye. B. X-ray uses x-rays.
   C. MRI uses a magnetic field and radiowaves. D. Correct!

3. On an IVP report, which structure is certain to be mentioned?
   a. brain   b. heart
   c. intestines   d. kidneys
   Answer: D
   Explanation: A. Intravenous pyelography uses dye to outline the kidneys.
   B. Intravenous pyelography uses dye to outline the kidneys. C. Intravenous
   pyelography uses dye to outline the kidneys. D. Correct!

4. Iodine-123 is used specifically to create an image of the _____.
   a. intestines   b. pituitary gland
   c. thyroid gland   d. heart
   Answer: C
   Explanation: A. Iodine-123 is taken up by the thyroid gland. B. Iodine-123 is taken
   up by the thyroid gland. C. Correct! D. Iodine-123 is taken up by the thyroid gland.

5. Which of the following procedures does expose a patient to x-rays?
   a. fluoroscopy   b. PET scan
   c. MRI scan   d. Doppler ultrasound
   Answer: A
   Explanation: A. Correct! B. A PET scan uses a radioactive radiopharmaceutical
   drug, not x-rays. C. An MRI scan uses a magnetic field and radiowaves.
   D. Ultrasound uses sound waves.

6. Which of the following is *not* related to measuring the amount of exposure to x-rays?
   a. rem   b. film badge
   c. dosimetry   d. half-life
   Answer: D
   Explanation: A. A rem is a unit of measurement of radiation exposure. B. A film
   badge detects exposure to x-rays. C. Dosimetry is measuring the amount of radiation exposure. D. Correct!